LABYRINTHS

A VOLUME IN THE SERIES

Critical Perspectives on Modern Culture

Edited by David Gross and William M. Johnston

ALSO BY RICHARD WOLIN

The Terms of Cultural Criticism: The Frankfurt

School, Existentialism, Poststructuralism (1992)

The Politics of Being: The Political Thought of

Martin Heidegger (1990)

Walter Benjamin: An Aesthetic of Redemption (1982)

EDITOR

Karl Löwith, *Martin Heidegger and European Nihilism* (1995)

The Heidegger Controversy: A Critical Reader (1991)

LABYRINTHS

Explorations in the Critical History of Ideas

RICHARD WOLIN

University of Massachusetts Press   Amherst

Copyright © 1995 by Richard Wolin

All rights reserved

Printed in the United States of America

LC 95-16844

ISBN 0-87023-989-9 (cloth); 990-2 (pbk.)

Designed by Mary Mendell

Set in Ehrhardt by Keystone Typesetting, Inc.

Printed and bound by Thomson-Shore, Inc.

Library of Congress Cataloging-in-Publication Data

Wolin, Richard.

   Labyrinths : explorations in the critical history of ideas /
Richard Wolin.

      p.   cm. — (Critical perspectives on modern culture)

   Includes bibliographical references and index.

   ISBN 0-87023-989-9 (alk. paper). —
ISBN 0-87023-990-2 (pbk.: alk. paper)

   1. Philosophy, German—20th century.

   2. Philosophy, French—20th century.

   3. Germany—Intellectual life—20th century.

   4. France—Intellectual life—20th century.

   5. Heidegger, Martin, 1889–1976—Influence.

   I. Title.   II. Series

   B3181.W75   1996

   193—dc20   95-16844

                   CIP

British Library Cataloguing in Publication data are available.

In memory of Ferenc Fehér,
1933–1994
scholar, dissident, critic, mentor

CONTENTS

PREFACE

Labyrinths: Explorations in the Critical History of Ideas represents a settling of accounts. For the most part I have sought to bring together reflections on a number of issues that have given rise to fairly intense intellectual debates in the course of recent years: the ideological basis of postmodernism, the Heidegger controversy, the de Man affair. All are issues I perceive as being intellectually related—although too often the level of polemic has tended to obscure the deeper matters of substance that underlie the debates. I do not expect all of my readers and critics to agree with the positions I've staked out in the interpretations that follow. But I do hope that they may be challenged by the way in which I have reformulated and recontextualized the disputes at issue. At stake is the translation and reception in a North American context of theoretical positions first articulated in a very different European (more specifically, Franco-German) milieu. Here is where I can provide some useful correctives and clarifications: by situating intellectual positions in their historical settings, one becomes more aware of their multifarious ramifications. The objective is thereby to broaden and deepen a more conventional set of theoretical assumptions about the complex interrelation of ideas, history, and political life. Such an undertaking requires remaining attuned to a variegated network of discursive levels: ethical, social, philosophical, national, and historical. That these levels are often compartmentalized and kept separate—a practice abetted by the academic division of labor—often makes it difficult to see filiations that are indispensable to a fair assessment of the political influence of ideas. It is precisely on this dimension of the "effective" history of ideas that I have elected to focus. As such, *Labyrinths* is in many ways a companion piece to *The Terms of Cultural Criticism*, which appeared three years ago and which treats a number of kindred problems and themes. If I have managed to make some of the ideational controversies of our day seem somewhat less labyrinthine, then I will consider my efforts in *Labyrinths* to have been a success.

I acknowledge the enthusiasm of David Gross and Will Johnston, editors of the "Critical Perspectives on Modern Culture" series, for a rather inchoate book project I outlined to them over a year ago. Both provided extremely useful, detailed suggestions on a first draft of the manuscript. In almost all cases, I took their proposals to heart. The final conception of *Labyrinths* has benefited greatly from their pertinent comments and criticisms. My revisions also profited greatly from the directives of an anonymous reviewer from a well-known university in upstate New York, whose identity has become somewhat less of a mystery to me in recent months. Thanks are also due to my perspicuous copyeditor, Betty S. Waterhouse.

I express my appreciation to Clark Dougan, editor of the University of Massachusetts Press, for his unwavering support for the project since its inception. He has made my dealings with the Press at every stage a pleasant experience.

A number of the chapters presented here have benefited from financial support provided by various fellowship agencies. Without their generous assistance, the volume would never have seen completion. I especially thank the Alexander von Humboldt Stiftung, the National Endowment for the Humanities, and the German Marshall Fund of the United States, all of whom provided crucial support at specific stages of the project.

I also express my gratitude to Allen Matusow, dean of Humanities at Rice University, for his extreme generosity in helping to support the publication of a book that ended up being somewhat longer than I'd originally intended.

Many of the chapters here have previously appeared in other venues. Although most of the texts have been substantially reworked, I thank the prior editors and publishers for their kind permission to reprint:

"Kulchur Wars: The Modernism/Postmodernism Controversy Revisited," *Telos* 62, 7 (4) (1984–85): 9–29; "The Cultural Politics of Neoconservatism," *Telos* 66, 19 (1) (1986): 115–24; "Reflections on Jewish Secular Messianism," *Studies in Contemporary Jewry* 7 (Oxford: Oxford University Press, 1991): 186–96; "Walter Benjamin Today," introduction to the second edition of *Walter Benjamin: An Aesthetic of Redemption* (Berkeley and Los Angeles: University of California Press, 1994), xix–xlviii; "Working through the Past: Habermas and the German Historians' Debate," introduction to Jürgen Habermas, *The New Conservatism* (Cambridge: MIT Press, 1989), vii–xxxi; "Carl Schmitt: The Conservative Revolution and the Aesthetics of Horror," *Political Theory*

20 (3) (1993): 424–47; " 'Over the Line': Reflections on Martin Heidegger and National Socialism," and "French Heidegger Wars," in *The Heidegger Controversy: A Critical Reader* (Cambridge: MIT Press, 1993), 1–22 and 272–300; "Democracy and the Political in the Thought of Hannah Arendt," a lecture given at the conference "Democracy: Identity and Difference," Villa Lanna, Prague, Czech Republic, 1994; "Antihumanism in the Discourse of French Postwar Theory," *Common Knowledge*, January 1995; "Deconstruction at Auschwitz: Heidegger, de Man, and the New Revisionism," *South Central Review* 11 (1) (1994): 2–22.

I dedicate this book to the memory of Ferenc Fehér, whose untimely death in June 1994 came as a shock to his many friends, supporters, and loved ones. Ours was a friendship that lasted some twelve years. It began as an exchange of letters about my first book on Walter Benjamin. At the time he cautioned me against my overcharitable evaluation of Benjamin's intellectual legacy: we live in a dangerously irrational age, Feri observed, and Benjamin's thought, whose greatness is beyond dispute, was hardly free of such tendencies and risks. Since then my work has benefited considerably from his timely and measured criticisms. For what there is of value in the book that follows, I am fully in Feri's debt. By dedicating it to his memory, I indicate, albeit belatedly, the profundity and extent of that intellectual indebtedness.

Lastly, I acknowledge the unstinting support of my wife, Melissa, throughout the various stages of my labors. Our exuberant two-year-olds, Seth and Emma, have been indispensable in keeping my priorities in life in perspective.

LABYRINTHS

INTRODUCTION:

OF LABYRINTHS, MINOTAURS, AND

LEFT HEIDEGGERIANISM

The problematic of *posthistoire* is not the end of history but the end of meaning.—Lutz Niethammer, *Posthistoire: Has History Come to an End?*

It may be difficult to be sure whether one is for or against rationality; things become a little clearer when one understands that the decision is also a choice for or against democracy.—Tzvetan Todorov, *On Human Diversity*

With the exception of "Kulchur Wars: The Modernism/Postmodernism Controversy Revisited," all of the essays in *Labyrinths* are of recent vintage. Though written for different contexts and occasions, they are in many respects thematically related. At issue are the origins and peregrinations of contemporary theoretical discourse: more specifically, the ways in which a certain German intellectual lineage that, in its prime, displayed affinities with fascism (namely, the Nietzsche–Heidegger–Carl Schmitt connection, which, needless to say, neither can nor should be *reduced* to its manifest political sympathies) was subsequently taken up by French intellectuals in the post–World War II period and, as it were, made canonical.

The intellectual filiations between the German radical-conservative critique of bourgeois civilization and a similar position presented by the post-'68 French Left have been increasingly noted of late. For example, in his short book on *posthistoire* Lutz Niethammer shows provocatively how a way of thinking about history that was once peculiar to German right-wing thought has rematerialized among postmodernists who purportedly take their stand on the Left. According to the paradigm of *Kulturkritik* represented by such thinkers as Oswald Spengler, Ernst Jünger, and Arnold Gehlen, we have reached the "end of history." The institutional features of the capitalist West have "crystallized" to the point where all traces of "otherness"—which they define aristocratically in terms of nobility, passion, substance, life, and heroism—have been banished. According to Niethammer, in the historical optic of postmodernism, the idea of the end of history has returned as a left-wing commonplace. The mistrust of significant historical change, as subtended by quasi-metaphysical "metanarratives," has become so pervasive, that the end of history or *post-histoire*, instead of being regarded with suspicion, is now strangely celebrated—along with the by now proverbial "fragmentation of the subject"—as a perverse form of deliverance. But this standpoint merely replaces the metanarratives of old with a new one: an inverse teleology of decline has supplanted a now discredited teleology of progress. Both perspectives rely on an overarching philosophy of history that, due to its abstractness, inevitably overshoots the complexity, specificity, and open-endedness of contemporary social struggles. Adding insult to injury, a number of theorists of the postmodern condition seek to include Walter Benjamin as one of their ideological forebears.[1]

Seconding Niethammer's reflections, the philosopher Manfred Frank emphasizes the ambiguous ideological patrimony of Nietzsche, who among postmodernists is often viewed naively as an *avant la lettre* deconstructionist. However, as a result of this exclusively textualist understanding of Nietzsche's influence and impact, the historico-political ramifications of his doctrines are woefully undervalued. As Frank observes: "Nietzsche's deconstructive thinking remains within an epistemological framework characterized by a vitalism and a social Darwinism specific to its time, welcomed, in particular, by the so-called 'irrationalists' (from Klages to Spengler and Alfred Baeumler), and the extreme right (from Gentile to Rosenberg, and even the 'Nouvelle Droite' of today)."[2] In a more polemical vein, Frank attempts to specify the determinate philosophical pedigree linking this checkered intellectual tradition with the "French connection" that has in recent decades incorporated so many features of the German "critique of reason" initiated by Nietzsche:

> In aspects of recent French philosophy that follow structuralism we encounter a degenerate species of dionysian irrationalism which (like Nietzsche and Spengler before it) rediscovers the unity and end of the Western tradition, calls out a joyous "yes" to the savagery and cruelty of life, and declares its hatred of the achievements of rationality and of the Cartesian cogito in hate-filled tirades analogous to the ones one already found in the work of Klages.

"Certainly," Frank continues, "most of these 'new thinkers' are no more fascist than was Klages; that doesn't prevent the fact that, as was earlier the case with the old [German] right, today it is primarily the 'Nouvelle Droite' that cheers it on."[3]

Following a rather surprising transatlantic intellectual migration that took place during the 1970s, this Germanic theoretical lineage, now outfitted with a French accent, became ensconced in the American academy. It was heralded as "critical," "oppositional," and "radical"—claims that probably said more about the impoverished state of contemporary American radicalism (or, more precisely, about its academic *displacement*) than anything else. As Todd Gitlin remarked perceptively, for the last twelve years, while the Republicans have been taking over the country, the theoretical left has been taking over course syllabi in English departments.[4]

One of the paramount ironies of the American reception of this Franco-German lineage is that purportedly marginal texts (by Derrida and others) came to occupy the "center" and were soon accorded iconic status. Too often, these texts and their methodological prescriptions were not so much critically appropriated as apotheosized. To question their fundamental presuppositions was regarded by supporters as akin to heresy—something I would discover firsthand in a rather acrimonious public dispute with Derrida in the *New York Review of Books*.[5] The truly outlandish aspect of this by now well-rehearsed debate lay in its denouement: the urgent petition, signed by some forty Derrida-acolytes (a conspiracy of the independent-minded, as it were), claiming that the master could do no wrong. The surreal quality of this feeble appeal, signed by not a few academic notables, lay in the following: the world was faced with Serbian ethnic cleansing, famine in Africa, the unraveling of the Soviet Union, an uprising in the Middle East, and the incipient democratization of Eastern Europe, South Africa, and South America, but politically committed U.S. academics would only spring into collective action should the honor and integrity of deconstruction—an academic growth industry—be impugned. In the end, as in the nonacademic spheres of American life, self-interest will out.

The Heidegger affair emerged in the late 1980s following new revelations concerning the extent and profundity of the philosopher's Nazi attachments. One of its unintended consequences was that it highlighted the fallacies of exclusively textualist readings of philosophy. This approach had been consecrated in the celebrated deconstructionist claim *il n'y a pas de hors texte* (there is nothing outside the text).[6] This view resulted in the studied neglect of those *nontextual* dimensions of life—history, politics, and society—that, owing to formalist prejudices, had been traditionally downplayed by literary and philosophical scholarship. With the controversies surrounding the Heidegger affair, one witnessed a return of the repressed: it now seemed patently self-defeating to ignore or minimize the manifest political implications of Heidegger's thought. Similarly, it is clear why the French intellectual public was so taken aback by Heidegger's Nazi past: for decades the interpretation of his work had been governed by highly decontextualized, strictly textual readings, in consequence of which the overtly political resonances of his thought (long self-evident to a German public) remained undetectable. When the basis of reading becomes the negative semiotics of Derridean grammatology, according to which one must focus on the way *hymen, trace, différance, supplément,* and so on, ensure a priori that texts remain nonequivalent to themselves, there does not remain much room for political or social concerns. The latter are redolent of the metaphysical tyranny of the referent. The Heidegger affair (as well as that of Paul de Man, which quickly followed) brought about the "revenge of the referent," as it were. One could no longer evade the realms of politics and history entirely while still making cogent theoretical judgments—as many of the somewhat desperate rearguard attempts to save Heidegger soon proved. Often, even more egregious than the initial misreadings of his thought, where its ethical and political ambivalences were ignored, were the subsequent attempts to exonerate him: to wit, Derrida's own efforts to deconstruct the opposition between Nazism and non-Nazism, making Nazis such as Heidegger into non-Nazis, and non-Nazis ("humanists" and others who had dared criticize Heidegger) into virtual or honorary Nazis.[7]

In the last analysis, the Heidegger controversy severely put to the test one of the theoretical linchpins of so-called poststructuralism: the embrace of philosophical antihumanism, a singularly Heideggerian inheritance. When understood as part of a critique of Eurocentrism, liberalism, patriarchy, and so forth, philosophical antihumanism—the critique of "man"—seemed a valuable construct. Yet, suddenly, the constellation had changed. It was now beyond dispute that the progenitor of that critique, Heidegger, was an avowed Nazi; and that his Nazism, moreover, far from being a contingent biographical episode, was related to his philosophy in essential ways. Heidegger's French defenders were now faced with the paradoxical task of demonstrating that Heidegger's antihumanism, which poststructuralism had so readily embraced, bore no relation to his Nazism. They were confronted with the even greater, counterintuitive challenge of showing how Heidegger's antihumanism even laid the groundwork for a *critique* of Nazism. In order to make this work, they had to interpret the *Nazis* as the real humanists, and philosophical antihumanism (or the critique of "man") as the proper antidote. Thus, as Philippe Lacoue-Labarthe informs us in *Heidegger, Art, and Politics:* "Nazism is a humanism insofar as it rests upon a determination of *humanitas* which is, in its view, more powerful—i.e., more effective—than any other."[8]

There is much one might say about the foregoing statement. Fundamentally, it seriously misconstrues the thrust of European counterrevolutionary thought, from de Maistre to fascism, which, in a resolutely anti-Enlightenment spirit, strove forcibly to eliminate the humanistic legacy of 1789, or, simply, European liberalism.[9] In truth, there was nothing remotely humanistic about this political movement in any meaningful sense of the term. To interpret Nazism and its legacy as humanistic is either an intentional misreading or crassly ideological. Here, too, at issue are the perils of an exclusively textualist, ahistorical reading of Nazism and its proper historical background.

What has undone deconstruction in the eyes of many who were once sympathetic is that, in spite of itself, it has turned into another "ism" (as in "deconstructionism"): a veritable school, replete with canonical authors and texts, its own entrenched institutional power bases, its own imperious precepts as to how one must go about reading a text. All of this proves that a negative semiotics of reading such as Derrida's, despite perfunctory affirmations of interpretive free play and creative misreading, can be just as intolerant vis-à-vis competing paradigms as other approaches to criticism. Deconstruction has passed over from a sophistic-critical phase, which rightfully generated much enthusiasm, to one that is dogmatic-authoritarian. Derrida, who ended his contentious debate with Searle by prescribing an "Ethics for Discussion," has shown himself incapable of living up to his own precepts[10]—as painfully evidenced in "Biodegradables: Seven Diary Fragments," Derrida's overwrought response to the de Man affair, where he did not even deign to address his critics by name.[11]

The consequences of these developments for the Derridean faithful will not necessarily be easy to accept: deconstruction is merely one school of interpretation among many; neither the only school, nor, as its supporters claim, a critical *via regia*. Deconstruction certainly has much to teach us about the rhetoricity or figuration of texts, but so do other more conventional methods and approaches in opposition to which deconstruction first established itself. As such, deconstruction is part of a new constellation of critical thought;[12] taken by itself, it is far from self-sufficient. What deconstruction has de facto achieved in the last two decades is a certain academic-institutional self-aggrandizement— little more, little less. In this respect, its critical pretensions notwithstanding, it has failed to differentiate itself substantially from other competing ivory-tower tendencies and trends. Its institutional fate is part and parcel of a more general academic sublimation of political radicalism. From this perspective, it is far from accidental that, circa the mid-1980s, as deconstruction's emancipatory rhetoric began to ring hollow, politically oriented criticism turned toward the legacy of Foucault and the paradigm of the New Historicism.[13]

The Heidegger affair was central in reconfiguring the shape of contemporary theory because it brought to the fore the dilemmas involved in the "total critique" of Western reason, a standpoint that soon became de rigueur for post-1968 French philosophical radicalism. Whereas Heidegger had imbibed this standpoint via the conservative revolutionary critique of modernity—a critique that, as the chapter on Carl Schmitt seeks to show, was avowedly fascistic—the French version claimed solidarity with a left-wing radicalism. Here, *les extrêmes se touchent.*

Heidegger's total critique of modernity was indeterminate and unnuanced. According to this perspective, the modern world had succumbed to a fate of total *Seinsverlassenheit* (abandonment by Being [*Sein*]) that was merely the flip side of its total *Gottesverlassenheit* (abandonment by the gods). Following Hölderlin, he deemed the contemporary era a wholly "destitute time" (*dürftiger Zeit*), a forlorn epoch trapped between the departure of the old gods and the "not yet" (*noch nicht*) of the gods to come. In "Overcoming Metaphysics" (1946) he describes the present age as characterized by "the collapse of the world," "the devastation of the earth," "the unconditional objectification of everything present"; in sum, it is an age of total perdition.[14] But, as Pierre Bourdieu has shown, as a piece of social analysis, Heidegger's description is merely a philosophically attired version of the standard German radical-conservative denunciations of a moribund and corrupt bourgeois *Zivilisation*.[15] It is integrally related to the analogous inculpations of "reason," "liberalism," and "civilization" that one finds in the writings of Klages, Jünger, Spengler, Schmitt, Hans Freyer, and a host of other lesser known foes of Germany's fledgling Weimar democracy.

It is the same standpoint of "total critique"—of "reason," "democracy," "bourgeois society," and so forth—that Heidegger's French heirs have adopted and disseminated in an uncritical manner. Essentially, the central tenets of a right-radical *Kulturkritik* have been assimilated and propagated for purportedly left-wing ends. Either way, however, the goal is not so much to transform contemporary democracy from within (and who but the neoconservatives discussed in Chapter 2 would deny that it is in sore need of transformation?), but to surpass it with something totally Other: the will to power, Being, sovereignty, or *différance*. A radical critique of reason will tolerate nothing less.

According to the standpoint of total critique, the criticisms do not redress the specific empirical failings of contemporary democratic practice; instead, they take aim at a more fundamental, transcendental level. The entire set of normative values that democracy privileges—fairness, justice, equality, and so forth—are radically called into question, though one crucial difference distinguishes the two camps. The conservative revolutionaries of the 1920s favored a protofascistic *Volksgemeinschaft*. The poststructuralists, conversely, taking a page from the writings of Georges Bataille, favor an *an-archic community;* they want their "unavowable" or "inoperative" community to be based on the values of "expenditure" (*la dépense*), otherness, or difference.[16] It is in this sense that Derrida, in his essay on Carl Schmitt, obliquely appeals for a conception of democracy that "does not yet exist," one that would orient itself "beyond the homo-fraternal and phallogocentric schema" that has been characteristic of democracy to date.[17]

What raises suspicions, however, is that the critique of the logos or logocentrism on which deconstruction has staked so much was in fact initiated by Germany's young conservatives in the 1920s. In fact, it was Ludwig Klages who in *Der Geist als Widersacher der Seele* (*The Intellect as Antagonist of the Soul*) first coined the term *logocentrism*. Some of the affinities between the two approaches are uncanny. They need to be explored and not wished away. With Fredric Jameson's recent avowal of "secret admiration" for Heidegger's involvement with the Nazis, which he finds "morally and aesthetically preferable to apolitical liberalism," they have assumed frightening proportions.[18] Here, the (self-defeating) logic of "left fascism" repeats itself: if bourgeois society cannot be overthrown from the left, let it be overthrown from the right.[19]

There is certainly nothing wrong with criticizing or calling into question rationality or reason. As Karl Popper has convincingly shown, the process whereby explanations or reasons are doubted or shown to be false is intrinsic to the process through which reason as a whole may be said to progress.[20] Conversely, to question the legitimacy of reason *simpliciter* suggests that we bid farewell to that which has proved the only basis, however partial and flawed, for adjudicating questions of legitimacy in general. The alternatives that lie in the wake of the total critique of reason have been tried and are bleak. They have generally appeared as variations on a Nietzschean motif that, in the 1970s, was vigorously adopted by Foucault: the idea that the *will to knowledge* is merely a cover for the *will to power;* that claims to validity or truth are merely camouflaged or sublimated claims to power; that *power is all there is and all there ever will be*. From this perspective, the question of how we define the difference between the legitimate versus illegitimate exercise of power, a theme that subtends some two millennia of ethico-political discourse, can no longer be raised. In the seventeenth century Hobbes, whose doctrine of the "state of nature" was much admired by both Schmitt and Nietzsche, set forth the new antinormative, modern-skeptical understanding of the relation between truth and power when he decreed, in a spirit not dissimilar to Foucault: "Auctoritas, non veritas, facit legem" (when questions of law or political legitimacy are at issue, it is authority, not truth, that matters). In the chapters that follow on Martin Heidegger and Carl Schmitt, I have tried to indicate precisely where a consequent abandonment of questions pertaining to matters of validity and justification leads when issues of social theory are at stake.

Historically, the total critique of reason has gone hand in hand with anti-democratic tendencies. Both constitute attempts to eliminate the Enlightenment's secular "religion of humanity" and reaffirm the irreducibility of otherness or difference. According to this standpoint, the attempt to subsume the particular under the general, the spirit of universality and cosmopolitanism, must be violently rejected as hostile to life. As Maistre, a progenitor of both counter-Enlightenment and counterrevolutionary ideology, as well as (along with J. G. Herder) the West's first theorist of "difference," famously observed: "In my life I have seen Frenchmen, Italians, Russians, and so on. I even know, thanks to Montesquieu, that one can be Persian. But as for *man*, I declare I've never encountered him; if he exists he is unknown to me."[21] There are, moreover, strong political affinities between the late eighteenth-century revolt against reason and the vitalist rebellion of a century later led by Nietzsche, Sorel, and the Italian elite-theorists Pareto and Mosca. Here, too, a protofascistic dismissal of democratic equality in favor of a return to what Nietzsche celebrated as *Rangordnung* (hierarchy or rule by elites) predominated.[22]

In evaluating the implications of the intellectual lineage under discussion, it is useful to contrast the positions of Husserl and Heidegger when the Nazis seized power. In 1935, after an initial period of silence, Husserl delivered a lecture entitled "Philosophy and the Crisis of European Humanity." The speech displayed a clear awareness of the momentous transformation undergone by Europe in the period of fascism's implacable rise. Husserl presented an unflinching defense of the rational and universalistic aspects of the Western tradition. He realized that the governments of Hitler and Mussolini, which had attracted numerous followers throughout Europe, posed an unprecedented challenge to everything that that legacy stood for. Although Husserl was not naive about the manifest limitations of that tradition, his lecture was anything but apologetic. As he remarked at one point: "I too think that the European crisis derives from the perversions of rationalism, but there is no reason to say that rationalism is bad in itself or that it is of secondary importance in human life as a whole."[23]

Heidegger, of course, had come to a series of very different conclusions. These were the years in which he spoke about the "glory and greatness of the [German] awakening" as well as "the inner truth and greatness of National

Socialism."[24] More important, however, such occasional political judgments were rooted in a philosophical standpoint that increasingly devalued the whole of Western reason as "onto-theological"—hence, valueless and nihilistic. Instead, statements such as the following became increasingly representative of his position: "Thinking begins only when we have come to know that reason, glorified for centuries, is the most stiff-necked adversary of thought."[25] But, as the historian of fascism Zeev Sternhell has observed: "A recognition of the existence of an area not controlled by reason and an acknowledgment that it cannot be explored by rational means alone is one thing; the intellectual and political exploitation of antirationalism is quite another."[26] Nor did the propagation of a radical critique of reason and universality take place in a social and political vacuum. Instead, if one analyzes closely the doctrines propounded by the prophets of fascist ideology—the writings of Gobineau, Pareto, Sorel, Jünger, and so forth—one sees that a rejection of the tradition of Enlightenment rationality is a sine qua non.[27] It would be shortsighted and dishonest to downplay the contributions that such intellectual tendencies made toward paving the way for the European catastrophe. As Sternhell also notes: "The political revolt that reached its climax in the period between the two world wars (we are referring not only to fascism and Nazism but to all the expressions of the 'national revolution' in France, Spain, and Portugal) would not have been possible without a long period of intellectual preparation. The cultural revolt preceded the political one in every part of Europe. Fascism was the hard core of the cultural revolt and succeeded in translating it into a political force."[28]

In his book dealing with these issues Derrida seeks to show not only that it was a surfeit of humanism that induced Heidegger to support Nazism 1933; he suggests that Husserl's Vienna discourse of 1935, which contains a reference to the culture of Eskimos and Gypsies as existing outside the Western tradition, was in effect equally racist and chauvinistic. This is Derrida's way of throwing down the gauntlet to liberal humanism's good conscience. That Husserl, who was Jewish, suffered persecution at the hands of the Nazi regime (with the full cooperation, one might add, of his former student Heidegger, in his new capacity as "Rector-Führer" of Freiburg University) makes such an equation especially macabre. Indeed, to compare Heidegger's fanatical support for Hitler ("Let not doctrines and 'ideas' be the rules of our Being. The Führer alone *is* the present and future German reality and its law," remarks Heidegger on one occasion)[29] with Husserl's extremely modest defense of Western reason is to equate incomparables. It reveals, one is tempted to say, a marked incomprehension of the political implications of intellectual discourse. As Tom Rockmore has correctly pointed out: "Husserl's rejection of National Socialism, weak as it unfortunately was, shines like a beacon in comparison with the more typical philosophical effort to embrace, or at least to cooperate with, Hitler's movement, above all by Martin Heidegger."[30] When all is said and done, Husserl would have been incapable of writing lines such as the following, which were part of Heidegger's lectures on logic in 1934: "Negroes are men but they have no history. . . . Nature has its history. But then negroes would also have history. Or does nature then have no history? It can enter into the past as something transitory, but not everything that passes away enters into history. When an airplane's propeller turns, then nothing actually "occurs" [*geschieht*]. Conversely, when the same airplane takes Hitler to Mussolini, then history occurs."[31] Moreover, it is important to realize that this passage, shocking though it may seem, does not merely represent an unthinking, aphilosophical aside on Heidegger's part; instead, when read in context, it is intended as a fundamental illustration of Heidegger's doctrine of *Geschichtlichkeit* or "historicity"—of the comprehension of history qua "authenticity."

Heidegger's failing was not so much in having called into question the shortcomings and inadequacies of Western reason. Many other thinkers and cultural critics of the modern era, beginning with the romantic movement, have enhanced our consciousness concerning the biases and extremes of Western cultural development.[32] Inflexible rationalism is hardly preferable to dogmatic irrationalism.[33] Heidegger's philosophical misstep lay in his opting, like so many of his countrymen and women, for a position of total critique; that is, in his assumption that the enterprise of reason could not be salvaged from within, but instead, needed to be cast aside in favor of, as he was fond of calling it, an "other beginning." Without a normative *point d'appui* to rely on in the modern world of total perdition, his thinking seemed to call for the extreme solutions and measures that he embraced in fact.

But what holds for the right-wing critique of the modern world must apply to the left-wing critique as well. Here, too, the extremes often coalesce. The more closely one examines the intellectual disposition of German thinkers of the interwar generation—on both sides of the political spectrum—the more one encounters profound generational commonalities. In the chapters that follow on Jewish secular messianism, on Walter Benjamin, and on the political thought of Hannah Arendt, I identify similar generational failings, despite the fact that my own intellectual sympathies are much closer to the positions they represent.

Although Benjamin, the Frankfurt School, and Arendt share many of Heidegger's critical positions on the inadequacies of modernity and the paradigm of instrumental reason, rarely did they take these criticisms as far as he did;

especially in Heidegger's later work, we see a rejection of reason in favor of an avowedly mythological "poeticizing gnosis."[34] Perhaps it was their Jewishness, their subterranean, seldom avowed affinities to "rational religion" and the taboo against images, that prevented them from taking the final step of casting off civilizing reason in favor of myth. Thus, as Horkheimer and Adorno insist in *Dialectic of Enlightenment* (a work that is otherwise unsparingly critical of modernity's historical outcome): "We are wholly convinced—and therein lies our *petitio principii*—that social freedom is inseparable from enlightened thought."[35] Far from being an abstract negation of Enlightenment, the Frankfurt School's philosophical project always aimed at "enlightenment about Enlightenment": it sought to promote theoretical reflection on the limitations of Enlightenment for the sake of strengthening the very concept. And thus they always insisted that their "critique of enlightenment [was] intended to prepare the way for a *positive notion of enlightenment* which [would] release it from entanglement in blind domination."[36]

This contrast between the Frankfurt School's qualified critique of reason—a critique that aims at revising and broadening, but not at dismissing the concept—and a radical critique such as the one purveyed by Heidegger and his heirs helps us understand more precisely what is at stake in the discourse of total critique. One of the main problems with this discourse is that it fails to distinguish among rationality types: insofar as they partake of reason, all are equally tainted, equally damnable. In the last analysis, this position, whether one finds it represented in the later Heidegger or Foucault (who, in an interview, goes so far as to conclude: "La torture, c'est la raison")[37] ends up subsuming all species of reason under the genus of instrumental reason. No matter whether one consults Heidegger's critique of *das Gestell* (enframing), Derrida's critique of logocentrism, or Foucault's critique of power/knowledge, the end result is the same: salvation can never be found within a revised concept of reason, but only outside it. All rationality types—theoretical-scientific, moral-practical, and aesthetic—are reduced to the same pernicious logocentric bases.

But this narrowing of theoretical focus potentially excludes too much. It is erroneous, following Heidegger's lead, to view all social action in the modern world (with the possible exception of that of a few privileged *Dichter* and *Denker*) as exclusively "instrumental" or "logocentric." The excesses of instrumental reason in the workplace, government, and cultural life should certainly be criticized. But countervailing tendencies in the realms of politics, art, and everyday life must also be emphasized. Otherwise one inevitably loses sight of the determinate gains of those social protest movements that have gone far toward redefining our contemporary notion of the political: the struggle for civil rights, the women's movement, and the antiwar movement. All have been guided by a concept of reason that is both practical in the sense of Kant's moral law ("Act in such a way that you always treat humanity, whether in your own person or in the person of any other, never simply as a means, but always at the same time as an end") and emancipatory.[38] What we need is a theoretical perspective that is non–one-dimensional, one that is capable of taking the variegated nature of social action into account: those aspects of social action that are potentially emancipatory as well as those that are repressive. One of the main problems of the philosophical lineage I have been discussing is that it has succumbed to the more resigned conclusions of *posthistoire* ideology: the idea that, in a postmodern era in which all metanarratives have been abandoned, the concept of utopia must also be cast aside; or the related conviction that the notion of emancipation itself is derisory, if not dystopian. In all of these respects it is necessary to uphold the utopian aspirations of the 1960s in the face of the fashionable, fin-de-siècle *Kulturpessimismus* that is so often brandished by that decade's neo-Nietzschean theoretical heirs.

PART I

KULCHUR WARS:

THE MODERNISM/POSTMODERNISM

CONTROVERSY REVISITED

Literary theory has come to be identified with the political left; but while it is true that a good many of its practitioners hail from that region, it is much less obvious that theory itself is an inherently radical affair. One might, indeed, argue exactly the opposite. It would be possible to see semiotics as the expression of an advanced capitalist order so saturated with codes and messages that we all now live in some vast stock exchange of the mind in which gobbets of packaged information whizz past us at every angle. Just as money breeds money in finance capitalism, having long forgotten that it was supposed to be the sign of something real, so the Saussurean sign broods on itself and its fellows in grand isolation from anything as lowly as a referent. One hears that in the United States there is now a fairly well-beaten path from the postgraduate semiotics course to Wall Street. . . . And it is not hard to see much of what passes for postmodernism as consumerism at the level of the intellect.—Terry Eagleton, "Discourse and Discos"

It is well known that in his introduction to the *Collected Essays on the Sociology of World Religions* (1920)[1] Max Weber grapples with the problem of the cultural specificity of the West. He phrases his inquiry in the following way: Why is it "that in Western civilization, and in Western civilization only, cultural phenomena have appeared which (as we like to think) lie in a line of development having universal significance and value"?[2] He continues to cite a wealth of cultural phenomena—theology, the rational concept, standardized methods of scientific experimentation, rational harmonious music, extensive utilization of perspective in painting, bureaucratic conduct of the organizational sphere, and the systematic rational pursuit of economic affairs—that are unique to the West yet illustrative of its self-avowed universality.

Yet the historical emergence of these various cultural developments by no means occurred simultaneously. It is to Judaism that we owe the advent of monotheism (or, as it has sometimes been termed, "rational religion"), to ancient Greece the birth of the rational concept, to the Renaissance the emergence of the principles of scientific experimentation and perspective in the arts, and to the Reformation the appearance of the Protestant ethic's inner-worldly asceticism, which becomes the hallmark of the extraordinary rationalization of life-conduct characteristic of the capitalist spirit. Only when all of the aforementioned variables have been allowed to establish themselves and combine into a single comprehensive ethos—usually placed by Weber within the category of "rationalization"—does modernity in the full sense of the term emerge. And although it crystallizes in the course of the fifteenth, sixteenth, and seventeenth centuries, it attains its definitive form in the eighteenth century, with the transition from the absolutist to the democratic era. As Jürgen Habermas has pointed out, it is during this period that the absolute breach between traditional and modern societies transpires.[3] For it is in this age that the transition from societies based on cosmological worldviews to those based on de-centered or differentiated worldviews occurs. From this point on, society is no longer characterized by the predominance of a single, monolithic value-system that pervades and structures its various partial subsystems. Instead, these subsystems may now pursue their own inherent independent logics. This development allows for an unprecedented proliferation of autonomous value-spheres that, in many respects, becomes the signature of the modern age. The primary value-spheres that are released in this process are those of science, morality, and art.[4] Each of these spheres becomes "rationalized" insofar as each no longer needs to invoke a priori the authority of an antecedent and determinative cosmological standpoint to legitimate itself. Instead, each becomes self-validating. Henceforth, the legitimacy of each is certified in terms of a set of internally generated criteria. While in principle Weber acknowledged the validity of all three spheres, in his scientific work he concentrated on the first form of rationality, instrumental or formal reason, whose predominance he viewed as the defining feature of modern culture.[5] Ultimately, he undermined his own pluralistic conception of modernity by judging the other two value-spheres—morality and art—in terms of criteria taken over from the scientific sphere and then branding these as formally irrational.[6] Thus, for Weber, moral choices do not partake of a logic of truth: they are ultimately decisionistic, a matter of pure choice. In the last analysis, they defy rational justification.

Today it would be an understatement to claim that the legacy of modernity has fallen under suspicion; in truth, it has fallen victim to a frontal assault from all quarters. The writings of the utopian socialists in the early nineteenth century still exuded the optimism characteristic of Enlightenment philosophies of history.[7] By the end of the century such confident expectations, still a driving motif in Marx's work, had succumbed to the disillusionment of "decadence," "vitalism," and "nihilism." These intellectual currents, which dominate the fin-de-siècle, signal a decisive historical rejection of the normative legacy of modernity. Their most formidable exponent, Nietzsche, is often celebrated as the spiritual progenitor of contemporary attempts to escape from the encumbrances of modern rationalism[8]—attempts that, by virtue of this much heralded breach, are associated with the banners of postmodernity and postmodernism.[9] In this chapter I shall focus on the third of the aforementioned three value-spheres—the sphere of aesthetic rationality—in order to gauge its significance in the modernism/postmodernism debate.

I

When we speak of art in terms of its import for the paradigm of modernity, we refer to the unfettered right of the artist to independent self-expression. We moderns assume this right to be self-evident, whereas in fact it is essentially an achievement of recent origin, postdating centuries in which art was fully implicated in the legitimation of what Weber termed traditional authority—be it in the form of myth (Homer's *Iliad*), religion (medieval Christian painting), or the divine right of kings (courtly art). This embeddedness of art in traditional worldviews is what Walter Benjamin has described as its "cult function." To "cult" he opposes the "exhibition value" of art: the fully secularized status it acquires in the course of the eighteenth century, when art comes to play a constitutive role in the formation of the bourgeois public sphere.[10]

In *Structural Transformation of the Public Sphere* Habermas analyzes the essential role played by art as a vehicle for generating postconventional social identities: identities that no longer assume the unquestioned validity of traditional societal norms and values. With special reference to the eighteenth-century epistolary novel, he demonstrates the indispensable role played by fiction in the public conveyance of subjective experiences (and thus in the process of identity formation) for the rising bourgeois class. While Habermas recognizes the truncated character of the humanitarian values flaunted in works such as *Pamela, La Nouvelle Héloïse* and *Werther*—the values of love, education, and freedom remained confined to the private sphere of *Innerlichkeit* or inwardness—he deems these values themselves authentically universalistic.[11] However, he is wholly without cynicism with regard to the eighteenth-century public sphere as an ideal model of communicative praxis, despite the fact that its original universalistic promise is revoked once the victorious bourgeois class turns conservative when faced with the prospect of having to extend its values beyond the boundaries of its own class interests. In Habermas's account, the original promise of the bourgeois public sphere ultimately becomes a tale of lost illusions: its progressive potential is revoked through a process of increasing commercialization, culminating in the "culture industry" of late capitalism.[12]

Habermas's depiction of the classical bourgeois public sphere is pertinent insofar as it convincingly demonstrates the impressive communicative potentials of postconventional or autonomous art. Nevertheless, these communicative capacities are increasingly curtailed in the course of the nineteenth century as autonomous art becomes progressively esoteric. "Esotericization" is the corollary on the autonomy side of the ledger for a bourgeois art that, having separated into "high" and "low" spheres, on the opposite side, as *divertissement*, regressed to "cult"—entertainment and amusement. Thus, in the bourgeois era, art undergoes a process of dichotomization. Although so-called high art remains faithful to the principle of aesthetic autonomy (the process of authentic subjective self-expression), it succeeds in this task at the expense of its former claim to generalizability, which then attaches to the lower sphere of entertainment art.[13]

The considerable tension that is generated between these two spheres accounts for the dynamism that becomes the hallmark of aesthetic modernism. The increasing commodification of what was once popular culture, the vast proliferation of entertainment media, compels autonomous art to undergo a series of radical self-transformations in order to remain abreast of the tide threatening to engulf it from below and thereby remain faithful to the precepts of aesthetic autonomy. The developmental history of bourgeois culture becomes a story of abandoned ideals. In literature it can be traced from the *Bildungsroman* (e.g., Goethe's *Wilhelm Meister*), where the prospect of a reconciliation with reality remains intact, to the novel of disillusionment (e.g., Stendhal's *The Red and the Black*), in which the hopes of the *Bildungsroman* are disconsolately abandoned, to the modern novel of consciousness (Proust, Joyce), where contact with an empirical world perceived as inimical to spirit is relinquished and the novelist thrown back on the resources of her own subjectivity. Since this process entails a progressive renunciation of the bourgeois world of "objective spirit" and correspondent subjectivization of narrative structure (the radical shift from the third person singular to first person singular narrative voice), the domain of "generalizable experiences" on which the bourgeois literary public sphere was originally predicated is placed at risk. This is a developmental tendency that culminates in the birth of literary modernism. Its defining characteristics are an increased self-referentiality, autonomy of literary signifiers (writing is about words, not things in the world), disruption of linear time, and rejection of the classical ideal of the rounded, integral work.

At the same time, in recent years an important controversy has arisen over the periodization of literary modernism in relation to the so-called avant-garde spurred by Peter Bürger's *Theory of the Avant-Garde*.[14] According to Bürger, at issue is a transformation from quantity to quality within the value-sphere of bourgeois autonomous art. Whereas one of the signal features of aesthetic modernism was a concerted assault on any and everything traditional—in the well-known words of Rimbaud, "Il faut être absolument moderne"—these attacks, for all their vehemence, ultimately fell short of challenging the bourgeois "institution of art" as it was originally constituted in the eighteenth century. That is, despite their radicalism, the works of literary modernism in the last instance remained thoroughly aestheticist. Not so, however, the works of the historical avant-garde: futurism, constructivism, dadaism, and, most important, surrealism. For the avant-garde is distinguished not so much by an attack on traditional works of art as by an attack on the ideal of *works of art per se;* that is, as autonomous aesthetic products entirely separated from the domain of life-praxis. It is the principle of aesthetic autonomy itself that is called into question by the historical avant-garde: the affirmative ideal of culture as a sphere of beautiful illusion in which the values denied in the realm of daily or material life can be safely enjoyed.[15] To be sure, bourgeois aestheticism, most commonly associated with the mid-nineteenth century doctrine of art for art's sake, was always a phenomenon laced with ambivalence. Affirmative though it may have been, it retained an indefeasible critical moment. Its harmonious images always threatened to indict the prosaic material world in which the ideal had little place. In Bürger's view, the avant-garde rebelled viscerally against ineffectual, aestheticist modes of negation. And in polemical opposition, it adopted the program of a reintegration of art in the domain of life-praxis: the beautiful illusion of art should be transposed to the sphere of real life. In this sense, the avant-garde no longer produced works of art, but instead "provocations."[16]

A few critical remarks concerning Bürger's scheme of classification are in order.[17] It is undoubtedly fruitful to distinguish between literary modernism and the twentieth-century avant-garde—a distinction often wanting in Anglo-American criticism, where the two are usually subsumed under the rubric of modernism. The avant-garde launches an assault on traditional aesthetic comportment that modernism would find difficult to countenance. And it is quite apparent that literary modernism, for all its iconoclasm and railing against the constraints of tradition, remains committed to several key pillars of bourgeois aestheticism—most important, to the principle of the completed work of art as an end in itself. In this respect modernism remains consistent with a line of development stemming from art for art's sake.

Nevertheless, Bürger's definition of the avant-garde as seeking "the overcoming of art in life-praxis" is too rigid. His explanation remains plausible in the cases of Russian constructivism and Italian futurism, which seek to turn art into a comrade-in-arms in the processes of industrialization and political mobilization.[18] Their links to historical programs of modernization yield products that desperately seek to avoid being works of art. The same might well be said of the dadaist ready-mades and *objets-trouvés* (Duchamp's "fontaine"). However, once the attitude of "épater le bourgeois" itself becomes an aesthetic program, its provocations cease to shock. It, too, soon finds a ready-made niche in museums, catalogues raisonnés, and modern art history syllabi.

The aesthetic program for merging the domains of art and life-praxis stands under the sign of the ephemeral. As Adorno once remarked with reference to the Brechtian aesthetics of "commitment": engaged works of art "merely assimilate themselves sedulously to the brute existence against which they protest—in forms so ephemeral that from the very first day they belong to the seminars in which they inevitably end."[19] In Adorno's view ephemeralness results when the concept of the integral work of art is relinquished for the sake of extra-aesthetic effect. However (and this is where Bürger's analysis goes astray), this is not the sign under which surrealism stands. Bürger fails to acknowledge that, for all the notoriety André Breton's claim concerning the need to "practice poetry" has received, in many respects surrealism remains faithful to the program of aesthetic autonomy. To this day its works retain a type of exemplary status. Thus, in 1929 Breton sought to preserve the sovereign powers of the surrealist imagination against Aragon's willingness to place them at the beck and call of the communist movement.[20] Whether one considers a poem by Eluard, a romance by Breton, or a painting by Dalí, all function at a distant remove from the found objects of dada. The latter possesses a shock-effect that, in most cases, dissipates after the initial act of reception. The surrealist works (which, admittedly, have become in their own way "canonical") are aesthetic enigmas that invite decipherment. One need only recall that, in his "Surrealism" essay, Benjamin, a prescient observer of the Parisian avant-garde, feared that the movement would remain incapable of transcending its "autonomous" phase, in which it lingered under the sway of romantic artistic prejudices; and that, as a result, it would be unable to accommodate itself to the "constructive, dictatorial side of revolution [!]"[21]

In order to conceptualize surrealism properly, in relation to both bourgeois aestheticism (art for art's sake) and the more engaged avant-garde, Bürger's theoretical framework would be in need of a third term: de-aestheticized autonomous art. This category suggests that surrealism's uniqueness lies in its having simultaneously negated the aura of affirmation characteristic of art for art's sake, while nevertheless refusing to abandon the modern requirement of aesthetic autonomy. This requirement ensures that the truth-content of surrealism, unlike that of fraternal avant-garde currents, will not evaporate immediately in the moment of reception. Surrealism must be understood therefore as a still aesthetic attack on bourgeois aestheticism. It consciously divests itself of the beautiful illusion, the aura of reconciliation, projected by art for art's sake, while refusing to overstep the boundaries of aesthetic autonomy, beyond which art degenerates to the status of merely a thing among things. Even Bürger, basing himself on Benjamin's theory of allegory, ultimately recognizes the means surrealism employs to distinguish itself from "auratic" (possessing an aura) art: a renunciation of the aestheticist ideal of the rounded, integral work of art in favor of the notion of the fragmentary work. In other words, *surrealism proffers fragmentary works of art that are nonetheless still works.* In this respect, it remains, in spirit and in fact, much closer to the domain of modernism proper than to its immediate historical precursor, dada.

In the 1950s the historical avant-garde entered into a state of profound crisis. The dilemma to which it fell victim may be diagnosed as follows: so dependent had it become on elements of shock, provocation, scandal, and rupture that, once these techniques had been routinized, they too would become new artistic conventions. In essence, newness itself had become traditional: it became a new aesthetic canon, achieving a bourgeois respectability that would have been anathema to its original partisans.[22] For quite some time now, it has no longer been unusual—it has even become de rigueur—to see nonfigurative images adorning the offices of corporate presidents. One of the first to note the co-optation of modernism was Lionel Trilling, who, rather than abet the domestication of the modernist challenge, refused to teach it in university seminars.[23] Compounding the avant-garde's identity crisis is the fact that its central principle of construction, montage, would become the standard modus operandi of the advertising industry. In its attempts to compel the audience to recognize the pseudo-uniqueness of its wares, shock-effects would become one of its staples.[24] In sum, the historical avant-garde seemed threatened with normalization and obsolescence from both above and below.[25] For all of these reasons, Hegel's controversial thesis concerning the "end of art" would seem once again to have become extremely topical.[26]

Of course, Hegel formulated this verdict with respect to the transition from neoclassicism to romanticism. To him it had become apparent that the avowedly subjective and idiosyncratic character of romantic art had made the monumentalism of Greek classicism forever a thing of the past. Yet art persevered and, despite its present crisis, continues to persevere. The question thus arises: What is the status of the avant-garde legacy in relationship to the various postmodern forms that became its heir and successor?

II

Perhaps the most basic historical point of reference for the phenomenon of postmodernism is the American reception of the European avant-garde following the Second World War. For the abstract expressionists were decisively influenced by the surrealist community-in-exile during the war years.[27] Noted for the techniques of "tachism" or "action painting," their methods seemed to be a visual corollary to the surrealist technique of automatic writing. The emphasis on conscious construction was renounced. The renunciation of figuration was carried to an extreme, and the last vestiges of "representation" or "subject matter" were extirpated (this in keeping with an assault, dating back to cubism, on the inherent illusoriness of the striving for three-dimensionality or perspective on a two-dimensional surface). The aural complement to these developments was the aleatory music of John Cage, with its analogous penchant for compositional contingency.

The New York School remained sufficiently indebted to its historical antecedent, surrealism, to qualify as a transitional stage on the path leading from the avant-garde to postmodernity. It maintained one foot in each camp, as it were. But one thing separating this school from the historical avant-garde was its lack of concern with the relationship between art and everyday life that had been so central to the earlier movements. This refusal to problematize art's relation to daily life suggests affinities with the more aestheticist qualities of surrealist painting. Abstract expressionism's alienation from politics and everyday life has its sociological origins in the one-dimensionality of the cold war years.

In its rejection of the form-giving capacities of the artist via the randomness of tachism and aleatory music, abstract expressionism carried the avant-garde attack on the romantic aesthetics of genius to an extreme. For this reason it stands under the sign of the "eclipse of subjectivity" (there is a strikingly comparable tendency in the *nouveau roman*), a trend that will become increasingly definitive of the postmodernist sensibility.[28]

It is not, however, until the 1960s that the phenomenon of postmodernism appears full-blown on the American cultural scene. Here, too, the visual arts stand in the forefront, riding the crest of momentum provided by the New York School. In this decade it is almost impossible to keep pace with the kaleidoscopic changes in artistic fashion: pop, op, conceptual, and body art, minimalism, happenings, and so on. All of these trends reproblematize the relationship between art and daily life in a manner reminiscent of the historical avant-garde (e.g., Robert Rauschenberg's neo-dadaism) and in polemical opposition to abstract expressionism's refusal to do so. At the same time there comes to pass a final breach with the absorption and concentration demanded of the viewer by modernist works of art. Few conceptual demands are placed on the recipient. Instead, the effect conveyed by these works is often one of unadulterated immediacy. In essence, they reproduce the fleetingness of dadaism, minus the shock, which has become institutionalized and domesticated.

One might even go so far as to say that in this phase, the avant-garde program of the reintegration of art and life-praxis has been stood on its head. This program aimed at the reconciliation of culture and material life once the latter itself had been transformed through the forces of aesthetic intoxication. Conversely, postmodernist art often enough assumes an ethos of cheerful adaptation. The radical oppositional stance adopted by the historical avant-garde versus traditional bourgeois aestheticism has been relinquished. A quiescent spirit of harmony and affirmation has been placed in its stead. The peaceful coexistence between art and reality is proclaimed. Thus, postmodernism behaves as if the radical transformation of material life sought by the avant-garde has already been achieved. But since this is not in fact the case, what results instead is merely the false sublation of autonomous art. The new marriage between art and facticity can be seen in the choice of artistic subject matter for pop: the detritus of everyday life reemerges, transfigured, glorified, literally larger than life in Warhol's silk screens, which become indistinguishable from an ad campaign (Warhol had an early career in advertising). Pop's return to figuration indicates postmodernism's new being-at-home-in-the-world. Postmodernism has declared metanarratives and first philosophy to be obsolete; thereby, however, it risks discarding conceptual resources that might be of value in penetrating and demystifying the current crisis.

In the *Sociology of Art History* Arnold Hauser describes the regressive tendencies of pop:

Pop art denies the autonomy and immanence of the individual work. The picture of a girl in a swimming costume by Roy Lichtenstein shows no more individual traits than Andy Warhol's cans. Their simple unequivo-

cality and formulaic nature, their sharp outlines and monotones, their
schematic drawing and composition which lacks any tension—everything
about them contradicts the individuality of the work of art in general and
points to its reproducibility in this particular case. . . . Pop painting thus is
not only commercial in spirit like the other forms of pop art, but also uses
techniques of the commercial media, placards, magazine illustrations, and
newspaper advertisements. . . . It does not depend upon the impressing of
actual articles but on their schematized representation in media of commercial advertising. . . . Instead of immediate reproductions, it consists of
quotations from a text which already represents the material of reality as
translated into artifacts. We can see in this second-hand retreat from the
original data just as many signs of fear of coming into contact with natural
reality as of the expression of the perception that nothing is left for us of
the originality and immediacy of nature. . . . Pop painting denies the
mechanized and standardized character of bourgeois civilization, just as
decisively as dada, but without letting the political point of the movement
come to the forefront and, falling into a total nihilism in the face of the
products of the system, raises suspicion. It accepts its forms as the elements of a milieu in which we do not necessarily take delight, but which
must be accepted because there is no alternative.[29]

Here, Hauser has captured three key elements of pop qua manifestation of
postmodernism: (1) the renunciation of constitutive subjectivity and, hence,
of the "individuality" of works (infinite reproducibility); (2) the reconciliation made with the world of commodity fetishism (commercialism); (3) a pronounced sense of politico-cultural resignation (no alternatives—no *sur*reality—
to the existing order). At the same time, in their proximity to mass culture, in
their orientation toward consumption, these works exude a pseudopopulist
ethos which suggests that the gap between (high) art and life has been definitively bridged, and that aesthetic cultural democracy has been realized in the
here and now. Yet, beneath such illusions lies the following unwritten credo: the
frivolity of a *société de consommation* should be matched by the frivolity of art.

Though the initial influence of postmodernism was felt most keenly in the
sphere of the visual arts, it by no means remained confined to this sphere.
Instead there was scarcely an artistic domain untouched by the new cult of
aesthetic immediacy. One thinks of the neo-dadaist sculptures of Rauschenberg, poetic "word salads" of beat inspiration, "living theater," the "new journalism" of Tom Wolfe, the novels of William Burroughs and Donald Bar-
thelme, the fusion of classical and pop styles in the music of Philip Glass, as
well as the ahistorical architectural eclecticism of Michael Graves and Philip

Johnson. In a spirit not dissimilar to that of Hauser, Irving Howe has perceptively characterized the anti-intellectualism and ahistoricism characteristic of
postmodernism:

> We are confronting, then, a new phase in our culture, which in motive and
> spring represents a wish to shake off the bleeding heritage of modern-
> ism. . . . The new sensibility is impatient with ideas. It is impatient with
> literary structure of complexity and coherence, only yesterday the catch-
> words of our criticism. It wants instead works of literature—though litera-
> ture may be the wrong word—that will be as absolute as the sun, as
> unarguable as orgasm, as delicious as a lollipop. . . . It has no taste for that
> ethical nail-biting of those writers of the left who suffered defeat and
> would never accept the narcotic of certainty. It is sick of those magnifica-
> tions of irony that Mann gave us, sick of those visions of entrapment to
> which Kafka led us, sick of those shufflings of daily horror and grace that
> Joyce left us. It breathes contempt for rationality, impatience with mind.
> . . . It is bored with the past: for the past is a fink.[30]

The postmodernist devaluation of classical modernism has led to a corresponding valorization of mass culture, especially among left-wing critics uncomfortable with modernism's elitism. Often spurred by the "cultural studies"
approach of Stuart Hall and the Birmingham School, it is a position that self-
consciously rejects the Frankfurt School's path-breaking exposé of the "culture industry" in *Dialectic of Enlightenment*.[31] Instead of emphasizing the one-
dimensional process whereby a conformist culture is unilaterally foisted upon
unwitting masses, cultural studies explores the way cultural meanings are
refigured and transfigured in the process of being received. It is alleged that the
images and meanings of the culture industry are reappropriated, even revolu-
tionized, in the reception process itself. Thus, in *No Respect*, Andrew Ross
sets forth what he calls a modest, "dialectical" reading of "popular culture"
(the preferred term among its partisans): "In short, we cannot attribute any
purity of political expression to popular culture, although we can locate its
power to identify ideas and desires that are relatively opposed, alongside those
that are clearly complicit, to the official culture."[32] Despite his attempts to
advance the terms of this debate, Ross fails to answer the question: What
happens when popular culture *becomes* the official culture? What happens when
the images of the Hollywood blockbusters, MTV, and CNN take on the character of a "hyper-reality," before which all traditional claims to cultural nega-
tivity, such as those once staked by modernism and the avant-garde, fade into
insignificance?

In *Uncommon Cultures* Jim Collins cites a number of cultural spectacles from the 1970s and 1980s—*The Texas Chainsaw Massacres, The Outlaw Josey Wales, Robocop,* as well as Queen's MTV video, *Radio Gaga*—which he claims have actually *embraced* the critique of one-dimensional society once purveyed by the Frankfurt School.[33] The administrative conspiracy among elites from the corporate, government, and military spheres, Collins argues, has in fact become an object of polemical attack in these videos and films. As true as these allegations may be from a descriptive standpoint, one can also turn the argument around: so formidable have the culture industry's powers of absorption and co-optation become that they now possess the foresight and wherewithal to incorporate the terms of their own critique. The culture industry—to be sure, no longer the monolith portrayed by Horkheimer and Adorno in the 1940s and 1950s—has been able to detect the changing winds of public opinion in a post-counterculture, post-Watergate era. Correspondingly (and with negligible or dubious public impact) the critique of its own political-economic basis has become one of its staples. In lieu of its meaningful democratization, its impact and influences remain those of an ersatz or pseudo-public sphere. Moreover, if one takes a closer look at the inculpation of administrative elites in the films praised by Collins (*Robocop* or Clint Eastwood's popular, vigilantist "Dirty Harry" series), one sees that the "criticisms" of mass society, far from being by any stretch of the imagination "progressive," are articulated from the standpoint of the highly conventional, nostalgia-ridden American ethos of rugged individualism. As such, these films promote a return to an earlier and simpler order of American values, one free of the demands of political activism or racial conflict; an order of values that, in its own way, is hardly less problematic or more oriented toward emancipatory political ends than the industrial-political nexus it seeks to indict.

In part, this new valorization of popular culture stems from the correct perception that the social situation of culture has undergone a number of qualitative alterations since the Frankfurt School's original critique. Following the 1960s modern industrial societies ceased to correspond to the "one-dimensional" or "totally administered world" depicted by the first generation of critical theorists.[34] Instead, the Frankfurt School's "end of reason" prognosis foundered as a result of the vigorous protest movements associated with the counterculture and the New Left. Here, the irony is that it was precisely the critique generated by Adorno, Marcuse, et al., announcing that there was "no exit" from the contemporary historical impasse, that fueled the imagination of so many political radicals of the era.

Late capitalism of the cold war era was a period of well-nigh stifling conformism and—apart from occasional rumblings on the fringes—cultural ac-

commodation. From this standpoint the political (antiwar movement and feminism), social (civil rights movement), and cultural (counterculture) turbulence
of the next decade would seem virtually unimaginable. The social movements
of the 1960s challenged the political-cultural hegemony of the social system in
many constructive respects. Far from being reducible to the status of system-
stabilizing "feedback loops,"[35] their legacy constitutes a watershed in contemporary political discourse. Despite the concerted attempt in the 1980s to
remobilize traditional conservative values (cold war politics, religious funda-
mentalism, supply-side economics, a culturally conformist modernism), it is
impossible simply to efface or roll back this influence. The healthy cynicism
raised about traditional bureaucratic party politics and an imperialist foreign
policy, the new emphasis on multiculturalism and environmental limits to
growth—all remain a crucial and indispensable part of this legacy.

At the same time one must be careful not to overestimate the advances that
have been made, and one must be prepared to appraise their fragility realistically. In the cultural domain, especially, the balance remains precarious. To
be sure, the tenuous breakthrough of oppositional public spheres that emerged
with the counterculture and student movement allowed for the articulation of
paramount social concerns (the challenge to traditional sex roles, for example)
that led to the removal of a set of debilitating cultural taboos. Nevertheless, in
many ways the result has been the proliferation of a cultural pseudodemocracy
with the substance of democracy withheld. We have witnessed the triumph of
cultural difference in semblance, whereas the authentic realization of the values
feigned by the cultural sphere in the sphere of material life itself has not come
to pass. In no small measure, the search for cultural otherness or polyvalence
has been institutionalized (the music industry representing the apotheosis of
this phenomenon), offering us the omnipresent illusion of emancipation ("ours
is a culture in which anything is permitted") in order to deny more effectively
its realization.

I offer only the barest anecdotal evidence of this phenomenon. Doubtless,
thousands of other examples could be invoked. Shortly after the urban riots of
the mid-1960s, which were apotheosized in Jim Morrison's hit, "Light My
Fire," one of the Detroit auto manufacturers felt confident enough to utilize
The Doors' insurrectionary ode as the theme music for a television ad.[36] And
on a more contemporary note: as I write (fall 1994), the Miller Brewing Company is airing a commercial featuring the Buffalo Springfield anthem, "For
What It's Worth." The ad includes the well-known lyrics: "Somethin's happen
here. What it is ain't exactly clear. . . . You better stop, children, what's that
sound, everybody look what's goin' round." The marriage between rock and

advertising is certainly nothing new. But this case is a bit more interesting than most. Following the opening two lines just quoted, the lyrics that encapsulate the song's political message have been conveniently elided: "There's a man with a gun over there, tellin' me what I ought to wear." The 1960s abide, but Madison Avenue dictates the rhythms of popular memory.

All of which suggests that, in the present context, one should not be too quick to consign the Frankfurt School critique of mass culture to irrelevance. The new myth propagated by the culture industry pertains to its untrammeled pluralism: the taboos of a one-dimensional society have been lifted, and for it no theme remains too risqué. Clearly, there can be little that is authoritarian or manipulative about a society with such vast parameters of cultural tolerance. Is mass culture the phantasmagoria of changing fashion, the repetition of the always-the-same under the guise of the "new" as described by Walter Benjamin in connection with the dawn of our modern *société de consommation* (namely, the glittering world of the Paris arcades)?[37] Or has it evolved to a point where, as the enthusiasts of popular culture suggest, we need merely tap into the veins of utopian promise that lie in wait beneath the encrusted surface?

Today one can no longer proclaim à la Adorno that whatever emerges from the sphere of mass culture is inherently retrograde and "affirmative" (though this was a conclusion from which Adorno himself began to shy away in later years).[38] To be sure, there exist significant moments of alterity and contestation amid the vast expanses of cultural conformism in the fields of film, literature, and popular music, moments that point beyond the usual repetition-compulsion and standardization of culture industry products. At the same time, in the last two decades the predominant tendency has been the co-optation of the oppositional impulses of the counterculture. For the most part, its contentious claims have been transformed into the cultural chic of narcissistic, middle-class "life-styles"; its values have merely become grist for the mill of a society of consumption, in which the goals of vocational success and of familial privatism have triumphed over those of a more engaged public culture. Thus, the long-term historical consequences of the counterculture's assault on the sphere of decaying traditional values has been a period of relative stabilization, in which the semiotics of cultural radicalism, rather than being suppressed outright, have been largely incorporated within the value-system they sought to overturn, resulting in the *semblance* of democratization—a pseudocultural pluralism—minus the *substance*. Conversely, the veritable transformation of material life as originally demanded by the New Left has failed to come to pass. The net result of these trends has been the false sublation—or reconciliation—of the former antagonism between culture and material life. The "adversary culture" maligned for decades by cultural conservatives has virtually ceased to exist.[39]

Should these conjectures prove reliable, it would suggest a healthy skepticism about the current vogue concerning the latently emancipatory character of mass culture. It is by no means a vogue of recent vintage. Back in the early 1960s Leslie Fiedler was sounding the death-knell of classical modernism and singing the praises of hitherto neglected genres of mass culture ("B" movies, science fiction, detective novels) in essays such as "Cross the Border—Close the Gap" and "The New Mutants."[40] A *Journal of Popular Culture* has emerged, imploring us to take the manifestations of consumer culture as seriously as critics once took works of high culture. These products should indeed be taken seriously; but not quite for the rather unabashedly celebratory reasons frequently suggested by the journal's contributors. Even critics with former critical theory allegiances, such as Fredric Jameson, have come around to according the products of the culture industry a degree of utopian potential on a par with the works of modernism. For Jameson, mass culture must be grasped "not as an empty distraction or 'mere' false consciousness, but rather as a transformational work on social and political anxieties and fantasies which then must have some effective presence in the mass cultural text in order subsequently to be 'managed' or repressed."[41] He concludes that mass culture contains a "utopian or transcendent potential—that dimension of even the most degraded type of mass culture which remains implicitly, and no matter how faintly, negative and critical of the societal order from which, as a product and a commodity, it springs."[42]

Yet, while the apostles of popular culture are predisposed to view it as a repository of spontaneous dissent and refusal, they have been at a loss to determine whether the attitudinal changes it induces have been of sustained public or critical value. In *Understanding Popular Culture*, John Fiske devotes a chapter to the sense of "empowerment" gained by teenage girls upon viewing Madonna music videos.[43] Whatever the merits of such claims, one must seriously question whether the proliferation of clone-like "wanna-bes," more firmly than ever ensconced in a consumer-oriented cultural identity, furthers the type of critical individuation that the notion of empowerment suggests. Moreover, other studies indicate that the attitudinal changes fostered by mass culture tend to be extremely short-lived and ephemeral. Often it is the case that the medium remains the message: the audience is not so much concerned with the content of what it views; instead, it is simply oriented toward escape, distraction, or leisure pursuits. In this respect, one of the most time-honored and salient features of the culture industry has not changed: it continues to be geared toward the values of an administered cultural hedonism. An orientation toward consumption and leisure remains the industrially driven *spiritus et animus* behind the majority of culture-industry products.

Making a virtue of a necessity with regard to the omnipresence of cultural reification cannot but strike one as a hollow solution. The mass "anxieties and fantasies" which, according to Jameson, the culture industry is able to channel and distort, can by no means simply be lauded in their pristine original state. They too are thoroughgoing results of preexisting mechanisms of socialization. To treat them as "ciphers of Utopia" is therefore misleading: the precipitate upon decipherment—unsocialized desire—is far from politically reliable. This program is reminiscent of the traditional socialist faith in the immediate spontaneity of the masses; yet even Brecht realized that it was only by way of the avant-garde techniques of "alienation" and "interruption" that standardized patterns of perception could be broken down, and the homilies of epic theater conveyed.

The culture of postmodernism possesses many ambivalences. Even Warhol's iconography of American consumerism and celebrity are replete with irony: they hold up a mirror to our own cultural narcissism and excess, daring us to recognize our own foibles, but, at the same time, betting we won't. Thus, as not a few critics have observed, postmodernism practices subversion and complicity in almost the same breath.[44]

Yet a number of critics have viewed the moment of complicity as predominant. Hal Foster laments postmodernism's profound ahistoricism. Marx once said, "We recognize only one science, the science of history." Foster fears that once the past is read ahistorically and cultural phenomena are radically decontextualized, we will be deprived of the basis for critique, which has always depended on an acute historical understanding:

> the use of pastiche in postmodern art and architecture deprives styles not only of specific context but also of historical sense: husked down to so many emblems, they are reproduced in the form of partial simulacra. In this sense, "history" appears reified, fragmented, fabricated—both imploded and depleted (not only a history of victors, but a history in which modernism is bowdlerized). The result is a history-surrogate, at once standard and schizoid. Finally, such postmodernism is less a dialectical supersession of modernism than its old ideological opponent, which then and now assumes the form of a popular front of pre- and anti-modernist elements.[45]

Even Jameson's initial enthusiasm for postmodernism qua mass culture appears to have undergone a substantial revision. In a much-cited essay, he argues (somewhat deterministically) that postmodernism is the cultural form appropriate to late capitalism. Particularly astute are his observations concerning postmodernism's cultural "depthlessness": its studious avoidance of the complexities and tensions of high modernism, its preference instead for light-hearted citation or pastiche.[46] Once irony becomes ensconced as a credo, what is the point of taking seriously the tasks of cultural criticism or social contestation? Would not such seriousness merely constitute a regression to the out-moded modernist cult of aesthetic profundity? One of the high points of Jameson's essay consists of a comparison between archetypal works from each artistic mode: Van Gogh's *Peasant Shoes* (modernism) and Warhol's *Diamond Dust Shoes* (postmodernism). As opposed to the Van Gogh image, which invites hermeneutical decipherment (e.g., Heidegger's famous commentary in "The Origin of the Work of Art"), Warhol's shoes are wholly inert. They tend consciously to rebuff all efforts at depth-psychological interpretation or historical criticism:

> Andy Warhol's "Diamond Dust Shoes" evidently no longer speaks to us with any of the immediacy of Van Gogh's footgear; indeed, I am tempted to say that it does not really speak to us at all. Nothing in this painting organizes even a minimal place for the viewer, who confronts it at the turning of a museum corridor gallery with all the contingency of some inexplicable natural object. On the level of the content, we have to do with what are now far more clearly fetishes, in both the Freudian and the Marxian senses. . . . Here, however, we have a random collection of dead objects hanging together on the canvas like so many turnips, as shorn of their earlier life world as the pile of shoes left over from Auschwitz or the remainders and tokens of some incomprehensible and tragic fire in a packed dance hall. There is therefore in Warhol no way to complete the hermeneutic gesture and restore to these odd-ments that whole larger lived context of the dance hall or the ball. . . .[47]

At issue is the rampant commodification of life in a "society of the spectacle" ("All life in societies in which modern conditions of production reign announces itself as an immense accumulation of *spectacles*"—Guy Debord), the triumph of a society in which images supplant the things themselves: a society in which reification has been "perfected."[48] These developments call for vigorous critique. Instead, postmodernism, by renouncing the depth-dimension of (modernist) interpretive rigor, by resting content with superficies and simulacra, ends up celebrating them. Echoing Nietzsche, postmodernism denies the dialectical tension between essence and appearance, announcing instead that "appearance is all there is." As Jameson continues:

> Andy Warhol's work in fact turns centrally around commodification, and the great billboard images of the Coca-Cola bottle or the Campbell's soup

can, which explicitly foreground the commodity fetishism of a transition to late capital, *ought* to be powerful and critical political statements. If they are not that, then one would surely want to know why, and one would want to begin to wonder a little more seriously about the possibilities of political or critical art in the postmodern period of late capital.[49]

The zero-degree aesthetic of postmodernist art engenders a wholesale loss of affect. It generates a surface-oriented aesthetic universe that is conducive to a drastic, post-Freudian withdrawal of emotional cathexis. Whereas one of modernism's signatures (in this connection, Jameson appropriately invokes Edvard Munch's *The Scream*) involved the theme of artistic alienation—the irreconcilable opposition between the artistic sublime and the prosaicism of society as a whole—postmodernism does away with this antagonism. In its emotionally flattened landscapes, one is, as it were, deprived of the capacity to feel one's own alienation. And this is the entire point of a society of spectacles, in which cheerful images of adjustment and reconciliation abound. Postmodern culture, its characteristic tropes of hypercynicism and irony notwithstanding, too readily and in good conscience buys into these images. Standing Hegel on his head for good, it ceaselessly proclaims that appearance is all there is.

THE CULTURAL POLITICS OF

NEOCONSERVATISM

It was inevitable that the neoconservative reaction of the 1980s would spread from politics to culture. It did this with a vengeance in the pages of the *New Criterion*, the journal of cultural criticism launched in September 1982 by Hilton Kramer, former art critic for the *New York Times*. The ideological slant of the journal was boldly enunciated in the very first number. "Standards," "values," and "morality" were to be preserved over and against the onslaught of countervailing tendencies: in truth, tendencies that possessed *different* standards and values from Kramer and his like-minded guardians of cultural purity. It is fascinating to encounter repeatedly in the journal's pages the claim that *its* criteria of aesthetic judgment are nonideological—or, strictly aesthetic, hence, pure—whereas the world of art criticism at large is sullied by vulgar ideologues, politicos, and irredeemable philistines.[1] The *New Criterion* appeared on the scene, with the banner of righteousness held high, in order, in Kramer's words, to "distinguish achievement from failure, to identify and uphold a standard of quality, and to speak plainly and vigorously about the problems that beset the life of the arts and the life of the mind in our society." What is written in journals other than Mr. Kramer's own is blithely dismissed as "either hopelessly ignorant, deliberately obscurantist, commercially compromised, or politically motivated." Elsewhere, "criticism at every level . . . has almost everywhere degenerated into one or another form of ideology or publicity or some pernicious combination of the two."[2] It is indeed a night in which all cows are black.

However, the aesthetic values propagated by the *New Criterion* are woefully predictable and familiar. Frankly, there is nothing in the least "new" about the "criteria" that are repeatedly invoked by Kramer et al. The journal seeks to glorify a thoroughly conventional and eviscerated version of the modernist canon. Bourgeois high culture is historically rehabilitated as an irrefragable repository of aesthetic integrity. Any deviations from this sacrosanct tradition of cultural achievement are pilloried with inquisitorial zeal. Unsurprisingly, all traces of so-called low or popular culture merit only the most relentless excoriation. The sociohistorical conditions that result in the polarization between high and low culture—namely, the capitalist commodification of value, which compels art to resort to increasingly rarefied and hermetic modes of expression in order to escape integration—remain imperceptible in Kramer's account. Given his self-understanding as "cultural critic,"[3] the acknowledgment that material factors of any sort might interfere with the purity of the cultural sphere would be strictly inadmissible. Yet, as Walter Benjamin emphasized nearly fifty years ago, "the concept of culture, as the substantive concept of creations which are considered independent, if not from the production process in which they originate, then from a production process in which they continue to survive, carries a fetishistic trait. Culture appears in a reified form."[4]

Kramer's concerted attempt to separate culture from the realm of material life reifies culture as a store of disembodied, eternal verities. Its immediate relationship to society, the life-world, and the formation of individual identities in the sense of the German *Bildung* is occluded in favor of a belletristic boosterism. Shorn of its experiential substance as a formative influence on the life-processes of individuals, culture is abstractly worshiped, resulting in the perpetuation of the "secular religion of art," as Benjamin termed art for art's sake. Paradoxically, the advent of secularized art in the modern era implies a definitive break with the concept of art as an object of religious veneration. Instead, implicit in the logic of cultural secularization, culminating in so-called autonomous art, is a claim to the *democratization* of culture. As confirmed elitists, Kramer and his cohorts view this prospect with dread, insofar as the advent of a truly democratic culture (as opposed to the Hollywood/Madison Avenue–administered variant) would deprive them of their vaunted position of privilege. In their position, it is not hard to glimpse the specter of (bourgeois) self-interest intruding upon the professed image of the disinterested aesthete.

Kramer insists repeatedly that the *New Criterion*'s standpoint is nonideological and objective, in comparison with the rampant left-wing politicization of culture. As opposed to such tendencies, Kramer's journal identifies with the values of "expert intelligence," "connoisseurship that concentrates its principal interest on aesthetic quality," and a "cultural elitism that serves the public interest"—presumably by continuing to allow Kramer and his fellow cognoscenti to arbitrate forcibly standards of taste.[5] However, if ideology may be defined as socially engendered false consciousness, it may be safely said that the *New Criterion* is copiously ideological. Rather than taking its claims to value-neutrality at face value, it is essential to understand the journal's timely appearance on the cultural scene as part of the larger sociopolitical phenomenon of neoconservatism.

To be sure, the *New Criterion* has never attempted to conceal its partisanship for the conservative ideological shift and its politics, an admission that squares poorly with its condemnation of competing cultural tendencies as ideological. The argument cuts both ways. Throughout its pages, the standard fare of neoconservative rhetoric is constantly reiterated. The absolute negative point of reference for the neoconservative cultural criticism is, of course, the political upsurge of the 1960s. As Kramer remarks at one point: "We are still living in the aftermath of the insidious assault on mind that was one of the most repulsive features of the radical movement of the Sixties. The cultural consequences of this leftward turn in our political life has been far graver than commonly supposed. In everything from the writing of textbooks to the reviewing of trade books, from the introduction of Kitsch into museums to the decline of literacy in the schools to the corruption of scholarly research, the effect on the life of culture has been ongoing and catastrophic."[6]

The politicization of life in the 1960s becomes the radical evil universally responsible for all subsequent cultural failings, with the possible exception of New York subway system breakdowns. Curiously, Kramer writes not a word about 1980s right-wing kitsch: *Red Dawn, Rambo,* the *Rocky* series, and so forth. Kitsch, moreover, derives from German cultural debates of the 1920s, not the 1960s; it is a phenomenon whose origins can be traced to the separation of high and low art at the close of the eighteenth century. It is clear that the specter of a politically active citizenry, standing up en masse to an immoral war, unwilling to stomach a plebiscitary democracy in which professional politicians reign, represents a devastating threat to an elitist philosophy of politics and culture, which requires instead a quiescent and pliable public. Here it is of interest to note that the neoconservative preference for government by elites conflicts with the pseudopopulism of its rhetoric, in which the evils of "big government" and "rule from Washington" are lamented.

In his book on the neoconservatives, Peter Steinfels describes a key element of their worldview as follows: "The current crisis is primarily a cultural crisis, a matter of values, morals, and manners. Though this crisis has causes and consequences on the level of socioeconomic structures, neoconservatism, unlike the Left, tends to think these have performed well. The problem is that our convictions have gone slack, our morals loose, our manners corrupt."[7] Steinfels's account accords well with the aforementioned appeal to "standards of quality" and the "values of high art," the raison d'être of the *New Criterion*.

Yet, not only does one find in the journal's pages the predictable paeans to the values of high culture, but implicit endorsements of the cultural policies of Republican politics as well. Unsurprisingly, public funding for the arts comes under heavy attack, and the private sector is typically viewed as the panacea for cultural as well as social problems. To be sure, public funding of the arts is an issue fraught with political difficulties. Ultimately, it fosters a regression behind the democratization of art achieved in the eighteenth century, in the form of a restoration of the constraints of artistic patronage. At the same time, when the potential for artistic democratization (i.e., the freeing of individual artists from the constraints of traditional authority, be it courtly or religious) is negated by the subjection of all art to the requisites of the commodity form, judicious employment of public funds to shelter artists from the vicissitudes of the market has much to commend it.

Despite his pretensions to the contrary, it is clear that the real motive behind Kramer's scorn for public support of the arts is ideological: in his view, the arts tend to be dominated by unpatriotic leftists, and eliminating public funding for the arts is the best way to ensure that they are purged. Such displays of political paranoia have become only too typical of the neoconservative mentality, and comparable examples abound in the *New Criterion*. The more one reads, the more one realizes that the mission of the *New Criterion* has little to do with promoting ideals of cultural excellence. Instead, the main preoccupation of the journal seems to be that of settling old political scores. "The truth is, it would be easier for a camel to pass through the eye of a needle than for a serious conservative writer to win a major literary prize in this country today," laments Kramer at one point.[8] Little does he realize, his observation, if correct, likely says more about the paucity of the conservative imagination than about left-wing conspiracies.

As might be expected, the *New Criterion* line on higher education is vintage William Bennett, with a generous dose of Accuracy in Academia thrown in for good measure. Like the authoritarian personality of old, the neoconservative mentality has little tolerance for ambiguity. The enemy must be identified quickly, accurately, then presumably rooted out. "There are three movements at work in American humanities departments which have replaced, or soon will replace, the ethos of the liberal humanists of my generation," observes Norman Cantor in an article entitled "The Real Crisis in the Humanities Today."[9] "These are Marxism, feminism, and the methodologies of structuralism and deconstruction. It is to these three movements and their ideological implications that we must turn for a real understanding of the crisis of the humanities today." There follows in essence an academic "hit list."[10] According to Cantor, the historians Lawrence Stone and Eugene Genovese must be given close scrutiny. Stone, the former head of the Davis Center for Historical Studies at Princeton, possesses "extensive patronage powers in the historical profession. Similarly, Genovese's appointment at Rochester gave him an influential position in the academic establishment." One must be especially wary of the pseudohumanistic "Western Marxism," which attempts to "reintroduce idealism into the Marxist system" and whose central tenet is that of "cultural mediation." "Critical theory," one learns, "is now an integral part of the American university curriculum."[11] What we are offered is a 1980s version of a "Marxist (or occasionally a feminist) under every bed."

Ranking high on the hit list are Marxist humanist scholars Martin Jay, Mark Poster, Eugene Lunn, and Fredric Jameson: "their work in intellectual history or literary criticism has taken the place, for many bright students in the humanities, of the liberal-humanist scholarship that characterized the 1960s." Journals such as *Social Text, October,* and *Telos* also must be carefully monitored. The tone and the level of Cantor's argumentation manifest delusions of paranoia reminiscent of McCarthyism. If Marxists have migrated to the universities (as, for example, Roger Kimball argues in *Tenured Radicals*), the neocons should be pleased. After all, what more innocuous locus could be found for political radicals than the ivory towers of academe?

The claim that left-wing intellectuals have fostered hedonistic life-styles that have plunged the moral fiber of the American way of life into an abyss is a long-standing kernel of neoconservative mythology often associated with the "new class" thesis. A much-discussed term in recent sociological literature,[12] the new class refers to the growing stratum of intellectuals who now find themselves in positions of economic and political power, bolstered by the advent of a technologically oriented "society of information." The claim that this grouping of individuals can be said to constitute anything resembling a "class" (the bearers of "cultural capital" in Alvin Gouldner's words, its membership ranges from university professors to corporate executives to computer programmers) seems dubious. On the other hand, the argument that its members tend toward narcissistic patterns of consumption rings true. Nevertheless, the alacrity with which this group participates in life-styles oriented toward conspicuous consumption disqualifies it as the subversive "adversary culture" of neoconservative lore. However loosely it is defined, this new class, given such conformist habits of consumption, hardly stands as a repository of the radical, "post-materialist values" that the neoconservatives fear.[13] Moreover, its orientation toward "self-actualization" (one of the distinguishing traits of a postmaterialist value-orientation according to political scientist Ronald Inglehart) is usually satisfied by a variety of fadlike, pop-psychological trends that facilitate narcissistic withdrawal rather than active political contestation.

The attempt by Kramer and his cohorts to blame a hedonistic counterculture for depleting the moral foundations of the late capitalist society is another standard component of neoconservative conventional wisdom. As originally set forth in Daniel Bell's *The Cultural Contradictions of Capitalism* (1976), this thesis holds that there is a structural incompatibility between the achievement mentality of capitalism, which is based on the rational forbearance embodied in the Protestant ethic, and the values of the cultural sphere, which promote an interest in sensual fulfillment, experiential immediacy, and expressive rather than goal-oriented subjectivity.

But the problems with this analytical scheme are twofold. First, cultural modernism's unquenchable desire for new experiences cannot be so neatly detached from the sphere of economic action: the ceaseless dynamism that necessitates the dismantling of all traditional ways of life, the disruption of all fixed values and norms, the obsessive concern with progress and development at all costs—all of these values correspond to the entrepreneurial ethos, the Faustian striving in which "all that is solid melts into air."[14] In all these respects, the dynamism of cultural modernism—its unceasing quest for the "new"—merely parallels the dynamism of modernity as a socioeconomic phenomenon. However, the limitation of Bell's argument is that it risks falling victim to a confusion of cause and effect. It unjustly condemns the cultural sphere for the attempt to provide elements of sensuousness and fulfillment that capitalism systematically denies. Moreover, the crucial economic transition from a society of production to a society of consumption is occluded in this account, though it is precisely this changeover that fosters an ethos of consumer indulgence ultimately fatal to Protestant self-renunciation. In all these respects, the cultural sphere is unfairly blamed for the advent of a profligate consumer ethos that was crucial to the *stabilization* of capitalism after the crisis of overproduction in 1929.[15] From this point on, an administratively engendered demand for consumer goods ("consumerism") was intended to offset future crises of overproduction.

Kramer's own account of how the cultural sphere, under capitalism, undermines the motivational foundations of the economic sector is misleading in comparison with Bell's. Because Kramer would like to save twentieth-century modernism, qua touchstone of aesthetic value, from being implicated in sociopolitical turmoil, he refuses to concede any link between the counterculture of the 1960s and aesthetic modernism. Instead, he holds 1960s radicalism alone accountable for what he and his neoconservative brethren view as contemporary moral laxness. Bell's account is more honest in that it views the counter-culture as merely one in a series of modernist assaults against the hypocrisy and repression characteristic of the culture of capitalism. Indeed, the very notion of a counterculture must be traced back to the Paris of Baudelaire and the advent of bohemianism as an oppositional life-style.

Kramer's appreciation of the modernist legacy is misleading insofar as it seeks to preserve a modernism shorn of its radical sensibilities. The iconoclastic thrust of the modernist heritage is neutered and domesticated in his account. By employing the overarching concept of "modernism" to refer to both the literary modernism of Joyce, Proust, Woolf, Kafka, etc., as well as to the revolutionary energies of the historical avant-garde (dadaism, futurism, expressionism, and surrealism) which, as Peter Bürger has shown, was less concerned with creating new literary or artistic "styles" than in challenging the bourgeois "institution of art" in its entirety, Kramer blurs a number of crucial differences between these two currents. The result is the creation of the homogeneous and aesthetically pure modernist canon in which the real social challenges posed by the modernist/avant-garde legacy to the institutional bases of the established social order evaporate in a cloud of aestheticist affirmation. In Kramer's framework, the entire modernist heritage is viewed as a single, undifferentiated continuum—fundamentally, an extension of art for art's sake. What is lost sight of is that, given the pressing nature of the European cultural crisis leading up to and precipitating World War I, the aestheticist credo of *l'art pour l'art* (art as the realm of "beautiful illusion") became insupportable to artists on a vast scale. Because Kramer insists upon viewing art strictly in *intra-aesthetic* terms, excluding all wider social and cultural mediations, he remains incapable of appreciating the extent to which art overlaps positively with other spheres of life, thereby actively influencing, defamiliarizing, and challenging conventional worldviews.

Kramer's aesthetic canon of orthodox high modernism offers little that is surprising or controversial. He reveres Cézanne, Picasso, Matisse, Mondrian, on the one hand; the abstract expressionists Gorky, Rothko, and Motherwell on the other. He is hostile toward virtually all artistic tendencies that postdate abstract expressionism. Unsurprisingly, all postmodernist trends become a privileged object of scorn. Kramer is aware of the "routinization of the avant-garde": the fact that a once adversarial culture has established a peaceable modus vivendi with the bourgeois society it once vehemently opposed. Yet the conclusions he draws from this realization are strangely inconsistent. For the inner contradictions of modernism—its inaccessibility, elitist self-understanding, implicit neglect of questions of content—that led to its assimilation and rejection by the postmodernists remain for him untroubling. Consequently, modernism's demise is not merely a testament to bourgeois society's capacity to assimilate difference; it also suggests elements of modernism's own intrinsic failings.[16] Since Kramer, however, is unwilling to address the shortcomings of modernism, his perspective is vitiated by a bad historicism: he remains a partisan of modernism "the way it really was"—as a fossilized object of historical veneration. Having acknowledged modernism's social integration, he observes: "Yet modernism, though now stripped of the nearly absolute authority it formerly wielded in artistic matters, is anything but dead. It survives as a vital tradition—the only real vital tradition that the art of our time can claim as its own. The revenge of the Philistines is anything but complete."[17] What Kramer fails to recognize is that any discussion of the modern as a "tradition"—even as a "vital tradition"—remains a contradiction in terms, since one of the most fundamental characteristics of the modern in general is to be *antithetical to all tradition*. Once the modern becomes something traditional, as it does in Kramer's hands, it has already lost the battle, as it were. Kramer refuses to think through the failings of modernism;[18] instead, he merely regresses to traditional modernist values in a moment of cultural insecurity.

The main problem with Kramer's approach is that it is both belletristic and affirmative. The socially critical role of art, which is one of its central raisons d'être, its capacity to negate the world as it is and thereby to provide alternative models of discourse, is wholly eclipsed in this perspective. Instead, art is reduced to the level of an innocuous, self-referential pastime suitable for the enjoyment of elites. Limited to this affirmative function, art is charged with providing illusory images of transcendence, in compensation for the failings and deficiencies of the world such as it is. Kramer believes that by artificially elevating art to the rarefied sphere of "eternal cultural values" fit for consumption by the few, he can remove all suspicion of art's ideological taint. The irony is that Kramer thereby only compounds the problem. In his schema, art is all the more reduced to a type of "socially engendered false consciousness," insofar as it is entrusted with the mission of providing a semblance of reconciliation despite existing social contradictions. However, by glossing over social antagonisms with a veneer of harmony and well-being, art becomes fully ideological. Even at the zenith of aesthetic affirmation with art for art's sake, the *promesse de bonheur* registered a moment of social protest: it contained the promise of a better world that, in contrast to the indigent state of the existing one, would serve as a powerful indictment of the latter's deficiencies. But since Kramer elects to bypass entirely the critical dimension of aesthetic semblance (*Schein*), one is left with the idea of art as rank consolation for the shortcomings of the material world. The content of art is reduced to diversion *simpliciter*.

Here a curious irony enters into play. Kramer's avowed mission all along has been to redeem art from the base domain of "low" culture, to save high art from the clutches of "philistines" and "kitsch." Yet, because he remains so averse to considering either the cognitive or social dimensions of aesthetic experience, all he is left with is art as a variety of kitsch—a conclusion implicit in his image of art as a diversion from the realm of material interests (albeit, an exalted diversion). Kramer's appreciation of art returns aesthetics to the sphere of the culinary or "banausic." In his hands high art becomes merely the flip side of culture-industry pap. It becomes an object of consumption for cultural elites— but an object of consumption nevertheless. This debasement of art echoes clearly in Kramer's notion of "connoisseurship,"[19] which is inseparable from associations with the culinary sphere. Moreover, in Kramer's conception of the art critic as connoisseur, the tainted origins of bourgeois criticism—its nineteenth-century links to the realm of commodity consumption—are discernible: the idea of the critic as a "purveyor of cultural goods," who assists consumers to discriminate in their choice among the available cultural commodities. The critic who fancies himself above the fray of commodification is ultimately fully in league with it. He attempts to assert that his estimable judgments are suprahistorical—hence, nonideological and sovereign—when in fact they are, like all "social facts," thoroughly mediated by the values of the reigning social totality. As Adorno has remarked of such cultural critics: "The prerogatives of information and position permit them to express their opinion as if it were objectivity. But it is solely the objectivity of the ruling mind. They help to weave the veil. . . . If cultural criticism, even at its best with Valéry, sides with conservatism, it is because of its unconscious adherence to a notion of culture, which, during the era of late capitalism, aims at a form of property which is stable and independent of stock-market fluctuations."[20]

But perhaps the greatest deficiency of affirmative cultural criticism is its shameless fetishization of the concept of culture itself: its treatment of culture as something independent, divorced from the life-process of society. In truth, culture is valuable only when it remains true to its implicit critical capacities. Its independence from society allows it the breathing-space required to reflect on society with critical acumen, rather than to turn its back on the social world in the celebration of eternal verities. Indeed, it is precisely when viewed *sub specium aeternis* that culture becomes in truth ideological, the window-dressing that lends a false veil of humanity to an otherwise inhuman society. What becomes unconscionable about affirmative cultural criticism is that "where there is despair and measureless misery, [the cultural critic] sees only spiritual phenomena, the state of man's consciousness, the decline of norms."[21] In this conception of the mission of criticism, culture becomes high-brow consolation for the anguish of worldly suffering—a *divertissement* for sophisticates. This view is only a hair's breadth removed from the connoisseurship for "serious music" displayed by Nazi concentration camp administrators after a busy day stoking the ovens.

These are the circumstances to which Adorno alluded when he reflected on the possibilities of writing poetry after Auschwitz.[22] After the Holocaust, would not every trace of affirmative sentiment be guilty of providing false consolation? Nevertheless, Adorno was quick to point out that to despair of culture would in the end be tantamount to surrendering to the forces of barbarism, which culture must strive to offset. It is precisely for such reasons that the concept of culture must be saved from the clutches of Kramer and his kind.

REFLECTIONS ON JEWISH
SECULAR MESSIANISM

The past carries with it a temporal index by which it is referred to redemption. There is a secret agreement between past generations and the present one. Our coming was expected on earth. Like every generation that preceded us, we have been endowed with a *weak* messianic power, a power to which the past has a claim. That claim cannot be settled cheaply.—Walter Benjamin, "Theses on the Philosophy of History"

It seems to me particularly noteworthy that the messianic idea, the third element in that trilogy of Creation, Revelation, and Redemption, exercises unbroken and vital power even today. Creation, so closely linked to the conviction of the existence of God, has to an extraordinary extent receded or vanished from contemporary consciousness. Outside the fundamentalist minority, Revelation persists only in enlightened or mystical reinterpretations which, no matter how legitimate they may be, no longer possess the original vehemence which promoted its enormous influence in the history of religion. Yet the messianic idea has maintained precisely this vehemence. Despite all attenuations it has proved itself an idea of highest effectiveness and relevance—even in its secularized forms. It was better able to stand a reinterpretation into the secular realm than the other ideas. Whereas more than 100 years ago such reinterpretation was still regarded as an utter falsification of the Jewish idea of Redemption and messianism—and just by the defenders of the historical school in Judaism—it has become the center of great visions in the present age.—Gershom Scholem, "Reflections on Jewish Theology"

I

In a celebrated essay, Isaac Deutscher describes a prominent Jewish personality-type, the "non-Jewish Jew." In the modern era the non-Jewish Jew has been responsible for a unique and productive extension of the Jewish sensibility to the realm of secular concerns. According to Deutscher:

The Jewish heretic who transcends Jewry belongs to a Jewish tradition. You may, if you like, see Akher [a *Midrash* heretic] as a prototype of these great revolutionaries of modern thought: Spinoza, Heine, Marx, Rosa Luxemburg, Trotsky, and Freud. You may, if you wish to, place them within a Jewish tradition. They all went beyond the boundaries of Jewry. They all found Jewry too narrow, too archaic, and too constricting. They all looked for ideals and fulfillment beyond it, and they represent the sum and substance of much that is greatest in modern thought, the sum and substance of the most profound upheavals that have taken place in philosophy, sociology, economics, and politics in the last three centuries.[1]

For Deutscher, it is not the Jewishness of the forenamed thinkers that accounts for their status as intellectual innovators. Instead, in his eyes, their claim to greatness may be best understood in terms of their having made a definitive break with their Jewish past. Indeed, the first three he names were all converts to Christianity. And the author of *The Future of an Illusion* never made a secret of his equation of religion with superstition *simpliciter*. In Deutscher's estimation, therefore (and it is at this point that the selectivity of his list begins to become apparent), these cosmopolitan intellectuals were able to achieve renown and influence only insofar as they were able to *transcend* their own Jewishness. Hence, their greatness must be explained *sociologically* and not in terms of the transposition of a religious sensibility to the realm of secular affairs. Spinoza's pantheism, Heine's solidarity with the persecuted and oppressed, Marx's longing for a this-worldly transcendence of alienation—all may be explained in terms of the Jew's traditional position on the sociocultural fringe. Their genius may be explained externally, as a by-product of the protagonists' social situatedness. In Deutscher's view the deracinated Jew, forced to the cultural margin, becomes as it were an internationalist *avant la lettre*. As he explains:

> They were a priori exceptional in that as Jews they dwelt on the borderlines of various civilizations, religions, and national cultures. They were born and brought up on the borderlines of various epochs. Their mind matured where the most diverse cultural influences crossed and fertilized each other. They lived on the margins or in the nooks and crannies of their respective nations. Each of them was in society and yet not in it, of it and yet not of it. It was this that enabled them to rise in thought above their societies, above their nations, above their times and generations, and to strike out mentally into wide new horizons and far into the future.[2]

There can be no arguing with the descriptive cogency of Deutscher's account. Similar interpretations concerning the historical uniqueness of Jewish intellectual life have been proffered often enough in the past. Still, it is those components of the non-Jewish Jew's experience that Deutscher intentionally passes over in silence that one would like to know more about. Can one really understand the non-Jewish Jew by abstracting from all religious contents, influences, and motifs, however broadly these might be conceived?

Deutscher rules out the possibility of an affirmative answer to this question. His worldview, one suspects, has been preformed. His own internationalism and progressivism suggest that the attempt to provide a positive answer to the question just posed would be retrograde. In his view, only by freeing himself from what is specifically Jewish can the Jew truly be fulfilled. In this way alone can he attain the status of humanity in general, or, what Marx referred to as "species-being." Deutscher persists in the belief that the definitive answer to the Jewish question was provided by the young Marx in his *Jugendschrift* of the same title: the self-sacrifice of Jewish identity on the altar of a socialist future. However, as the century draws to a close, can we not detect in Marx's answer to the Jewish question of some 150 years ago more than a faint anticipation of the handling of the "minorities question" in Eastern Europe's now obsolete People's Republics?

II

Were Deutscher to have expanded his list of non-Jewish Jews to include that generation of uniquely gifted, Central European apostles of messianic socialism who came of age at the time of World War I—a list that would include Walter Benjamin, Ernst Bloch, Gustav Landauer, Georg Lukács, Herbert Marcuse, as well as other members of the Frankfurt School—he might have been more hard-pressed to make good his atheological explanation. For he then would have been compelled to explain what Scholem, in "Reflections on Jewish Theology," calls the peculiar resilience of the messianic idea. According to Scholem, this was an idea that maintained its vehemence insofar as it "was better able to stand a reinterpretation into the secular realm than the other ideas."[3] In its pure form, this Central European intellectual type might best be described by the term Bloch applied to the sixteenth-century champion of radical social reform, Thomas Münzer: they were *theologians of revolution*.

How can one account for the fact that the messianic idea was able to renew its effectiveness and relevance at this particular juncture in the history of European Jewry by undergoing a fundamental modification; namely, by becoming secularized? What were the peculiar affinities between messianism, socialism, and the Central European Jewish intelligentsia that brought forth this historically unprecedented synthesis of theological and revolutionary motifs? And, given that the hopes for historical-messianic renewal shared by this generation of intellectuals were so brutally quashed by the parallel triumphs of Nazism and Stalinism, is there any possibility that this vision of utopian fulfillment can provide inspiration for our own very different historical circumstances?

III

The social situation of Central European Jewry that figures so prominently in the portrait of the non-Jewish Jew sketched by Deutscher is a factor that no analyst concerned with the phenomenon of Jewish secular messianism can afford to ignore. Were one to require further proof of this thesis, one need only examine matters from the *ex negativo* standpoint of the Western European countries, in which virtually no traces of this secular messianic spirit are to be found.[4] Whereas circa 1900, postrevolutionary promises of universal equality had gone far toward alleviating the plight of Western European Jews, the assimilationist dreams of their Central European counterparts seemed all but dashed amid recurrent waves of increasingly virulent anti-Semitism. As a result, for Central European Jewry the liberal option seemed to have played itself out, and the historical alternatives appeared to be the either/or of socialism or Zionism. Thus, at a time when hopes for assimilation were dashed, the only possibilities seemed to lie either in the radical political transformation of existing Central European societies—which the socialists hoped would be a prelude to the radical transformation of the world itself—or the pursuit of a Jewish identity elsewhere.

The historical dynamic behind such thinking has been described by Anson Rabinbach:

> In the years approaching the First World War, the self-confidence and the security of German Jewry was challenged by a new Jewish sensibility that can be described as at once radical, secular and Messianic in both tone and content. What this new Jewish *ethos* refused to accept was above all the optimism of the generation of German Jews nurtured on the concept of *Bildung* as the German Jewish mystique. They were profoundly shaken by political anti-Semitism and the anti-liberal spirit of the German upper classes, which for them called into question the political and cultural assumptions of the post-emancipation epoch. Especially irksome was the

belief that there was no contradiction between *Deutschtum* and *Judentum;* that secularization and liberalism would permit the cultural integration of Jews into the national community.[5]

But this explanation itself needs explaining. In the fifty years prior to World War I the Central European monarchies underwent an unprecedented economic transformation. Within this relatively brief span of time, Germany, for example (the changes were not quite so far-reaching in the case of Austria-Hungary), vaulted from a predominantly agrarian nation to one of the world's leading industrial producers. Nor would these changes leave the foundations of traditional German social structure unaffected. Whereas in 1870, some 70 percent of Prussian Jews lived in small villages, by 1927, this was true of only 15 percent.[6] Clearly, many Jews had taken advantage of the new opportunities for social mobility and professional advancement provided by Germany's industrial revolution. At the same time, Jews increasingly took the blame for changes in German society that had upset the traditional class structure. Thus, the evils of industrialization and urbanization were unjustly attributed to unnatural Jewish influences. Nor was this new wave of anti-Jewish sentiment confined to so-called traditional or "vulgar" anti-Semitism. It was shared by a large segment of the German *Bildungsbürgertum,* as well as the mandarin intelligentsia, which had suffered a decline of status and influence as a result of the triumph of commercial and material values that were part and parcel of Germany's rapid economic expansion.

IV

Lukács's preface to *The Theory of the Novel* (1962) provides important insight into the intellectual origins of Jewish secular messianism. There he coins the phrase "romantic anti-capitalism" to describe a generation of German intellectuals who were psychologically traumatized by the repercussions of rapid industrialization. In response, they focused nostalgically on the prospects for a restoration of precapitalist social relations. As Fritz Ringer has observed, "The German academics related to the [economic] dislocation with such desperate intensity that the specter of a 'soulless' modern age came to haunt everything they said and wrote, no matter what the subject. By the early 1920s they were deeply convinced that they were living through a profound crisis, a 'crisis of culture,' of 'learning,' of 'values,' or of the 'spirit.' "[7] For this generation, the distinction between *Gemeinschaft* and *Gesellschaft* popularized by Tönnies' 1887 classic work of this title possessed a type of canonical status.[8]

Lukács characterizes the legacy of his 1914–15 study as follows:

The Theory of the Novel is not conservative but subversive in nature, even if based on a highly naive and totally unfounded utopianism—the hope that a natural life worthy of man can spring from the disintegration of capitalism and the destruction, seen as identical with that disintegration, of the lifeless and life-denying social and economic categories.

The standpoint of the work aimed at a fusion of "left" ethics and "right" epistemology (ontology, etc.). . . . From the 1920s onwards this view was to play an increasingly important role. We need only think of Ernst Bloch's *Der Geist der Utopie* (1918, 1923) and *Thomas Münzer als Theologe der Revolution,* of Walter Benjamin, even of the beginnings of Theodor W. Adorno, etc.[9]

Lukács's characterization of the romantic anti-capitalist type clarifies several ambiguities of the secular messianic worldview. For one, it suggests ironically that the representatives of the secular messianic spirit (of course, Lukács's own name should be added to the list) share an affinity with the German conservative mandarin intelligentsia from which they were rather systematically excluded. Both groups were profoundly influenced by the *Kultur / Zivilisation* dichotomy, where *Kultur* symbolized the predominance of higher, spiritual values and *Zivilisation* was associated with the crude materialistic orientation of the decadent capitalist West. Both groups tended to conflate the political and economic aspects of "liberalism." As a result a vehement denunciation of capitalism frequently entailed an equally unnuanced rejection of parliamentary government. Because of this concerted mutual rejection of political liberalism, neither party would prove a likely candidate to come to the aid of Germany's fledgling Weimar Republic. In both its "left" and "right" variants, therefore, the romantic anti-capitalists bore the marks and prejudices of Germany's status as a "belated nation": above all, a principled, existential refusal to adapt to the demands of political modernity.[10]

But of equal interest in Lukács's remarks is his characterization of the perspective of *The Theory of the Novel* (and by extension, that of Benjamin, Bloch, and the others) as "subversive"—a claim that could certainly not be made on behalf of the mandarin intelligentsia. Undoubtedly, it was this dimension of their thought that made it an object of fascination to a more recent generation of critical intellectuals. Out of this multifaceted collective oeuvre emerges a remarkably dramatic and persuasive critique of capitalist civilization in virtually all its aspects.

Lukács describes the intellectual orientation of the secular messianic standpoint as a combination of "left" ethics and "right" epistemology. With this verdict (despite its manifest polemical intentions) he reaches an essential insight, which nevertheless remains undeveloped. The "left ethics" derive from leading contemporary theoreticians of revolutionary socialism. Their point of departure was not the deterministic Marxism of the Second International, but the "left-wing communism" of Gustav Landauer, Sorel, and the Dutch council communists, whose views the Bolsheviks would soon view as heretical. "Right epistemology" harks back to the emancipatory thrust of the Jewish messianic idea. Thus, only when these two factors—revolutionary socialism and the messianic idea—are thought of in tandem can the radical trajectory of Jewish secular messianism be fully appreciated.

v

It was in the writings of Walter Benjamin and Ernst Bloch that the idea of secular messianism achieved its full radicality. As Rabinbach has observed, "There were others, of course, who embodied the new Jewish spirit, but only Bloch and Benjamin—initially without any mutual influence—brought, in varying degrees, a self-consciously Jewish and radical messianism to their political and intellectual concerns."[11]

The historical sources for this secular messianic renewal are variegated. Of no small importance was Franz Rosenzweig's *The Star of Redemption* (1916), which brought renewed attention to the redemptive aspects of the Jewish religious tradition. Of greater significance, however, were Martin Buber's *Three Speeches on Judaism* (1909, 1911). Buber's emphasis on the existential and mystical components of Jewish religiosity, his critique of the stale convention of the rational-rabbinical tradition, established the terms of debate for an entire generation of Jews interested in probing the spiritual implications of their faith. The direct influence of Buber's writings on the early Benjamin has been well documented.[12] Finally, both Benjamin and Bloch were well acquainted with the work of Franz von Baader, in whose writings the cabalistic tradition figured prominently.[13]

The content of the Jewish messianic idea has been best described by Scholem. At its center lies the delicate tension between a restorative and a utopian dimension. As Scholem notes, "the messianic idea crystallizes only out of the two of them together. . . . [E]ven the restorative force has a utopian factor, and in utopianism restorative factors are at work." Thus, the messianic idea "can take on the form of the vision of a new content which is to be realized in a future that will in fact be nothing other than the restoration of what is ancient, bringing back that which had been lost; the ideal content of the past at the same time delivers the basis for the vision of the future." Still, while the vision of the new order receives its inspiration from the old, "even this old order does not consist of the actual past; rather, it is a past transformed and transfigured in a dream brightened by the rays of utopianism."[14]

"The world is not true, but it will successfully return home through human beings and through truth," declares Bloch.[15] "Origin is the goal," proclaims Benjamin, citing Karl Kraus. In both of these remarks there echoes the messianic image of redemption as a recaptured past. Yet, as Scholem indicates, this primal past—an "original leap" or "Ursprung"—is not something that one intends to restore to its pristine, original condition. Instead, the very process of conjuring forth the past in a contemporary historical setting serves to activate and release dormant potentials that lie concealed in the past. The past is not merely recaptured; it is rendered dynamic—in the sense of a living tradition— as a result of this fructifying contact with the utopian potentials that are secretly at work in the historical present.

But the desire to realize the sublimity of the messianic idea amid the profane continuum of historical life immediately presents a dilemma both epistemological and theological in nature. Those who dwell in this continuum can have only the dimmest presentiment of the manner in which the messianic idea might apply to the realm of secular affairs: the two spheres proceed according to entirely different, even mutually opposed, logics. In truth, the categories of reason and logic fail to conceptualize the consequences of the messianic age for the historical present. When viewed in relation to the customary concepts of the human understanding, redemption proves to be a category of absolute transcendence; thus, there is no prospect of bringing about an organic transition between the historical and messianic eras. There are no (Hegelian) precepts of mediation that would be capable of bridging the gap.

Scholem explains the absolute dichotomy between the profane and messianic spheres of life in the following vivid account:

> It is precisely the lack of transition between history and the redemption which is always stressed by the prophets and apocalyptists. The Bible and the apocalyptic writers know of no progress in history leading to the redemption. Redemption is not the product of immanent developments such as we find it in modern Western reinterpretations of messianism since the Enlightenment where, secularized as the belief in progress, messianism still displayed unbroken and immense vigor. *It is rather transcendence breaking in upon history, an intrusion in which history itself perishes, transformed in its ruin because it is struck by a beam of light shining into it from an outside source.* . . . The apocalyptists have always cherished a

pessimistic view of the world. Their optimism, their hope, is not directed to what history will bring forth, but to that which will arise in its ruin, free at last and undisguised.[16]

And thus, "there can be no preparation for the Messiah. He comes suddenly, unannounced, and precisely when he is least expected or when hope has been long abandoned."[17] Or, as Benjamin puts it in his "Theses on the Philosophy of History," for the Jews, "every second of time was the strait gate through which the Messiah might enter."[18]

VI

The messianic idea tended to catalyze the Jewish imagination in times of unprecedented hardship or catastrophe, such as the expulsion from Spain in 1492, in whose wake the Lurianic cabala was composed. As Scholem reminds us, "Jewish messianism is in its origins and by its nature—this cannot be sufficiently emphasized—a theory of catastrophe. [It] stresses the revolutionary, cataclysmic element in the transition from every historical present to the messianic future."[19] The neo-Kantian Ernst Cassirer viewed all such reliance on myth and supernatural imagery as historical regression.[20] It is clear, however, that at unusually trying moments in the life of the Jewish people, when the traditional, rational content of Judaism failed to address their true spiritual needs, the messianic idea provided a crucial element of cultural and religious cohesiveness. Through it alone could Jews seemingly render comprehensible—and bearable—historical experiences of disproportionate severity.

The proliferation of secular messianism circa World War I undoubtedly derives from an analogous historical dynamic. As hopes for Jewish equality in Central Europe were crushed, and thus prospects for a secular, this-worldly solution to the Jewish question blocked, only a recrudescence of messianic sentiment seemed to offer new hope. The Great War itself, moreover, was a cataclysm that shook the very foundations of post-Enlightenment European self-confidence. The secular heirs of the messianic tradition were among those who sought to give new meaning to this waning spiritual legacy.

Yet, the prerequisite for the resurgence of messianic longing in a secular guise was the viability of the "socialist idea." Only when the redemptive impulse of traditional Jewish messianism encountered the socialist belief in the imminence of a secular millennium were the foundations of modern messianism truly established. Those twin descendants of the Enlightenment, utopian socialism and historical materialism, both believed they could discern the contours of a society of freedom, solidarity, and plenty. However, theorists such as

Bloch and Benjamin (as well as Lukács, in his own fashion) were soon convinced that an infusion of messianic thought alone could rescue the socialist idea from the crisis of Marxism that was evident in the reformist character of the contemporary socialist parties. As Bloch observes, in Marxism, "the economy has been sublated, but the soul and the faith it was to make room for are missing." "The soul, the Messiah, the Apocalypse which represents the act of awakening in totality—these impart the ultimate impulses to action and thought, and constitute the a priori of all politics and culture."[21] And, as is well known, in 1940 Benjamin recommends that historical materialism "enlist the services of theology" should it wish to be victorious.[22]

What Scholem refers to as the "revolutionary, cataclysmic element" in the transition from the profane era of history to the sublimity of the messianic future plays a prominent role in the thinking of both Benjamin and Bloch. Thus, for example, in his "Theologico-Political Fragment" (a fascinating gloss on *Geist der Utopie*) Benjamin identifies the "cardinal merit" of Bloch's 1918 work as its having "repudiated with utmost vehemence the political significance of theocracy."[23] Theocracy suggests that the messianic kingdom could be realized *within* the profane continuum of history. But, as Benjamin points out emphatically, "nothing historical can relate itself on its own account to anything messianic." The method of world politics, therefore, must be nihilism: it must promote the downfall and ruination of all that is merely historical, forsaken, and profane.[24] Only in this way can the path to the messianic future be cleared. Consequently, in their "revolutionary nihilism," both Benjamin and Bloch find inspiration in the doctrines of Sorel. Benjamin praises Sorel's notion of revolutionary or "law-creating violence," which he contrasts favorably with the conservative idea of "law-preserving violence" that characterizes the modern state.[25] And in a celebrated bon mot, Bloch characterizes the ethical stance appropriate to the present age as the "categorical imperative with revolver in hand."[26]

Via the influence of Benjamin, the standpoint of secular messianism would come to play an important role in the critical theory of the Frankfurt School. The rejection of progressivist, evolutionary philosophies of history in *Dialectic of Enlightenment* bears the distinct traces of the messianic critique of the homogeneous and empty continuum of historical life developed by Benjamin. Like Benjamin, and in contrast to Marx and Hegel, the critical theorists ceased to believe in the historical prospects of redemption. The positive side of the messianic idea—such as explicit or allegorical visions of redemption—is lacking in their work. Both Horkheimer and Adorno thereby always maintained respect for the antimessianic *Bilderverbot* (taboo against images).

Nevertheless in Adorno's work the messianic strategy of negative theology

remains prominent. Negative theology suggests the unredeemed—and unre-
deemable—character of the profane continuum of historical life. Adorno, however, proceeds to historicize this idea: his concepts of the "totally administered
world" or "context of total delusion" refer to a specific historical period: twentieth-century state capitalism. Negative theology suggests that, the immanent
historical dynamic toward freedom having been suspended, the nature of redemption can only be deduced *ex negativo:* that is, by completely reversing the
signs of the degraded historical present. Only when we realize Adorno's profound indebtedness to negative theology as a theoretical strategy can we appreciate the brilliance, unrelenting severity, and truly radical character of his
cultural criticism.

The passage of his work that best conveys this weak messianic approach
appears at the end of *Minima Moralia,* where Adorno observes: "The only
philosophy which can be responsibly practiced in the face of despair is the
attempt to contemplate all things as they would present themselves from the
standpoint of redemption. Knowledge has no light but that shed on the world
by redemption: all else is reconstruction, mere technique. Perspectives must be
fashioned that displace and estrange the world, reveal it to be, with its rifts and
crevices, as indigent and distorted as it will appear one day in the messianic
light. To gain such perspectives without velleity or violence, entirely from felt
contact with its objects—this alone is the task of thought."[27]

VII

Ironically, it was the man who single-handedly rescued so much of the Jewish
messianic heritage from the oblivion of forgetting, Gershom Scholem, who was
often quickest to warn of the dangers that lurk in attempts to recklessly impose
a messianic perspective on the course of secular events. As he remarks in a 1975
interview: "I've defined what I thought was the price the Jewish people have
paid for messianism. A very high price. Some people have wrongly taken this to
mean that I am an antimessianist. I have a strong inclination toward it. I have
not given up on it. But it may be that my writings have spurred people to say
that I am a Jew who rejects the messianic idea because the price was too high."
He continues: "I think that the failure to distinguish between messianism and
secular movements is apt to trip up movements of this sort. Such a mix-up
becomes a destructive element. The misapplication of messianic phraseology
injected a false note into the minds and self-image of the devotees of those
secular movements."[28]

The messianic idea in its modern secular guise has provided a wealth of insight and illumination concerning some of the contradictions and dilemmas of contemporary human life. Above all, it has encouraged men and women to confront a series of troubling existential questions concerning the irrational, transcendence, and hope that have been repressed and rejected by modern rational and scientific habits of thought. It would be a rationalist delusion to think that these questions would recede from human consciousness of their own accord; or that they, too, would prove pliable material for contemporary methods of social engineering. In keeping these so-called ultimate questions of human existence to the fore of modern historical consciousness, Jewish secular messianism has accorded new relevance and meaning to a variety of traditional religious preoccupations.

Nevertheless, the reservations indicated by Scholem concerning a premature effacement of the boundary separating the messianic from the historical seem well placed. As a telos transcending contemporary historical consciousness that descends on the latter suddenly from above, the messianic category of redemption knows no compromises with the merely incremental gains of secular historical life. From this privileged, suprahistorical vantage point, all that is "merely" historical—customs, morality, political forms, and so forth—deserves simply to perish. Scholem has alluded to the prominence of the catastrophic or apocalyptical character of salvation in the messianic tradition. And we have seen how both Benjamin and Bloch, borrowing a page from Sorel, were attracted to the "purifying" capacities of violence. Here, of course, there is a perfect fit between messianism and the modern revolutionary tradition as a whole, as it descends from Robespierre and the Jacobins.[29] As Scholem points out, Benjamin, especially in his later writings, too readily collapsed the barrier separating religious and political concepts; a charge that, mutatis mutandis, could be made with respect to the other apostles of revolutionary messianism: Ernst Bloch, Theodor Adorno, and Herbert Marcuse. The compelling critique of a "damaged life" (Adorno) that emerged from their work is purchased at no small cost: a potentially ruinous confusion of theological and historical levels of analysis, in consequence of which prospects for incremental human betterment in the here and now are discounted and undervalued.

The problem is one that Benjamin recognized in the aforementioned "Theologico–Political Fragment": "The quest of free humanity for happiness runs counter to the messianic direction."[30] In other words, the ends of human freedom and social utopia often operate at cross-purposes. Yet, as one sees so often in the course of Jewish history, for this generation of political apocalyptists, the taboo against graven images has proved difficult to respect.

WALTER BENJAMIN TODAY

I

One of the key concepts in the thought of the later Benjamin is that of *Aktualität* or (cumbersomely translated into English) "contemporary relevance." The first collection of essays devoted to an understanding of his work, *Zur Aktualität Walter Benjamins*, highlighted precisely this dimension of his thought.[1] Like the "truth-content" of the work of art, on which Benjamin reflects in his essay on Goethe's *Elective Affinities*, his relevance is not something that is simply *vorhanden*, or immediately available. In Benjamin's case, too, "truth-content" comes only by way of an outer veneer, a "material content" (*Sachgehalt*). Here, material content refers to the fact that his oeuvre was conceived under a very precise set of historical circumstances: the tumultuous years spanning the outbreak of two catastrophic world wars; a period in whose aftermath many of the self-evidences of European civilization were seemingly left hanging by a thread; an era dominated by the political extremes of Communism and fascism, for which the survival of democracy seemed at best remote. Is it, then, any wonder that from Benjamin's very earliest intellectual stirrings eschatological motifs occupied a position of prominence in his thought? Indeed, a profound spirit of apocalyptical imminence pervades both his youthful and mature writings.

Ours, conversely, is an epoch that has seen too much of apocalypse—world war, death camps, the Soviet Gulag, Hiroshima, Vietnam. It is an age understandably weary of fanciful, eschatological political claims. It is an era that has become enlightened—or so one would like to believe—about the folly and zeal of political theology: the notion that the kingdom of ends might be realized on earth via secular political means. We have become properly mistrustful of redemptory political paradigms.[2] In Kantian terms, the excesses of political messianism have taught us to be wary of all attempts to fuse the "noumenal" and "phenomenal" realms. Indeed, the idea that the foremost issue in the domain of secular political life is justice or fairness, and that questions of salvation must be relegated to the private sphere as the province of individual conscience, is one of the quintessential legacies of political modernity.[3]

As Irving Wohlfarth has pointed out: "To apply Benjaminian categories to the present without also trying to rethink them in the light of intervening history is . . . not merely to remain trapped within the coordinates of his thought, but to arrest the recasting process that it sought to initiate."[4] His caveat is directed to those who succumb to an ever-present danger of Benjamin scholarship: the danger of overidentification. Those who seek to follow in Benjamin's footsteps run the risk of becoming mesmerized by the aura of his life and thought. Before they can be appropriated, his ideas must be subjected to an alienation-effect; their spell must be broken, they must be stripped of their aura. To this end, they must be unflinchingly brought into contact with other intellectual traditions as well as new historical circumstances. Only through such a confrontation might they prove their worth. The greatest disservice one could do to Benjamin's theoretical initiatives would be to accord them the status of received wisdom, to assimilate them uncritically or whole-sale. His mode of thinking, both alluring and elusive, invites commentary and exegesis, which must not be confused with adulation.

For all of these reasons, the attempt to appropriate Benjamin's intellectual legacy under dramatically different historical circumstances is far from simple. To begin with, one would have to do justice to the fact that his interpretation of history remains inalienably wedded to a problematic of unremitting cataclysm and catastrophe, as the following observations indicate:

> That things have gone this far *is* the catastrophe. Catastrophe is not what threatens to occur at any given moment but what is given at any given moment.[5]

> If the abolition of the bourgeoisie is not completed by an almost calculable moment in economic and technical development (a moment signaled by inflation and poison-gas warfare), all is lost. Before the spark reaches the dynamite, the lighted fuse must be cut.[6]

> Counterpart to [Auguste] Blanqui's worldview; the universe is a locus of perpetual catastrophe.[7]

And in his legendary discussion of the "angel of history"—perhaps the defining image of his entire work—Benjamin affirms that "where we perceive a chain of events [the angel] sees one single catastrophe which keeps piling wreckage upon wreckage and hurls it in front of his feet."[8] He identifies the storm responsible for this catastrophe simply with "progress." Hence, for

Benjamin, it is the responsibility of the critic to "brush history against the grain." For if left to itself, the immanent course of history will never produce redemption. That is why the historical materialist must "blast open the continuum of history." Only in this way can she activate its veiled redemptory potentials, which Benjamin (with a clear allusion to the mystical *nunc stans*) associates with *Jetztzeit* or the "time of the now."

To be sure, there are certain strains of postmodernist thought that approximate Benjamin's bleak understanding of history as a *Verfallsgeschichte* or a "history of decline": Foucault's cheerless image of a "carceral society," say, or Baudrillard's concept of the omnipresence of "simulacra." But often they purvey inordinately dispirited images of contemporary society that are wholly denuded of the utopian sensibility infusing Benjamin's work.[9]

At least Benjamin tried to uphold a vision of utopian possibility that resides beyond the fallen and desolate landscape of the historical present. Postmodernism, conversely, by fetishizing the notion of *posthistoire,* conveys a sense that all attempts to actualize elements of the past for the sake of an emancipated future are a priori consigned to failure. For example, the concept of "historicism" proper to postmodern architectural theory intends less a meaningful actualization of the past than an avowedly random historical pillaging of it. In Benjaminian terms, the past is less "cited" as a "now-time" ("a sign of messianic cessation of happening")[10] than as a purely ornamental adornment. The end result in most cases is a reaestheticized version of the modern.

With postmodernism, moreover, the very concept of emancipation is relegated to the dustbin of unserviceable metaphysical concepts. But thereby, too, the crucial metaphysical distinction between essence and appearance is abandoned. Once these terms are relinquished, one risks surrendering the capacity to make significant conceptual distinctions. For postmodernism, as was already true in Nietzsche, appearance is all there is. For Benjamin, conversely, appearance is the realm of "phantasmagoria": it bespeaks the spell of commodity fetishism, that degenerate utopia of perpetual consumption that must be demystified and surmounted. But then, since Benjamin never made a secret of his predilection for metaphysical, even theological modes of thought, the attempt to reconcile his thinking with the antimetaphysical stance of postmodernism has always been somewhat strained.[11]

Since Benjamin was engaged in some of the pivotal aesthetic controversies of our time, he is at present a logical candidate for inclusion in the burgeoning cultural studies canon. Yet it may be that the attempt to understand contemporary culture in accordance with Benjamin's eschatological theory of history— which is predicated on the notion of the present as a perpetual "state of emergency"—obfuscates more than it clarifies. For while in 1940, following

Nazism's initial successes, Benjamin could with some plausibility characterize "the 'state of emergency' in which we live [as] not the exception but the rule,"[12] this claim can at best have metaphorical meaning when applied to the historical present.[13] Conversely, if today the "state of emergency" is understood literally rather than metaphorically, one risks systematically underestimating the existing possibilities for political intervention and criticism. The result can be—and often is—a paralysis and marginalization of left-wing oppositional practice. A position that proceeds from the assumption that the capitalist state is inherently fascist or totalitarian is predestined to inefficacy. Moreover, it commits the mistake of generalizing such concepts to the point where they are rendered both trivial and meaningless—precisely the opposite of the effect that an understanding of totalitarian political forms should strive to promote.

If Benjamin's eschatological temperament places him at odds with the modest political aims of contemporary democratic practice, it nevertheless serves as an important corrective to the postmodernist embrace of *posthistoire*.[14] Postmodernism has not only abandoned "metanarratives." In its anti-Hegelianism, it has also rejected one of the basic premises of dialectical thought: the idea that, despite its apparent indigence, the contemporary social situation might yield something qualitatively better. The desire to perceive hope beyond despair—a central feature of Benjamin's redemptory approach to cultural history—is a sentiment alien to the disillusioned mood of postmodernity. The very concept of *posthistoire* suggests that the Enlightenment project of reconciling history and reason (a project that still finds a prominent echo in Hegel's thought) is illusory if not dystopian. Yet not even Benjamin, for all his reservations about "progress," was so antagonistically disposed toward Enlightenment ideals. He went so far as to provide himself with the following methodological watchword for the *Passagenwerk,* one that would have been worthy of Kant or Condorcet: "To make arable fields where previously only madness grew. Going forward with the sharp axe of reason, refusing to look left or right, in order not to succumb to the horror that beckons from the depths of the primeval forest. The entire ground must be made arable by reason in order to be purified from the jungle of delusion and myth. That is what I would like to accomplish for the nineteenth century."[15]

II

Because Benjamin's intellectual sensibility was profoundly shaped by the experience of the interwar years, it was conditioned by an acute sense of historical collapse that parallels Nietzsche's no less apocalyptical diagnosis of "European nihilism" in *The Will to Power.* "What does nihilism mean?" inquires Nietzsche. "*That the highest values devaluate themselves.* The aim is lacking; 'why?' finds no answer."[16] And with this summary pronouncement on the utter untenability of inherited European values, Nietzsche initiated a line of radical *Kulturkritik* that would often prove as influential for those on the left as on the right.[17]

It is far from surprising, therefore, that in the notes and drafts to the *Passagenwerk*, Benjamin betrays a fascination for Nietzsche's doctrine of eternal recurrence. It was an idea he thought he could make serviceable for his critique of nineteenth-century historical consciousness: in it he found an appropriate antidote to the bourgeois belief in progress in an epoch—the era of imperialism or high capitalism—where there was no longer anything "progressive" about the rule of this class. Moreover, it was an idea that seemed in accord with Benjamin's own conception of the nineteenth century as the site of a mythic proliferation of commodity fetishism: a "phantasmagoria." Like Benjamin, Nietzsche was a staunch critic of historicism. Yet, for this reason (and due to the archaicizing predilections of his thought), he glorified the mythological implications of eternal recurrence. Conversely, although Benjamin believed that the concept expressed a fundamental truth about the nature of bourgeois society (as a society that, owing to the inescapable compulsions of the commodity form, remained essentially indebted to myth), for him it was a truth from which humanity needed to be free. Hence, the great methodological emphasis in the Arcades Project on the idea of awakening—awakening from a dream or from the compulsions of myth.

Benjamin's fascination with the concept of "nihilism" helps us account for the peculiar relationship in his thinking between periods of "decline" and "redemption"—an association suggestive of the doctrines of negative theology. One of the first to perceive the import of these two poles in his thought was Gershom Scholem, who observes that "an apocalyptic element of destructiveness is preserved in the metamorphosis undergone in his writing by the messianic idea. . . . The noble and positive power of destruction—too long (in his view) denied due recognition thanks to the one-sided, undialectical, and dilettantish apotheosis of 'creativity'—now becomes an aspect of redemption."[18] The relation between these two concepts, moreover, goes far toward explaining the—at first glance peculiar—link he always emphasized between his theologically oriented 1925 *Origin of German Tragic Drama* and the quasi-Marxist Arcades Project.[19] Both works seek to highlight manifestations of cultural decline (mourning-plays and arcades) in order to cull from them dormant potentials for transcendence.

One might say that, in a Nietzschean spirit, Benjamin identifies with the doctrines of "active nihilism": the conviction that if something is falling, it should be given a final push.[20] Only at the point where the process of cultural decay is consummated might a dialectical reversal occur. Already in his surrealism essay (1929), Benjamin speaks rhapsodically of "the Satanism of a Rimbaud and a Lautréamont." Along with Dostoyevsky, their writings give birth to "the cult of evil as a political device . . . to disinfect and isolate against all moralizing dilettantism."[21] Their work represents a thoroughgoing renunciation of the "affirmative character of culture" (Marcuse) as practiced by bourgeois aestheticism. It breaks definitively with a cultural practice, from romanticism to art for art's sake, that provides the literary precipitate of experience in recompense for the experience itself. It stands as a subterranean, nonliterary literary complement (insofar as their works have ceased to be "literature") to the wave of anarchism that first made its appearance in mid-nineteenth-century Europe. For it was the anarchists who first initiated a concept of radical freedom that expressed a total refusal to compromise with the blandishments of the existing social regime. In sum, their work signifies the advent of a spirit of *intransigent cultural nihilism,* in consequence of which bourgeois art begins to divest itself of its "aura": the idea that the beautiful illusion of art is meant to provide aesthetic compensation for society's failings. Their attitude would culminate in the tradition-shattering ethos of the twentieth-century avant-gardes: dadaism, futurism, and, of course, surrealism. Of Breton and company Benjamin famously observes: "No one before these visionaries and augurs perceived how destitution—not only social but architectonic, the poverty of interiors, enslaved and enslaving objects—can be suddenly transformed into *revolutionary nihilism*";[22] that is, into an attitude of thoroughgoing and uncompromising cultural radicalism.

It is the same sensibility that provokes Benjamin's profound identification with the "destructive character" who appreciates "how immensely the world is simplified when tested for its worthiness for destruction." The destructive character is anything but goal-oriented and is devoid of an overarching vision of the way the world should be. "He has few needs, and the least of them is to know what will replace what has been destroyed."[23] It was in the same spirit that he enthusiastically cited a remark of Adolf Loos: "If human work consists only of destruction, it is truly human, natural, noble work."[24]

These sentiments also account for what Benjamin found attractive about communist politics. From the very beginning, he acknowledged his profound disinterest in communist goals. Nor was he at all moved by communism's crude epistemological stance. On one occasion he openly mocks the "inadequate materialist metaphysic" of diamat ("dialectical materialism"), which, needless to say, remained incompatible with Benjamin's abiding interest in the relationship between politics and theology.[25] Instead, Communism attracted him as an approach to political radicalism, as a form of "activism" that valued action for its own sake. Moreover, in Benjamin's eyes it was a politics that viewed the totality of inherited social forms nihilistically, with a view to their imminent destruction.

Benjamin would employ the theme of "anthropological nihilism" as one of the subheadings for the Arcades Project. He was aware, however, that by flirting with this problematic his thought had entered into dangerous proximity to a fascist sensibility that had already triumphed in Germany and Italy and that threatened to engulf Europe. Fascism, too, placed great emphasis on the need to destroy: an avowedly nihilistic "aesthetics of horror" formed a key component of the fascist worldview.[26] Hence, Benjamin saw the need to distance his own "conservative revolutionary" tendencies—his inclination to view radical destruction as a necessary prerequisite for cultural renewal—from those of his protofascist contemporaries such as Gottfried Benn, C. J. Jung, Ernst Jünger, Ludwig Klages, and Carl Schmitt.

Thus, to the anthropological nihilism of the conservative revolutionaries, Benjamin counterposes his own notion of "anthropological materialism." Not only was this theory intended as a counterweight to the "aesthetics of horror" purveyed by Benn, Jünger, et al.; it was also meant as a forceful rejoinder to the values of Western humanism as propagated by the representatives of German idealism. The events leading up to World War I had shown how readily the German idealist tradition could be chauvinistically reinterpreted; for example, in the concept of Germany qua *Kulturnation,* which the mandarin intelligentsia employed as a justification for Germany's entitlement to geopolitical hegemony within Europe.[27]

Anthropological materialism was Benjamin's way of attempting to substitute, as he put it, a "more real humanism" for the bankrupt, sham humanism whose ineffectuality under current historical circumstances seemed self-evident. It was a way of denigrating humanity in its current, degraded state in order to prepare the ground for its final, eschatological renewal; just as, according to Benjamin, in order "to understand a humanity that proves itself by destruction," one must appreciate Klee's *Angelus Novus,* "who preferred to free men by taking from them, rather than make them happy by giving to them."[28] These remarks, from Benjamin's essay on Karl Kraus, represent an essential complement to his discussion of the angel of history in the "Theses" and demonstrate how integral the relationship between destruction and renewal was for his thought.

As a basis for real humanism, anthropological materialism differed from the scientific materialism of orthodox Marxism. Benjamin had already introduced the concept in his surrealism essay, the fount of so much of his later thought. He associates it with the "nihilistic poetics" of Büchner, Nietzsche, Rimbaud, and, of course, the surrealists themselves. As such, it is essential to the key concept of that essay: profane illumination. It expresses Benjamin's "revisionist" conclusion that revolution is less a question of socializing the means of production than a matter of bodily collective exaltation; in essence, society must become "surrealized," it must become a *collective locus of profane illumination*. As Benjamin concludes his essay: "Only when in technology body and image so interpenetrate that all revolutionary tension becomes bodily collective innervation, and all the bodily innervations of the collective become revolutionary discharge, has reality transcended itself to the extent demanded by the *Communist Manifesto*." It is the tradition of anthropological materialism, culminating in the surrealist effort to efface the boundaries separating art and life, that alone has realized concretely what it might mean "to win the energies of intoxication for the revolution."[29]

An interest in the relation between "revolution" and "intoxication" gets to the very heart of Benjamin's cultural-revolutionary program for the Arcades Project. It also goes far toward explaining why his momentous encounter with surrealism in the 1920s would become the key influence in defining that program.

III

The proximity in which Benjamin's destructive-regenerative critique stands to analogous tendencies on the German Right bears further examination. It is a proximity that has been widely noted but rarely analyzed in detail. Perhaps the first to detect its import was Scholem, who once observed that Benjamin "had an extraordinarily precise and delicate feel for the subversive elements in the *oeuvre* of great authors. He was able to perceive the subterranean rumbling of revolution even in the case of authors whose worldview bore reactionary traits; generally he was keenly aware of what he called 'the strange interplay between reactionary theory and revolutionary practice.' "[30]

Habermas has pointed to a similar phenomenon: Benjamin's marked fascination with authors and ideas that had become standard points of reference for the right-wing critique of modern society: "Benjamin, who uncovered the prehistoric world by way of Bachofen, knew [Alfred] Schuler, appreciated Klages, and corresponded with Carl Schmitt—this Benjamin, as a Jewish intellectual in 1920s Berlin, could still not ignore where his (and our) enemies stood." This insight leads Habermas to conclude that Benjamin's theory of experience would be best described as a "conservative revolutionary hermeneutic."[31]

Like Bloch, Benjamin realized that the left's unreflective progressivism was in danger of neglecting the value of those "noncontemporaneous" elements whose revolutionary promise was being commandeered by the forces of political reaction: elements pertaining to the values of tradition, *Gemeinschaft*, myth, religiosity, and so forth; elements that had been brusquely marginalized by the rush toward modernity, which, in his view, left the world a disenchanted, impoverished, well-nigh meaningless place. It was, therefore, only natural that Benjamin would seek to mobilize potentials for the critique of modernity that had been provided by reactionary thinkers. They alone realized the latent capacity to heal the lacerated social totality of modernity. Such an alliance of convenience suggested itself to Benjamin insofar as the right-wing critique of "Zivilisation" (a characteristic term of disparagement for a generation that grew up under the tutelage of Nietzsche and Spengler, though one that Benjamin carefully avoided) proved more intransigent, more thoroughgoing, and less willing to compromise with the normative presuppositions of the modern world than left-wing criticism. In the last analysis, both Social Democrats and Communists (let alone liberals and "mere" democrats, who, from the rarified standpoint of theological criticism, are hardly worth mentioning) proved over-enamored with the logic of "progress," with which Benjamin believed one needed to break at all costs—even that of forming problematical theoretical alliances.

To be sure, Benjamin went to great lengths to transform elements of the conservative revolutionary critique of modernity in order to make them serviceable for a left-wing political agenda. But with the advantage of historical distance, one realizes just how much of an overlap exists between the cultural left and right in the case of the interwar generation. For critically minded German intellectuals of this period, the vitalistic critique of *Zivilisation* had become an obligatory intellectual rite of passage.

It is in this spirit that recent critics have justifiably tried to show the parallels between *Lebensphilosophie* and the philosophy of history adumbrated by Horkheimer and Adorno in *Dialectic of Enlightenment*. It would be wrong to emphasize the similarities at the expense of the differences: unless these differences, which are no less important, are taken into account, the two approaches risk becoming in essence "the same," which is far from being the case.[32] But in fact both Klages and *Dialectic of Enlightenment* purvey an anthropologically rooted critique of civilization, in which the central culprit is "ratiocination"—a faculty that places humanity at odds with both inner and outer nature. In essence, contemporary civilization suffers from an excess of "intellect" over "life." A reconciliation with nature—both inner and outer—is the telos that guides both approaches to *Kulturkritik*.[33]

These sentiments, far from being alien to Benjamin, are central to his work (see, for example, the important fragment, "On the Doctrine of the Similar"). I have argued elsewhere that the philosophy of history of *Dialectic of Enlightenment* is, via the mediation of Adorno, a specifically Benjaminian inheritance.[34] The critique of progress, the understanding of history as loss and decline, as well as the central theme concerning the interrelationship between enlightenment and myth, would be inconceivable without the precedent of his "Theses on the Philosophy of History" and other texts.

But unless one specifies precisely what aspects of the vitalist critique Benjamin deemed worthy of appropriation, one risks proceeding by insinuation rather than sound argument. For example, we know that his theory of the "decline of the aura" was in part derived from a member of the George-circle, Alfred Schuler. Yet, in Benjamin's work Schuler's ideas appear radically transformed, to the point where Schuler's predominantly mythological interpretation of it is barely visible.

A similar claim can be made in the case of what Benjamin may have found of value in the work of Carl Schmitt. Schmitt's work emphasizes the paramountcy of the "state of exception" (*Ausnahmezustand*) in determining sovereignty. It was an approach that Benjamin found methodologically suggestive for understanding the endemic political instability depicted in seventeenth-century tragic drama. Yet, the existence of a fairly ingratiating 1930 letter to Schmitt notwithstanding, to claim that Benjamin's understanding of contemporary politics was substantively indebted to Schmitt (as indeed some have) is to exaggerate.[35]

But in the case of Benjamin and Klages, there is something much more essential at stake. Benjamin was an enthusiast of Klages early on. In 1913 Klages delivered a famous lecture on "Man and Earth" at Hohe Meissner, a legendary German youth movement site. Because of its provocative anticivilizational and ecological themes, the lecture subsequently acquired canonical status among youth movement members. Benjamin visited Klages in Munich the next year and invited him to speak to the Berlin youth movement group (the Free Student Society) over which Benjamin presided.

Benjamin later developed a keen interest in Klages's 1922 work *On Cosmogonic Eros*, praising the book in a letter to Klages of the following year. Moreover, his essay on Johann Jakob Bachofen (1935) is punctuated by a long discussion of Klages whom he praises on a number of counts.[36] According to

Benjamin, the chthonic theory of archaic images (*Urbilder*) Klages develops in his 1922 work stands opposed to "representations" or the domain of the rational concept. Representations pertain to the "intellect" (*Geist*), which is characterized by "utilitarian views" and an interest in "usurpation." The image, conversely, is a direct expression of the soul and relates to the domain of "symbolic intelligence." As such, it stands opposed to the abstract intellectualism of the rational concept, which, from the perspective of *Lebensphilosophie*, represents the basis of a mechanistic and soulless bourgeois *Zivilisation*. On all these points, it would seem, Benjamin could not be more in agreement with Klages.

It is not hard to discern what it was about the vitalistic critique of modern life Benjamin sought to appropriate for the ends of left-wing *Kulturkritik*. Despite his explicit reservations about Klages's perspective (he calls it a "system without issue that loses itself in a threatening prophecy addressed to a humanity that has allowed itself to be misled by the insinuations of the intellect"), he concludes his discussion with the following words of praise: "It is true that despite its provocative and sinister side, this philosophy, by virtue of the shrewdness of its analyses, the profundity of its views, and the level of its discussions, is infinitely superior to the appropriations of Bachofen that have been attempted by the official professors of German fascism."[37]

Benjamin would remark to Adorno that the Bachofen manuscript, in which he attempts to work out in detail his relation to Klages, bore great relevance to their most intimate shared theoretical concerns ["Es ließe sich bei dieser Gelegegenheit viel zu unseren eigensten Dingen sagen"].[38] And in an earlier letter, Adorno had already noted that Klages's "doctrine of the 'phenomenon' in the 'Reality of Images' [a chapter from volume 3 of *The Intellect as Antagonist of the Soul*] stands in the closest proximity to our questions."[39] He goes on to observe that "it is precisely here that the boundary line between archaic and dialectical images lies, or, as I once stipulated against Brecht, a materialistic theory of ideas."

In essence, the success of Benjamin and Adorno's mutual philosophical project hinged on a successful materialist articulation of the doctrine of dialectical images. It was Klages who, as Adorno acknowledges in the lines just cited, had unquestionably gone the farthest in the direction of outlining a doctrine of images that was decidedly opposed to the predominant, rationalist approaches to the theory of knowledge: neo-Kantianism, positivism, and scientific Marxism. Yet in his theory such images appeared as eternal, timeless embodiments of the human soul. With Klages, the image possessed an avowedly transhistorical, mythological status. For Benjamin and Adorno, therefore, the key to redeeming Klages's theory lay in *historicizing* the doctrine of images: to break decisively with their timeless, ahistorical, mythological character by saturating them with historical content. Whereas Klages and other representatives of *Lebensphilosophie* viewed the contemporary cultural crisis as the manifestation of an eternal cosmological struggle between "reason" and "life," Adorno and Benjamin sought to give the crisis historical definition and scope by revealing it as a crisis of capitalism. To the imagistic theory of truth per se, however, they had few specific objections. Instead, they viewed it as a valuable epistemological alternative to the fatal rational-scientific biases of late capitalist society.

In this approach, one sees in *in nuce* the methodological plan for Benjamin's Arcades Project as well as Adorno's own mature theory of knowledge—which, following Benjamin's lead, he would characterize as thinking in "constellations."[40] It should come as little surprise, then, if Benjamin, in one of the more revealing (if characteristically terse) methodological directives for the Arcades Project, remarks: "to link heightened visuality [*Anschaulichkeit*] with the Marxist method" (*Gesammelte Schriften*, 5:578). Here, "visuality" signifies a clear reference to the theory of images.

And thus, one of the conceptual keys to the project's completion lay in a risky merger of Marx and Klages. Because of their nondiscursive nature, Benjamin viewed images as potentially superior to rational theories of cognition, which only aggravate the post-Enlightenment march of "disenchantment." Yet, the important twist added by Benjamin's theory of modernity suggests that, contra Weber and Marx, the disenchantment of the world is accompanied by a *reenchantment:* by a resurgence of mythological forces in modern garb. This reenchantment of the world was integrally related to the quasi-utopian wish-images that pervaded the phenomenal manifestations, the cultural superstructure, of modern capitalism: manifestations such as world exhibitions, iron constructions, panoramas, interiors, museums, lighting, photography—not to mention the arcades themselves, the consummate dream-images of nineteenth-century commodity culture.

In *Dialectic of Enlightenment*, Horkheimer and Adorno would explicitly adopt Benjamin's view concerning the entwinement of myth and Enlightenment, arguing that in the modern era Enlightenment degenerates into myth (e.g., the myth of "scientific progress"), just as myth is already a form of Enlightenment (an early form of world-demystification). Yet, in Benjamin's case, the idea of a recrudescence of mythical elements in the modern era was a concept of distinctly Klagean provenance. For Klages, the archaic images corresponded to a primeval soul-world that stood opposed to the progressive disintegration of experience in modernity. However, owing to this atrophy of experience, under present social conditions these images were only accessible once the conscious mind was caught off guard: in daydreams, trances, or when confronted with experiences that disrupted the normal patterns of rational thought. In his essay "On Dream-Consciousness," a work that Benjamin admired,[41] Klages sought to provide a phenomenological account of the everyday circumstances that could lead to renewed contact with archaic images:

> if in the stillness of the night we hear an automobile pass by and the sound gradually trails off into the distance; when viewing fireworks from afar or noiseless sheet-lightning; when returning to one's native surroundings after a several year interim marked by a perhaps stormy life; or, conversely, when visiting places of uncommon strangeness; . . . often when traveling by train, assuming that one has a compartment to oneself; occasionally in moments of great exhaustion, of hopeless despondency, of unbearable pain, as well as usually after taking whatever type of narcotic.[42]

Here, moreover, the parallel with Jünger's theory of experience, as developed in books such as *The Adventuresome Heart*, is quite relevant. All three, Benjamin, Klages, and Jünger, were concerned with the diminution of the potential for qualitative experience following the world-historical transition from *Gemeinschaft* to *Gesellschaft*. Like Benjamin, Jünger feared that an increasingly mechanized modern cosmos and the progressive industrialization of the life-world would banish prospects for superior, self-transformative experiences. Karl-Heinz Bohrer has convincingly shown how Benjamin's identification with the shock-aesthetics of the twentieth-century avant-garde resembles Jünger's attraction to extreme situations (*Grenzfälle*), rapture, and transgression—whose paramount instance was proximity to death in war.

In a recent essay, Axel Honneth has commented on the parallels between the "anthropological materialism" on which the theories of experience of both Benjamin and Jünger are based:

> Jünger's anthropological materialism seized on extraordinary states, which, as in Benjamin, are circumscribed with the help of categories casually adopted from Bergson: in situations of danger, which originate from the child's natural helplessness, in the warrior's confrontation with the danger of being killed, and for those intoxicated in the maelstrom of the loss of self—in these situations a series of self-evident values or "standards of the heart" are revealed from the magical perspective. . . . These moments of magical rapture have a privileged status. . . . Again and again, Jünger's diary-like notes end in the description of corresponding situa-

tions of magical rapture: intoxication, sleep, and the danger of dying are for him keys to that one experience that in a unique way establishes a correspondence between soul and world because it is not shaped by an attitude of instrumental control.[43]

Of course, Jünger and Benjamin take their concern for the atrophy of historical experience in radically different directions. As an aristocratic radical in the tradition of Nietzsche,[44] Jünger's magical realism pushes in the direction of a restoration of the values of social hierarchy and martial heroism. Only at the end of *The Adventuresome Heart* does he divulge the figure on whom he places his hopes: the "Prussian anarchist." "Armed only with the categorical imperative of the heart," he roams through the forlorn landscape of the historical present as the apocalyptic standard-bearer of a new social order.[45] In *The Worker* (1932) Jünger argues that an enfeebled modernity can be redeemed only if society as a whole is reorganized along military lines. Benjamin finds this line of thinking abhorrently fascistic, as his scathing review of the 1930 anthology edited by Jünger, *War and Warriors* ("Theories of German Fascism") suggests.[46] Instead, he places his hope in a messianic theory of history— a marriage, as it were, of cabala and Marx—whereby the promises of redeemed life are generalized and rendered profane.

At the same time, both Benjamin and Jünger are convinced that a surfeit of consciousness (a peculiarly modern affliction; in *The Genealogy of Morals*, Nietzsche already speaks of the virtues of "active forgetting") works to the disadvantage of heightened states of experience, whose prerequisite seems to be a capacity to dissolve the self in ever greater experiential totalities: the "collective unconscious" (Jung), the cosmos (Klages), the Parmenidean "one," and so forth.

In his remarks on Freud and Bergson in "On Some Motifs in Baudelaire," Benjamin makes precisely this point. He laments the fact that in the modern world the powers of consciousness must be enhanced as a defense against the shocks of everyday life (a problem that is especially acute in the modern metropolis, the locus classicus of shock experience). As a result of this need for a constantly vigilant consciousness, our natural and spontaneous capacities for experience are necessarily diminished.

This diminishment accounts for the great methodological significance that Benjamin attaches to the celebration of involuntary (nonconscious) memory in Proust. Only the systematic labor of involuntary memory can recover memory traces that have been lost to conscious remembrance owing to the institutionalized struggle for self-preservation that modern society has become. It also accounts for the importance of Bergson (who occupies a similar niche of honor in Jünger's work), who was the first to consider memory as the key to the theory of experience (though Benjamin would sharply criticize Bergson's alienation from genuine historical experience).

According to Benjamin, the attempt to wrest a genuine concept of experience from the benumbing uniformity of modern *Zivilisation* has proceeded in two opposed directions. The first stems from *Lebensphilosophie,* which extols the notion of *Erlebnis.* Its characteristic features are: (1) a steadfast aversion to sociohistorical categories and concerns; and (2) a corresponding tendency to seek refuge in the manifestly ahistorical spheres of nature and myth (a late inheritance of German romanticism). These tendencies culminate in the doctrines of Jung and Klages who, Benjamin observes, "made common cause with fascism." "Towering above this literature," he counters, "is Bergson's early monumental work, *Matter and Memory.* . . . The title suggests that it regards the structure of memory as decisive for the philosophical pattern of experience. Experience is indeed a matter of tradition, in collective existence as in private life." Proust is the proper heir to Bergson: he realized that, whereas an experienced event is finite, "a remembered event is infinite because it is key to everything that happened after it and before it."[47] In the Arcades Project, Benjamin sought to use rapidly fading historical memories as precisely such a key.

It is at this point that the dilemma involved in Benjamin's later theory of experience, whose consummation was to have been the Arcades Project, becomes clear. The dilemma may be stated as follows. Benjamin's project focused on a critique of modernity from the standpoint of a theory of experience. To this end, he received very little theoretical aid and comfort from thinkers on the left. Instead, their Panglossian conviction that "history was on their side" (in the "Theses," Benjamin caustically observes that "nothing has corrupted the German working class so much as the notion that it was moving with the current") showed that they were committed to an Enlightenment vision of progress that, in its essentials, barely differed from the bourgeois worldview they were seeking to counter. Moreover, the "cult of labor" that had been established by the Social Democrats (and presciently exposed by Marx in his "Critique of the Gotha Program") amounted to little more than a socialist version of the Protestant ethic. Benjamin found the alacrity with which the established left-wing parties proclaimed the exploitation of nature as a desirable and valid goal especially appalling. It represented a betrayal of the noninstrumental, poetic vision of a reconciliation between humanity and nature that had been proposed by utopian socialists such as Fourier.

It is a stark and incontestable reality that Benjamin found he had more in common with the theoretical strategies of right-wing intellectuals than he did with contemporaries on the left. If one were interested in an uncompromising critique of modernity from the standpoint of the diminution of experiential wholeness (a standpoint which, to be sure, always entailed a somewhat romanticized vision of the past), the position represented by Weimar's numerous and influential *Zivilisationskritiker* ("critics of civilization") seemed to have much to recommend it. Early on, Benjamin would in a letter to Scholem speak of a "theoretical confrontation with Bachofen and Klages [as] indispensable."[48] A few years later he would characterize *The Intellect as the Antagonist of the Soul* as "a great philosophical work," despite the avowedly anti-Semitic leanings of the book's author.[49]

Benjamin's concept of the "collective unconscious"—one of the methodological keys to the Arcades Project—was explicitly derived from Jung. In the mid-1930s, as the fascistic implications of Jung's theories became apparent, Benjamin came to view a theoretical self-clarification vis-à-vis Jung as an imperative task. He alludes to this project in a 1937 letter to Scholem: "I wish to secure certain methodological fundaments of 'Paris Arcades' via a confrontation with the theories of Jung—especially those of the archaic image and the collective unconscious."[50] His proposed study of the differences separating his utilization of these concepts from that of Jung and Klages was rebuffed by the Institute for Social Research. Undoubtedly, Horkheimer et al. were convinced that an engagement with Jung and Klages, even for the sake of broadening the potentials of left-wing *Kulturkritik*, was wholly unacceptable under current historical circumstances, in which the link between vitalism and fascist ideology were present for all to see.[51] Adorno had already vehemently criticized Benjamin's uncritical reliance on their theories in "Paris, Capital of the Nineteenth Century" (the Arcades Exposé)—especially with reference to Benjamin's attempt to view the classless society of prehistory as a "golden age": "Thus disenchantment of the dialectical image leads directly to purely mythical thinking, and here Klages appears as a danger, as did Jung earlier."[52]

To say that Benjamin found many aspects of the national revolutionary critique of modernity methodologically congenial, that he perceived figures such as Jung, Klages, Schuler, and Max Kommerell (the latter three were all members of the George-*Kreis*)[53] as kindred intellectual spirits, should not be treated as evidence that the Arcades Project was inherently flawed. Though he assimilated their views, they were by no means the only major influences: the surrealists, the utopian socialists, Proust, and Baudelaire were equally significant. In different ways, all contributed to Benjamin's unique and brilliant research program of the 1930s: a secular redemption of modern mythology; a materialist recovery of the phenomenal manifestations of the nineteenth century "dreaming-collective."[54]

Moreover, Benjamin hardly appropriated the doctrines of the Weimar Republic's antidemocratic intellectuals *tel quel*. Instead, he sought to transform them in accordance with his own idiosyncratic theoretical perspective and needs. He was convinced that their theories had addressed the problem of the breakdown of experience in the modern world in a way that the intellectual paradigms of Enlightenment provenance—neo-Kantianism, social scientific empiricism, logical positivism, historicism, and so forth—had not. The anti-intellectual intellectuals of Germany's conservative revolution agreed that "thinking was no longer the highest vocation of humanity, rather experiencing, feeling, seeing . . . and the actualization of myth."[55]

From his earliest writings on experience, knowledge, and language, Benjamin displayed a considerable measure of sympathy for such views, though he was also keenly aware of their destructive potential. This accounts for his figurative or "imagistic" recasting of the theory of knowledge in the *Trauerspiel* book as a theory of constellations. A similar impulse explains his reliance on the dialectical image as the methodological crux of the Arcades Project: in his view, a theory of knowledge that was graphically oriented possessed a distinct epistemological advantage over approaches that relied on discursive or propositional truth alone. From the standpoint of the philosophy of life, therefore, one could accede to realms of experience and knowledge that exclusively rational modes of cognition had, to their own detriment, left unexplored. In all of these respects, it is clear that the vitalist fascination with archaic images, the unconscious, dreams, shocks, collective forms of experience, and states of ecstasy in which the unity of the self dissolves, represented for Benjamin an important complement to what he found of value in the profane illuminations of the surrealists. Reactionary thought, too, contained "energies of intoxication" that needed to be won over for the revolution. But in this case, it would not be a *Revolution von Rechts* (revolution from the right).[56]

Could the effort to recast historical materialism as a theory of experience be successful? Would it be possible to weld together two perspectives that have traditionally been at odds without succumbing to the risks, as Benjamin says in his surrealism essay, of a "poetic politics"?

Many have been skeptical of such attempts. In his extremely lucid evaluation of Benjamin's thought and legacy, Habermas expresses a dissenting view. The attempt to reconcile historical materialism and a redemptory hermeneutics must fail, he observes, "because the materialist theory of social development cannot simply be fitted into the anarchical conception of now-times [*Jetzt-zeiten*] that intermittently break through fate as if from above. Historical materialism, which reckons on progressive steps not only in the dimension of productive forces but in that of domination as well, cannot be covered over with an anti-evolutionary conception of history as with a monk's cowl."[57]

In other words, in his writings of the 1930s Benjamin tried to reconcile the irreconcilable: a theory that takes claims concerning progressive historical development seriously (claims for which Benjamin certainly did not show much patience) and a messianic view of history that believes, conversely, that only those breakthroughs are meaningful that present themselves as *ruptures* with the continuum of history as it has been constituted thus far. In Habermas's view, then, a theory of experience and historical materialism are not inherently incompatible. They do operate at cross-purposes, however, when both are subtended by a messianic perspective that perceives the realms of historical and messianic time as constitutionally opposed. Benjamin could counter (and does) by claiming that the messianic-utopian potentials on which a materialist theory of experience focuses are wholly *immanent* and thus in no way dependent on a deus ex machina, such as "the coming of the Messiah." The description of "now-time" as a moment of "messianic cessation of happening" in the "Theses on the Philosophy of History" must therefore be understood metaphorically. Even if this claim were true, it still leaves unanswered Habermas's initial question as to whether a theory that is so antithetically disposed toward the claims of social evolution—on which, clearly, Marxism stakes so much—can be reconciled with historical materialism as it has been traditionally conceived.

In order to answer the question of whether Benjamin's theory of experience remains ultimately compatible with the claims of Marxist thought, we must turn to a consideration of the thirteen-year undertaking that Benjamin hoped would reconcile these two approaches: the Arcades Project.

IV

The hermeneutic difficulties of approaching the Arcades Project are compounded by its status as a torso. The editors of Benjamin's collected works insinuate a false integrity by referring to it as the "Passagen-Werk." It would be perhaps more accurately dubbed the "Passagen-*Arbeit*" in order to suggest that, instead of constituting a whole, it represents a work-in-progress, on which Benjamin labored fitfully from 1927 until shortly before his death in September 1940 (moreover, this was the designation that Benjamin himself used in his letters to describe his study).

There are those who would like, following a well-established German liter-ary tradition, to celebrate its fragmentariness; an attitude that would seem especially apt in the case of Benjamin, for whom a preoccupation with frag-ments and ruins became, as it were, a literary signature. Yet, to romanticize its inconsummate character serves only to further mystify a document whose hermeticism implores sober decoding. Otherwise one risks consigning Ben-jamin's oeuvre to the belle-lettrism he deplored.

The text is patently unreconstructable as a whole. Many of its "files" (*Kon-voluten*)—in all, thirty-five, organized according to subject-headings—consist largely of uncommented citations that Benjamin intended either as references or material ultimately to be incorporated into the finished version. Benjamin's own commentaries (e.g.: "The dialectical image is a flashing image. Thus, the past must be seized as a flashing image in the now of recognizability")[58] are characteristically lapidary, but, for that reason, far from easy to decipher. Though the massive quantities of citations he assembled are highly suggestive, it is largely a matter of conjecture as to how they would have been fashioned into a coherent whole. For that matter, there has been ample speculation, far from irrelevant, as to whether the project, which had gone through so many alterations in methodology, form, and substance, was in principle completable, so refractory and unwieldy had those vast quantities of citations become.

A minor scholarly tempest was unleashed when two researchers, upon pe-rusing a batch of newly discovered Benjamin manuscripts found among the literary estate of Georges Bataille, concluded that, in the late 1930s, Benjamin had simply *abandoned* work on the Arcades Project and instead decided to concentrate his energies exclusively on the Baudelaire book. As evidence for their case, they contended that as of 1938, Benjamin's notes were entered exclusively under the Baudelaire rubric (file J).[59] These claims have been vig-orously contested by the editors of Benjamin's collected works and others.[60] Yet, what one can indeed conclude from an examination of Benjamin's Paris manuscripts is that the Arcades Project was even further away from completion than expected: of the 600-odd titles Benjamin had inventoried in the course of his many years of research, only one-third had been consulted; and, of these, only fifty or so had actually been incorporated in the "Notes and Materials" section of the *Passagenwerk*.[61]

Whereas in the 1935 "Exposé" the work on Baudelaire constituted only one chapter among six (the other five were arcades, panoramas, world exhibitions, the interior, and barricades), in 1937, at the urging of the Institute for Social Research, it grew into a separate book, only one part of which was ever brought to completion ("Paris of the Second Empire in Baudelaire"). Susan Buck-Morss speculates that Benjamin was so committed to the Arcades Project that all six chapters might have eventually been turned into independent books.[62] But considering that only one-third of the Baudelaire study was ever written, what chance might he have stood of completing, along with it, five additional *Passagenwerk*-derived monographs, even had his material conditions of life been optimal?

Moreover, in evaluating the project one must keep in mind that Benjamin's own intentions changed several times. The first surrealist-inspired version was called "Paris Arcades: A Dialectical Fantasy." There Benjamin refers to the arcades as "the architectural constructions in which we relive, as if in a dream, the life of our parents and grandparents, just as the embryo in the womb relives the life of animals."[63] In these early notes for the Arcades Project, Benjamin seemed much more infatuated with the manifest content of his material—its potential for enchantment à la surrealism—than with the moment of revolutionary awakening. But the essential conception of the nineteenth century as a modern mythology was in place. Unlike bourgeois and Marxist theories of history that viewed technology as emancipatory and progressive, Benjamin viewed it as responsible for a recrudescence of myth. It succeeded in creating a dream-landscape and consciousness, a type of kitsch-dominated, retrograde utopia. The moment of "ambiguity" would prove crucial, since it expressed the fact that this modern mythology was not something purely and simply regressive; it contained a utopian moment. It was the duty of the historical materialist to flush out this element. Therein lay the indispensable role of the dialectical image. It would establish a unique and revolutionary relation to the past. Unlike the positivist mentality of nineteenth-century historicism, which aimed at a reconstruction of the past as such, the dialectical image sought to situate the past in relationship to the revolutionary needs of the historical present. It was concerned with the "actualization" (*Vergegenwärtigung*) of the past rather than re-creating it "as it really was."

In the early 1930s Benjamin had virtually ceased his labors on the "Paris Arcades." When he resumed his work in 1934, his conception had changed dramatically. The earlier subtitle, "A Dialectical Fantasy," had been dropped. Whereas the first version of the project had focused exclusively on the arcades, in the new formulation, the arcades, while still central, were demoted to merely one chapter among six. Moreover, in its new incarnation, "Paris, Capital of the Nineteenth Century," the project took on a less literary and more historical focus. Benjamin seemed determined not to allow himself to succumb, as had the surrealists, to the magic spell of modern mythology. This was a spell that needed to be broken; at the same time, to break the spell entailed a profound redemptory moment. Qua fairy tale, modernity contained a promise of happiness it fell to the critic to redeem.

But the question remains: Did Benjamin in his unfinished masterwork ever really free himself from an infatuation with the modern mythology that had been incited by the works of surrealist authors such as Breton, Aragon, and others? Were his dialectical images sufficiently disenchanted to actually *break* the magic spell? Or did they merely perpetuate it, thereby purveying a type of "enchantment to the second power"? These are difficult questions to answer given the inconsummate status of the Arcades Project. But they are nonetheless inescapable if one is to accede to the essence of what Benjamin hoped to achieve.

We know that Benjamin, inspired by the surrealists, had intended "montage" as the project's methodological key. Montage—a juxtaposition of disparate elements, in which no one element takes precedence over another—was meant as the organizing principle of the dialectical images. Benjamin had always been unambiguous on this point:

> Method of this work: literary montage. I have nothing to say. Only to show. I will make off with nothing valuable and allow myself no clever turns of phrase. Only the refuse and waste: which I will not inventory but instead allow to come into their own in the only way possible: I will make use of them.

> This work must raise the art of citing without quotation marks to the highest level. Its theory is most intimately linked to that of montage.[64]

Precisely what Benjamin might have meant by "literary montage" as an organizing principle is open to interpretation. Adorno understood this idea quite literally, thereby confirming his direst fears: that Benjamin intended to construct the Arcades Project as a montage of citations divested of supporting commentary. In retrospect, this view seems untenable, not least of all insofar as the arcades-related texts that have survived, such as "The Paris of the Second Empire in Baudelaire" (which Benjamin once referred to as a "miniature model" of the Arcades Project) are hardly devoid of commentary (though it certainly remains sparse).[65]

Nevertheless, Adorno's misgivings about the potential for abuse that lay in an excessive reliance on montage were well founded. They address the fact that at times Benjamin tended to view the theoretical implications of his material (the "refuse and waste" he refers to above) as nearly self-evident, which was far from true. When Adorno in the late 1940s first gained access to the "Notes and Material" to the Arcades Project, he expressed these reservations quite pointedly in a letter to Scholem:

> At the beginning of the previous year [1948] I finally received the arcades material that had been hidden in the Bibliothèque Nationale. Last sum-

mer I worked through the material exhaustively, and problems arose that I must discuss with you. The most difficult aspect is the extraordinary inattention to theoretically formulated ideas as opposed to the enormous store of excerpts. That may in part be explained from the idea that was explicitly expressed on one occasion (and which to me is problematical) that the work should be merely "assembled" [*montieren*]; that is, compiled from citations, such that the theory leaps forth without one having to append it as interpretation. Were that to have been possible, only Benjamin himself would have been able to accomplish it; whereas I have always been faithful to the standpoint of the Hegelian phenomenology of spirit, according to which the movement of the concept, of the matter at hand, is coincident with the explicit thought process of the reflecting subject. Only the authority of sacred texts would stand as a refutation of this conception, and the Arcades project has avoided precisely this idea. If one takes, as I would like, the montage idea not entirely *à la lettre*, it could have easily turned out that Benjamin's ideas could have been formed from countless citations.

   A further difficulty consists in the fact that although there exists a general plan for the work and a careful ordering of the material according to subject headings, there is no really detailed schema that, for example, would have permitted one to complete the construction as Benjamin had intended. On the other hand, the *unorganized* publication of the material would not in the least be helpful, insofar as, as things now stand, in no way does the intention leap forth.[66]

Even had Benjamin abandoned the idea of montage in the strict sense—that is, as a theoretically unadulterated array of citations—as now seems likely, it was far from clear that the basic theoretical difficulties of the work would thereby have been resolved. On the one hand, as Adorno points out in his letter, only the late Benjamin himself could have reconstituted the massive compilation of data as a meaningful whole. The ordering schemas he left behind—the two versions of "Paris, Capital of the Nineteenth Century" as well as the some thirty-five subject headings to the "Notes and Materials" section—remained too fragmentary or allusive to serve as a reliable guide.

   Moreover, it seems that even though in the course of his research Benjamin may have realized the potential risks involved in pure montage, he was never able to distance himself sufficiently from his fascination with this principle, which had become the hallmark of the 1920s avant-garde (surrealism, Soviet film, etc.).

In his correspondence of the mid-1930s, a related methodological keyword began to crop up: construction. As he remarks in a 1935 letter to Gretel Adorno: the "constructive element" would form the necessary complement to the compilation of materials. This was also his response to Theodor Adorno's objections to the division of chapters in the 1935 Exposé: "The arrangement [of the chapters] lacks the constructive moment. . . . The constructive moment signifies for this book what the philosopher's stone means for alchemy."[67]

That Benjamin insisted on drawing analogies with medieval science to explain what was at stake in the Arcades Project did not bode well for its fidelity to materialist principles. It also illustrates some of the perils of an approach that is committed to thinking in images: their indeterminacy cannot compensate for conceptual failings. In the last analysis, "construction" merely referred to the arrangement of materials. Fundamentally, it was as ascetic toward commentary as was montage. Moreover, the directives Benjamin gave as to how such an arrangement should proceed ("Articulating the past historically means . . . seizing hold of a memory as it flares up in a moment of danger") for their part lacked specificity.[68]

The materialist turn he sought to give concepts taken over from Jung and Klages, which were of central theoretical importance to the Arcades Project, would also prove ineffective. Jung's theory of the "collective unconscious" would play a key role in the 1935 Exposé, as would the notion of dream-consciousness, which seemed to be derived in equal measure from surrealism, Klages, and Bloch. Benjamin was clearly enamored with Marx's famous claim in a letter to Ruge that "the world has long been dreaming of something that it can possess in reality only if it becomes conscious of it." He cites it approvingly in the section on "Theory of Knowledge" in the Arcades Project and goes on to claim that "The utilization of dream elements in awakening is the textbook example of dialectical thought."[69] His theory of dream-consciousness has much in common with Bloch's notion of "dreaming toward the future." It is precisely in this sense that he employs Michelet's saying, "Every epoch dreams its successor," as a motto to introduce the central statement of method in the Exposé. The allegory-laden, commodity utopias of the nineteenth century engendered a proliferation of dream- and wish-images, a phantasmagoria, that humanity would be able to "possess in reality only if it becomes conscious of it." Benjamin associated the act of "becoming conscious" with the moment of awakening from the dream; it was an act that at the same time, entailed a realization of the utopian potential contained in the dream.

In this way, Benjamin sought to recast the relationship between base and superstructure in orthodox Marxism. No longer was the superstructure a mere reflection of the base. Instead, it appeared as its "expression";[70] an expression, however, that proved in crucial aspects to be *in advance of the base*, insofar as, qua phantasmagoria, its wish-images foreshadow the utopia of a classless society.

Here is how Benjamin sought to fuse together the concepts of wish-image, dream, collective unconscious, and classless society in the 1935 Exposé:

> To the form of the new means of production, which to begin with is still dominated by the old (Marx), there correspond images in the collective consciousness in which the new and the old are intermingled. These images are wish-images, and in them the collective seeks not only to transfigure, but also to transcend, the immaturity of the social product and the deficiencies of the social order of production. In these wish-images there also emerges a vigorous aspiration to break with what is out-dated—which means, however, with the most recent past. These tendencies turn the image-fantasy, which gains its initial stimulus from the new, back upon the primal past. In the dream in which every epoch sees in images the epoch which is to succeed it, the latter appears coupled with elements of prehistory—that is, of a classless society. The experiences of this society, which have their store-place in the collective unconscious, interact with the new to give birth to the utopias which leave their traces in a thousand configurations of life, from permanent buildings to ephemeral fashions.[71]

Benjamin viewed it as his task in the Arcades Project to unlock, via the employment of dialectical images, the utopian potential that lay dormant in the phenomenal manifestations of nineteenth-century cultural life. Whereas Klages had sought to highlight the recurrence of *archaic images* in modern life, the images from the primal past that Benjamin sought to cull were the purportedly "materialist" images of a classless society. But the theory of the trans-historical persistence of archaic images was, in its essence, Klagean. The memory-traces of a classless society had been stored in the "collective unconscious" (Jung) and were then reactivated in the phantasmagoria of high capitalism. Marx once observed that humanity only sets itself tasks that it can solve. Benjamin believed that its most valuable potentials first appeared (albeit encoded) in dream form. If the phenomenal forms of nineteenth-century life represented a collective dream, then Benjamin's Arcades Project was a type of monumental *Traumdeutung*.

As the 1930s drew to a close, the prospect that Benjamin's work would have a historical effect dwindled considerably. The rising tide of European fascism deprived Benjamin's study of its anticipated audience, just as it would soon deprive him of his life. As the parameters of historical possibility narrowed, the eschatological motifs in his thought took on increasing prominence. His ideas would be received, if at all, only by an unnamed future witness. Of course, this eschatological focus would culminate in the "Theses on the Philosophy of History," which, as a strategy of historical remembrance amid catastrophe, is intimately related to the concerns of the Arcades Project.[72]

In his notes to the *Passagenwerk* Benjamin never made an effort to conceal the centrality of theological concerns. In his reflections on theory of knowledge, he observes: "My thought is related to theology as a blotter is to ink. It is totally absorbed by it. If it were up to the blotter, however, nothing of what has been written would remain"[73]—an indication of both the extraordinary power and the dangers of the theological understanding of history to which Benjamin had been so profoundly attracted since his youth. The centrality of theology also meant that the question of redemption was foremost to him in his understanding of the past. Among the "elementary principles of historical materialism" he lists the following bold claim: "The object of history is that for which knowledge enacts its redemption [*Rettung*]. . . . The authentic conception of historical time is wholly based on the image of salvation [*Erlösung*]."[74]

In the "Theses" Benjamin would speak of a "secret agreement" that exists between "past generations and the present one." He emphasizes that "the past carries with it a temporal index by which it is referred to redemption."[75] This is the reason he insisted on the methodological primacy of remembrance, as opposed to a concept of "progress" that would be superficially future-oriented. He invested this faculty with profound theological powers, for only via remembrance could the "secret agreement" between generations (i.e., between the living and the departed) be redeemed. Through it alone could criticism reactivate that "temporal index of redemption" that lay dormant in the past. For similar reasons he would insist that socialism is "nourished by the image of enslaved ancestors rather than that of liberated grandchildren."[76]

The version of historical materialism that Benjamin envisioned—one whose victory, according to the imagery of Thesis 1, was contingent upon enlisting "the services of theology"—was, therefore, eschatological in the strong sense. The lines between the dawning of a classless society and the advent of the Messiah were blurred to the point where the claims of Marxism overlapped with those of the Last Judgment: the wicked would be duly punished and the righteous dead would be resurrected.

It is fair to conclude that when in the course of his reflections on the philosophy of history Benjamin invoked the coming of the messianic era ("every second of time [is] the strait gate through which the Messiah might enter")[77] he was not speaking metaphorically. In the notes to the Arcades Project he insists that the dialectical recuperation of cultural history must reach a point where "the entire past has been brought into the present in a historical apocatastasis";[78] that is, a messianic retrieval of everything and everyone. His intentions were not merely directed toward a revamped historical materialism, but toward a full-blown political messianism:

> In the Jewish apocalyptic and Neoplatonic-Gnostic traditions, apocatastasis refers to the restoration of an original paradisiacal state brought about by the coming of the Messiah. With this restoration, things would resume their proper relations to each other, the displacements that characterized the "dream condition of the world" would be undone. The goal of Benjamin's "dialectics of cultural history" is thus the abolition of the prevailing context of expression in favor of the original context of Being. . . . Thus Benjamin transfers the catastrophic and redemptive elements coexistent in the apocalyptic doctrine of apocatastasis into the secular realm of history.[79]

It was precisely this tendency to attribute eschatological, redemptory force to the powers of theory that would lead to misunderstandings in his dealings with the more empirically oriented Institute for Social Research. In a letter of the late 1930s, Horkheimer would attempt to temper Benjamin's inclination toward speculative grandiosity with the following hardheaded reminder: "Past injustice has occurred and is done with. The slain are really slain. . . . If one takes the idea of openendedness seriously, then one must believe in the Last Judgment . . . the injustice, horror, and pain of the past are irreparable." To which Benjamin offers the following unrepentant response:

> The corrective to this way of thinking lies in the conviction that history is not only a science but also a form of remembrance. What science has 'established' can be modified by remembrance. Remembrance can make the openended (happiness) into something concluded and the concluded (suffering) into something openended. This is theology; however, in remembrance we have an experience that forbids us from conceiving history fundamentally atheologically, even though we would hardly be able to write it in theological concepts that are immediately theological.[80]

Benjamin's shift in the late 1930s toward an avowedly apocalyptical-messianic perspective is especially evident in his second draft of the Arcades Exposé, written in 1939. In the later version the section on "Daguerre or the Panoramas" was deleted, leaving five instead of six projected chapters. More important, though, Benjamin added a new introduction and conclusion, which in the estimation of the editors of his works, "contain . . . perhaps Benjamin's most lucid remarks concerning the theoretical goals of the *Passagenwerk*."[81]

Of greatest theoretical significance in the new version were Benjamin's meditations on a relatively obscure prison-writing by the professional revolutionary Auguste Blanqui. The text, entitled *L'éternité par les astres*, became for Benjamin an intellectual discovery of the highest order. He describes his momentous first encounter with it in a January 1939 letter to Horkheimer:

> One must concede that on first glance the text seems inept and banal. Still, the awkward reflections of an autodidact contained in the first part are preparation for speculation about the universe that no one but this great revolutionary could provide. If hell is a theological object, then one could call such speculation theological. The view of the world that Blanqui outlines is infernal, insofar as he takes his data from the mechanistic natural science of bourgeois society; it is at the same time a complement to the society that Blanqui in the twilight of his life was forced to recognize as victorious over himself. What is so disturbing is that this sketch lacks all irony. It presents an image of unreserved submission [*Verwerfung*]. . . . Its theme, eternal recurrence, has the most remarkable connection to Nietzsche.[82]

What Benjamin found of great value in Blanqui's otherwise unexceptional treatise was his vision of contemporary society as characterized by an infernal-mythological compulsion-to-repeat—hence the affinities with Nietzsche's doctrine of eternal recurrence. This was of course a theme that stood in close proximity to one of the Arcades Project's main concerns: to portray the cultural superstructure of high capitalism as a type of modern mythology, thereby unmasking the secret affinities between modernity and prehistory.

Blanqui wrote this extremely dispirited text in 1872 while imprisoned in Fort du Taureau following the suppression of the Paris Commune. It is the testimony of a beaten man, one who has recently seen his most cherished hopes for humanity's future brutally crushed. Undoubtedly, Benjamin found himself attracted to Blanqui's cosmic pessimism for reasons that were as much biographical as theoretical: the sense of hopelessness that pervades Blanqui's text was one with which Benjamin identified profoundly.

The key passage in this fable of eternal recurrence reads as follows: "There is no progress. . . . What we call progress is immured on each planet and vanishes with it. Everywhere and always, the same drama, the same decor, on the same narrow stage, a clamorous humanity, infatuated with its greatness, believing itself to be the entire universe and living in its immense prison, soon about to sink with the globe that has brought the burden of its pride into such a contemptuous state. The same monotony, the same immobilism on the other stars. The universe repeats itself endlessly and runs in place. Eternity plays imperturbably in the infinity of its representations."[83]

For Benjamin, Blanqui's vision represented a profound confirmation of the theory of history of the Arcades Project—a portrait of the phantasmagoria of modernity as governed by a hellish-mythological compulsion to repeat: "Blanqui's cosmic speculation teaches that humanity will be prey to the anxiety of myth for so long as the phantasmagoria has a place in it."[84] According to Benjamin, the failure of the nineteenth century—and, by implication, of the twentieth as well—was that, "The century did not know how to respond to the new technological innovations with a new social order."[85] That is, it allowed the potentials embodied in the new forces of production to remain trapped in outmoded (capitalist) relations of production. The cultural expressions of this society were able to project a utopian future, albeit, in a distorted dream-form. In the Arcades Project, Benjamin sought as it were to capture the "rational kernel" of these utopian wish-images and dream-states. In his valorization of Blanqui's profound cosmological gloom, the signature interrelationship in his work between decline and salvation—*Verfall* and *Erlösung*—is once again plainly manifest.

The attempt to bring a messianic theory of history to bear on the course of secular world history is fraught with danger. This is not the locus where Benjamin's actuality should be sought out today. Benjamin dwelled amid exceedingly dark times. He thought that an infusion of secular messianism would help historical materialism compensate for its intrinsic theoretical rigidity as well as for the lack of imminent revolutionary possibility. To think about the prospects for social change in such terms today would for the most part lead astray. Benjamin's boyhood friend Scholem, who went on to become the century's greatest authority on the tradition of Jewish Messianism, well understood the dangers inherent in conflating the secular and the messianic: "I think that the failure to distinguish between messianism and secular movements is apt to trip up movements of this sort. Such a mix-up becomes a destructive element. This misapplication of messianic phraseology injected a false note into the minds and self-image of the devotees of those secular movements."[86]

Conversely, to reassert Benjamin's lifelong, frenetic quest for happiness and fulfillment *within* the parameters of a democratically constituted society would be an achievement worth emulating. Until such a condition has been achieved, the actuality of his thought will remain keen.

WORKING THROUGH THE PAST: HABERMAS AND THE GERMAN HISTORIAN'S DISPUTE

There are not two Germanies, an evil and a good, but only one, which, through devil's cunning, transformed its best into evil . . .—Thomas Mann, *Germany and the Germans*, (1945)

I consider the continued existence of National Socialism *within* democracy potentially more threatening than the continued existence of fascist tendencies *against* democracy.—Theodor Adorno, "What Does Coming to Terms with the Past Mean?"

The 1980s were extremely significant in the political life of the Federal Republic of Germany. In 1982 thirteen years of Social Democratic rule (1969–82) came to an end in favor of a coalition headed by the conservative Christian Democrats. Led by Chancellor Helmut Kohl, the Christian Democrats have subsequently been returned to office (along with their junior partners, the Free Democrats), in 1987, 1991, and 1994. In many ways this political transformation of the 1980s signified a delayed confirmation of the *Tendenzwende* or ideological shift first visible in Germany in the mid-1970s.

At issue in the Historians' Debate is Germany's *Aufarbeitung der Vergangheit* or "coming to terms with the past." For years, the "German question" as perceived by politicians of Western Europe had been, "How can German aggressiveness be curbed?" But after 1945, this question took on an entirely different, more sinister meaning. It was rephrased to read, "How could the nation of Goethe, Kant, and Schiller become the perpetrator of 'crimes against humanity?' " Or simply, "How was Auschwitz possible?" One could justifiably say that the very "soul" of the nation was at stake in the answer to this question. The development of a healthy, nonpathological national identity would seem contingent on the forthright acknowledgment of those aspects of the German tradition that facilitated the catastrophe of 1933–45. And that is why recent efforts on the part of certain German historians—bolstered by an era of neoconservative stabilization—to circumvent the problem of "coming to terms with the past" are so disturbing. What is new about this situation is not simply the attempt to provide dishonest and evasive answers to the "German question" as stated above, but to declare the very posing of the question itself null and void.

Historically, the problem of coming to terms with the past has not been an easy one. In the first decade and a half of the Federal Republic's existence—the so-called latency period of the Adenauer years, which lasted from 1949 until 1963—the nation as a whole did very little of it. Instead, the Nazi experience was regarded as a *Betriebsunfall*, an "industrial accident," for which no one could be said to bear direct responsibility. Very little about the Third Reich was taught in schools. On those occasions when questions of historical culpability did arise, the "captive nation" theory was frequently invoked: it was the evil genius, Hitler, who had seized control of the German nation and led it to ruin; an explanation that conveniently absolved rank-and-file Germans from their share of responsibility for the catastrophe. As the cold war progressed, Nazi pasts were quickly forgotten. Suddenly, the anti-Communism of ex-Nazis was perceived as a valuable ideological asset. Many of these attitudes were directly fostered by the occupying Allies, whose sights were now fixed on the enemy to the East.

Fundamentally, the wrong lesson seemed to have been learned from twelve years of Nazi rule. There was not only a rejection of the jingoistic-genocidal politics, (that had, after all, brought in its wake unprecedented misery for the Germans, too); the nation seemed to reject politics in toto, which, in the post-Hitler era, seemed irrevocably contaminated by the Nazi experience. These were years of overwhelming political apathy. German political energies, which had once been so robust, were entirely sublimated toward the ends of economic reconstruction. The result is well known: the creation of the *Wirtschaftswunder* or economic miracle, which catapulted the Federal Republic, within years of its foundation, to the position of one of the world's leading industrial powers. But democratic societies do not come into being overnight. And many features of the Adenauer regime—the political docility of the general populace, the fact that so many officials from the Nazi years readily found positions of power and influence in his government—suggested that the essential structure of the traditional "Obrigkeitsstaat" (the authoritarian state of Bismarckian vintage) remained in place beneath the veneer of democratic respectability.[1] Thus, for example, in their classic study *The Civic Culture,* Almond and Verba were able to show the deep ambivalence felt by most Germans toward democratic politics—a form of government that, after all, they had been compelled to adopt by the victors.[2]

Such conclusions were generally confirmed by social-psychological studies of German character structure in the 1950s. In his incisive analysis of the results of one such study, Theodor Adorno noted that many of the attitudes displayed revealed character traits that were highly neurotic: "defensive gestures when one isn't attacked; massive affect in situations that do not fully warrant it; lack of affect in the face of the most serious matters; and often simply a repression of what was known or half-known."[3] Instead of coming to terms with the past, the latter was consistently repressed through a series of familiar rationalizations: only five, not six million Jews had been killed; Dresden was as bad as Auschwitz; the politics of the cold war era confirmed what Hitler had always said about communism, which, in retrospect, justified the war he launched in the East—from here it is a short step to the conclusion that Hitler was right about a number of other matters as well; the fate of the "Eastern Germans" (those driven from the eastern territories at the war's end) was comparable to that of the Jews; and so forth.

The inability of the German nation during these years to express honest grief or remorse was brilliantly satirized in a scene from Günter Grass's *The Tin Drum*, where people require onion-cutting ceremonies to help them shed tears. As one pair of critics astutely observed regarding the German national character of the postwar years: "there is a determining connection between the political and social immobilism and provincialism prevailing in West Germany and the stubbornly maintained rejection of memories, in particular the blocking of any sense of involvement in the events of the Nazi past that are now being so strenuously denied."[4]

Certainly, much has changed in Germany since this initial period, largely through the efforts of the generation of the 1960s. Refusing to remain satisfied with the strategy of repression pursued by their parents, younger Germans pressed forcefully for answers to the most troubling questions about the nation's past.[5] However, just at the point when one is tempted to believe that genuine progress has been made concerning the confrontation with the Nazi years, one runs across studies such as Dieter Bossman's *Was ich über Adolf Hitler gehört habe* (What I have heard about Adolf Hitler; Frankfurt, 1977), revealing astonishing ignorance among German youth concerning their recent past. For example, upon being asked what Hitler had done to the Jews, some of Bossman's young interviewees responded as follows: "Those who were against him, he called Nazis; he put the Nazis into gas chambers" (thirteen-year-old); "I think he also killed some Jews" (thirteen-year-old); "He murdered some 50,000 Jews (fifteen-year-old); "Hitler was himself a Jew" (sixteen-year-old).

The work of mourning is essential not as penance, but as a prelude to the formation of autonomous and mature identities for both nations and the individuals who compose them. As Freud showed in his classic study, "Mourning and Melancholia," unless the labor of mourning has been successfully completed—that is, unless the past has been sincerely come to terms with—individuals exhibit a marked incapacity to live in the present. Instead, they betray a melancholic fixation on their loss that prevents them from getting on with the business of life. The neurotic symptom-formations that result, such as those described by Adorno above, can be readily transmitted to the character-structures of future generations, which only further compounds the difficulty of confronting the historical trauma that wounded the "collective ego." And thus, the injustices of the past tend to fade into oblivion—unmourned, and thus uncomprehended.

Instances of collective repression are, moreover, far from innocent. They prevent the deformations of national character and social structure that facilitated a pathological course of development—such as mass acquiescence to genocide and terror—from coming to light. Instead these abnormalities remain buried deep within the recesses of the collective psyche, from which they may reemerge at some later date in historically altered form. In Germany, these deformations are often discussed in terms of the persistence of authoritarian patterns of behavior that are a holdover from traditional, predemocratic forms of social organization.[6]

So long as this incapacity to confront the past exists, there results an inability to live realistically in the present. Thus, historically, one of the salient features of Germany as a nation has been a tendency toward a militant exaggeration of the virtues of nationalism as a way of compensating for its relatively late and precarious attainment of nationhood under Bismarck in 1871. Or, as Alexander and Margarete Mitscherlich have expressed it in their landmark study of postwar German character structure, *The Inability to Mourn:* "World-redeeming dreams of ancient greatness arise in peoples in whom the sense of having been left behind by history evokes feelings of impotence and rage."[7]

Such infantile fantasies of collective omnipotence have led, on not a few occasions, to false estimations of national strength and to some correspondingly catastrophic national defeats. Unless the historical reasons that have led to disaster have been explored, unless the labor of coming to terms with the past has been undertaken in earnest, one risks reenacting the historical cycle as a type of collective repetition-compulsion: one proceeds to invent new, more sophisticated rationalizations and defenses to protect the idealized image of national greatness from the traumatic blows it has most recently endured.

Thus, in the immediate postwar period, the theory arose that it was the German leaders alone who were to blame for the most heinous of Nazi crimes, thereby absolving rank-and-file Germans from responsibility. In truth, of course, the German populace had given their full and enthusiastic support to Hitler's war aims and policies; and without the alacritous and dedicated cooperation of large segments of German society—from industrialists and the judiciary to public officials and railway personnel—the Third Reich and its atrocities would hardly have been possible.[8]

It is within the context of this long-standing attempt to deny the Nazi past—as well as its possible repercussions for postwar German society—that the arguments of Habermas's adversaries in the Historians' Debate must be understood.[9] Their efforts to trivialize and thus, finally to have quit with, past German sins signify much more than a dubious act of historical reinterpretation: they constitute a calculated rewriting of history by virtue of which, as Adorno opines, "the murdered are to be cheated even out of the one thing that our powerlessness can grant them: remembrance."[10]

It is also important to recognize that the revisionist standpoint did not materialize overnight and by chance. Rather, it complemented a carefully orchestrated campaign on the part of the ruling Christian Democratic coalition to remove once and for all the stigma of the Nazi era, which was perceived as a troublesome blot on the honor of the nation. Thus, the cry heard frequently during the course of the 1986–87 election campaign was that Germany must once more become a "normal nation," a nation without a troublesome past.[11]

The centerpiece of this process of "normalization" was to have been the visit of the American president to the German military cemetery at Bitburg on May 8, 1985, the fortieth anniversary of the end of the Second World War and the Nazi dictatorship. Kohl, who had been shunned at the Allies' commemoration of the landings at Normandy the previous year (as would again occur in June 1994), had obtained a small degree of consolation in a ceremony with President Mitterrand at the site of Verdun, which thus became a type of dress rehearsal for Bitburg.

However, it was the Second, not the First World War that weighed heavily on the German conscience. Bitburg was to have symbolized the end of Germany's pariah status and return to the fold of political normalcy—a *coup de théâtre* that was to receive international sanction by virtue of the presence of Ronald Reagan, the "leader of the Free World." However, as is by now well known, the whole affair backfired spectacularly once it was discovered that forty-seven SS members were also buried there.[12] What was intended as a contrived display of German normalcy was thus transformed into a prime example of that country's inclination toward grievous lapses of historical memory.[13] Moreover, the American president only compounded the difficulties of the situation by making a series of embarrassing gaffes: he tried to justify his decision to visit the Bergen-Belsen concentration camp on the morning of his Bitburg trip with the explanation that the men buried in the two gravesites were both "victims"—a macabre equation of victims and perpetrators, to say the least. Then he made the inexplicable claim that "the German people have very few alive that remember even the war, and certainly none that were adults and participating in any way." Reagan himself was in his thirties during World War II.

Unflustered by the Bitburg debacle, the Christian Democratic leadership continued to make "normalization" one of the focal points of the 1987 federal election campaign. Such was the intention of CDU parliamentary president Alfred Dregger, as he argued vehemently against distinguishing between the victims and perpetrators of Nazism in a debate before the Bundestag over a new war memorial.[14] In a similar vein, Franz-Josef Strauss, head of the Christian Socialist Union (the Bavarian allies of the Christian Democrats), repeatedly urged in his campaign addresses that Germany must "emerge from the ruins of the Third Reich and become a normal nation again."

To many historians in the West, the claims of Habermas's adversaries in the Historians' Debate have been perceived as neonationalist provocations.[15] A good example of such provocation is the rationale for historical study provided by Michael Stürmer, one of the leading members of the revisionist contingent. Stürmer, a speechwriter for Kohl and a CDU adviser, believes that it falls due to historians to provide compensations for the potentially confusing array of value-choices that have arisen with the decline of religion and the rise of modern secularism. What is needed in order to stave off crises of social integration is a "higher source of meaning, which, after [the decline of] religion, only the nation and patriotism were able to provide." Hence, for Stürmer, it is the task of the historian to assist in the renewal of national self-confidence by providing *positive* images of the past. In his eyes, the historical profession is motivated by the "establishment of inner-worldly meaning."[16] For "in a land without history, whoever fills memory, coins the concepts, and interprets the past, wins the future."[17]

In his *Zweierlei Untergang: Die Zerschlagung des Deutschen Reiches und das Ende des europäischen Judentums* (Two types of defeat: The destruction of the German Reich and the end of European Jewry), Andreas Hillgruber suggests that, while scrutinizing Germany's collapse in the East toward the end of World War II, a historian is faced with the choice of "identifying" with one of three parties: Hitler, the victorious Red Army, or the German army trying to defend the civilian population from being overrun by Soviet troops.[18] In his eyes, the choice is self-evident: the brave German soldiers, desperately fighting to save the fatherland from the atrocities of the Red Army, win hands down. It is almost as though Hillgruber were attempting to apply literally the "positive" approach to historical study recommended by his colleague Stürmer.

But as Habermas points out in his essay "Apologetic Tendencies," Hillgruber in effect presents us with a series of false choices: why is it the obligation of the responsible historian to "identify" with *any* of the historical protagonists?[19] In fact, is it not her responsibility (in this case, some forty years after the events in question have occurred), instead of playing favorites, to arrive at an independent and morally appropriate verdict regarding events of the past? Moreover, Hillgruber can succeed in his choice of "protagonists" only by abstracting from some extremely gruesome facts: it was the same "heroic" German army in the East that established many Jewish ghettos from which the concentration camp victims were chosen, provided logistical support to the SS Einsatzgruppen charged with exterminating the Jews, that was responsible for the shooting of thousands of Jews in Serbia and Poland, and in whose hands some two million Soviet prisoners of war perished during the course of the war, either from famine or starvation.[20] It was this army that, as an integral part of Hitler's plans for European domination, served as the guarantor and accomplice to all Nazi atrocities in eastern Europe, from mass exterminations to the sadistic enslavement of the populations of the occupied territories. The sad irony to Hillgruber's thesis, of course, is that it was the brutal war of aggression in the East launched by the German army, a war that resulted in the death of some twenty million Soviet soldiers and civilians, that provoked the Red Army's revenge on German soil.

In addition to the important material questions that have arisen in the debate concerning the manner in which crucial episodes of the German past should be interpreted, equally important issues concerning the integrity and function of scholarship in a democratic society have emerged. Should the primary role of historical study in a democracy be to facilitate social integration via the "establishment of inner-worldly meaning," as Stürmer claims; an approach that results in the creation of positive images of the past? Or should scholarship assume a more skeptical and critical attitude vis-à-vis the commonplaces of a national past for which Auschwitz has become the unavoidable metaphor, thereby assisting concretely in the process of "coming to terms with the past?" Compelling support for the historical importance of the critical approach to historical scholarship has been provided by Detlev Peukert, who, in a recent essay, has argued that what was historically new about the Nazi genocide was that it received a theoretical grounding through a determinate conception of "positive" science; namely, the idea of basing science on racial categories.[21] Habermas's specific fear is that by subordinating scientific criteria to an identity-securing function, historical study risks falling behind conventional standards of liberal scholarship, resulting in the production of neonationalist "court-histories." Indeed, the very idea championed by Hillgruber that a historian must in some way identify with historical protagonists represents a throwback to the empathic historiography of German historicism: a school formed in the German mandarin tradition, for which the writing of history from a national point of view was a common phenomenon.[22]

However, the most sensational of the theses espoused by Habermas's opponents in the debate were undoubtedly those set forth by the Berlin historian and former Heidegger student Ernst Nolte. In an article that first appeared in English, Nolte had stooped to reviving a choice bit of Nazi anti-Semitic propaganda from the early days of the war: a September 1939 declaration by Jewish Agency President Chaim Weizmann urging Jews to support the cause of democracy in the impending world war justified Hitler's treating them as prisoners of war as well as subsequent deportations. Moreover, in the course of the same article, Nolte encourages readers to engage in the tasteless thought-experiment of trying to imagine what the history of Israel would look like were it written by victorious PLO conquerors.[23] Here, Nolte wishes to suggest by analogy that the history of the Federal Republic, which, following Nuremberg, has emphasized German historical responsibility and war guilt, has essentially been written by the victors. Such inculpation has deprived Germany of its capacity to act effectively in the historical present.

But it was Nolte's contention in a June 6, 1986, article that the atrocities perpetrated by Hitler at Auschwitz were merely an understandable, if exaggerated, response to a "more original Asiatic deed"—the Red Terror during the Russian Civil War—of which Hitler considered himself a potential victim, that proved the most offensive and ominous of the revisionist claims. Nolte's argument proceeds as follows:

> It is a surprising deficiency of the literature on National Socialism that it does not want to know or believe to what extent everything that National Socialism later did—with the exception of the technical method of gassing—was already described in the extensive [Soviet] literature of the early 1920s. . . . Did not the National Socialists, did not Hitler commit an "Asiatic" deed, only perhaps because he and his kind considered themselves as potential or real victims of an "Asiatic" deed? Was not the "Gulag Archipelago" more original than Auschwitz? Was not the "class

murder" of the Bolsheviks the logical and factual *prius* of the "race mur-der" of the National Socialists?[24]

As Nolte states in conclusion: the singularity of the Nazi crimes "does not alter the fact that the so-called [*sic*] annihilation of the Jews during the Third Reich was a reaction or a distorted copy and not a first act or an original."[25] Nolte goes on to enumerate an entire series of twentieth-century crimes in comparison with which the uniqueness of the Holocaust is reduced to a mere technological innovation, the gas chambers. By articulating these positions, Nolte succeeded in according a semblance of respectability to points of view that heretofore had only surfaced on the fringes of the German extreme right.

As Habermas is quick to point out, there is a method behind Nolte's mad-ness. With the stroke of a pen, the singularity of the Nazi atrocities is denied: they are reduced to the status of a "copycat" crime, and, at that, merely one among many. The gist of Nolte's transparent efforts to rewrite the saga of Auschwitz may be read as follows: why continue to blame the Germans? The Communists did it first anyway. And, after all, during the war we were fighting on the right side—at least in the East.

In making such arguments Nolte takes no cognizance of the historical uniqueness of the Holocaust. For the first time in history (and what one can only hope will be the last), a regime came to the sovereign conclusion that an entire group of people—the Jews—should cease to exist; that every man, women, and child belonging to this group should be targeted for extermina-tion. Once this policy was put into effect, there was nothing unsystematic or haphazard about it. It was indeed intended to be comprehensive: a "total" and "final" solution to the Jewish question.

In the face of Nolte's revisionist arguments, Habermas's response was guided by an awareness that it is Germany's willingness to deal forthrightly with the dark side of its national past that will determine the moral fiber of the nation in the future. Only the "analytical powers of remembrance" can break the nightmarish grip of the past over Germany's present. As he remarks in "On the Public Use of History":

> The more a collective form of life maintains itself through the usurpation and destruction of the lives of others, the greater is the burden of recon-ciliation, the labor of mourning and critical self-examination, that falls due to succeeding generations. And doesn't this precept itself forbid the attempt to downplay our undeniable responsibility through leveling com-parisons? . . . We in Germany . . . must keep alive the remembrance of the suffering of those who were slaughtered by German hands. Those who

died have all the more a claim to the weak anamnestic power of a solidarity that those who were born later can preserve only in the medium of an— always to be renewed, often despairing, yet always present—remembrance. If we brush aside this Benjaminian bequest, Jewish citizens— including the sons, daughters, and grandchildren of those who were murdered—would no longer be able to breathe in our country.[26]

One of the key theoretical arguments Habermas mobilizes in his refutation of the revisionist position is the distinction between conventional and postconventional identities.[27] Within the framework of developmental psychology, the formation of a postconventional identity indicates that an individual has acquired a capacity to evaluate his moral convictions in terms of general ethical maxims. Thus, beliefs concerning right and wrong are no longer decided by immediate and particularistic points of reference—the standpoint of one's peer group or nation—but instead by appeal to universal principles. Habermas views the revisionists' desire for a return to a conventional national identity as a potential regression behind the precarious gains the Federal Republic has made as a democratic nation since its inception forty-five years ago.

The "conventionalist" perspective comes through most forcefully in the positions of Hillgruber and Stürmer, whose arguments betray no small measure of nostalgia for a highly mythologized image of the old German Reich: Germany as master of *Mitteleuropa*, capable of mediating the interests of the nations to the West and East.[28] Their contributions to the debate are reminiscent of the traditional nineteenth-century argument for a German *Sonderbewußtsein*, suggesting a "special" historical course of development for Germany between East and West.[29] The same nostalgia is also implicit in Nolte's desire to minimize the historical significance of Auschwitz, thus paving the way for Germany's return to the status of a "normal nation." But the bankruptcy of the *Sonderbewußtsein* argument was definitively proved at Stalingrad and Auschwitz—the very names are infamous. In defiance of this historical lesson, one of the main strategies of Nolte and company has been to downplay the importance of the years 1933–45 in relation to the overall "positive" trajectory of German history as a whole. In fact, in his more recent work, Nolte has characterized the entire 1914–45 period as a thirty-year "European civil war" in order to imply equal culpability among the fascist and democratic nations.[30] But, as this chapter's opening citation from Thomas Mann reminds us, the desire to differentiate in cut-and-dried fashion between "good" and "bad" Germanies is based on a dichotomy that fails to hold up under closer historical scrutiny.

It is for this reason that Habermas emphatically insists: "That the Federal

Republic opened itself without reservation to the political culture of the West is the great intellectual accomplishment of the postwar period."[31] He is convinced that attempts to revive neonationalist dogmas—whose disastrous outcomes, moreover, are a painful matter of historical record—must be combated by the "only kind of patriotism that does not alienate us from the west": a patriotism toward the "principles of a democratic constitution."[32] Such allegiances, oriented toward "principles" rather than "ethnicity," would constitute the basis for a "postconventional patriotism." The constitutional state may therefore be viewed as a form of *postconventional political consciousness,* insofar as the inherent distinction between "law" and "right" (corresponding to a broader distinction between "fact" and "norm") mandates that all concrete legislation be evaluated in light of universal normative precepts embodied in the constitution itself.

Habermas associates the revisionist offensive in the Historians' Debate with a neoconservative backlash against the alternative, environmental, and anti-nuclear movements that crested in the mid-1980s. Of course, neoconservatism has been a phenomenon common to virtually all Western democracies over the course of the last decade. But, as Habermas explains in "Neoconservative Cultural Criticism in the U.S. and West Germany," the peculiarities of the German version are especially worthy of note, insofar as its roots are to be found in proto-fascist ideologies that date from the pre-war era.[33]

In a 1984 interview, Habermas recounted his shock as a university student in the late 1940s upon learning of the continuities between the leading intellectuals of the pre- and postwar eras. Many, including several of Habermas's teachers, had been enthusiastic supporters of the National Socialist regime.[34] Although since that time a new generation of thinkers has come to prominence in the Federal Republic, antidemocratic intellectual habits have been slow to die. In most cases, although the transition to democracy has been grudgingly accepted (something that could not have been said for the advocates of a German *Sonderweg* during the days of the Weimar Republic), the dissonances of modernity are perceived as placing such great burdens on the adaptational capacities of social actors, that the preservation of "order" (as opposed to "freedom") has become the foremost value in contemporary political life.[35] One of the concrete and highly controversial political expressions of this mania for order was the notorious *Berufsverbot* (vocational proscription) first decreed in 1972, which aimed at excluding political extremists, sympathizers, and other undesirables from the German civil service.[36] Those who are perceived as the intellectual and cultural standard-bearers of modernity (e.g., artists and critical intellectuals) come in for more than their fair share of the blame for failures of social integration. But in this way, as Habermas shows, the neoconservatives confuse cause and effect: disturbances of social integration that have their source in shortcomings of economic and political subsystems are mistakenly attributed to avant-garde artists and a "new class" of freethinkers.

It is considerations of precisely this nature that dominate the historiographical concerns of Stürmer and Hillgruber, in whose eyes history must take on the affirmative function of reinforcing national consensus. As Habermas remarks: "The neoconservatives see their role, on the one hand, in the mobilization of pasts which can be accepted approvingly and, on the other, in the neutralization of those pasts which would only provoke criticism and rejection."[37] The currency of *Ordnungsdenken*—a belief in "order" as a primary political value—in contemporary Germany, evident in an at times maniacal preoccupation with questions of internal security, is reminiscent of the typical historical justifications of a paternalistic *Obrigkeitsstaat* during the Second Empire. Its popularity cannot but provoke grave suspicions concerning the prominence of regressive tendencies in the political culture of the Federal Republic. At the time of the "German autumn" (1977), Chancellor Helmut Schmidt was compelled to wonder aloud whether the West Germans have "in their souls" a certain "hysteria for order" (*Ordnungshysterie*).[38] Such a belief might help to account for the continued prominence of the authoritarian political doctrines of Carl Schmitt in contemporary Germany.[39]

Since German reunification in the fall of 1990, the specters raised by the Historians' Debate have become even more real. It has become common to refer to the *Wende* or neonationalist shift of German political culture since the two Germanies became one, as decades of repressed German patriotism suddenly came to the fore. Following reunification, a spate of articles appeared suggesting that Germany must have the courage to become a "nation" once again, and that rank-and-file Germans must have the courage to be "Germans" again.[40] The new Germany, it is argued, must be capable of assuming responsibilities on the European and international political stage commensurate with its size and economic might. Many of the claims of Hillgruber, Stürmer, and, to a lesser extent, Nolte, have gained a new lease on life. Indeed, a frequently raised complaint is that a German nation abnormally preoccupied with traumas of its past will be unable to act effectively in the future.

The terms in which this debate over the future of German identity have been phrased are cause for concern. It seems that, as a rule, the word "nation" has been used as shorthand to connote the terms of a "conventional" rather than a "postconventional" national consciousness. In public debates the relatively liberal political culture of West Germany has increasingly been viewed with suspicion. Was it not, its detractors claim, excessively influenced by the "Western" political culture of the victors and occupiers, as well as by returned German-Jewish émigrés? And aren't such cultural influences essentially alien to "authentic" German traditions, to which one should return now that the artificial situation of a divided Germany has been overcome?[41] Correspondingly, a concerted effort has been made to rehabilitate a purportedly "unblemished" German conservatism, such as that espoused by the national conservatives and conservative revolutionaries during the Weimar period (e.g., Carl Schmitt, Martin Heidegger, and Ernst Jünger). That there was a considerable degree of overlap between their worldview and that of the Nazis is conveniently omitted. Jünger, at the ripe age of 98, recently presided over the opening of the Venice Biennale, bantering about the new battle between "gods and titans" that would mark the twenty-first century. Along with this recent resurgence of a young conservative mentality there has been a relativization of Nazism's misdeeds as well as a chauvinistic celebration of the virtues of "Deutschtum" or "Germanness"—throwbacks that call for a heightening of critical vigilance.

Not only has there been a notable resurgence of vicious right-wing extremism (as a result of which innocent foreign residents have either been driven from their homes or killed); but this new German racism has been justified by recent government policies and proclamations. Thus, in June 1993, the German parliament, with the support of the Social Democratic delegates, voted for a constitutional amendment to alter the terms of Germany's asylum law, previously the most liberal in Europe. In an insensitive rebuke to Germany's 7,000,000 foreign residents, Chancellor Kohl has repeatedly stated that Germany is not an "immigration nation." To this day, Germany is the only major European nation where citizenship is awarded on the basis of *jus sanguinis*. Thus, residents of Turkish origin who have been born and raised in Germany must formally apply for German citizenship, whereas so-called *Volksdeutsche*, or foreign nationals of German ancestry, can quality for citizenship immediately. These attitudes and policies suggest that although the vigilantist methods chosen by the extreme right might be slightly excessive, their xenophobic aim to rid Germany of foreign influences is one that the ruling powers fundamentally embrace. The sea-change in German political culture initiated in the course of the Historians' debate is one that should be monitored closely.

Since the early 1980s, Habermas has shown considerable interest in exploring the possible links between the politics of neoconservatism and the philosophical implications of what is known as postmodernism. In his view, it is far from coincidental that what were perhaps the two most significant intellectual trends of the 1980s emerged and flourished concomitantly.

His earliest thoughts on the relationship between the two date back to an influential essay of 1980 that appeared in English under the title "Modernity versus Postmodernity."[42] This article was itself a meditation on the conception of modernity advanced in the recently completed *Theory of Communicative Action* as it pertained to the contemporary political spectrum. In concluding the essay, he differentiates between three types of conservatism: "old conservatism," which longs for a return to premodern forms of life; "new conservatism," which accepts the economic and technological features of modernity, while attempting to minimize the potentially explosive elements of cultural modernism; and finally, "young conservatism," which he associates with postmodernism.

Habermas's historical point of reference for "young conservatism" is the generation of conservative revolutionary thinkers who dominated German intellectual life during the 1920s. Their foremost representatives were Ludwig Klages, Carl Schmitt, the Jünger brothers, and Oswald Spengler. Like the postmodernists of today, they were all immensely influenced by Nietzsche. Their writings were characterized by an uncompromising critique of the modern age that often relied on the strategy of rehabilitating archaic concepts: for example, Klages's idea of the "archaic image" or Ernst Jünger's notion of the "warrior." As the following remarks show, Habermas perceives significant commonalities between the young conservatives of the 1920s and contemporary postmodernism. By virtue of a shared archaism and aestheticism, both groups seek to break free of the normative presuppositions of modernity: autonomous subjectivity, liberal-democratic forms of government, a rational theory of knowledge, and so forth.

> The *young conservatives* embrace the fundamental experience of aesthetic modernity—the disclosure of a de-centered subjectivity, freed from all constraints of rational cognition and purposiveness, from all imperatives of labor and utility—and in this way break out of the modern world. They thereby ground an intransigent anti-modernism through a modernist attitude. They transpose the spontaneous powers of the imagination, the experience of self and affectivity, into the remote and the archaic; and in manichean fashion, they counterpose to instrumental reason a principle only accessible via "evocation": be it the will to power or sovereignty, Being or the Dionysian power of the poetic. In France this trend leads from Georges Bataille to Foucault and Derrida. The spirit [*Geist*] of Nietzsche that was re-awakened in the 1970s of course hovers over them all.[43]

   The theoretical bases of Habermas's critique are complex. They presuppose the theory of modernity developed in *Theory of Communicative Action* and foreshadow the lecture series that was first published in 1985 as *The Philosophical Discourse of Modernity*. Nevertheless, since Habermas's critique of neoconservatism stands in integral relation to his interpretation of postmodernism (see, for example, the essays "Modern and Postmodern Architecture" and "Following the Arrow into the Heart of the Present"), a brief discussion of the conceptual foundations of his position will facilitate understanding of the bases of his political judgments.

   Habermas's theory of modernity builds on Max Weber's conception of the "differentiation of the spheres": for Weber, modernity is chiefly characterized by the proliferation of "independent logics" in the value-spheres of science/technology, morality/law, and art.[44] In premodern societies, the development of autonomous cultural spheres was hindered by the predominance of all-encompassing, "cosmological worldviews" (religion, myth), in terms of which all social claims to value and meaning were forced to legitimate themselves. Only since the Enlightenment have these individual value-spheres become *self-legitimating;*[45] that is, for the first time in history, the realms of science, morality, and art have been in a position to develop their own inherent meanings.

   On the one hand, the gains of modernity have been indisputable: the institutionalization of professional science, universalistic morality, and autonomous art have led to innumerable cultural benefits; our capacities for technical expertise, political justice/ethical fairness, and aesthetic experience have no doubt been tremendously enhanced. *It is this point that separates Habermas most emphatically from the postmodernists:* he believes that to fall behind the threshold of possibility represented by the cultural achievements of modernity can only result in "regression": the species would literally have to "unlearn" valuable cultural skills that were only acquired very late and with great difficulty. And it is precisely such "regressive inclinations" among the postmodernists that he singles out for pointed criticism. By generalizing an *aesthetic* critique of modernity (first elaborated in the late nineteenth century by the artistic avant-garde and Nietzsche), the postmodernists show themselves capable of understanding the modern age solely in terms of *one* of its aspects: the aspect of *instrumental reason*, which then must be combated at all costs via the (aesthetic) media of provocation, transgression, and play. In this way, they may be considered heirs to Nietzsche's "total critique" of modern values. Like Nietzsche, they reject the method of "immanent critique," insofar as they proceed from the assumption that the values of modernity are irreparably corrupt.[46]

   What is lost above all in the heady whirl of postmodern *jouissance* is a capacity to appreciate the universalistic ethical qualities of modernity. It is facile to summarily dismiss the latter as "instrumental," since their very basis is the (Kantian) notion of treating other persons as "ends in themselves." And for this reason, Habermas can justifiably accuse the postmodernists of representing a disguised, yet profound *antimodernism:* because their criticisms of modernity as a "generalized instrumentalism" are so reductive, their "program" is governed by an irrepressible longing to be free of the requirements of modernity at all costs, with the "aesthetic moment" as the sole possible survivor.

On the other hand, Habermas himself has been extremely critical of the developmental trajectory of modernity as an empirical social formation. Hence, he believes that, historically speaking, its normative potentials have been inadequately realized. Above all, the various spheres have not developed in an equitable fashion. Instead, the cognitive-instrumental sphere has attained predominance at the expense of the other two spheres, which in turn find themselves marginalized. Instrumental reason, in alliance with the forces of the economy and state administration, increasingly penetrates the sphere of everyday human life—the "life-world"—resulting in the creation of "social pathologies." The basis of the life-world is intersubjectivity, not formal reason. In the life-world, social action is governed by an orientation toward reaching an *understanding* (i.e., communicative reason), not by a functionalist orientation toward *success* (i.e., the ends-means rationality of instrumental reason). The latter therefore violates the inner logic of the former by attempting to subject it to alien, "functionalist" imperatives that derive from the administrative-economic sphere. The term Habermas has coined to describe this process is felicitous: the *colonization of the life-world.*[47]

It is this point that separates Habermas most emphatically from the neoconservatives. They wish to preserve one-sidedly the economic, technical, and managerial achievements of modernity at the expense of its ethical and aesthetic components. From their standpoint, the bureaucratic colonization of the life-world is a positive development. By extending the functionalist logics of economic and administrative rationality to the life-world, technocratic imperatives of system-maintenance are furthered. Thus, neoconservative political views incline toward a theory of government by formally trained elites. From this perspective, popular or democratic "inputs" with regard to governmental decision-making having their origin in the life-world are perceived as an unnecessary strain on the imperatives of efficient political "management."

It is at this point that aspects of the neoconservative and young conservative (or postmodernist) position intersect, as potential complements to one another under the conditions of late capitalism. For if the latter's main contribution to the course of Western cultural development has been "specialists without spirit and sensualists without heart" (Weber) (i.e., reified personality types and social relations that correspond to them), then the global assault against modernity undertaken by the postmodernists under the banner of *différance* would appear to be a logical historical outgrowth of and response to this trend. That is, the aestheticist pseudoradicalism of postmodernism ("pseudoradical" because thoroughly depoliticized) may be viewed as a type of historical *compensation* for the overwhelming pressures of "theoretical and practical rationalism" (Weber again) that have been imposed by modernity as a social formation. In Heideggerian parlance, the postmodernist celebrations of *jouissance* thereby serve as a kind of "releasement" from the hyper-rationalized life-world of late capitalism. Yet, as a type of "compensation," such celebrations ultimately have a system-stabilizing effect, insofar as they provide apparent outlets for frustration while leaving the technical-political infrastructure of the system itself essentially untouched.

The postmodernists have been correctly characterized by Habermas as "young conservatives," inasmuch as they have abandoned any hopes of conscious social change. Indeed, the word "emancipation" seems to have been stricken from their vocabulary. Instead, their aestheticist perspective is content to fall behind the achievements of modernity. As Habermas warns: "The rejection of cultural modernity and the admiration for capitalist modernization [on the part of the neoconservatives] will corroborate a general anti-modernism ready to throw out the baby with the bathwater. If modernity had nothing to offer beside the praises of neoconservative apologetics, one could understand why parts of today's intellectual youth are returning (via Derrida and Heidegger) to Nietzsche, searching for salvation in the portentous moods of cultic rejuvenation of a young conservatism not yet distorted by compromise."[48]

Habermas's alternative to the extremes of neo- and young conservatism is the *rebirth of autonomous political subcultures* willing to struggle for the creation of new life-forms; life-forms that stand in opposition to the increasing pressures of bureaucratic colonization as well as the postmodernist desire to return to a premodern condition of cultural de-differentiation. "Success" for these political subcultures would mean the creation of new forms of social solidarity capable of linking "social modernization to *other*, non-capitalist paths." It is an alternative that can come to fruition only if "the life-world can develop out of itself institutions which restrict the systematic inner dynamic of economic and administrative systems of action":

At issue are the integrity and autonomy of lifestyles, for example, the protection of traditionally established sub-cultures or the alteration of the

grammar of dated forms of life. . . . In the micro-areas of communication . . . autonomous public spheres can take shape that enter into exchange with one another as soon as they make use of the potential for self-
organization and for the self-organized employment of communications
media. Forms of self-organization strengthen the collective capability to
act below the threshold at which organizational goals become detached
from the orientations and attitudes of the organization members and
become dependent on the self-maintenance imperatives of independent
organizations. . . . Autonomous public spheres would have to attain a
combination of power and intelligent self-limitation that would make the
self-regulating mechanisms of the state and economy sufficiently sensitive
to the goal-oriented results of radically democratic formation of public
will.[49]

With these words from "The New Obscurity," Habermas articulates a vision
of radical democratic practice which, coming amidst a chorus of fin-de-siècle
pessimism, one cannot but admire. As he has demonstrated in his contributions to the Historians' Debate, there is still much to be accomplished—
contemporary nay-sayers to the contrary—for the ethico-political program of
the Enlightenment, out of which that same radical democratic spirit first
emerged. As a new millennium approaches, inspiration can be found in his
program of a "social theory with a practical intent" tempered by the genuinely
egalitarian sentiment that in "discourses of Enlightenment, there can only be
participants."

PART II

CARL SCHMITT:

THE CONSERVATIVE REVOLUTION AND

THE AESTHETICS OF HORROR

Carl Schmitt's polemical discussion of political Romanticism conceals the aestheticizing oscillations of his own political thought. In this respect, too, a kinship of spirit with the fascist intelligentsia reveals itself.—Jürgen Habermas, "The Horrors of Autonomy: Carl Schmitt in English"

The pinnacle of great politics is the moment in which the enemy comes into view in concrete clarity as the enemy.—Carl Schmitt, *The Concept of the Political* (1927)

I

Only months after Hitler's accession to power, the eminently citable political philosopher and jurist Carl Schmitt, in the ominously titled *Staat, Bewegung, Volk,* delivered one of his better known dicta. On January 30, 1933, observes Schmitt, "one can say that, 'Hegel died.' "[1] In the vast literature on Schmitt's role in the National Socialist conquest of power, one can find many glosses on this one remark, which indeed speaks volumes. But let us at the outset be sure to catch *Schmitt's* meaning. For Schmitt quickly reminds us what he does *not* intend by this pronouncement: he does not mean to impugn the hallowed tradition of German *étatisme,* that is, of German "philosophies of state," among which Schmitt would like to number his own contributions to the annals of political thought. Instead, it is Hegel qua philosopher of the "bureaucratic class" or *Beamtenstaat* that has been definitively surpassed with Hitler's triumph; "bureaucracy" (cf. Max Weber's characterization of "legal-bureaucratic domination")[2] is, according to its essence, a bourgeois form of rule. As such, this class of civil servants (which Hegel in the *Rechtsphilosophie* dubs the "universal class") represents an impermissible drag on the sovereignty of the executive authority. For Schmitt, its characteristic mode of functioning, based on rules and procedures that are fixed, preestablished, and calculable, qualifies it as the very embodiment of bourgeois normalcy—precisely that "bourgeois normalcy" that Schmitt strove to transcend and destroy in virtually everything he thought and wrote during the 1920s. The very essence of the bureaucratic conduct of business is *reverence for the norm;* a standpoint that could not exist in greater tension with the philosophy of Schmitt himself, whom we know to be a philosopher of the exception—of the *Ausnahmezustand.* And thus, in the eyes of Schmitt, Hegel had set an ignominious precedent by according this putative universal class a position of preeminence in his political thought, insofar as the primacy of the bureaucracy tends to supplant sovereign authority.

But behind this critique of Hegel and the provocative claim that Hitler's rise coincides with Hegel's metaphorical death (a claim that, while true, should have offered, *pace* Schmitt, little cause for celebration), lies a further indictment. In the remarks cited, Hegel is simultaneously perceived as an advocate of the *Rechtsstaat,* of "constitutionalism" and "rule of law." Therefore, in the history of German political thought, the doctrines of this very German philosopher prove to be something of a Trojan horse: they represent a primary avenue via which "alien," bourgeois forms of political life have infiltrated healthy and autochthonous German traditions, one of whose distinguishing features is an authoritarian rejection of constitutionalism and all it implies. The political thought of Hegel thus represents a threat—and now we encounter another one of Schmitt's key terms from the 1920s—to German *homogeneity.*

Schmitt's poignant observation concerning the relationship between Hegel and Hitler thus expresses the idea that one tradition in German cultural life— the tradition of German idealism—has come to an end. A new set of principles, based on the category of *volkisch homogeneity* (and all it implies for the political future of Germany), has arisen to take its place.[3] Or, to express the same thought in other terms: a tradition based on the concept of *Vernunft* (reason) has given way to a political system whose new raison d'être is the principle of *authoritarian decision*—whose consummate embodiment was the *Führerprinzip,* the ideological basis of this post-Hegelian state. Schmitt's insight remains a source of fascination owing to its uncanny prescience: in a statement of a few words, he manages to express the quintessence of some one hundred years of German historical development. At the same time, this remark also remains worthy of attention insofar as it serves as a prism through which the vagaries of Schmitt's own intellectual biography come into unique focus: it represents an unambiguous declaration of his satiety with Germany's prior experiments with constitutional government and of his longing for a "total" or *Führerstaat* in which the ambivalences of the parliamentary system would be abolished once and for all. Above all, however, it suggests how readily Schmitt personally made the transition from one of the most influential intellectual antagonists of Weimar democracy to a wholehearted supporter of the National Socialist revolution. Herein lies what one might refer to as the "paradox of Carl Schmitt": a man who, in the words of Hannah Arendt, was a "convinced Nazi," yet "whose very ingenious theories about the end of democracy and legal government still make arresting reading."[4]

The focal point of our inquiry will be the distinctive intellectual habitus (Bourdieu) that facilitated Schmitt's alacritous transformation from respected Weimar jurist and academician to "Crown Jurist of the Third Reich." As a key to understanding the intellectual basis of Schmitt's political views, I suggest the importance of his elective affinities with the generation of conservative revolutionary thinkers, whose worldview was so decisive in turning the tide of public opinion against the fledgling Weimar Republic. As the political theorist Kurt Sontheimer has noted: "It is hardly a matter of controversy today that certain ideological predispositions in German thought generally, but particularly in the intellectual and political climate of the Weimar Republic, induced a large number of German electors under the Weimar Republic to consider the National Socialist movement as less problematic than it turned out to be." And even though the Nazis and conservative revolutionaries failed to see eye to eye on many points, their respective plans for a "new Germany" were sufficiently close that a comparison between them is able to "throw light on the intellectual atmosphere in which, when National Socialism arose, it could seem to be a more or less presentable doctrine." Hence, "National Socialism . . . derived considerable profit from thinkers like Oswald Spengler, Moeller van den Bruck and Ernst Jünger," despite their later parting of the ways.[5] It would not be much of an exaggeration to label this intellectual movement "protofascistic"; in many ways, its general ideological effect consisted in providing a type of "spiritual preparation" for the National Socialist triumph.

Schmitt himself was, properly speaking, never an active member of the conservative revolutionary movement. It would be fair to say that the major difference between Schmitt and this like-minded, influential group of right-wing intellectuals concerned a matter of form rather than substance: unlike Schmitt, most of whose writings appeared in scholarly and professional journals, the conservative revolutionaries were, to a man, nonacademics, who made names for themselves as *Publizisten;* that is, as "political writers" in that same kaleidoscopic and febrile world of Weimar *Öffentlichkeit* that was the object of so much scorn in their work. But Schmitt's status as a "fellow traveler" in relation to the movement's main journals (e.g., Hans Zehrer's influential *Die Tat*), activities, and circles notwithstanding, his profound intellectual affinities with this group of convinced antirepublicans are impossible to deny; to the point where, in the secondary literature, it has become more common than not to simply include him as a bona fide member of the group.[6]

The intellectual habitus shared by Schmitt and the conservative revolutionaries is in no small measure of Nietzschean derivation. Both subscribed to the immoderate verdict registered by Nietzsche on the totality of inherited Western values: those values were essentially *nihilistic.* Liberalism, democracy, utilitarianism, individualism, and Enlightenment rationalism were the characteristic belief-structures of the decadent capitalist West; they were manifestations of a superficial and materialistic *Zivilisation,* which failed to measure up to the sublimity of German *Kultur.* In opposition to a bourgeois society viewed as being in an advanced state of decomposition, Schmitt and the conservative revolutionaries counterposed the Nietzschean rites of "active nihilism"; or, in Nietzsche's terms, whatever is already falling should be given a final push. One of the patented conceptual oppositions proper to the conservative revolutionary habitus was that between the "hero" (or "soldier") and the "bourgeois." Whereas the former thrives on risk, danger, and uncertainty, the life of the bourgeois is devoted to petty calculations of utility and security.[7] This conceptual opposition would occupy center-stage in what was perhaps the most influential conservative revolutionary publication of the entire Weimar period, Ernst Jünger's 1932 *Der Arbeiter,* where the opposition assumes the form of a contrast between "the worker-soldier" and "the bourgeois." And if one turns, for example, to what is arguably Schmitt's major work of the 1920s, *The Concept of the Political* (1927), where the controversial "friend-enemy" distinction is codified as the raison d'être of politics, it is difficult to ignore the profound conservative revolutionary resonances of Schmitt's argument. Indeed, it would seem that such "resonances" permeate Schmitt's attempt to justify politics *primarily in martial terms;* that is, in light of the ultimate eventuality or (to utilize Schmitt's own terminology) *Ernstfall* of "battle" (*Kampf*) or "war."

Once the conservative revolutionary dimension of Schmitt's thought is brought to light, it will become clear that the continuities in his pre- and post-1933 political philosophy are stronger than the discontinuities. Yet, Schmitt's own path of development from archfoe of Weimar democracy to "convinced Nazi" (Arendt) is mediated by a successive series of intellectual transformations that attest to his growing political radicalization during the 1920s and early 1930s. He follows a route that is both predictable and sui generis: "predictable" inasmuch as it was a route traveled by an entire generation of like-minded German conservative and nationalist intellectuals during

the interwar period; sui generis, insofar as there remains an irreducible originality and perspicacity to the various *Zeitdiagnosen* proffered by Schmitt during the 1920s, in comparison with the at times hackneyed and familiar formula-
tions of his conservative revolutionary contemporaries.

The oxymoronic designation "conservative revolutionary" is meant to distinguish the radical turn taken during the interwar period by right-of-center
German intellectuals from the stance of their "traditional conservative" counterparts, who longed for a restoration of the imagined glories of the earlier
Germanic Reichs and generally stressed the desirability of a return to premodern forms of social order (e.g., Tönnies's *Gemeinschaft*) based on the aristocratic considerations of rank and privilege. The conservative revolutionaries
(and this is true of Jünger, Moeller van den Bruck, and Schmitt) conversely
concluded from the German defeat in the Great War that if Germany were to
be successful in the next major European conflagration, premodern or traditional solutions would not suffice. Instead, what was necessary was "modernization"; yet, a form of modernization that was at the same time compatible
with the (albeit mythologized) traditional German values of heroism, "will" (as
opposed to "reason"), *Kultur,* and hierarchy. In sum, what was desired was a
modern community. As Jeffrey Herf has stressed in his book on the subject, at
issue is not Germany's rejection of modernity, but instead its *selective embrace
of modernity.*[8] That is, the ultimate triumph of National Socialism, far from
being characterized by a disdain of modernity tout court, was marked simultaneously by an assimilation of "technological modernity" and a repudiation of
what one might call "political modernity": the values of political liberalism as
they emerge from the democratic revolutions of the eighteenth century. This
"selective embrace" describes the essence of the German *Sonderweg:* Germany's "special path" to modernity that is neither Western (in the sense of
England and France) nor Eastern (in the sense of Russia).

Schmitt begins his intellectual career in the 1910s as traditional conservative; namely, as a Catholic philosopher of state. As such, his early writings
revolved around a version of political authoritarianism in which the idea of a
strong state was defended at all costs against the threat of liberal encroachments. In his most significant work of the decade, *The Value of the State and the
Significance of the Individual* (1914), the balance between the two central concepts, state and individual, is struck one-sidedly in favor of the former term.
For Schmitt, the state, in executing its law-promulgating prerogatives, cannot
countenance any opposition. The uncompromising, antiliberal conclusion he
draws from this observation is that "no individual can have autonomy within
the state."[9] Or, as Schmitt unambiguously states elsewhere in the same work:

"the individual" is merely "a means to the essence, the state is what is most important."[10] Thus, although Schmitt displayed little inclination for the brand of jingoistic nationalism so prevalent among his German academic mandarin brethren during the war years, as Joseph Bendersky has observed, "it was precisely on the point of authoritarianism vs. liberal individualism that the views of many Catholics [such as Schmitt] and those of non-Catholic conservatives coincided."[11]

But, like other German conservatives, it was Schmitt's innate antipathy to liberal democratic forms of government, coupled with the political turmoil of the Weimar Republic, that facilitated his transformation from a traditional conservative to a "conservative revolutionary." To be sure, a full account of the intricacies of Schmitt's conservative revolutionary conversion would necessitate a year-by-year account of his political thought during the Weimar period, during which Schmitt's intellectual output was nothing if not prolific (he published virtually a book a year). Instead, for the sake of concision, and in order to highlight our chosen leitmotif of the "conservative revolutionary habitus," I have elected to concentrate on three aspects of Schmitt's intellectual formation that prove essential for understanding the aforementioned process of political transformation: (1) his sympathies with the vitalist (*lebensphilosophisch*) critique of modern rationalism; (2) what one might call Schmitt's "philosophy of history" during these years; and (3) Schmitt's protofascistic assimilation of the conservative revolutionary doctrine of the "total state." All three aspects, moreover, are integrally interrelated.

II

The vitalist critique of Enlightenment rationalism is of Nietzschean provenance. In opposition to the traditional philosophical image of man qua *animal rationalis*, Nietzsche counterposes his vision of "Life [as] will to power."[12] And in the course of this "transvaluation of all values," the heretofore marginalized forces of life, will, affect, and passion should reclaim the position of primacy they once enjoyed before the triumph of "Socratism." It is in precisely this spirit that Nietzsche recommends that in the future, we philosophize with our *affects* instead of with *concepts*. For in the culture of "European nihilism" that has triumphed with the Enlightenment, "the essence of life, its *will to power*, is ignored," argues Nietzsche; "one overlooks the essential priority of the spontaneous, aggressive, expansive, form-giving forces that give new interpretations and directions."[13]

It would be difficult to overestimate the power and influence this Nietzschean critique exercised over an entire generation of antidemocratic German intellectuals during the 1920s. The anticivilizational ethos that pervades Spengler's *The Decline of the West*—the defense of "blood and tradition" against the much-lamented triumph of forces of societal rationalization— would be unthinkable without that dimension of vitalistic *Kulturkritik* to which Nietzsche's work gave consummate expression.[14] Nor would it seem that the doctrines of Klages, as embodied in the title of his magnum opus from the late Weimar period, *The Intellect as Antagonist of the Soul* (1929–31), would have captured the mood of the times as well as they did had it not been for the irrevocable precedent set by Nietzsche's work. Indeed, the central opposition between "life" and "intellect," as articulated by Klages and so many other German "anti-intellectual intellectuals" during the interwar period, represents an unmistakably Nietzschean inheritance.

While the conservative revolutionary components of Schmitt's worldview have been frequently noted, the paramount role played by the philosophy of life (above all, by the concept of cultural criticism proper to *Lebensphilosophie*) in his political thought has escaped the attention of most critics. But a full understanding of Schmitt's status as a radical conservative intellectual is insep- arable from an appreciation of this hitherto neglected aspect of his work.

In point of fact, the influences of "philosophy of life"—a movement that would feed directly into the *Existenzphilosophie* craze of the 1920s (Heidegger, Jaspers, etc.)—are readily discernible in Schmitt's pre-Weimar writings. In one of his first published works, *Law and Judgment* (1912), Schmitt is concerned with demonstrating the impossibility of understanding the legal order in *exclu- sively* rationalist terms, as a self-sufficient system of legal norms à la "legal positivism." It is along these lines that Schmitt argues that in a particular case, a correct decision cannot be reached solely via a process of deduction or generalization from existing legal precedents or norms. Instead, he contends, there is always a moment of *irreducible particularity* to each case that defies subsumption under general principles. And it is precisely this aspect of legal judgment that Schmitt finds most interesting and significant. He goes on to coin a phrase for this "extralegal" dimension: the moment of "concrete indif- ference," the dimension of adjudication that transcends the previously estab- lished legal norm. In essence, the moment of "concrete indifference" repre- sents for Schmitt a type of vital substrate, an element of "pure life," that stands forever opposed to the formalism of law as such. And thus, at the very heart of bourgeois society, its legal system, one finds an element of "existential particu- larity" that defies the coherence of rationalist syllogizing or formal reason.

The concept "concrete indifference" is of more than passing interest insofar as it proves a crucial harbinger of Schmitt's later decisionistic theory of sovereignty. In its devaluation of the adequacy of existing legal norms as a basis for judicial decision-making, the category of "concrete indifference" points toward *the imperative nature of the juridical decision itself as a self-sufficient and irreducible basis of adjudication.* The vitalist dimension of Schmitt's early philosophy of law betrays itself in his thoroughgoing denigration of "legal normativism"—for norms are a product of abstract *Intelligenz,* and, as such, *lebensfeindlich* (hostile to life)—and the concomitant belief that the decision alone is capable of bridging the gap between the abstractness of law and the fullness of life.

The vitalist sympathies of Schmitt's early work become full-blown in his writings of the 1920s. Here, the key text is *Political Theology* (1922), in which Schmitt formulates his decisionist theory of politics. Or, as he remarks in the work's oft-cited first sentence: "Sovereign is he who decides over the state of exception [*Ausnahmezustand*]."[15]

One is tempted to claim that from this initial, terse yet lapidary definition of sovereignty, one may deduce the totality of Schmitt's mature political thought. It contains what we know to be the two keywords of his political philosophy during these years: "decision" and the "exception." Both in Schmitt's lexicon are far from value-neutral or merely descriptive concepts. Instead, they both entail a strong evaluative component; they are accorded an unambiguously positive value in the economy of his thought. And thus, one of the signatures of Schmitt's political thinking during the Weimar years will be a privileging of the *Ausnahmezustand* or "state of exception" vis-à-vis political normalcy.

Schmitt's celebration of the state of exception over conditions of political normalcy (which Schmitt essentially equates with the reign of "legal positivism" or, more generally, with "parliamentarianism") has its basis in the vitalist critique of Enlightenment rationalism. In his initial justification of the *Ausnahmezustand* in *Political Theology,* Schmitt leaves no doubt concerning the historical pedigree of such concepts. Following the well-known definition of sovereignty cited above, he immediately underscores its status as a "borderline concept"—a *Grenzbegriff,* a concept "pertaining to the outermost sphere."[16] It is precisely this fascination with "extreme" or "boundary situations" (what Karl Jaspers calls *Grenzsituationen*)—those unique moments of extreme peril or danger that become a type of existential "proving ground" for "authentic" individuals—that stands as one of the hallmarks of the sweeping critique of "everydayness" proffered by *Lebensphilosophie* in all its variants. In the *Grenzsituation,* "*Dasein* glimpses transcendence and is thereby transformed from possible to real *Existenz.*"[17] By according primacy to the "state of exception" as opposed to political normalcy, Schmitt tries to invest the emergency situation with a higher, existential significance and meaning.

According to the inner logic of this conceptual scheme, the *Ausnahmezustand* becomes the basis for a *politics of authenticity*. In contrast to conditions of political normalcy, which represent the unexalted reign of the "average," the "mediocre," and the "everyday," the state of exception proves capable of reincorporating a dimension of heroism and greatness so sorely lacking in the routinized, bourgeois conduct of political life.

Consequently, the superiority of the state as ultimate, decisionistic arbiter over the emergency situation is a matter that, in Schmitt's eyes, need not be argued for. According to Schmitt, "Every rationalist interpretation *falsifies the immediacy of life.*"[18] Instead, in his view, the state possesses the status of a fundamental, irrefragable, *existential verity,* as does the category of "life" in Nietzsche's philosophy. Or, as Schmitt remarks with characteristic pith in *Political Theology,* "The *existence of the state* is undoubted proof of its superiority over the validity of the legal norm." And thus, "the decision [on the state of exception] becomes instantly independent of argumentative substantiation and receives an autonomous value."[19]

But as Franz Neumann observes in *Behemoth,* given the fundamental lack of coherence of Nazi ideology, the rationales provided for totalitarian practice were often couched specifically in "vitalist" or "existential" terms. In Neumann's words,

> [Given the incoherence of Nazi ideology,] what is left as justification for the [*Grossdeutsche*] Reich? Not racism, not the idea of the Holy Roman Empire, and certainly not some democratic nonsense like popular sovereignty or self-determination. Only the Reich itself remains. It is its own justification. The philosophical roots of the argument are to be found in the existential philosophy of Heidegger. Transferred to the realm of politics, existentialism argues that power and might are true: power is a sufficient theoretical base for more power.[20]

In *Political Theology,* Schmitt is quite forthright concerning the vitalistic bases of his political thought. As he observes early on: "Precisely a *philosophy of concrete life* must not withdraw from the exception and the extreme case, but must be interested in it to the highest degree."[21] At issue in this judgment are "existential" considerations—the "choice" of a "worldview"—that simultaneously express an aesthetic sensibility; namely, an "aesthetics of horror" (*Ästhetik des Schreckens*), which has been defined by Karl Heinz Bohrer as propagating a temporal semantics of "rupture," "discontinuity," and "shock." According to Bohrer, whereas this modernist aesthetic of "suddenness" (*Plötzlichkeit*) is primarily of Nietzschean provenance, it is "renewed in the 1920s through the works of Max Scheler, Carl Schmitt, and Martin Heidegger."[22]

Only in light of this vitalist intellectual historical lineage and the aesthetics of rupture that underlie it does Schmitt's partisanship for the exception over the norm first become fully intelligible. Hence, what is important is not merely that the exception presents itself as superior to the norm. Rather, the temporal semantics of discontinuity and horror embraced by Schmitt culminates in the insight that "the norm is *destroyed* in the exception."[23] From the ashes of the norm, an ontologically higher condition of political life will emerge, as it were.

In *Political Theology*, Schmitt will attempt to justify his exaltation of the exception in terms explicitly culled from the vitalist aesthetics of "suddenness" or "rupture" described by Bohrer: "The exception is more interesting than the rule," observes Schmitt. "The rule proves nothing; the exception proves everything: It confirms not only the rule but also its existence, which derives only from the exception. In the exception the power of real life breaks through the crust of a mechanism that has become torpid by repetition."[24]

The "mechanism that has become torpid by repetition" is none other than a society of *bourgeois normalcy*, where, in Schmitt's view, positive law reigns supreme. This society of "normalization" (Foucault) must be subjected to an "aesthetics of rupture" (Bohrer), which is the point at which the exception enters upon the scene. For the exception alone qua "borderline concept" (*Grenzbegriff*) allows "the power of real life"—here, a type of existential *transcendens*—to explode the society of "mechanized petrification" (Weber) that bourgeois *Zivilisation* has wrought.[25] Only the will to power of "real life" possesses the capacity to break through the inertial character of society qua encrusted "mechanism." And it is precisely in this spirit that Schmitt will praise the Bergsonian origins of Sorel's apotheosis of violence. In Schmitt's estimation, Sorel's "reflections" on this concept are of value precisely insofar as they are grounded in a Bergsonian "theory of unmediated real life."[26]

In sum, Schmitt's partisanship for the moment of absolute decision, which can only emerge once conditions of political normalcy have been suspended in the *Ausnahmezustand*, represents a transposition of Kierkegaard's "teleological suspension of the ethical" from the moral to the political sphere.[27] For both thinkers, a fascination with "boundary situations" and an aesthetics of "rupture" or "suddenness" subtends a critique of "the present age" qua embodiment of an indigent condition of ethico-political normalcy.

Thus, Schmitt grounds the foundational concepts of his mature political philosophy in a fundamental existential value-judgment: a condemnation of the prosaicism of bourgeois normalcy combined with an exaltation of the capacities for "transcendence" embodied in the emergency situation. My employment of the word "transcendence," moreover, is far from accidental, insofar as it is one of Schmitt's most profound beliefs that "all significant concepts of the modern theory of state are secularized versions of theological concepts."[28] Thus, the state of exception in Schmitt's view represents nothing less than a "return of the repressed" in the form of a "return of the sacred." In keeping with the discourse of "political theology," the state of exception is to politics what the miracle is to theology.

But it is of equal importance in this connection to recognize the historical-contextual status of such arguments as set forth by the leading jurist of the Weimar Republic. It was precisely this vitalist/conservative revolutionary devaluation of political normalcy, on the one hand, coupled with an exaggeration of the value of "emergency powers," or government by executive decree (as embodied in the notorious Article 48 of the Weimar constitution), on the other, that was indispensable to the advent of Hitler's dictatorship. And thus, according to Franz Neumann, "the idea of the totalitarian state grew out of the demand [during Weimar] that all power be concentrated in the hands of the president."[29]

III

Schmitt's 1923 critique of parliamentarianism concludes with a chapter entitled "Irrationalist Theories of the Direct Use of Force." Unsurprisingly, the doctrines of Georges Sorel occupy pride of place in his analysis. Schmitt's barely concealed admiration for Sorel qua apostle of revolutionary violence and myth is fascinating in its suggestion of the many points shared by "left" and "right" variants of the critique of bourgeois normalcy. In one telling passage, Schmitt cites the views of the nineteenth-century Spanish counterrevolutionary stalwart, Donoso Cortés, with whom Schmitt himself identified profoundly. Donoso Cortés, interestingly enough, praises the doctrines of "radical socialism" as the only "worthy opponent" of his own counterrevolutionary ideology: it is these two standpoints alone that demand a total, *eschatological* break with bourgeois conditions of life. To be sure, in the eyes of Donoso Cortés, anarchist socialism was tantamount to radical evil, in league with the devil, and, as such, worthy of summary eradication. Yet, as Schmitt comments, "Today it is easy to see that both were their own real opponents and that everything else was only a provisional half-measure."[30]

Of course, as a twentieth-century "clerico-fascist," Schmitt's own intellectual sympathies are infinitely closer to the views of the nineteenth-century counterrevolutionary philosophers of state, Donoso Cortés, Bonald, and de Maistre. But this does not prevent him from mining the doctrines of Sorel, this "worthy adversary," for all that they are worth. What Schmitt appreciates about Sorel is the fact that in his celebrations of violence, the "warlike and heroic conceptions that are bound up with battle and struggle were taken seriously again . . . as the true impulse of an intensive life."[31] Sorel is thus praised as an apostle of Nietzsche, a proponent of "active nihilism," an unrelenting advocate of the powers of desublimated instinct, and of those martial virtues that have been allowed to atrophy owing to the predominantly rationalist temper of modern *Zivilisation*. The views that Schmitt attributes to Sorel (indeed, he never tries to conceal it) are very much his own. And thus, as Schmitt goes on to observe, "Whatever value human life has does not come from reason; it emerges from a state of war between those who are inspired by great mythical images to join battle. . . . Bellicose, revolutionary excitement and the expectation of monstrous catastrophes belong to the intensity of life and move history."[32] Here, the vitalist advocacy of "intensive life" flows seamlessly into the conservative revolutionary embrace of that mentality of *Sturm und Kampf* that would play such a pivotal role in the worldview of National Socialism.[33] Schmitt's confrontation with Sorel thus proves a crucial way-station on his path to a conservative revolutionary glorification of a militaristic, aggressive "total state"; a position to which he would accede unambiguously in his provocative work of 1927, *The Concept of the Political*.

But before concluding our discussion of Schmitt's relation to Sorel, it would perhaps be worthwhile to mention the point at which their respective paths diverge. Ultimately, Schmitt parts company with his confrère across the Rhine insofar as, in Schmitt's view, Sorel's Marxism threatens the "autonomy of the political." The problem with Sorel's apotheosis of violence is that violence is placed in the service of "unpolitical powers"; namely, the powers of a "social class," the proletariat. From Schmitt's perspective, this solution is too reminiscent of the evils of modernity that must be cured. For in the modern world, claims to political sovereignty have been usurped by the prepolitical interests of social classes; a phenomenon that comes to light in the interminable jockeying for position among the various interest groups in parliament. As Schmitt observes, the drawback of Sorel's position is that he "sought to retain the purely economic basis of the proletarian standpoint, and despite some disagreements, he clearly always began with Marx."[34]

The rejection of Sorel drives him into the arms of the aforementioned counterrevolutionary philosophers of state—albeit, a position from which Schmitt never really strayed. According to Schmitt's philosophy of history, political life since the seventeenth century has fallen into a state of permanent decline. Whereas in the age of absolutism, the twin pillars of state, God and sovereign, occupied their rightful niches of supremacy, since then, both have suffered debasement at the hands of the ascendant bourgeois class and its proletarian heir apparent. In the secularizing doctrines of the eighteenth and nineteenth centuries, the concept of "God" was supplanted by the idea of "man," and the majesty of the sovereign proper was irreparably decimated by the ideal of popular sovereignty. As a result, "the decisionistic and personalistic element in the concept of sovereignty was lost."[35] More generally, the sublime virtues of transcendence were sacrificed in favor of the prosaic terms of immanence. This concerted assault against traditional religiosity could only end in atheism, disorder, and "anarchic freedom." It was the chief merit of the Catholic philosophers of state to have confronted this situation head-on and to have never shied away from drawing the logical conclusion from this turn of events. Thus, since the legitimacy of the ancien régime had been irreparably damaged following the revolutions of 1848, from this point hence, *dictatorship alone* could save the world from the godless era of secular humanism. Schmitt's reflections on the implications of this new historical situation could hardly be less equivocal. Once again, he relies on the wisdom of Donoso Cortés to make his point:

> The true significance of those counterrevolutionary philosophers of state lies precisely in the consistency with which they decide. They heightened the moment of decision to such an extent that the notion of legitimacy, their starting point, was finally dissolved. As soon as Donoso Cortés realized that the period of monarchy had come to an end . . . he brought his decisionism to a logical conclusion. He demanded a political dictatorship. In . . . de Maistre we can also see a reduction of the state to the moment of decision, to a pure decision not based on reason or discussion and not justifying itself, that is, to an absolute decision created out of nothingness. But this decision is essentially dictatorship, not legitimacy.[36]

A politics of "dictatorship," grounded in a "decision *ex nihilo*," will also become Schmitt's solution to an era of relentless "depoliticization."[37]

Moreover, although the Marxist Sorel is correct in his estimation of the value of political myth-making, he is mistaken in his belief that the myth of proletarian *internationalism* will prove a source of inspiration to future generations of political actors. Instead, according to Schmitt, today we know that "the stronger myth is *national*" and that "the national myth has until today always been victorious."[38] Thus, it is the national myth as propagated by Mussolini and Italian fascism that represents the embodiment of all future hopes for the return of an authentic politics; it characterizes a politics in which the values of "intensive life" might once again come to the fore. As Schmitt observes: "The theory of myth is the most powerful symptom of the decline of the relative rationalism of parliamentary thought." Indeed, for the first time in the modern era, it raises the prospects of "an authority based on the new feeling for order, discipline, and hierarchy." Italian fascism thus represents the model to be followed by all future attempts to reverse the bourgeois sublimation of politics and realize an authentic "repoliticization" of modern life:

> Until now the democracy of mankind and parliamentarianism has only once been contemptuously pushed aside through the conscious appeal to myth, and that was an example of the irrational power of the national myth. In his famous speech of October 1922 in Naples before the march on Rome, Mussolini said, "We have created a myth, this myth is a belief, a noble enthusiasm; it does not need to be reality, it is a striving and a hope, belief and courage. Our myth is the nation, the great nation which we want to make into a concrete reality; for ourselves."[39]

IV

The work in which Schmitt's propagation of the conservative revolutionary aesthetics of horror becomes most apparent is his 1927 *The Concept of the Political*. In this text, the vitalist correlation between "violence" and "intensive life," which Schmitt first discovers in the theories of Sorel, receives its fullest elaboration. It would be a mistake, however, to view this key text of the late 1920s apart from a series of related writings from the late 1920s and early 1930s in which Schmitt elaborates his views on the "totalitarian" or "total state." The conclusions Schmitt reaches in this series of works represents both the consummation of his political thought during the Weimar period and a crucial anticipation of his later partisanship for the National Socialist cause.

I have already referred to the rudiments of Schmitt's philosophy of history during the Weimar period; this philosophy revolves around the theme of the "eclipse of the political." Thus, according to Schmitt, the salient feature of the past three centuries of European history has been the fact that political energies have been placed in the service of heteronomous, *nonpolitical* forces and interests; above all, in the service of bourgeois *economic* interests. With respect to the political, then, Schmitt describes recent historical trends as culminating in an "age of neutralizations and depoliticizations." All bourgeois encroachments on sovereignty, claims Schmitt, "aim with undeniable certainty at subjecting the state and politics partly to an individualistic, and thus private-legal morality, partly to economic categories—and thus robbing it of its specific meaning."[40] Schmitt's lamentations concerning the sublimation of politics in the modern world suggest his affinities with the "traditional conservative" political thought of fellow Germans Leo Strauss and Eric Voegelin; and with the nonconservative traditionalism of Hannah Arendt.

As we have seen from our earlier discussion of Schmitt's interest in Sorel, Donoso Cortés, and Italian fascism, Schmitt is constantly on the lookout for countervailing tendencies vis-à-vis the dominant historical trend toward neutralization/depoliticization. He believes he has discovered precisely such prospects in the logic of technological concentration that emerged in the aftermath of World War I. The outstanding characteristic of the Great War was that it gave the lie to the well-known Clausewitzian dictum "war is the continuation of diplomacy by other means"; in this respect, it set the tenor for all wars to come. Thus, according to Schmitt, as a result of recent trends, the insight of Clausewitz must be *reversed*. Now, instead of war standing in the service of politics, the era of "total war" heralded by the conflagration of 1914–18 suggests that all energies of modern political life stand in the service of war. It is precisely in this vein that Schmitt sees concrete prospects for the reemergence of the political in the modern world. Through a strange instance of the "cunning of reason," the bourgeois ideology of progress ultimately proves self-subverting. Forces of the modern economy that were originally directed against the "autonomy of the political" (i.e., against the values of the monarchical absolutism) now undergo a transformation from quantity to quality and reemerge as the guarantor of autonomous political energies. As Schmitt observes: "Economics is no longer *eo ipso* freedom; technology serves not only [the ends of] comfort, but instead just as much the production of dangerous weapons and instruments; its progress does not further *eo ipso* the humanitarian-moral perfection that was conceived of in the eighteenth century as 'progress,' and technical rationalization can be the opposite of economic rationalization."[41] For Schmitt, this assertion represents an objective description of current social trends in addition to being a statement of political preference.

Walther Rathenau once observed that in the modern world, not politics but economics has become "fate." According to Schmitt, however, Rathenau failed to realize the ultimate ramifications of this dictum, insofar as autonomous laws of economic-technological concentration have led to a situation in which the economy itself, of necessity, is repoliticized. One can see such tendencies developing throughout all Western industrialized societies, where the "nightwatchman state" of the nineteenth century has developed into the interventionist, "total state" of the twentieth century. Thus, according to Schmitt, the contemporary balance between state and society is conditioned by the fact that today, "*all* problems are potentially political problems."[42] Whereas formerly the state was subjected to alien, economic interests, now this situation has reversed itself, and the economy has itself become an object of political planning and control. The mastery of the new technological means (in the areas of economic production, warfare, and mass communications) has become, as it were, an imperative of survival for the modern state. As Schmitt observes, "Every political power is forced to take the new weapons in hand."[43] No state can, for example, afford to neglect the new technological means of influencing public opinion, such as cinema and radio. "Behind the idea of the total state," observes Schmitt, "stands the correct realization that the contemporary state possesses new mechanisms of power and possibilities of enormous intensity, whose ultimate significance and consequences we can barely anticipate."[44]

In his arguments for the total state, Schmitt betrays his theoretical indebtedness to the most prominent representative of the conservative revolutionary generation, Ernst Jünger, whom Schmitt praises as "a remarkable representative of the German *Frontsoldaten*." Or, as Schmitt avers in "The Turn toward the Total State" (1931), "Ernst Jünger has introduced an extremely pregnant formulation for this astonishing process [whereby the state extends itself to all spheres of society]: total mobilization."[45] In "Total Mobilization" and *Der Arbeiter*, Jünger argues that the distinguishing feature of modernity as an era of "total war" is that the entirety of society's resources—ideological, economic, scientific—are of necessity incorporated into the war effort; and that, consequently, the only form of political life proper to an era of "total mobilization" is that of a "total state." Thus, the new realities of struggle in an era of technological concentration dictate that society as a whole be fashioned after a military model. As Jünger observes in 1930:

> In addition to the armies who encounter one another on the battle-fields originate the modern armies of commerce, of food-production, of the armaments industry—the army of labor in general. . . . In this total incorporation of potential energies, which transforms the warring industrial states into volcanic forges, the beginning of the "age of work" [*Arbeitszeitalter*] is perhaps most strikingly apparent—it turns the World War into a historical phenomenon that is superior to the French Revolution in significance.[46]

I make the strong claim that in Schmitt's post-1927 writings (beginning with *The Concept of the Political* and including his various commentaries on the theme of the "fascist" or "total state") there exists a body of work and a complex of ideas via which one can trace the transformation of his authoritarian political philosophy of the early 1920s into a protofascistic, conservative revolutionary partisanship for a totalitarian state. In light of this assertion, it would seem that Schmitt's option for a totalitarian resolution of the political ills of Weimar was made in theory some six years before it was registered in actual fact (Schmitt joined the Nazi Party in March 1933). To be sure, the encomium to the glories of Italian fascism with which Schmitt concludes *The Crisis of Parliamentary Democracy* points strongly in this direction. But it is not until his writings of the late 1920s that analogous themes occupy a position of primacy in his work. It is at this point that Schmitt concludes, in a manner similar to Donoso Cortés some seventy years earlier, that in the modern era, the "integrity of the political" can only be maintained through a plebiscitary, fascist dictatorship. From this conclusion, it is only a short step to the *Gleich-schaltung* legislation Schmitt drafts with alacrity at the behest of the Nazis in April 1933.[47] Thus, already in 1929, with reference to developments in Italy, Schmitt, in an essay entitled "Wesen und Werden des faschistischen Staates," had concluded that, "the preponderance of fascism over economic interests . . . [signifies] the *heroic* effort to maintain and preserve the dignity of the state and of national unity vis-à-vis the pluralism of economic interests."[48]

V

Thus far, we have treated Schmitt's assimilation of the conservative revolutionary *habitus* as deriving from both his virulently antiliberal, decisionistic theory of sovereignty ("sovereign is he who decides on the state of the exception"), as well as his preoccupation with the vitalist theme of "intensive life." The latter preoccupation, it has been suggested, has its origins in an existential predilection for so-called boundary or extreme situations, which has been felicitously captured by Bohrer via the expression the "aesthetics of horror." It now falls due to us to examine how the motif identified by Bohrer is at work in Schmitt's 1927 work, *The Concept of the Political*—specifically, in Schmitt's glorification of "war" as the "highest instance" (or *Ernstfall*) of politics. Recall the opening citation to this chapter: "The pinnacle of great politics is the moment in which the enemy comes into view in concrete clarity as the enemy."[49]

Although it has become fashionable among Schmitt's defenders to refer to Schmitt qua proponent of political authoritarianism as the "Hobbes of the twentieth century," it is essential to clarify what attracted him to the political thought of Hobbes. The stakes at issue have been incisively summarized by Leo Strauss, who observes, "Schmitt goes back against liberalism to its originator, Hobbes, in order to strike at the root of liberalism in Hobbes' explicit negation of the state of nature."[50] It is not Hobbes qua theorist of the "social contract" whom Schmitt reveres, since this is the Hobbes who becomes the intellectual progenitor of Western liberalism. Rather, it is Hobbes the theorist of the state of nature qua state of war that Schmitt finds worthy of admiration. As such, for Schmitt, war or the eventuality thereof becomes the basis and guarantor of great politics; it is the ultimate *Grenzsituation*, as it were, in which the very existence of a people or *Volk* is put to the test. But there is no small irony here, insofar as Schmitt, the supposed defender of the autonomy of the political, thereby elevates a moment that for Hobbes epitomized the lawlessness and chaos of prepolitical existence (the state of nature) to the position of existential raison d'être of politics *tout court*. Thus, Schmitt's conceptual scheme in point of fact ends up by standing Hobbes on his head: the prepolitical *bellum omnium contra omnes* is turned into the essence of the political in general.

Without doubt, it is in his descriptions of war as the existential, ultimate instance of politics that Schmitt betrays most profoundly his intellectual affinities with the conservative revolutionary aesthetics of horror. With Jünger, "war is an intoxication beyond all intoxication, an unleashing that breaks all bonds. It is a force without caution and limits, comparable only to the forces of nature."[51] For Schmitt, similarly, "war, the readiness for death of fighting men, the physical annihilation of other men who stand on the side of the enemy, all that has no normative *only an existential meaning*."[52] Or, as Schmitt, in an observation strikingly redolent of Heideggerian *Existenzphilosophie* (*Being and Time* and *The Concept of the Political* both appear in the same year), affirms in *The Concept of the Political*, "The word struggle [*Kampf*], like the word enemy, is to be understood in its existential primordiality [*seinsmäßige Ursprünglichkeit*].[53] Similarly, the friend–enemy distinction in terms of which Schmitt seeks to ground his "concept of the political," must be understood "in [its] concrete, existential sense. . . . The concepts of friend, enemy, and struggle receive their real meaning especially insofar as they relate to and preserve the real possibility of physical annihilation. War follows from enmity, for the latter is *the existential [seinsmäßige] negation of another being*."[54]

Schmitt's proponents view his doctrines as praiseworthy in that they serve to defend the autonomy of the political in face of the modern denigration of politics in favor of "the social." Apparent textual support for such claims is evinced by Schmitt's repeated emphasis on the *specificity* of politics vis-à-vis the other realms of modern life. Thus, whereas "beauty" is the subject matter of aesthetics; "good and evil," that of morality; and "wealth," the focal point of economics, the inner logic of politics, so Schmitt claims, is grounded in terms of the friend-enemy dichotomy.

But it takes no special talent for hermeneutical decipherment to discern the speciousness of the claim for Schmitt as champion of political autonomy. In *The Concept of the Political*, it is clear that "politics" stands in the service of heteronomous, nonpolitical powers; namely, the powers of war. In no uncertain terms, in Schmitt's scheme, the autonomy of politics is sacrificed on the altar of war. There is no small irony here: Schmitt succumbs, mutatis mutandis, to the same charges of "occasionalism" that he levels against "political romanticism" in his book of 1919. Like the political romantics, Schmitt's decisionistic conception of politics proves devoid of intrinsic content and in need of an external pretext or "occasion" to realize itself; the occasion in this instance being the possibilities for existential self-realization embodied in struggle or war.

Upon closer scrutiny, Schmitt's attempt to separate politics from morality, allegedly in the name of preserving the autonomy of the political, also raises suspicions of intellectual chicanery. As we have seen, the separation of politics from morality in the name of a bellicose, social Darwinist ethos of "existential self-preservation" merely serves to deliver the political over to the "alien" powers of war and struggle. In this way Schmitt has rashly abandoned the classical doctrine of politics, according to which politics and morality are necessarily interrelated: according to this political lexicon, a "just" political order proves most conducive to a life of "virtue." An echo of this doctrine may be found in the tenets of modern liberal-democratic thought (e.g., J. S. Mill), where an absence of authoritarian political interference should prove conducive to the maximum development of individual talents and capacities. In both classical and modern theories, therefore, the proper end of political society is to varying degrees a conception of the good life. But in Schmitt's political philosophy, we are forced to abandon any concept of higher political ends. Instead (and here the reliance on Hobbes is once again instructive), his existential definition of politics in terms of the primacy of the friend-enemy grouping compels us to relinquish all claims to the good life and instead to rest content with "mere life" (i.e., existential self-preservation).

In a perceptive review-essay of Ernst Jünger's 1930 anthology *Krieg und Krieger* (War and warriors), appropriately titled, "Theories of German Fascism," Walter Benjamin analyzes the cult of violence promoted by Jünger et al. as a perverse extension of the bourgeois doctrine of art for art's sake.[55] The celebration of the "war experience" as an end in itself, the idea that what is important about war and struggle is not so much the ends that are being fought for, but the fact of struggle as an intrinsic good, is viewed by Benjamin as an endorsement of a fascist aesthetics of violence, of "violence for violence's sake." Schmitt's existential justification of war in *The Concept of the Political,* where what counts is not the specific ends being fought for (the concept of a "just war" would have no place in Schmitt's schema), but war as a touchstone and basis for political existence as such (for this reason, the prospect of a "world government," as implied by the Kantian doctrine of "perpetual peace," signifies for Schmitt "the end of politics"), must be viewed as of a piece with the "theories of German fascism" discussed by Benjamin in his 1931 review.

Schmitt remarks in the early months of Hitler's dictatorship that "to stand in the immediate presence of the political" means to stand in the presence of "intensive life." In the same breath, he assimilates Heraclitus's well-known aphorism (fragment 43) concerning "war" as "the father of all things" to the ends of National Socialist "struggle."[56] Yet this allusion to the integral relation between "intensive life" and "war" in no way symbolizes a "break" in his thinking; he has merely reiterated, under politically more propitious circumstances, the vitalist aesthetics of violence he had already embraced in the 1920s.

"OVER THE LINE":
REFLECTIONS ON HEIDEGGER
AND NATIONAL SOCIALISM

Given the significant attachment of the philosopher to the mood and intellectual habitus of National Socialism, it would be inappropriate to criticize or exonerate his political decision in isolation from the very principles of Heideggerian philosophy itself. It is not Heidegger, who, in opting for Hitler, "misunderstood himself"; instead, those who cannot understand why he acted this way have failed to comprehend him. A Swiss lecturer regretted that Heidegger consented to compromise himself with daily affairs, as if a philosophy that explains Being from the standpoint of time and the everyday would not stand in relation to the daily affairs in which it makes its influence felt and originates. The possibility of a Heideggerian political philosophy was not born as a result of a regrettable miscue, but from the very conception of existence that simultaneously combats and absorbs the "spirit of the age."—Karl Löwith, "The Political Implications of Heidegger's Existentialism"

Whoever does not want merely to judge Heidegger but also to appropriate initiatives and to learn from him must realize that in the thirties, Heidegger himself placed the decision about the truth of Being as he sought it in a political context.—Otto Pöggeler, afterword to the second edition, *Martin Heidegger's Path of Thinking*

I

In his marvelously thorough *New York Review of Books* essay on "Heidegger and the Nazis," Thomas Sheehan concludes by observing: "one would do well to read nothing of Heidegger's any more without raising political questions. . . . [One] must re-read his works—particularly but not exclusively those from 1933 on—with strict attention to the political movement with which Heidegger himself chose to link his ideas. To do less than that is, I believe, finally not to understand him at all."[1] Yet, ten years earlier, Sheehan had argued for a very different position: that the relationship between Heidegger's political commitment to Nazism and his philosophy itself was negligible; and that in any event, Heidegger's partisanship for National Socialism had been a short-lived affair, a regrettable, momentary *lapsus*, that was in no way a sincere expression of the philosopher's own innermost conviction. What was it that induced Sheehan to arrive at such a radical volte-face?

Above all, since the publication of the Heidegger biographies of Farias and Ott, the typical rationalizations that had been invoked in the past to minimize the extent of Heidegger's commitment to the Nazi cause have become wholly untenable. We now know that Heidegger's alliance with Nazism, far from being a temporary marriage of convenience, was grandiose and profound: at least for a short period of time, Heidegger labored under the delusion that he could play the role of "philosopher-king" to Hitler's *Führerstaat*—which, to many, has suggested parallels with Plato's ill-fated venture with the tyrant Dionysius at Syracuse.[2] As the philosopher Otto Pöggeler has phrased it, Heidegger sought "den Führer führen" (to lead the leader), Adolf Hitler, along the proper course so that the "National Revolution" might fulfill its appointed metaphysical destiny.[3] Heidegger believed that in its early manifestations, National Socialism possessed the capacity to initiate a great spiritual renewal of German *Dasein*. In it, he saw a potential countermovement to the fate of "European nihilism," of perpetual spiritual decline, as it had been diagnosed by the leading German "conservative revolutionary" critics of his generation—Oswald Spengler, Ludwig Klages, and Ernst Jünger—thinkers who, in essence, were merely following the powerful critique of Western modernity that had been outlined some forty years earlier by Friedrich Nietzsche.

To be sure, it appears that Heidegger's understanding of National Socialism had little in common with the ideology of genocidal imperialism via which the movement has left its gruesome imprint on twentieth-century history. But we know that he was sufficiently convinced of National Socialism's "inner truth and greatness"[4] to have acquired the reputation of a zealous propagandist on behalf of the new regime in its initial stages. And thus, following his acceptance of the rectorship at the University of Freiburg in May 1933, Heidegger traveled around Germany delivering speeches in favor of Hitler's policies. He also proved an enthusiastic supporter of *Gleichschaltung* legislation (the so-called Law for Reconstituting the Civil Service), which barred Jews and other undesirables from Germany's civil service, replacing them instead with party members. Lastly, it should be kept in mind that Heidegger was not merely a Nazi sympathizer, but was in fact found guilty of political crimes by a (favorably disposed) university peer review committee immediately following the war. As a result, he was banned from university life for close to five years. These crimes included denouncing political undesirables to the Nazi authorities, inciting students against "reactionary" (i.e., non-Nazi) professors, and enthusiastically transforming the university along the lines of the Nazi "leadership principle" or *Führerprinzip*.[5]

In December 1945, the aforementioned peer review committee contacted the philosopher Karl Jaspers for an evaluation of Heidegger's activities and character. Among Jaspers's most telling observations, one finds the following remarks:

> Heidegger is a significant potency, not through the content of a philo-sophical world-view, but in the manipulation of speculative tools. He has a philosophical aptitude whose perceptions are interesting; although, in my opinion, he is extraordinarily uncritical and stands at a remove from true science [*der eigentlichen Wissenschaft fern steht*]. He often proceeds as if he combined the seriousness of nihilism with the mystagogy of a magician. In the torrent of his language he is occasionally able, in a clandestine and remarkable way, to strike the core of philosophical thought. In this regard he is, as far as I can see, perhaps unique among contemporary German philosophers.
>
> It is absolutely necessary that those who helped place National Social-ism in the saddle be called to account. Heidegger is among the few pro-fessors to have done that. . . . In our situation [i.e., after the war] the education of youth must be handled with the greatest responsibility. . . . Heidegger's manner of thinking, which to me seems in its essence unfree, dictatorial, and incapable of communication [*communikationslos*], would today be disastrous in its pedagogical effects. . . . Heidegger certainly did not see through all the real powers and goals of the National Socialist leaders. . . . But his manner of speaking and his actions have a certain affinity with National Socialist characteristics, which makes his error comprehensible.[6]

And thus, in view of the extent and profundity of Heidegger's commitment to the National Socialist revolution, the question inevitably arises: To what extent is Heidegger's philosophy implicated in his ignominious life-choice of the early 1930s? It is presumably on the basis of such considerations that Jaspers, in the continuation of the remarks cited, recommends to university officials that Heidegger be suspended from the faculty for a period of several years after the war; and that Thomas Sheehan urges a careful reading of Heidegger's philosophical texts in light of his political beliefs. And it is undoubtedly as a result of a kindred set of concerns that Karl Löwith, in the opening epigraph to this chapter, suggests that, "it would be inappropriate to criticize or exonerate [Heidegger's] political decision in isolation from the very principles of Heideggerian philosophy itself."

Are, however, the preceding admonitions hermeneutically justifiable? Don't such interpretive practices risk imputing to Heidegger's philosophical doctrines a political content that only comes into view ex post facto? Isn't there, moreover, an even more serious risk at issue, one against which Heidegger's French defenders have stridently warned: the risk that we would judge the contributions of an undeniably great thinker exclusively on the basis of political motifs that are, strictly speaking, "extrinsic to thought"? We would thereby succumb to the practice of convicting the philosophy on the basis of a type of spurious "guilt-by-association."

It would be dishonest to deny the cogency of the foregoing caveats. And thus, it should be clearly acknowledged that to suggest that Heidegger's philosophy in its entirety would in some way be "disqualified" as a result of his political misdeeds—however egregious these might prove—would be an act of bad faith. The requirements of intellectual honesty demand that we judge a philosopher in the first instance on the merits of her thought.

Yet, it is precisely this comforting, artificial dichotomy between work and worldview that has been increasingly called into question of late in Heidegger's case.[7] There is undeniable evidence to suggest that Heidegger himself viewed his political commitments in the early 1930s as of a piece with his philosophy; that he considered his "engagement" for National Socialism as a type of a "political actualization" of the "existentials" (*Existenzialen*) of *Being and Time:* of categories such as "historicity," "destiny," "potentiality-for-Being-a-Self," and so forth. In the philosopher's own mind, his "existential decision" for National Socialism in 1933 signified a decision for "authenticity." And thus, in a 1936 conversation with Löwith, Heidegger agrees "without reservation" with the suggestion that "his partisanship for National Socialism lay in the essence of his philosophy."[8] Of course, in keeping with the foregoing caveats, such conclusions should in no way be interpreted to suggest that Nazism would somehow constitute the necessary political corollary of a work like *Being and Time.* However, that in the mind of its author, its conceptual framework proved readily compatible with the greatest form of political tyranny our century has known suggests the need for considerable critical reflection on the ethico-political substance of Heidegger's 1927 work.

It is in this vein that Otto Pöggeler—in a manner that parallels Sheehan's cautionary remarks—has suggested, "Was it not through a definite orientation of his thought that Heidegger fell—and not merely accidentally—into the proximity of National Socialism, without ever truly emerging from this proximity?"[9] Pöggeler thereby implicitly seconds Sheehan's suggestion concerning the imperative necessity of reexamining Heidegger's corpus for those potential intellectual shortfalls that might have precipitated his engagement for Nazism in the early 1930s. However, Pöggeler's remarks also imply the possibility that in his later years Heidegger may have never completely emerged from that "proximity" to National Socialism. But this allegation must stand as an intellectual-philosophical rather than a political judgment. We know that as of the mid-1930s Heidegger increasingly distanced himself from the realities of Nazism as a contemporary political movement. In his view, the "inner truth and greatness" of its historical potential (as an expression of "the encounter between planetary technology and modern man")[10] was perverted by usurpers and pretenders; for example, by those proponents of racial-biological National Socialism such as Ernst Krieck and Alfred Baeumler, who had, at Heidegger's expense, gained control of the "philosophical direction" of the movement. Heidegger explains the ideological basis for his support of National Socialism as follows: "I . . . believed that the movement could be spiritually directed onto other parts and . . . felt such an attempt could be combined with the social and overall political tendencies of the movement. I believed that Hitler, after he assumed responsibility for the *whole Volk* in 1933, would grow beyond the party and its doctrine and everything would come together, through a renovation and a rallying, in an assumption of Western responsibility. This belief proved erroneous, as I recognized from the events of 30 June 1934."[11]

Although Heidegger was extremely critical of "historically existing" National Socialism (his criticisms become quite explicit at times in his lectures of the late 1930s and early 1940s), he seems never to have abandoned his earlier conviction that the dawn of the movement itself (or the "National Awakening" as it was referred to among its supporters) contained seeds of true greatness. It is thus fairly clear that, to the end of his days, Heidegger never abandoned his faith in the movement's authentic historical potential, its "inner truth and greatness." Thus, in his 1945 apologia written for a university denazification commission, Heidegger, instead of critically distancing himself from his earlier beliefs, merely reaffirms his original pro-Nazi convictions: "I saw in the movement that had just come to power [in 1933] the possibility of a spiritual rallying and renewal of the *Volk* and a way of finding its western-historical destiny." And when questioned some twenty years later in a *Spiegel* interview about the elegy to the "Glory and greatness of the [National] Awakening" with which he concluded his 1933 Rectoral Address, Heidegger can only reply—again, without a modicum of contrition—"Yes, I was convinced of that."[12] His refusal to come forth with an unambiguous public disavowal of his earlier political ties, moreover, has been a source of great irritation and dismay, even among those seeking to defend his legacy.[13] It is an omission that lends additional credence to Pöggeler's suggestion that Heidegger continued to work "without ever truly emerging" from his fateful proximity to Germany's National Revolution.

II

Pöggeler's claim that it was through a "definite orientation of his thought that Heidegger fell . . . into the proximity of National Socialism" may well prove indispensable for understanding the philosophical bases of Heidegger's political involvement. His subsequent observation that Heidegger may have never truly emerged from that proximity suggests a much greater measure of continuity between the "early" and "later" Heidegger than is usually admitted. Wherein might this continuity lie? The critical issue may well hinge on a "historicization" of our understanding of Heidegger's philosophy. That is, on an appreciation of the extent to which his philosophy is implicated—almost despite itself—in a set of intellectual presuppositions shared by the German radical-conservative intelligentsia of his era.[14] Certainly the brilliant philosophical démarche that is *Being and Time* is in no way reducible to the aforementioned "historical" elements. And in this respect many of the contributions Heidegger has made toward recasting the traditional forms of philosophical questioning remain unimpugnable. Yet if it is true that in the philosopher's own mind there existed an essential relation between fundamental ontology and (a, to be sure, idealized version of) National Socialism, it becomes all the more important to identify those aspects of his thinking that led to this fateful political partisanship.

The essential element linking the early and the later Heidegger—and that dimension of his thought that gives determinate content and meaning to Pöggeler's suggestive remarks concerning Heidegger's precarious political "proximity"—is Heidegger's *critique of modernity*. In essence, Heidegger fully subscribes to the critical indictment of the totality of modern life-forms (associated with the traits of prosaic and materialistic, bourgeois *Zivilisation*) that has been a mainstay of German conservative *Kulturkritik* since the nineteenth century. This position received its consummate and most intellectually sophisticated articulation in Nietzsche's work. There, a far-reaching critique of modern philosophy, politics, and culture—which are viewed essentially as manifestations of decline—is combined with a nostalgic idealization of the prephilosophical (i.e., pre-Socratic) Greek polis and the quasi-apocalyptical expectation that a nihilistic Western modernity will soon be supplanted by a new heroic ethos, in which the much-vaunted "self-overcoming of nihilism" reaches a point of crystallization.

All three "spheres"—philosophy, politics, and art—suffer from the same affliction: a surfeit of subjectivity. Thus, modern philosophy, since Descartes, has become "epistemology," narrowing the scope and purview of philosophical questioning to *res cogitans* (thinking substance): the new solipsistic *fundamentum inconcussum* that substitutes for the divine guarantees of scholasticism. Politics has become "liberalism," which means that the standpoint of the self-enclosed, monadic individual has emerged as its absolute point of reference. A greater antithesis to the classical polis, in which the individual good was always subordinated to the good of the whole, could scarcely be imagined. Finally, modern art, from romanticism to art for art's sake, has assumed a predominantly effete, private, and self-referential character. It has thereby forfeited that monumental quality that once suffused Greek architecture and tragedy, and that was capable of spiritually uniting the polis and its citizens. Or, as Nietzsche himself formulates his indictment of aesthetic modernism with unabashed candor: "*L'art pour l'art:* the virtuoso croaking of shivering frogs, despairing in their swamp."[15]

Heidegger shares this resolutely antimodernist worldview to an extreme. And if one is sincerely interested in understanding the political implications of his thought, it would be difficult to overemphasize the absolute centrality of this perspective, which served as the ideological prism, as it were, through which he interpreted the political events of the twentieth century. Despite the criticisms that are directed toward Nietzsche in the lectures of 1936–41, Heidegger never breaks entirely with the fundamental terms of this—in essence, Nietzschean—"conservative revolutionary" critique of modernity. And thus, on one essential methodological point, Heidegger and Nietzsche show themselves to be in complete agreement: in the conviction that the decline of modernity has "progressed" so far that it can no longer be redeemed by the methods of immanent criticism; that is, in the manner of earlier critics of modernity qua "bourgeois society," such as Hegel, Tocqueville, and Marx, who still believed that the value-orientations of this society were capable of redemption from within. Instead, for both Nietzsche and Heidegger, only the categories of "total critique" will suffice to capture the essence of this Fichtean era of "absolute sinfulness."

Thus, Heidegger, while proceeding from a significantly different philosophical orientation, shares with Nietzsche a number of essential value-premises. Among them: the aforementioned glorification of the pre-Platonic polis (Heidegger's emphasis of course falls on pre-Socratic philosophy rather than, as with Nietzsche, on Attic tragedy); and, perhaps most important, the conviction that it is art rather than science that indicates the path along which an authentic "overcoming" (*Überwindung*) of modern nihilism must proceed. This conviction explains the seminal role played by the concepts of *poesis* and "poetic dwelling" in Heidegger's later philosophy.[16] Here, too, it would be fruitful to compare Nietzsche's youthful enthusiasm for Greek tragedy and the music of Wagner with Heidegger's parallel enthusiasm for Hölderlin in the *Erläuterungen zu Hölderlins Dichtung* (Commentaries on Hölderlin's poetry). According to Heidegger, as Sophocles was to ancient Greece, Hölderlin is to modern Germany. And thus, "The essential disposition [*Grundstimmung*], that is, the truth of the *Dasein* of a nation [*Volk*], is originally founded by the poet."[17] Or, as Heidegger remarks elsewhere, the poet is the "voice of the *Volk*."[18]

That Heidegger shares the *Zeitdiagnose* proffered by Nietzsche, according to which European culture is viewed as essentially moribund and nihilistic, accounts for the distinctive ideological tenor of the value-judgments he sets forth concerning modern forms of life. Thus, for example, in the *Spiegel* interview, Heidegger summarily dismisses modern literature (*heutige Literatur*) as "predominantly destructive": in contrast to the poetry of Hölderlin or the art of the Greeks, it lacks grounding in the historical life of a people.[19] Or, as Heidegger observes elsewhere, in a thinly veiled attack against the spirit of "cosmopolitanism": "Does not the flourishing of any genuine work depend upon its roots in a native soil?"[20] Similarly, in the Nietzsche lectures of the late 1930s, while flirting with the Wagnerian ideal of the *Gesamtkunstwerk* (collective work of art), he reaffirms his conviction that art must serve as the foundation of the *Volksgemeinschaft* (the Nazi term for the German "National Community"): "With reference to the historical position of art, the effort to produce the 'collective artwork' [*Gesamtkunstwerk*] remains essential. The very name is demonstrative. For one thing, it means that the arts should no longer be realized apart from one another, but that they should be conjoined in *one* work. But beyond such sheer quantitative unification, the artwork should be a celebration of the *Volksgemeinschaft:* it should be *the* religion."[21]

Heidegger emphatically seconded the historian Jacob Burckhardt's opinion that the institution of democracy was responsible for the downfall of the ancient polis. Thus, in *What is Called Thinking* (1954), he approvingly cites Nietzsche's characterization of "modern democracy" as a "degenerate form of the state" (*Verfallsform des Staats*).[22] Further, Heidegger summarily dismisses political liberalism, which is "*tyrannical* insofar as it requires that everybody be left to his own opinion."[23]

His criticism of the inadequacies of modern "science" (in the German sense of *Wissenschaft*) dates from the 1929 Freiburg inaugural lecture "What is Metaphysics?" and the celebrated debate with Cassirer in Davos, also in 1929, over the legacy of neo-Kantianism. In the former work, Heidegger laments the lack of existential rootedness and unity afflicting the various contemporary sciences: "The scientific fields are still far apart. Their subjects are treated in fundamentally different ways. Today this hodgepodge of disciplines is held together only by the technical organization of the universities and faculties and preserves what meaning it has only through the practical aims of the different branches. The sciences have lost their roots in their essential ground."[24] In the debate with Cassirer, he risks, in two crucial respects, crossing "over the line" separating "scientific" from "nonscientific" statements; that is, the "line" separating falsifiable from nonfalsifiable claims to truth. First, in his proclamation of the equiprimordiality of "truth" and "untruth." Or, as Heidegger phrases it: "On the basis of finitude man's Being-in-the-truth is simultaneously as Being-in-the-untruth. Untruth belongs to the innermost core of *Dasein*." Second, in his attempt to link the "question of Being" itself to a specific ideological perspective or, as he calls it, a "determinate worldview": "In what way must a metaphysic of *Dasein* be initiated?" inquires Heidegger. "Does not a determinate worldview lie at its basis? It is not philosophy's task to provide a worldview; however, to do philosophy [*Philosophieren*] indeed *already presupposes* such a worldview."[25] Over the next few years, as the crisis of the Weimar Republic reached its point of no return, Heidegger would make few efforts to conceal the "determinate worldview" that subtended his own manner of doing philosophy.[26]

There is a direct conceptual lineage between the criticisms of "science" voiced in these "purely philosophical" writings of the late 1920s and the dubious political positions Heidegger would espouse four years hence in the 1933 Rectoral Address, where he openly mocks the existence of the "much-ballyhooed 'academic freedom'" and redefines the "will to science" (*Wille zur Wissenschaft*) as "a will to the historical-spiritual mission of the German *Volk* that knows itself in its State."[27] In dicta such as these, Heidegger is only a hair's breadth removed from the militant appeals for "politicized science" that swept Nazi Germany during these years. For Heidegger, "Mere intelligence is a semblance of spirit, masking its absence."[28] And thus, the "sham-culture" (*Scheinkultur*) of Western *Zivilisation* will be overcome only if the "spiritual world" of the *Volk* is grounded in "the deepest preservation of the forces of soil and blood."[29] Such conclusions derive from an all-too-familiar rejection of the spirit of modernity, which fosters values that are "cosmopolitan" and, as such, alien to the "forces of soil and blood" that Heidegger—anachronistically—views as a precondition for historical greatness.

It is this critique of "science" and "intelligence" as part of the "sham-culture" of modernity that provides the crucial moment of intellectual continuity between Heidegger's philosophical writings of the late 1920s and his pro-Nazi texts of the early 1930s. And in retrospect, it is perhaps this dimension of his thought that strikes one as most problematic—yet highly symptomatic. The critique of "science" is perfectly indicative of the way in which "philosophy" and "ideology" become inextricably commingled in Heidegger's post-1927 thinking. Moreover, a great danger haunts this immoderate rejection of all inherited *Wissenschaft,* one that will beset the entirety of his subsequent philosophical oeuvre: the danger that Heidegger's own philosophizing will "cross the line" separating warranted philosophical assertion from unverifiable, ex cathedra pronouncements. More and more, especially in the later writings, Heidegger's philosophical comportment resembles that of a prophet who views himself as standing in a position of immediate access to Being. Increasingly, his discourse threatens to make its stand beyond the realm of philosophical statements that are capable of being discursively redeemed. In celebrating the ineffability of Being (or, according to Heidegger's quasi-theological answer to the *Seinsfrage* in the 1946 "Letter on Humanism": "Yet Being— What is Being? It is *It* itself"),[30] Heidegger risks promoting an intellectual method and style whose distinguishing feature is its "nonfalsifiability." Nor is the credibility of his standpoint furthered by claims such as the following: "Thinking begins only when we have come to know that reason, glorified for centuries, is the most stiff-necked adversary of thought.[31] And thus, when faced with philosophical disquisitions that claim a privileged relation vis-à-vis the mysterious destinings of *Seinsgeschick,* the claims of critical philosophy— that is, of a post-Kantian thought that is capable of reflecting in earnest on its own foundations—must go by the board.

Heidegger's thinking, therefore, appears to be afflicted by a twofold debility: a disdain of traditional methods of philosophical argumentation, which emphasize the nonesoteric, generalizable character of philosophical contents and judgments; and an empirical deficit that follows from his rejection of the individual sciences. Inevitably, the question must arise: Did not a certain metaphysical hubris, stemming in part from a philosophically conditioned neglect of empirical findings (e.g., the disciplines of history and the social sciences) adversely affect the philosopher's capacity for political discernment? When the trajectory of concrete historical life is restyled according to the logic of a self-positing "history of Being," whose ethereal "sendings" (*Schickungen*) seem impervious to counterfactual instances, political judgment is deprived of any verifiable touchstone.

In this regard, Karl Löwith has contributed the following sober reflections on Heidegger's methodological afflictions: "Philosophical reflection on the whole of what exists in nature, which is the world . . . cannot merely 'pass science by' without falling into the void. It is easily said, and it would be a relief, if philosophical thought were to dwell beyond what is provable and refutable; if, however, the realm of [Heideggerian] 'essential thinking' were to surpass all proof and refutation, then philosophy would have to do neither with truth nor with probability, but rather with uncontrollable claims and allegations."[32]

III

It is clear that as of the early 1930s, Heidegger sought to immerse the "question of Being" in the vortex of contemporary political events. Heretofore, the most telling evidence to this effect has been the 1933 Rectoral Address, where Heidegger explicitly interweaves key categories from *Being and Time* with the rhetoric of Germany's National Revolution. But a further example of his conviction that philosophy and contemporary politics were necessarily interrelated has recently come to light with the publication of his 1934 lecture course on logic.[33]

"We want to *convulse* logic," Heidegger begins. "We bid farewell to the tawdry arrogance that views logic as a merely formal affair," he continues, leaving no doubt that traditional approaches to the subject must be wholly rejected. Formal approaches to logic are part of a shallow "intellectualism" (*Intellektualismus*) against which Heidegger also polemicizes in "What is Metaphysics?" and the Rectoral Address.

Instead, Heidegger wishes to endow logic with existential substance. He thereby seeks to relate it directly to the categorial framework established in *Being and Time*, to the "question of Being." The chief failing of traditional metaphysics lay in its attempt to conceive of Being as "presence," that is, nontemporally. By seeking to relate Being to "temporality" in his 1927 work, Heidegger sought to redress this condition. Being is not something static, merely given, or present-at-hand (*vorhanden*) like a thing; as an "event" (*Ereignis*) it has a history. *Dasein* or human being is "ecstatic": it projects itself into the future on the basis of decisive appropriations of its past. Yet Heidegger once affirmed that it was precisely the theory of historicity in *Being and Time* that represented the philosophical basis for his commitment to National Socialism.[34] As Heidegger remarks there, anticipating the political precepts he would develop six years later in the Rectoral Address and other texts: "If fateful *Dasein*, as Being-in-the-world, exists essentially in Being-with-others, its historicizing is a cohistoricizing and is determinative for it as *destiny*. This is how we designate the historicizing of a community, a Volk."[35]

Returning to the claims of his 1934 lecture course, we now see more clearly what it meant for Heidegger to give formal logic an existential or historical turn in the sense of "historicity." In this respect, one would do well to keep in mind Löwith's remarks, cited at the chapter's outset, suggesting that it was hardly an act of self-misunderstanding that led Heidegger to relate his ontologically derived theory of historicity to contemporary political events. Instead, in many respects, this was precisely the point of Heideggerianism qua philosophy of existence. At issue was not merely another version of contemplative "first philosophy" or traditional "science," but a doctrine of authenticity that demanded temporal-historical realization.

In the lectures on logic, as in the Rectoral Address, what this means more specifically becomes clear: the National Revolution needs a theory of historicity such as Heidegger's in order to elevate itself philosophically, just as the theory of historicity needs Nazism—or a political movement like it—to reverse the tide of European nihilism and establish the political basis for a recovery of "Greco-Germanic *Dasein*." The philosophical chauvinism involved in the latter conception corresponds to the serious judgmental incapacities subtending both Heidegger's initial commitment to Nazism and, later, his failure to distance himself from the movement's alleged "inner truth and greatness."

Thus, in his Nietzsche lectures, Heidegger reads the fall of France (1940) in ontological-historical terms: it represents the appropriate historical destiny for a nation that has remained wedded to an outmoded concept of metaphysics, Cartesianism. Conversely, Germany's *Blitzkrieg* victory is a testimony to the powers of *active nihilism*, "which does not confine itself to witness the slow collapse of the existent [but] intervenes actively to reverse the process."[36] Only a nation like Germany that embodies the principles of Nietzsche's superman, Heidegger continues, "is capable of an unconditional 'machine economy' and vice versa: the one needs the other in order to establish an unconditional domination over the earth."[37] Here, Heidegger's argument is taken directly from Jünger's reading of Nietzsche in *The Worker:* only a total or totalitarian state can adequately harness the nihilistic powers of modern technology for ends of historical greatness or "active nihilism."

In the 1934 course on logic, Heidegger gives us a more precise, "existenziell" view of what authentic historicity entails. "Negroes," he begins, "are men but have no history. . . . Nature has its history. But then Negroes would also have history. Or does nature then have no history? It can enter into the past as something transitory, but not everything that fades away enters into history.

When an airplane's propeller turns, then nothing actually [*eigentlich*] 'occurs.' Conversely, when the same airplane takes Hitler to Mussolini, then history occurs."[38]

Turning to the 1935 *Introduction to Metaphysics*—the same text in which we find the aforementioned eulogy to the "inner truth and greatness of National Socialism"—Heidegger proffers his own historical-ontological (*seinsgeschichtlich*) *Zeitdiagnose:*

> The spiritual decline of the earth is so far advanced that the nations are in danger of losing the last bit of spiritual energy that makes it possible to see the decline (taken in relation to the history of "Being"), and to appraise it as such. This simple observation has nothing to do with *Kulturpessimismus*, and of course it has nothing to do with any sort of optimism either; for the darkening of the world, the flight of the gods, the destruction of the earth, the transformation of men into a mass, the hatred and suspicion of everything free and creative, have assumed such proportions throughout the earth that such childish categories as pessimism and optimism have long since become absurd.
>
> We are caught in a pincers. Situated in the center, our *Volk* incurs the severest pressure. It is the *Volk* with the most neighbors and hence the most endangered. With all this, it is the most metaphysical of nations. . . . All this implies that this *Volk*, as a historical *Volk*, must move itself and thereby the history of the West beyond the center of their future "happening" and into the primordial realm of the powers of Being. If the great decision regarding Europe is not to bring annihilation, that decision must be made in terms of the new spiritual energies unfolding historically from out of the middle.[39]

The foregoing historical commentary in no way represents an extraneous, nonphilosophical digression from the primary ontologico-metaphysical question at issue. In point of fact, Heidegger's lectures and texts of the 1930s and 1940s abound with kindred sweeping historico-philosophical judgments. It is clear that, for Heidegger, our very capacity to pose the *Seinsfrage* itself is integrally tied to our ability to overcome the contemporary historical crisis— "the darkening of the world, the flight of the gods, the destruction of the earth, the transformation of men into a mass"—and in this overcoming, history and politics will undeniably play a primary role. For if the "clearing" (*Lichtung*) that is a prerequisite for the emergence of Being is a temporal clearing, this means that the "presencing" of Being is essentially a historical presencing—a *Seinsgeschichte*. In this sense, as Heidegger makes undeniably clear, the "question of Being" is, according to its essence, a historical question. This is a conviction that follows directly from one of the most central (anti-Platonic) insights of *Being and Time:* that Being's coming to presence is inexorably a *temporal* coming to presence. Yet, this is only another way of saying that the emergence (or self-concealment) of Being is essentially a question of historicity. For Heidegger, too, "readiness is all"; that is, all depends on our readiness to heed the call of Being. However, our receptivity to Being is ineluctably tied to our current state of historical-ontological preparedness. When Heidegger, a few paragraphs after the preceding citation, observes: "That is why we have related the question of Being to the destiny of Europe, where the destiny of the earth is being decided—while our own [i.e., Germany's] historic *Dasein* proves to be the center for Europe itself,"[40] he betrays unambiguously the historical-ontological rationale behind his partisanship for what he will refer to as "Western-Germanic historical *Dasein.*"[41]

Astonishingly, references to the "historical singularity of National Socialism" persist as late as 1942.[42] And that "singularity," moreover, is in no way viewed negatively; that is, as a "regression" vis-à-vis historically received principles of justice, morality, and truth. Instead, it points to National Socialism's "inner truth and greatness," which Germany and the Germans proved too weak to realize. To the bitter end, Heidegger holds out in his belief that the "overcoming of nihilism was announced in the poetic thinking and singing of the Germans."[43] Or, as he opines in 1943: "The planet is in flames. The essence of man is out of joint. Only from the Germans can there come a world-historical reflection—if, that is, they find and preserve their 'Germanness' [*das Deutsche*]."[44] Thus, according to Heidegger's neo-ontological reading of contemporary history, Germany still represents the "saving power" of Western humanity, instead of its scourge. In "Overcoming Metaphysics," Nazism, rather than signifying a "totalitarian deformation" of Western modernity, is merely its nihilistic "consummation."

But can't this astounding theoretical myopia—in truth, part of a grandiose and elaborate strategy of denial—at least in part be attributed to Heidegger's own efforts toward self-exculpation? For if it is "Western metaphysics" that is in fact responsible for the devastating "events of world history in this century,"[45] then certainly Germany as a nation (which Heidegger persists on viewing as the vehicle of our salvation) need bear special responsibility neither for the European catastrophe nor for its "crimes against humanity." It is in this vein that his insensitive response to Herbert Marcuse's query as to why he never bothered to condemn such "crimes" publicly must be understood. Or, as Heidegger observes, in a monumental instance of bad faith, with reference to the annihilation of millions of European Jews: "if instead of 'Jews' you had written 'East Germans,' then the same holds true for one of the Allies, with the difference that everything that has occurred since 1945 has become public knowledge, while the bloody terror of the Nazis in point of fact had been kept a secret from the German people."[46]

Given Heidegger's penchant for dogmatic historical judgments and the equation of incomparables, it is hardly surprising if, upon turning to the text of a 1949 lecture, we find the following observations: "Agriculture is today a motorized food industry, in essence the same as the manufacture of corpses in gas chambers and extermination camps, the same as the blockade and starvation of countries, the same as the manufacture of atomic bombs."[47] But here, too, the essential point is philosophical, not biographical: such travesties of historical reasoning in no way represent tangential asides; instead, they go to the essence of the incapacities of the "history of Being" as a framework for historical understanding.

IV

Few thinkers can claim so auspicious a philosophical debut as could Heidegger with *Being and Time*. But already in that work, one finds a characteristic disdain of traditional methods of philosophical argumentation. At crucial junctures, Heidegger's modus operandi tends to be "evocative" rather than "discursive." And thus, according to Ernst Tugendhat, "The procedure of explication through the sheer accumulation of words [*Worthäufung*] is frequent in *Being and Time*; it is connected with what I have called the *evocative method*"—a method that is characterized by the employment of neologisms whose conceptual self-evidence is merely assumed rather than argued for.[48] It is this method that provoked Adorno's polemical ire in *The Jargon of Authenticity*, where it is alleged that Heideggerian *Existenzphilosophie* "sees to it that what it wants is on the whole felt and accepted through its mere delivery, without regard to the content of the words used." Insofar as "the words of the jargon sound as if they said something higher than what they mean . . . whoever is versed in the jargon does not have to say what he thinks, does not even have to think it properly."[49] All of which is to say that Heidegger's ambivalences about "Wissenschaft," or about traditional discursive methods of philosophical argumentation, are already fully apparent in his magnum opus of 1927. Moreover, as a number of critics have pointed out, Heidegger's imperious use of philosophical terminology is far from unrelated to his distasteful political leanings. And thus it falls due to inquire as to whether in Heidegger's case a certain "linguistic authoritarianism" does not in fact prove the harbinger of a distinctly authoritarian political disposition. Or, as the German political scientist Alfons Söllner has remarked, echoing Adorno's suspicions: "the authoritarian sense or nonsense of Heideggerian philosophy lies in its jargon and its linguistic gestures."[50]

In his post hoc attempts to account for his involvement with the politics of German fascism, Heidegger never made a secret of the fact that in 1933, he "expected from National Socialism a spiritual renewal of life in its entirety, a reconciliation of social antagonisms, and a deliverance of Western *Dasein* from the dangers of Communism."[51] To be sure, Heidegger's expectations were ultimately disappointed. But our discussion thus far has sought to make clear that the aforementioned political desiderata derive directly from Heidegger's philosophical program itself; specifically, they result from that program's radicalization in the late 1920s, as Heidegger becomes increasingly convinced of the essentially nihilistic tenor of Western "science"—a term that for him becomes synonymous with the totality of inherited intellectual paradigms *simpliciter*. It is the radicality of this critique that convinces Heidegger of the necessity of "extreme solutions" and the need to make a total break with value-orientations of European modernity. He believed (erroneously, as it would turn out) that National Socialism offered the prospect of an awakening of Germany's "epochal" historical mission, which he incongruously equates with a "repetition" of the "Greek beginning." Even after the German collapse of 1945, he would perversely insist that if only the right pressures had been brought to bear on the movement in its early stages, everything might have turned out for the better: "[Who knows] what would have happened and what could have been averted if in 1933 all available powers had arisen, gradually and in secret unity, in order to purify and moderate the 'movement' that had come to power?"[52]

With the advantage of some sixty years of historical hindsight, it is easy for us to condemn Heidegger's actions and beliefs. Pre-Nazi Germany was exposed in rapid succession to a demoralizing defeat in World War I, an exacting peace treaty, catastrophic inflation, political chaos, and a severe economic depression. The historically available progressive political options were indeed few.

What cannot but give cause for dismay, however, is Heidegger's repeated insistence after the war that, if only the proper forces had been brought to bear on Germany's National Revolution, matters would have been entirely different. Such a claim is extremely difficult to uphold. As indicated above, Heidegger dates his disillusionment with the National Socialist program from 30 June 1934. Yet, even in the regime's first few months, the brutal characteristics of totalitarian rule were as plain as noonday: the Reichstag lay in flames, parliament had been dissolved, the Social Democratic Party had been banned, the trade unions had been forcibly disbanded, Jews had been dismissed from the civil service (university teaching included), civil liberties had been suspended, and as of the Enabling Act of 24 March 1933, Hitler was in essence governing by decree. That Heidegger felt sufficiently comfortable with the trappings of totalitarian rule to emerge as Germany's most prominent academic spokesman for the new regime helps place his political actions in the proper historical perspective. No doubt he at least in part shared the sentiments of the German shopkeeper who, when questioned by an American researcher about Germany's devastating loss of freedom under Hitler, responded: "You don't understand. Before we had parties, elections, political campaigns and voting. Under Hitler, we don't have these anymore. Now we are free!"

As late as 1936 (that is, two years after his putative withdrawal of support for the regime) Heidegger could remark in a lecture course: "These two men, Hitler and Mussolini, who have, each in essentially different ways, introduced a countermovement to nihilism, have both learned from Nietzsche. The authentic metaphysical realm of Nietzsche has, however, not yet been realized."[53] His later claims to have offered "spiritual resistance" to Nazism are surely exaggerated.

V

It would be facile to dismiss the Nietzschean-inspired, conservative revolutionary critique of modernity that so influenced Heidegger's political views as "reactionary" or "protofascistic," even if it was precisely this intellectual paradigm that very much facilitated Germany's "spiritual preparation" for National Socialism.[54] Simplistic intellectual classifications always fall short of the demands of complex historical circumstances. Moreover, it could easily be shown how, mutatis mutandis, a surprisingly similar critique of modernity was shared by the radical left.[55] That Nietzsche's critique, as well as Heidegger's appropriation of it, is capable of sensitizing us to the "excrescences of modernity"—to the ways in which the rationality of progress, as buttressed by categories of formal or technical reason, begins to take on an apparent life of its own, divorced from the needs of the historical actors who originally set it in motion—remains undeniable. Yet, by highlighting the failings of modernity to the exclusion of its specific advances (which Hegel, to take merely one example, in the wake of the democratic revolutions of the eighteenth century, identifies with "progress in the consciousness of freedom"), this critique proves, in the last analysis, woefully imbalanced and myopic. It thereby seemingly invites the political extremism that it embraces in point of fact. For if the "present age" is indeed one of total perdition—"the collapse of the world," "the devastation of the earth," "the unconditional objectification of everything present," is how Heidegger describes it in "Overcoming Metaphysics"[56]—then "extreme solutions" alone would be warranted, even mandated, to combat the manifold failings of modernity. Even after the war, Heidegger steadfastly refused to abandon the conviction that "democracy" (along with Christianity and the constitutional or *Rechtsstaat*) is a mere "half-measure" (*Halbheit*), from which no real solution might emerge.[57] Here, too, it behooves us to keep in mind Pöggeler's question as to whether Heidegger "ever truly emerged" from the ideological proximity in which he felt so at home during the early 1930s.

Germany's political dilemmas have often been described in terms of its status as a "belated nation"; that is, in terms of its delayed assimilation of the constituent features of political modernity: national unification, an autonomous civil society, and parliamentary government.[58] Earlier, I suggested the need for a historicization of Heidegger's philosophical project. Could it be that Heidegger's own philosophical shortcomings parallel those of his nation's own historical formation? That his thought, too, in significant respects fails to make the transition to modern standards of philosophical and political rationality? It is likely that the most significant long-term repercussions of the Heidegger controversy will be concerned with these and related themes.

Postscript

The theme of Heidegger's relationship to National Socialism has been vexed insofar as it is inevitably fraught with overdeterminations: hardly a current of modern thought exists that does not have a profound vested interest, for or against, in the fate of Heidegger's doctrines. With so much at stake for so many, the process of sorting out, with some measure of fairness, what remains of philosophical value from what has been historically surpassed can never be an easy one. In the preceding essay, I have hazarded a few pointers and suggestions concerning avenues of future investigation that may be fruitful.

Amid the din of opinion for or against Heidegger, much of it shrill and partial, there is the voice of a Heidegger contemporary one would due well to heed—that of the political philosopher Leo Strauss. In a set of recently published lecture notes on the problem of Heidegger's existentialism that date from the mid-1950s, Strauss was able to go directly to the heart of the matter.

On the one hand, Strauss states without hesitation that Heidegger is not merely a great thinker, but "the only great thinker of our time"—so forceful and insurmountable was, in his estimation, Heidegger's challenge to all inherited philosophical schools and models. On the other hand, Strauss had no trouble in defining, with a few choice words, the philosophical stakes involved in Heidegger's grandiose "decision" for Hitler in 1933:

> Heidegger became a Nazi in 1933. This was not due to a mere error of judgment on the part of a man who lived on great heights high above the low land of politics. Everyone who had read his first great book [*Being and Time*] and did not overlook the wood for the trees could see the kinship in temper and direction between Heidegger's thought and the Nazis. What was the practical, that is to say, serious meaning of the contempt for reasonableness and the praise of resoluteness except to encourage that extremist movement? . . . In 1953 he published a book, *Introduction to Metaphysics*, consisting of lectures given in 1935, in which he spoke of the greatness and dignity of the National Socialist movement. In the preface written in 1953 he said that all mistakes had been corrected.
>
> The case of Heidegger reminds one to a certain extent of the case of Nietzsche. Nietzsche, naturally, would not have sided with Hitler. Yet there is an undeniable kinship between Nietzsche's thought and fascism. If one rejects, as passionately as Nietzsche did, conservative constitutional monarchy, with a view to a new aristocracy, the passion of the denials will be much more effective than the necessarily more subtle intimations of the character of the new nobility, to say nothing of the blond beast.[59]

Strauss's incisive remarks constitute a worthy point of departure for all future discussions of the relationship between German philosophy and the experience of fascism.

FRENCH HEIDEGGER WARS

I believe one's point of reference should not be to the great model of language (*langue*) and signs, but to that of war and battle. The history which bears and determines us has the form of a war rather than that of a language: relations of power, not relations of meaning.—Michel Foucault, "Truth and Power"

Few events in recent memory have shaken the world of French letters as has the appearance of Victor Farias's book, *Heidegger et le Nazisme.* Through an extremely thorough and painstaking (and for French Heideggerians, clearly painful) labor of documentation, Farias has single-handedly given the lie to all the inventive rationalizations contrived by French Heideggerians—as well as those set forth on several occasions by Heidegger himself—over the course of the last four decades trivializing the Master's alacritous participation in the "National Awakening" of 1933. It is no secret that since the collapse of the previous two dominant intellectual paradigms of the postwar era—existentialism and structuralism—Heideggerianism, as a philosophy of "difference," has enjoyed unquestionable pride of place. It is no small irony that Farias's book, while hardly a theoretical tour de force, may well have paved the way for a new epistemological break in the volatile world of Parisian cultural life.

Yet one outcome of the tumultuous events surrounding Farias's book may be discerned already: from this point hence, in France and elsewhere, intellectuals in all walks of life will never be able to relate to Heidegger's philosophy "naively"; that is, without taking into consideration the philosopher's odious political allegiances. In this respect, the debate spawned by *Heidegger et le Nazisme* is destined to become an inescapable point of reference for all future discussions of Heideggerianism and its merits. Were the relationship between the philosopher and his politics nonintegral, if one could make a neat separation between the philosophical oeuvre and the political engagement, then this outcome would be prejudicial. All persons, great thinkers included, are capable of errors of political judgment, even egregious ones. However, the more one learns about the Heidegger–National Socialism nexus, the more one is ineluctably driven to conclude that the philosopher himself perceived his Nazi involvements not as a random course of action, but as a logical outgrowth of his philosophical doctrines. A careful correlation of the early philosophy with the political speeches of the 1930s[1] leaves no doubt concerning the fact that Heidegger himself viewed his National Socialist activities as a concrete exemplification of *eigentliches Dasein* (authentic existence). That is, Heidegger himself makes a great effort to justify his participation in the Nazi movement in terms of categories carefully culled from his magnum opus of 1927, *Sein und Zeit.*

Why Heidegger? Why in France? Why now? Have the true intellectual stakes of the debate been exaggerated beyond reason by an unprecedented degree of media hype (in newspapers, journals, and highly publicized television debates)? Or is it true that beneath the layers of publicity surrounding the controversy, the Farias revelations have indeed unleashed questions of major intellectual import?

Paris was the logical staging-ground for such a debate if one takes seriously the oft-quoted maxim: "Today, Heidegger lives in France." Without question the major repercussions of the debate stand to be felt in Parisian intellectual circles, where Heideggerianism has been so dominant in the postwar years. One must also consider that the two major cultural and political *événements* in France during the last few years have both been Holocaust-related: *Shoah,* Claude Lanzmann's magisterial film about the death-camps; and the trial of Klaus Barbie, which received intensive media coverage since his return to France in 1983. Moreover, despite the fact that significant debates over Heidegger's Nazi past have surfaced in France on at least two previous occasions,[2] Farias's documentation incorporates the pathbreaking findings of the Freiburg historian Hugo Ott;[3] it is principally the additional revelations brought to light by Ott's archival work in Freiburg that have, as it were, transformed quantity into quality. As a result of Ott's researches, the full extent of Heidegger's dedication to the National Socialist cause has attained the status of an undeniable fact; whereas previously, the incomplete documentation of the case, coupled with Heidegger's own disingenuous accounts of his activities, made it fairly easy for his devoted supporters to parry any possible blows to the Master's reputation.[4]

Thus, with the appearance of the Farias book,[5] French perceptions regarding Heidegger's political loyalties in the early thirties have definitively changed: his zealous involvement with the NSDAP, which could formerly be denied or trivialized, has now assumed the status of a permanent taint. The traditional contingent of French Heidegger defenders is at present scrambling to salvage what can be salvaged; and his long-standing detractors are basking (at least momentarily) in the glory of *Schadenfreude,* since what they have been suggesting all along now seems a proven fact. We shall return to Farias's study, as well as to the fascinating debate it has unleashed, after clarifying precisely those aspects of Heidegger's activities as rector that conflict with the hitherto standard accounts.

One of the most reprehensible aspects of Heidegger's conduct concerns his duplicitous efforts to misrepresent the full extent of his past misdeeds. In his two published apologiae,[6] Heidegger consistently argues that he accepted the rectorship not out of ideological loyalty to the National Socialist cause, but in order to preserve university autonomy in face of the threat of rampant politicization by Nazi extremists. In support of this claim, Heidegger cites the title of his *Rektoratsrede,* "The Self-Affirmation of the German University." Or, as he remarks in an interview in *Spiegel,* "Such a title had not been risked in any rectoral address up to that time." But the facts of the case unearthed by Ott and others show that this explanation could not be farther from the truth.

In fact, the opposite is the case: Heidegger was a zealous advocate of *Gleichschaltung* at the university level, and the university "reforms" carried out under his direction at Freiburg were among the earliest and most radical among German universities in the months following Hitler's seizure of power. One of the most damning indictments of Heidegger's conduct was a personal telegram he sent to Hitler, dated May 20, 1933, that read as follows: "I faithfully request the postponement of the planned meeting of the executive committee of the German University League until a time when the especially necessary *Gleichschaltung* of the leadership of the League is effectuated."[7] Within a few months of his assumption of the rectorship, he assisted in the redrafting of the university constitution at the provincial level. Subsequently, the rector would be appointed by the state minister of culture—thus bypassing the normal democratic channels of the university senate, which had heretofore always selected the rector by an open vote—and assume the new title of "Führer" of the university. These and related events show Heidegger to be an early and devoted apostle of the Nazi *Führerprinzip.*

A closer look at Heidegger's Rectoral Address of May 27, 1933, reveals a vast discrepancy between the implied theme of the title—an apparent plea for university autonomy at a time when Nazi *politische Wissenschaft* (politicized scholarship) predominated—and its actual political message, which on many counts harmonized with Nazi rhetoric and objectives.[8] The address is replete with references to the *Führerprinzip* and a community of followers to be led. The "will to knowledge" that determines the essence of the university is defined as "the will to the historical-spiritual mission of the German *Volk* [which] arrives at self-knowledge in the State." "Science and German destiny must come to power simultaneously," Heidegger goes on to observe. In his crass glorification of "German destiny," Heidegger not only panders to the reigning authorities, but also embraces a fatalism that turns the very idea of intellectual autonomy into a travesty. Or, as he notes in a similar vein: "all knowledge about things remains delivered over in advance to the supremacy of fate."

Such remarks are part and parcel of Heidegger's general polemic against the superficiality of "so-called academic freedom." In a philosophical work of two years hence, he would lament the fact that the "Sauberung" (cleansing) of the German university—here, a transparent euphemism for *Gleichschaltung*—had not gone far enough.[9] Similarly, in the Rectoral Address of 1933, Heidegger insists that the realm of the intellect must not be reduced to the status of a free-floating "cultural superstructure." Instead, it draws its true strength from "erd- und bluthaften Kräfte" (the powers of earth and blood).

"German students are on the march," observes Heidegger. "They seek leaders." He leaves no doubt that this march proceeds according to a military rhythm. Students must fulfill their obligation to the *Volksgemeinschaft* by giving service (*Dienst*): "labor service," "military service," and—trailing behind in third place—"service in knowledge." Extrapolating from the philosophical framework of *Being and Time*, Heidegger suggests that it is "the questioning of Being in general [that] compels the *Volk* to labor and struggle [*Arbeit und Kampf*]." Together, the German students and teachers form a "Kampfgemeinschaft" (fighting community). "All volitional and intellectual capacities, all powers of the heart and capabilities of the body must be developed *through* struggle, heightened *in* struggle, and preserved *as* struggle," Heidegger concludes. Such usage of the word *Kampf* in 1933, two months after passage of the Enabling Act allowing Hitler to rule by decree, and one month after the nationwide institution of the first anti-Jewish decrees, left very little to the imagination of the audience.

Although the Rectoral Address consists of an uneasy admixture of Nazi rhetoric and Greek philosophical references, the latter seem to be carefully tailored to suit the political exigencies of the day. To take one example: Heidegger concludes the address with an epigram from Plato's *Republic* (497d), which he chooses to render as follows: "Alles Grosse steht im Sturm." He cites this remark following the aforementioned celebration of the virtues of *Kampf* and a concluding appeal to "the historical mission of the German *Volk*." When one recalls that the initials "SA" stands for *Sturm*abteilung (the SA was well represented at Heidegger's inaugural lecture, moreover) and that one of the most virulently anti-Semitic Nazi journals was called *Der Stürmer*, it appears that Heidegger's choice of epigrams was far from accidental.[10]

In sum, rather than struggling to preserve the autonomy of the university from external political encroachment, Heidegger zealously delivered it over to the Nazi movement. His university reforms in the province of Baden were widely considered model instances of political *Gleichschaltung* to be emulated by universities throughout the Reich.

That the inaugural discourse of May 27, 1933, was hardly an excrescence is evidenced by the fact that it was only one of many agitational addresses on behalf on the "National Awakening" delivered by Heidegger that year. What is fascinating about these speeches as intellectual documents is that they represent a hybrid of existentialist categories drawn from *Being and Time* and National Socialist rhetoric of the basest sort.

For example, in his May 26, 1933, speech in honor of the National Socialist hero Albert Leo Schlageter, who had been executed for acts of sabotage against French occupation troops ten years earlier, Heidegger celebrates Schlageter's death in terms reminiscent of one of the key categories of fundamental ontology: *Sein-zum-Tode* or Being-toward-Death. Schlageter, Heidegger tells us repeatedly, died "the cruelest and greatest death." But, as those familiar with *Being and Time* well know, to endure such a death is one of the hallmarks of authenticity.

Heidegger played an especially vigorous role as a propagandist on behalf of Hitler's November 12, 1933, referendum on Germany's withdrawal from the League of Nations. In one early November speech entitled "German Students!" Heidegger begins by claiming that "the National Socialist Revolution brings about a total transformation of our German *Dasein*." He concludes by observing that "the Führer himself is the present and future German reality and its law. . . . Heil Hitler." Many of the speeches of this period emphasize the need for "decision" (*Entscheidung*) in a manner highly redolent of one of the most important categories of *Being and Time*: that of *Entschlossenheit*. Heidegger leaves no doubt concerning the fact that a yes-vote in the plebiscite—a "decision" for the Führer—is in truth a demonstration of the "authenticity" of the German *Volk*.[11]

Another disquieting aspect of Heidegger's tenure as Rektor-Führer concerns his employment of political criteria to judge university appointments and dismissals. In a letter to the Baden state ministry concerning an appointment in the field of church history, Heidegger singles out "fulfillment of National Socialist educational goals" as one of his primary criteria for the position.[12]

In another case—that of the future Nobel-prize winning chemist Hermann Staudinger—Heidegger voluntarily played the role of informer, by seizing on rumors that Staudinger had been a pacifist during World War I (i.e., some fifteen years earlier!) and alerting the National Socialist Ministerial Counsel, Eugen Fehrle, in Karlsruhe. Soon the Gestapo became involved in the investigations, and Heidegger, asked by the local authorities for his personal judgment of Staudinger's case, stated that the civil service reform measures, demanding the dismissal of undesirables, should definitely be applied in the case at hand. Staudinger was forced to submit a letter of resignation. After a series of humiliating obeisances, he was allowed to retain his position—no thanks to the efforts of the new Rektor-Führer.[13]

Finally, in the heat of a controversy concerning a "political (i.e., pro-Nazi) appointment" to the deanship of the Division of Law and Social Science, Heidegger offered the following policy statement: "Since the first days of my acceptance of office, the defining principle and the authentic (if only gradually realizable) goal [of my rectorship] is the fundamental transformation of scholarly education on the basis of the forces and demands of the National Socialist state. . . . What will survive of our transitional labors is uncertain. . . . The sole certainty is that only our unbending will toward the future gives meaning and support to the merest effort. The individual by himself counts for nothing. The fate of our *Volk* in its State counts for everything."[14]

At the center of the recent French controversy is of course the book by Victor Farias. On the one hand, Farias deserves credit for having ignited a long overdue debate over the tabooed theme of the political dimension of Heidegger's work. On the other hand, his argument concerning Heidegger's Nazi ties is so brazenly tendentious that he has in the end ironically undermined his own case. For Farias, there are no gray areas; the question of Heidegger and Nazism is an open-and-shut case. National Socialism was not a political credo that Heidegger adopted opportunistically and then abandoned when it proved a political liability. Instead, for Farias, Heidegger was *born* a Nazi and remained one until the end of his days. To be sure, Farias is able to muster an impressive amount of evidential support to show that (1) Heidegger's provincial Catholic background in the German town of Messkirch predisposed him toward a "national revolutionary" solution to the evils of modernity; and (2) his partisanship for Nazi principles continued long after the point when his enthusiasm for the historical movement itself had waned (at least into the early forties). But to accept the results of Farias's inquiry at face value would be to conclude that both Heidegger's life and thought are so irredeemably colored by Nazi convictions that nothing "uncontaminated" remains worth salvaging. In this respect, the book is truly a *livre à thèse*, and this proves to be its ultimate undoing. It is so negatively disposed toward its subject that the outcome—a rousing condemnation of Heidegger as dyed-in-the-wool Nazi—is a foregone conclusion. Various commentators have compared Farias's strategy of argumentation (which frequently consists of juxtaposing the pro-Nazi sentiments of Heideggerian intimates or associates with those of the Master himself) with the tactic of "guilt by association"—by no means an unfair accusation. In this respect, Farias has done a great disservice to his own cause. There is really little objective need for exaggeration or hyperbole: the facts of the case are disturbing enough and speak for themselves. The strategy of unnuanced, wholesale condemnation has left Farias extremely vulnerable to attacks from the Heideggerian faithful, who have been able to seize on the prejudicial character of his inquiry as a clever way of delegitimating his efforts and avoiding coming to grips with the troubling substantive concerns that have in fact arisen.

The *thèse* of this *livre à thèse* is fairly simple: that Heidegger was not merely a Nazi, but a *radical Nazi*, by which Farias means a supporter of the Röhm faction or SA. As he comments in the opening pages of his book: "Martin Heidegger's adherence to the NSDAP in no way resulted from an improvisational opportunism or tactical considerations. . . . Heidegger opted for the wing represented by Ernst Röhm and the SA and sought to place this variant of National Socialism on a proper philosophical footing, in open opposition to the biological and racial faction led by Alfred Rosenberg and Ernst Krieck" (16–17). Were Farias to make this argument stick, he would thereby also rather handily dispel some evidence that might prove troubling to a more simplistic attempt to equate Heidegger with National Socialism; for example, the fact that Heidegger was at a later point the object of calumnious attacks by the ideologists Rosenberg and Krieck (the Nazi Rektor-Führer at Frankfurt University, who was also a philosopher). Hence, by aligning Heidegger with the SA, Farias can plausibly explain his later difficulties with certain Nazi authorities such as Rosenberg and Krieck by claiming that such polemics were a result of Heidegger's former SA allegiances.[15] Farias tries to prove his case by showing that Heidegger, on numerous occasions, cultivated especially close ties with the various German Student Associations in the early 1930s, which were at this point "gleichgeschaltet" and closely allied with the SA. However, the evidence Farias offers on this score is largely circumstantial and far from convincing. As Hannah Arendt has shown in her contribution to the Festschrift for Heidegger's eightieth birthday,[16] the philosopher always had a large student following dating back to his Marburg years in the early 1920s. Moreover, since he was apparently convinced of the retrograde character of the German university system (as is suggested by his polemics against "so-called academic freedom" in the early thirties), it follows logically that he would look to the German youth of the period as a possible source of revitalization. Of course, there is no sidestepping the fact that in 1933, it was a "Fascist youth" to whom Heidegger directed his not infrequent appeals on the subject of national rejuvenation.

In any event, Farias's contention that Heidegger was a radical Nazi and Röhm adherent is far from persuasive. However, an interesting sidelight on the Heidegger–SA theme is shed in a remark by Heidegger in "The Rectorship, 1933–34: Facts and Thoughts,"[17] where he claims to have relinquished any and every illusion concerning the authenticity of the National Socialist movement as of June 30, 1934, the "Night of the Long Knives." What is fascinating about Heidegger's admission is that it can be interpreted in either of two ways: either the brutality of the Röhm purge finally enlightened him concerning the base realities of National Socialism; or else, the destruction of the SA signaled for him the defeat of National Socialism in its radical, heroic strain. The fact that in 1935 Heidegger could still counterpose the "inner truth and greatness of the National Socialist movement" to the "works that are being peddled about nowadays as the philosophy of National Socialism"[18] suggests that he himself continued to distinguish (as he would in a *Spiegel* interview some thirty years later) between the movement's original historical potential and its later bastardization, which subsequently accounted for Heidegger's own withdrawal of active support. Yet, even if Heidegger's political sympathies indeed lay with the Röhm faction, the case for Heidegger as a hard-core SA adherent is one for which Farias has failed to provide adequate proof.

A final illustration of the manner in which Farias undermines the credibility of his own argument (and one frequently cited by his opponents) pertains to the eighteenth-century prelate Abraham à Sancta Clara, a native son of Heidegger's own Messkirch. A prolific writer who gained a position of tremendous influence at the court of the Hapsburgs (as well as the model for the Capuchin preacher in Schiller's *Wallenstein*), Abraham was also a virulent anti-Semite. It so happens that the first published writing of the young Heidegger in 1910 was composed on the occasion of a monument erected in the honor of this local hero. Farias devotes an entire chapter (39–55) to this otherwise uninteresting bit of Heidegger juvenilia. That Heidegger has no special words of praise for Abraham's anti-Semitism is to Farias a matter of indifference. However, Farias pursues the tenuous connection between these two sons of Messkirch relentlessly, ending his book with a discussion of a 1964 speech delivered by Heidegger at Messkirch once again in honor of the eighteenth-century monk. In his speech, Heidegger quotes an observation by Abraham that "Our peace is as far from war as Sachsenhausen from Frankfurt" (Farias, 293). Of course, by invoking Sachsenhausen, Abraham (and Heidegger) are referring to the district of Frankfurt. But Farias cannot let pass the opportunity for some ruminations on the workings of Heidegger's unconscious, by linking the Frankfurt quarter with the concentration camp of the same name outside of Berlin. Farias's amateur Freudianism suggests that Sachsenhausen is a metonymic trope for Auschwitz, the logical historical outgrowth of Abraham's anti-Semitism; and thus, that Heidegger's statement is a merely a sinister instance of parapraxis. But such feeble efforts at lay analysis fall short of producing the resounding indictment Farias has been seeking for some three hundred pages.

Finally, the Farias book is extremely weak from a philosophical standpoint. This would not be a damnable failing if the author had been content to stick primarily with biographical themes. But instead, he chooses to indict not only Heidegger the man—who, following the researches by Ott, has become an easy target—but also Heidegger the thinker. At this level of analysis, the questions at issue become decidedly more complex, and Farias lacks the intellectual wherewithal to broach these matters with the requisite degree of prudence and sophistication. Because Heidegger as a man may have been rotten to the core does not mean one can, mutatis mutandis, make the same argument concerning his philosophy. If the canon of great works were to be decided on the ad hominem grounds of the ethical character of the authors, we would conceivably be left with little to read. On occasion, Farias concocts specious parallels between Heidegger's work and his politics, but these insights for the most part have the status of unsystematic afterthoughts; and, when the stakes are so high, off-handed remarks won't do. Farias leaves us with the impression that there is a necessary link between Heidegger's thought and his Nazism; and that as a result, Heideggerianism as a philosophical enterprise is essentially flawed or invalid. While the relationship between thought and politics in Heidegger's case may well turn out to be paramount, Farias has not shown us wherein this linkage consists, nor why it may be fatal to the Heideggerian project. The conclusions are suggested instead by insinuation and innuendo.

Within days of its appearance in October 1987, Farias's book was the subject of full-page essays in both *Le Monde* (by Roger-Pol Droit, October 14) and *Libération* (Robert Maggiori, October 16). Both articles sent shock-waves throughout Parisian intellectual circles. The *Libération* article seemed especially damning, and its headline—"Heil Heidegger!" in two-inch, boldface type—set the tone for the debate in its early stages. The conclusions drawn in both essays were strikingly similar: "How will we ever be able to read Heidegger/Dr. Jekyll again without surreptitiously thinking of Heidegger/

Mr. Hyde?" inquires Droit. "It falls due to all those who are professional philosophers, and not for fun but out of concern for truth, to '*think Heidegger*' along with that which the inquiry of Farias has revealed," urges Maggiori.

There followed the predictable attempts at "damage control" on the part of the Heideggerian faithful.[19] But at this point the Farias revelations proved too extensive to refute. Several respondents, including Jacques Derrida in an interview published in *Nouvel Observateur,* attempted to downplay the importance of Farias's findings by claiming they had been known in their essentials for a long time.[20] But this strategy of argumentation all but sidesteps the truly provocative nature of Farias's contribution: even if many of the individual episodes had been known to Heidegger specialists, little of the evidence was publicly available, especially in the non-German-speaking world. Hence, Farias's study was the first both to render the disturbing truths concerning Heidegger's hidden past accessible to public scrutiny and to attempt to account for their systematic interconnection. In this respect, though his execution may have been flawed, he has unquestionably opened up important new perspectives. To gainsay his work as "nonoriginal" is simply to argue in bad faith. (Moreover, if knowledge of these "facts" was as widespread as Derrida and others claim, then why were they not made available to the public at an earlier date? Had these troubling facts been . . . suppressed?)

For certain French Heideggerians, the Farias book will forever be viewed as a small-minded and rancorous assault on a great philosophical legacy.[21] Or, as Heidegger himself was fond of saying: "When they can't attack the philosophy, they attack the philosopher." The philosopher and Heidegger translator Pierre Aubenque asks plaintively: "What is the *ethical* status, as far as our traditional judgments about inquisition and censure are concerned, of a book that openly presents itself as an enterprise of denunciation, and especially the denunciation of a thinker, above all, when this denunciation is in a large measure calumnious?" François Fédier attempts to explain the hue and cry concerning Heidegger's Nazi ties psychologically, as an instance of "ressentiment": it is reducible to "the rage of mediocrities against Heidegger—I've seen it at work my entire life."[22] Henri Crétella contends that there can be no integral relation between Heidegger's thought and Nazism, since the latter was predicated "on a refusal to think." He then seeks to turn the tables on Farias by claiming that "there are two ways to declare a taboo on thinking: a vociferous, frenzied way, and another, gently anesthetizing way." Whereas the former mentality, which Crétella identifies as the "historical meaning" of Nazism, has been vanquished, the second, which is the "essential meaning" of Nazism, survives in inquiries such as that of Victor Farias.[23]

On the other hand, many commentators have been genuinely disturbed by the recent facts that have come to light about Heidegger's National Socialist past, recognizing that to harp ceaselessly on Farias's purported methodological failings is to beg the major question at issue: namely, to what extent might Heidegger's personal misdeeds jeopardize the legacy of his philosophical project? A common theme among those who have chosen to acknowledge the gravity of Farias's revelations relates to the philosopher's obstinate refusal to utter the barest word of contrition about his Nazi past or about the Holocaust in general.[24] As Maurice Blanchot observes: "Each time that he was asked to recognize his 'error,' he maintained a rigid silence, or said something that aggravated the situation. . . . it is in Heidegger's silence about the Exterminations that his irreparable error lies" (Blanchot goes on to cite Heidegger's arrogant remark to the effect that Hitler had failed *him* by reneging on the original radical potential of National Socialism).[25] In a similar vein, the philosopher Emmanuel Levinas observes: "Does not this silence, even in peacetime, about the gas chambers and the death-camps—something beyond the realm of all 'bad excuses'—attest to a soul that is in its depths impervious to compassion [*sensibilité*], is it not a tacit approval of the horrifying?"[26] Even Heidegger's most talented and original disciple, Hans-Georg Gadamer, has freely admitted that in his political engagement, "Heidegger was not a pure and simple opportunist"; rather, "he 'believed' in Hitler."[27]

Equally fascinating have been a series of related discoveries that have surfaced as unintended outgrowths of the main debate itself. The most momentous of these "spillover" disclosures concerns the man who for thirty-five years was France's most stalwart Heidegger advocate, Jean Beaufret. Beaufret, a Heidegger translator, intimate, and interlocutor—as well as a former Resistance-fighter—who published several volumes of his "Conversations with Heidegger" before his death in 1982, is perhaps best known to the English-speaking world as the addressee of Heidegger's important "Letter on Humanism"—a fifty-page rejoinder to a series of questions posed by Beaufret in 1945 on the relationship between fundamental ontology and humanism (Heidegger's response is also a pointed rebuttal of Jean-Paul Sartre's defense of the humanist tradition in "Existentialism is a Humanism"). Whenever questions had been raised in years past concerning Heidegger's unsavory political allegiances, Beaufret had always been in the forefront of his defenders; and his credentials as an ex-*résistant* lent an aura of unimpeachable moral sanctity to his pro-Heideggerian proclamations.

As it turns out, however, Beaufret seems to have had a hidden agenda: he was a covert supporter of Robert Faurisson, the French historian who denies the existence of the gas chambers specifically and the Holocaust in general.[28] In two letters dated November 22, 1978, and January 18, 1979 (recently made available in Faurisson's journal, *Annales d'histoire revisionniste*), Beaufret expresses adamant support for Faurisson's "project" and sympathizes with him for the criticism he received from the press. At one point Beaufret observes: "I believe that for my part I have traveled approximately the same path as you and have been considered suspect for having expressed the same doubts [concerning the existence of the gas chambers]. Fortunately for me, this was done orally."[29] That the major French Heidegger interpreter of the postwar era was a closet supporter of Faurisson's thesis concerning the nonexistence of the Nazi death-camps casts serious doubt (to say the least) concerning his "objectivity" as an intrepid Heidegger champion.

Another disturbing circumstance that has recently come to light concerns Heidegger's long-standing friendship with the notorious Eugen Fischer, who in 1927 became director of the Institute of Racial Hygiene in Berlin. Fischer was one of the principal architects of the National Socialist racial theory, and thus in essence laid the intellectual groundwork for the Final Solution. Born in 1874, Fischer established his credentials in 1913 with a book on the "problem of the bastardization of the human species." This work drew important lessons from German colonial racial legislation in Southwest Africa, where, as of 1908, marriages between Europeans and natives were forbidden, and those that had already been contracted were declared null. However, the true solution to the problem of miscegenation envisioned by Fischer is the "disappearance" of those of mixed race through a diabolical "process of natural selection."

Fischer was active in the early years of Nazi rule, helping to promulgate legislation aimed at "protection against the propagation of genetic abnormalities," on the basis of which more than 60,000 forced sterilizations were performed in 1934 alone. His institute in Berlin was also the inspiration behind the Nuremberg racial laws of 1935, forbidding intermarriage (as well as sexual contact of any sort) between Jews and non-Jews. A leading theorist of eugenics and a forceful proponent of "a biological politics of population," Fischer has been described as "one of the linchpins of the execution of the bureaucratic and ideological methods that facilitated [Nazi] genocide." It may help put things in perspective to add that Dr. Joseph Mengele was a "researcher" at Fischer's Institute.

Relations between Heidegger and Fischer were loose, but nonetheless interesting. Both hailed from the same region in Baden. Both participated in a Leipzig congress in November 1933 to promote the cause of "German science." The two remained in contact for the duration of Heidegger's rectorship.

And it may have been in no small measure due to Fischer's influence that the racial measures promoted by Heidegger during his tenure as rector that have been chronicled by Farias—a questionnaire concerning racial origin distributed to all professors; an obligatory lecture for all instructors on the importance of racial purity; the establishment of a "department of race" at the university run by the SS—followed a model set forth by his fellow *Schwarzwalder.*

In 1944, at the age of fifty-five, Heidegger had been drafted into the *Volksturm*—a reserve unit composed of older German men as well as underaged youth—as was not uncommon for men his age during the war's later stages. Only a personal telegram sent to the Gauleiter of Salzburg spared Heidegger from service. The sender of the telegram was none other than Eugen Fischer. It read: "With all due respect for the imperatives of the hour and those of the *Volkssturm* . . . I am in favor of freeing from armed service Heidegger, an exceptional and irreplaceable thinker for the nation and the Party."[30]

That ties between the two remained cordial over the years is suggested by the fact that in 1960, Heidegger sent Fischer a copy of his book *Hebel, der Hausfreund,* with the inscription, "For Eugen Fischer, with warm Christmas greetings and best wishes for the New Year."[31]

It would certainly be unfair to judge Heidegger by the company he kept, no matter how sinister. Yet, the Heidegger–Fischer episode is of interest insofar as it suggests that, because of his ties with Fischer, the philosopher may well have been aware of the Nazi preparations for genocide (as well as other crimes) at a relatively early date—something his supporters have always denied.

Two of the leading French Heideggerians, Jacques Derrida and Philippe Lacoue-Labarthe, have been in the forefront of the philosophical debate concerning the question "whither Heideggerianism?" in the aftermath of the Farias controversy. Unlike the base Heidegger-apologists (Fédier, Aubenque, Crétella), who have seized on the purportedly tendentious nature of Farias's study in the hope of fostering a return to "business as usual," Lacoue-Labarthe and Derrida have been willing to confront these troubling biographical themes head-on (Derrida, for example, speaks of Heidegger's "terrifying silence" about the past in the February 9, 1988, issue of *Le Monde*). Their intention, however (the methodological validity of which can hardly be denied), is to allow the vultures to feed on Heidegger the contingent, empirical individual (what *is* an author, anyway?), while saving the philosophical oeuvre itself— especially Heidegger's work following *die Kehre* (the "Turn"), where, so the argument runs, Heidegger freed himself from the vestigial anthropocentrism that is still so prominent in *Being and Time.*

Ironically, both Lacoue-Labarthe and Derrida published book-length "responses" to Farias well before his manuscript ever appeared: they are respectively entitled *La Fiction du politique* and *De l'esprit: Heidegger et la question* (both appeared in 1987).[32] Both Lacoue-Labarthe and Derrida had heard tell of the troubling revelations from the other side of the Rhine (Ott's work being the major source) and decided to stake out a position on the philosophical implications of these findings in advance of the storm that would soon be unleashed. Since these two books contain the major *prises de position* on the question of Heidegger and politics by the two leading representatives of Heideggerianism working in France today, they are worth discussing at some length.

La Fiction du politique is simultaneously an unflinching arraignment of Heidegger's Nazism and a bold endorsement of (post-*Kehre*) Heideggerian orthodoxy. Unlike the tiresome apologists, who would give anything to go back to "life before Farias," Lacoue-Labarthe pulls no punches when addressing the fatal interrelation between philosophy and politics that led to Heidegger's 1933 "engagement." His approach is characterized by a refreshing willingness to weigh seriously the continuities between Heidegger's early philosophical writings and his National Socialist convictions in the early thirties. His assertion that "contrary to what has been said here and there, Heidegger's engagement is *absolutely coherent* with his thought" apparently leaves little room for equivocation. But what Lacoue-Labarthe gives with one hand, he takes away, cleverly, with the other: the insight just cited pertains only to the pre-1935 Heidegger. The post-1935 Heidegger emerges virtually unscathed.

Lacoue-Labarthe's argument, which parallels Derrida's in its essentials, proceeds as follows. The problem with the early Heidegger is that he suffers from a surfeit of metaphysical thinking. Even though he has gone to great lengths to distance himself from the tradition of Western metaphysics in *Being and Time* and other early works, insisting that this tradition must be subjected to the purifying powers of *Destruktion*, the break proves in the end to be insufficiently rigorous. Metaphysical residues abound: most notably, in the *Dasein*-centered paradigm of *Being and Time*, where, when all is said and done, a human subject (albeit, a non-Cartesian, existentially rooted subject) once again provides privileged access to ontological questions. Thus, in the last analysis, *Being and Time*, despite the profound insight with which the book opens (the question concerning "the Being of beings"), simply relapses into conventional onto-theological modes of thought; its anthropomorphic *démarche* is really little more than a warmed-over version of traditional metaphysical humanism. Now that Nietzsche's insight concerning the death of God has been acknowledged, the topographical locus of the metaphysical *archē* has merely shifted: a transcendent dwelling-place has merely been exchanged for an immanent one, and Dasein, in its "decisive resolve toward authentic Being-for-Self," has become the new focal point of metaphysical inquiry. The fact that the second volume of *Being and Time* was never written can thus be explained by the fact that Heidegger, circa 1935, came to view the entire existential framework of his 1927 work as essentially flawed; that is, as perilously beholden to the paradigm of metaphysical humanism he had been at such pains to counteract.

What, however, do such ethereal philosophical questions have to do with Heidegger's attachments to the base realities of Nazi politics? Everything in the world, according to Lacoue-Labarthe and Derrida. Through a brilliant piece of hermeneutical chicanery, they intentionally seek (unlike the blatant apologists) to link the philosophy of the early Heidegger with his pro-Nazi phase in order the better to save him: the early Heidegger, whose thought is in any case oversaturated with superfluous metaphysical residues,[33] can be safely jettisoned in order that the posthumanist Heidegger—the Heidegger of the Nietzsche lectures and the "Letter on Humanism"—can be redeemed unscathed. And thus by an ingenious interpretive *coup de maître*, the troubling "question" of Heidegger and politics can be neatly brushed aside, since the post-1935 Heidegger abandoned the philosophical paradigm that led to his partisanship for Hitlerism in the first place.

The "defense" proffered by Lacoue-Labarthe and Derrida is certainly not without merit. It therefore behooves us to examine it in more detail before passing judgment on its worth. I focus on the linchpin of the argument: the counterintuitive claim that it was an excess of metaphysical thinking that led to Heidegger's Nazism.[34] At the same time, it is of interest to note the extent to which this reading of Heidegger conforms verbatim with the philosopher's own interpretation of his intellectual/political trajectory. It is a strikingly orthodox reading of Heidegger.

The Lacoue-Labarthe–Derrida interpretation is of a piece with Heidegger's reevaluation of his own philosophy in his Nietzsche lectures of 1936–39. Previously, Heidegger had accepted Nietzsche's work at face value, viewing the latter as Nietzsche had understood himself: as a great subverter of metaphysical humanist nostrums and a critic of that "nihilism" to which traditional Western values inevitably led. It was fundamentally the debacle of Heidegger's Nazi experience that led him to reconceptualize his previous, uncritical relationship to Nietzsche. Just as Heidegger understood Nietzsche's efforts toward a "transvaluation of all values" as a philosophical answer to nihilism, he had greeted the National Socialist Revolution as a political antidote to nihilism. In viewing the Nazi movement through a Nietzschean frame of reference, Heidegger endowed it with all the attributes of a salutary, world-historical challenge to Western nihilism and to the "decadent" values that are its necessary historical accompaniment: liberalism, individualism, philosophical subjectivism, mass society, *technē*, value-relativism, and so forth; in short, he perceived it as that panacea for the aporias of modernity allusively prophesied by Nietzsche's Zarathustra. The Nazis were the heroic "new pagans" that would save the West from a seemingly irreversible process of Spenglerian decline.

In fact, it is fascinating to note that Heidegger maintained this perspective until the end of his life. That he never "renounced" the National Socialist experiment was neither an accident nor an oversight. Instead, if one examines "The Rectorship: 1933–34," the 1966 *Spiegel* interview, as well as *An Introduction to Metaphysics*, it is clear that Heidegger continued throughout his life to distinguish "the debased historical actuality" of Nazism from its "true historical potential." He originally developed this distinction in *An Introduction to Metaphysics* where, as previously noted, he takes pains to differentiate between "the inner truth and greatness of the National Socialist movement" and the inauthentic "works that are being peddled nowadays as the philosophy of National Socialism." The former he defines in terms of "the encounter between global technology and modern man"; that is, the "inner truth and greatness" of Nazism is to be found in its nature as a world-historical alternative to the technological-scientific nihilism bemoaned by Nietzsche and Spengler. What is shocking about this claim is that the second half of this sentence (concerning the "encounter between global technology and modern man") was added parenthetically to the text of the 1953 edition of these lectures of 1935. Thus, not only has Heidegger refused to omit the original distinction between the "historical" and "essential" forms of Nazism in the later edition; he has in fact reemphasized the value of this distinction eighteen years later by adding a clarification through which he seeks to reinforce the original distinction itself.

Heidegger's dogmatic nonrepentance is further illustrated by his long-standing conviction that the National Socialist movement (and he personally) had been "betrayed" by the Führer himself. That is, it was Hitler who, owing to a failure of nerve, ultimately abandoned the original "antinihilistic" thrust of the movement (which was its raison d'être, according to Heidegger), by curbing its more radical tendencies. Thus, according to the testimony of the writer Ernst Jünger, Heidegger claimed after the war that Hitler would be resurrected and exonerate Heidegger, since he (Hitler) was guilty of having misled him.[35] That Heidegger never made a profession of guilt concerning his role in the "German catastrophe" follows logically from this reasoning, since, in the last analysis, the fault lay with the National Socialist movement itself—which had failed to live up to its true historical potential—rather than with him. This whole "strategy of denial" on Heidegger's part is fully consistent with the rather exalted mission he assigns to the National Socialist *Führerstaat* in his Rectoral Address of 1933, where the latter is hailed as a bellicose reinvention of the Greek polis. Since the National Socialist state failed to live up to the metaphysical goals Heidegger had set for it, it was the Nazis, not Heidegger, who were ultimately at fault.[36]

To return to the Lacoue-Labarthe–Derrida contention that it was a "surplus of metaphysical thinking" that accounted for Heidegger's National Socialist leanings: according to this argument, Heidegger finally came around to realizing in the late 1930s that Nietzsche, instead of having delivered a death-blow to Western metaphysics, was in truth the last metaphysician. The post-Cartesian version of metaphysics largely consisted of an exaltation of human will; and Nietzsche's thought, for all its criticisms of philosophical humanism, was ultimately of a piece with this tradition, since its central category, "the will to power," is likewise a glorification of will. It is precisely such an exaltation of "will" that is, according to Heidegger, at the root of Western *technē* and the triumph of modern technology. This celebration of will is at the very heart of the modern cultural project of "human self-assertion" (Blumenberg). Hence, National Socialism, which originally presented itself in Heidegger's eyes as a countermovement to the nihilism of the Western "will to *technē*"—and thus as a world-historical alternative to the nihilism so reviled by Nietzsche—in the end proved to be only a different historical manifestation of that same nihilism, in the same way that Nietzsche's strident critique of metaphysics itself ultimately rests on metaphysical foundations. The equation according to which Heidegger proceeds, therefore, is: National Socialism = Nietzscheanism = metaphysics. If it was an infatuation with Nietzsche (more specifically, with the latter's critique of nihilism) that led to Heidegger's embrace of National Socialism, then it was ultimately Western metaphysics that was at fault, since this was the intellectual framework that stood behind Nietzsche's thought. Heidegger had been misled and duped (first by Nietzsche, then by the Nazis), but he was not "responsible for," let alone "guilty of" any misdeeds.

A similar interpretive "strategy of containment" is pursued by Derrida in *De l'esprit*. Derrida, unlike Lacoue-Labarthe, believes that he can succeed in getting the *early* Heidegger partially off the hook. The sticking point is the keyword in Derrida's title, "l'esprit" (or *Geist*). Derrida argues that the frequent positive allusions to "spirit" in the political speeches of 1933 indicate a sharp departure from *Being and Time*, where this category is systematically criticized. A "metaphysics of spirit" was a Hegelian trope, a telltale metaphysical residuum that Heidegger the philosopher had long since renounced. Therefore, the utilization of this outmoded philosophical rhetoric was by definition discontinuous with the philosophy of *Being and Time,* despite the fact that the latter remained partially beholden to prejudicial Cartesian nostrums (above all, in treating *Dasein* as the *archē* through which the "question of Being" could be unlocked). As Derrida himself explains the rationale behind his "spirited" defense of Heidegger: one must preserve the "possibilities of rupture" in a "variegated Heideggerian thought that will remain for a long time provocative, enigmatic, worth reading." In his rectoral address, "Heidegger takes up again the word 'spirit,' which he had previously avoided, he dispenses with the inverted commas with which he had surrounded it. He thus limits the movement of deconstruction that he had previously engaged in. He gives a voluntaristic and metaphysical speech [whose terms] he would later treat with suspicion. To the extent that [Heidegger's discourse] celebrates the freedom of spirit, its exaltation [of spirit] resembles other European discourses (spiritualist, religious, humanist) that in general are opposed to Nazism. [This is] a complex and unstable skein that I try to unravel [in *De l'esprit*] by recognizing the threads in common between Nazism and anti-Nazism, the law of resemblance, the fatality of perversion. The mirror-effects are at times vertiginous."[37]

The illogical conclusion we are left to draw from the line of argument pursued by both Lacoue-Labarthe and Derrida is that it was a surfeit of metaphysical humanism (later abandoned) that drove Heidegger into the Nazi camp! But in the end, this interpretive tack amounts only to a more sophisticated strategy of denial. The entire specificity of the relationship between Heidegger's philosophy and National Socialism is theorized away once the distinction between "humanism" and "antihumanism" is so readily blurred. The *Volk* for which Heidegger became the spokesman in 1933 is a particularistic entity, unlike the category of "mankind" with which one associates traditional humanism. In addition, any trace of personal or German national responsibility is conveniently effaced once the triumph of National Socialism is attributed to a nebulous, impersonal force such as "planetary technology," "metaphysical thinking," "nihilism," or the "will to will."[38] Since Nazism proves in the last analysis to be merely a particular outgrowth of the rise of "planetary technology" (which itself is a mere "symptom" of the "forgetting of Being" that has victimized the history of the West since Plato), the historical specificity of the Hitler years becomes, in the overall scheme of things, a minor episode. From this perspective, it would be presumptuous of Martin Heidegger, the lowly "shepherd of Being," to assume culpability for a metaphysical process (the forgetting of Being) for which he can hardly be held responsible. If you want someone to blame, knock on Plato's door. He's the one, after all, who, by distinguishing between the forms and the sensibles, kicked off the entire onto-theological muddle in the first place. In fact, Heidegger deserves our ceaseless praise for attempting to reverse this odious process; albeit, within the limits of *Gelassenheit* or "releasement" (which substitutes for the overly "voluntaristic" category of *Entschlossenheit* in the later Heidegger), according to which matters can only be made worse if men and women assert their "wills" to try to change things. As Heidegger confesses in the *Spiegel* interview (in a line that theologians have ever since cited with glee), at this point in history, the domination of "will," "metaphysics," and "technē" has gone so far that "only a god can save us!"

That the "antihumanist" philosophical framework of the later Heidegger can hardly be deemed an unqualified advance, as Lacoue-Labarthe and Derrida would have it, is indicated by a telling remark made by Heidegger in 1949 (well after his alleged *Kehre*): "Agriculture today is a motorized food industry, in essence the same as the manufacture of corpses in gas chambers and extermination camps, the same as the blockade and starvation of countries, the same as the manufacture of atomic bombs."[39] This cynical avowal—by the man who has staked a claim to being the leading philosopher of our time—gets at the very crux of Heidegger's later philosophy as a critique of *technē*. That the Freiburg sage can simply equate "the manufacture of corpses in gas chambers and extermination camps" with mechanized agriculture is not only a shockingly insensitive affront to the memory of the victims of the Nazi death-camps. It is not only a gruesome equation of incomparables. It serves once more to deny the specifically German responsibility for these crimes by attributing them to the dominance of an abstract, all-encompassing, world-historical process. It suggests, moreover, that other Western (as well as non-Western) nations who engage in mechanized food production, "blockades," and the manufacture of nuclear weapons, are in essence no different than the SS lieutenants who herded Jews into the gas chambers. It illustrates an extreme myopia concerning the various uses to which technology can be put in the modern world, an incapacity to distinguish between its beneficial and destructive employment. It is in sum a simplistic demonization of technology. That the later Heidegger's philosophy is to such a great extent predicated on a demonization of "technique" as exemplified by the 1949 observation just cited suggests a glaring flaw in his theoretical framework.

Essentially, Heidegger is a philosopher who is not at home in the modern world. Thus, it comes as little surprise that, when pressed by his interlocutors during the course of the *Spiegel* interview for a tidbit of philosophical wisdom concerning a possible solution to the dilemmas of the modern age, Heidegger can only answer emphatically in the negative: whatever the solution may be, "it is not democracy"; instead, "only a god can save us." His devaluation of the modern project of human autonomy is so extreme, that he will only admit to a deus ex machina solution—in the most literal sense of the term. The powers of human intelligence and volition are so thoroughly downplayed, the modern ideal of self-fashioning subjectivity is so far devalued, that all we are left with is an appeal to myth that is abstract, irrational, and sadly impotent.

DEMOCRACY AND
THE POLITICAL IN THE THOUGHT
OF HANNAH ARENDT

Hannah Arendt has justifiably been lauded as the greatest political thinker of the twentieth century. The merits of her totalitarianism book alone, which to this day remains a classic, would be enough to secure such a claim. However, when one considers the fact that she complemented this study with two other great contributions to modern political philosophy, *The Human Condition* (1958) and *On Revolution* (1963), how formidable an intellectual legacy she has bequeathed becomes evident. Perhaps one can speak of Leo Strauss in the same breath. The names of Antonio Gramsci, Carl Schmitt, Eric Voegelin, and Michael Oakeshott also come to mind. But after that, one would be hard pressed to name political thinkers of equal stature.

Laudations aside, the more specific question as to which aspects of her thought are worth building on today remains to be answered. What both fascinates and frustrates about her work is that, in so many respects, it defies categorization: Arendt is neither a liberal nor a conservative, reactionary nor radical, classicist nor modernist.

Many rightly believe that the key to Arendt's political thought is to be found in *The Human Condition;* more specifically, in the concept of *action* she develops in that work. I shall be devoting considerable attention to the relevance and implications of this notion for her political philosophy in general. My basic claim is that the roots of Arendt's political thought are to be found in the values of the pre-Platonic polis. In her view, there the values of the political properly so called were allowed to flourish, as yet uncorrupted by orientations proper to the spheres of "contemplation" (the Platonic *bios thēoretikos* which tends to downgrade the values proper to the sphere of action) or *technē*. To be sure, the framework she adopts provides a highly fruitful and suggestive basis for understanding the failings of modern politics, dominated as they are by the prepolitical spheres of economy and public administration. In the end, however, her perspective remains overantiquarian. Illuminating though it may be in many respects, her adherence to a Periclean–Athenian model of politics means that her perspective is seriously at odds with the terms and requirements of political practice in the modern world.

I

The centrality of Arendt's first book, *The Origins of Totalitarianism* (1951), for the subsequent development of her political thought is beyond dispute. In this study Arendt would define the problem that would preoccupy her in all her future work: the nightmarish threat to human freedom posed by modern forms of political rule. The Greeks believed they had categorized all possible forms of rulership: monarchy, democracy, tyranny, and oligarchy. In the twentieth century, however, totalitarianism appeared as a qualitatively new form of political domination. The totalitarian state mandated the absorption of all enclaves of social autonomy—very often, via the means of terror.

For Arendt, totalitarianism represented not only a new form of political rule, but something much more radical: a conscious effort to transform the very fabric of human nature. The concentration camps—our century's signature institutions—became the laboratories in which this cynical experiment would be carried out. Totalitarian rule constituted an attempt to realize Circe's dream: to reduce men and women, via terror, to the condition of animals. It strove to create a society of conditioned reflexes: Pavlov's dog, who salivates not when he is hungry but when his master rings a bell, would be the model.[1] In Arendt's view, totalitarian societies embodied an unprecedented threat insofar as they threatened to negate what was most essentially human: the capacity for spontaneity or free action; a capacity that, for the Greeks, was one of the traits that distinguished human life from that of lower species.

The diminution of prospects for free action in modern societies would become the guiding thread for much of Arendt's mature work. It was a tendency she viewed as operative not merely in the twentieth-century dictatorships, but (following Tocqueville) also in modern democracies, in which the horizons of political expression, too, had radically contracted. Modern democracy bore all the hallmarks of mass society. Politics properly speaking had become a matter of public administration, in which "action," in Arendt's understanding of the term, played a negligible role.

Profound though it was, Arendt's understanding of totalitarian rule was far from unflawed. In retrospect her attempt to portray totalitarianism as the logical culmination of political modernity—rather than, say, as a terrible excrescence—seems overteleological. This is especially true of the first two parts of her study, "Anti-Semitism" and "Imperialism." Arendt underestimates the fact that, in the majority of cases, neither imperialism nor anti-Semitism (in-

stances of which were extremely widespread) blossomed forth into the totalitarian politics per se. In what way, then, can these two phenomena be said to
embody the "elements" or sine qua non of totalitarian rule as Arendt describes
them? Anti-Semitism, moreover, played virtually no role in the totalitarian
deformation of the Soviet regime under Stalin. Conversely, it remained the
ideological basis of National Socialism; so much so that the policies and politics
of Nazi rule remain incomprehensible without recourse to its avowedly racist
self-understanding.

In retrospect, by conflating the German and Soviet variants of totalitarianism (the cursory treatment the Soviet model receives seems appended as an
afterthought), the book seems eminently beholden to the ideological context of
the cold war. And while it would be foolish to deny the many similarities
between the two regimes, the term "totalitarianism" itself fails to distinguish
their essentially different economic and ideological bases. As one commentator
has remarked, "By understanding Nazism in terms not of its specifically German context but of modern developments linked to Stalinism as well, Arendt
was putting herself in the ranks of the many intellectuals of German culture
who sought to connect Nazism with Western modernity, thereby deflecting
blame from specifically German traditions."[2]

Thus, at a crucial point, the attempt to understand totalitarianism as the
fundamental or most representative expression of political modernity breaks
down. To be sure, Nazi Germany and the Soviet Union may have been totalitarian in Arendt's sense. Yet, totalitarianism as she describes it was hardly a
pan-European phenomenon. Even the fascist regimes that were in certain
respects comparable to Hitler's Germany, such as Mussolini's Italy or Franco's
Spain, remained in essence single party, authoritarian dictatorships; which is to
say they fell short of being the all-consuming political entities we customarily
associate with totalitarianism.[3]

When all is said and done, the success of totalitarianism in Germany and
Russia cannot be strictly explained, as Arendt implies, in terms of the logic of
political modernity. Instead, in both cases one must equally take into account
the formidable persistence of quasi-feudal, authoritarian traditions. That both
nations were *latecomers* to (rather than "exemplars" of) political modernity
may have played a much more significant role in their aversion to parliamentary
forms and embrace of dictatorial rule.[4]

II

Arendt was a student of both Jaspers and Heidegger. It would be surprising,
therefore, were the marked imprint of their theories not evident in her political

thinking. Indeed, the influence of their thought on her concept of action—her alternative to the impoverished bourgeois definition of liberty as "negative freedom"—is pronounced. In many ways, *Existenzphilosophie* was the crucible in which her theory of action was formed. As Martin Jay has remarked: "To stress this link [between Arendt and *Existenzphilosophie*] is useful not because it establishes some sort of guilt by association, but rather because it provides the historical context in which her apparently uncategorizable position begins to make sense."[5]

Though it was the formative philosophy of her youth, Arendt remained peculiarly silent about *Existenzphilosophie* in her later years. In a 1946 *Partisan Review* essay on this theme, however, she praises *Existenzphilosophie* for "having reached a consciousness, as yet unsurpassed, of what really is at stake in modern philosophy."[6] What aspects, then, of the philosophies of Jaspers and Heidegger would prove most influential for Arendt?

In the case of Jaspers, it was the theory of boundary or limit-situations (*Grenzsituationen*) that had the greatest impact on Arendt's political thought. Limit-situations represent moments of existential risk—proximity to death, danger, or crisis—in which the meaning of one's life, one's personal authenticity as it were, comes distinctly into view. If we transpose the values of the limit-situation to the political sphere proper (Arendt's realm of "action"), we will have gone far toward determining the normative features of politics that Arendt reveres. For Arendt, there is nothing in the least prosaic or routine about politics as a species of "action." In this regard, she laments, action has all but disappeared from contemporary politics. For Arendt politics as an expression of action becomes a type of existential proving ground; it becomes a test of the capacity of individual actors for heroism or great deeds. It is a page taken verbatim out of Plutarch's *Lives*.[7]

We know that for Heidegger, too, politics was a sphere of authenticity: it pertained to a Nietzschean "great politics" as opposed to the routinized politics that characterize bourgeois rule. "The time for petty politics is over," remarks Nietzsche in *Beyond Good and Evil;* "the very next century will bring the fight for the dominion of the earth—the *compulsion* to great politics."[8] These were very much the normative terms through which Heidegger justified his commitment to National Socialism in 1933; that is, as a return to a type of great politics, a politics of authenticity.[9]

For Arendt, too, politics meant "great politics." The avowedly Homeric dimensions of action that were of such importance for Nietzsche—the emphasis on heroism, striving, agon, and individual distinction—for her, too, embodied the unique contribution of the Greeks to modern political life. Thus, in *The Human Condition*, Arendt construes political action in a manner wholly consistent with the virtues of political existentialism (and thus, with the Nietzschean–Heideggerian lineage) just discussed: "action can be judged only by the criterion of greatness because it is in its nature to break through the commonly accepted and reach into the extraordinary, where whatever is true in common and everyday life no longer applies because everything that exists is unique and *sui generis*."[10] From this standpoint it is clear that it is not democracy per se but the *agora* that she prizes; for the first time in history, the Greeks provided a space, an opening, in which superior individuals could display their prowess. As Margaret Canovan has observed: "As we explore [Arendt's] theory, the action and self-disclosure that apparently started as general human capacities seem to be narrowed down until they become rare human achievements"— a view that well captures the elitist and aristocratic biases of Arendt's conception of the political.[11]

The more we probe the theoretical bases of Arendt's understanding of politics, the more we see the extent to which it remains indebted to specific Heideggerian-ontological presuppositions. For Arendt, as for Heidegger, the polis, the site of the political, provides a "clearing" (*Lichtung*), in which action comes to expression.

In this connection it is important to realize that in Arendt's view it is not so much the ends of politics that occupy pride of place—happiness, the public weal, justice, and so forth—but certain *aesthetic* qualities. In keeping with the aforementioned motif of the Heideggerian clearing, Arendt views politics very much as a stage on which great individuals might display themselves. The political arena becomes a setting in which great persons reveal their uniqueness and worth by virtue of their capacity to speak and act. As Arendt observes: "In acting and speaking, men show who they are, reveal actively their unique personal identities and thus make their appearance in the human world."[12] It is for this reason that in *The Human Condition* she refers to theater as "the political art *par excellence;* only there is the political sphere of human life transposed into art. . . . [theater] is the only art whose sole subject is man in his relationship to others."[13] Similarly, in "What is Freedom?" she writes that "performing artists—dancers, play-actors, musicians and the like—need an audience to show their virtuosity, just as acting men need the presence of others before whom they can appear; both need a publicly organized space for their 'work,' and both depend upon others for the performance itself."[14]

In Arendt's view, action and politics, as distinct from labor and work, must be wholly noninstrumental or non-goal-oriented. She observes that "action almost never achieves its purpose"; in other words, it must be considered primarily as an end in itself.[15] Once it is viewed instrumentally, as a means to a determinate end, its purity will have been corrupted. Even were it to be thought of as a means to achieving the ends of justice or social equality, politics qua action would thereby forfeit its distinctiveness and degenerate to the level of productive activity or "labor."

Following from this marked devaluation of the ends of action or questions of political content—inferior considerations that threaten to sully the realm of politics by associating it with base, utilitarian concerns—Arendt's concept of the political assumes distinctly decisionistic hues. Thus, it is not so much the "what" or "wherefore" of politics that matters, but rather the "how." The great are judged by *who they are,* remarks Arendt, in a patently aristocratic spirit; that is, on the basis of certain existential attributes that, in action, are permitted to shine forth for all to see. Only the vulgar, she goes on to observe, are judged by the prosaic criterion of what they have done.[16]

In Heidegger, similarly, the concept of "resolve" (*Entschlossenheit*) abstracts entirely from the *ends* of action. Thus, one could be "resolutely" a fascist, a Bolshevik, or anarchist; but not a democrat, since, as a form of mass rule, democracy pertains to the degraded sphere of everydayness. Democracy is, one might say, constitutionally inauthentic. Like Arendt's concept of action, "decision" for Heidegger reflects the sheer quantum of will or conviction subtending our worldly engagements. It abstracts entirely from the specific content or ends of those commitments themselves. (Thus, the witticism popular among Heidegger's students in the 1920s: "I'm resolved, but to what end I know not.")

In Heidegger's case, decisionism leads to a celebration of ontological politics. The ends of politics are not conceived of in terms of justice or fairness; instead, they become an extension of Heideggerian "unconcealedness" (*Unverschlossenheit*), the disclosure of truth. They serve to ground and maintain the "openness of an open region," as Heidegger characterizes the "clearing" (Lichtung) as a locus for the "event" (*Ereignis*) of truth.[17]

For Arendt, too, politics possesses a quintessential ontological function: it is the supreme act of human self-revelation or self-disclosure. Thus, in the first instance, the vocation of politics concerns certain existential criteria: it is the fundamental way in which we express our distinctiveness as human beings. In *The Human Condition,* Arendt speaks of the "revelatory character of action and speech, in which one discloses oneself without ever either knowing himself or being able to calculate beforehand whom he reveals."[18] One of the primary virtues of action, therefore, is its unforeseeableness, its sheer unpredictability— so far removed is it from the vulgar, material sphere of *technē* or production.

Unlike Heidegger, however, Arendt considers personal authenticity to be necessarily tied to the existence of a public realm, the political equivalent of Heidegger's clearing. Tyranny forecloses this space and is therefore unacceptable. To engage in a provocative thought experiment, one might inquire: Could a fascist public sphere preserve the dramaturgical model of politics advocated by Arendt? In view of the wholesale degradation of the political in the modern world, where social "interests" have come to monopolize political decision-making, and basing one's response on the conceptual framework established in *The Human Condition,* one would be hard-pressed to rule out this possibility. In many respects fascism attempts to reassert the autonomy of the political over the economic (which is, after all, one of the key desiderata of Arendt's political theory). Her own thoroughgoing critique of the modern party system, in which the administration of needs takes precedence over the ends of self-realization, suggests that, in any event, her real political options are few.[19]

The aestheticist tenor of Arendt's theory of action is reinforced by her emphasis on the concepts of natality and novelty, which inhere in the act of founding a state. More generally, though, one of the essential attributes of action is that it certifies the "insertion of the new." Nevertheless, as a criterion for action, "newness" remains quasi-formal. It abstracts from the particular content or ends of a given form of political rule, and, in principle could be compatible with a wide variety of regimes.

Another consequence of Arendt's embrace of natality and newness is a corresponding devaluation of normal politics or political normalcy (such dismissal is one of the hallmarks of political existentialism). Action in Arendt's sense of the word strives after glory and distinction: "Action needs for its full appearance the shining brightness we once called glory."[20] As such, great individuals alone, and not the hoi polloi or common run of men and women, possess a true capacity for action. But, if this is true, then normal politics—grassroots organizing, voting, debating, deliberating, caucusing, not to mention the other aspects of collective will–formation that are characteristic of civil society—are relegated to the status of a second-order political good. They fall considerably short of Nietzsche's "great politics" or the agonistic struggle for glory that distinguished political life among the Greeks. Admittedly, there is little heroism involved in the day-to-day routine of parliamentary democracy.

To be sure, Arendt's critique of the routinized and bureaucratic nature of modern politics is extremely well placed. It is the one-sided nature of her argument, its either-or quality, that makes it so difficult to reconcile with the requirements of modern democratic practice. Her embrace of natality as a paramount political value threatens to consign all latecomers or subsequent political actors to the subaltern sphere of political everydayness or inauthenticity. This conclusion is driven home clearly in her discussion of the American Revolution, where the glory of the founding forms a pointed contrast with the dull familiarity of postrevolutionary, legislative business-as-usual.

Arendt's concerns with natality, founding, and newness come to a head in her valorization of revolution—one of the strangest features of a political thought that is so otherwise oriented to the values of the ancient polis. Needless to say, her partisanship for revolution is far from unqualified. In those cases where the political goals of revolution have been superseded by the needs of what Arendt calls the "life-process"—the locus classicus being the way in which the "social question" led to the French Revolution's Jacobin *virement* (turning)—the revolutionary process negates itself (similar criticisms of course could be made of the Russian Revolution).

Arendt values revolution insofar as it transcends political normalcy. Revolutions stand out as instances of "pure action"; they constitute an existential break with "governmentality," which she associates with the predictability and regimentation of the party system. As such, revolutions provide an eruption of the new amid the prose of the world. Within the framework of political existentialism and as a species of "great politics," revolutions embody a transposition of Kierkegaard's teleological suspension of the ethical from the moral to the political sphere. The air they breathe is that of a "boundary situation." Similarly, in the case of fellow political existentialist Carl Schmitt, great politics facilitates contact with "intensive life" (*intensives Leben*). It emerges only with a state of emergency (*Ausnahmezustand*), in which the values of political normalcy are suspended and, in Schmitt's words, "the power of real life breaks through the crust of a mechanism that has become torpid with repetition."[21]

For Arendt it is the fleeting glory of the revolutionary councils in St. Petersburg (1905), Munich (1918–19), and Budapest (1956) in which the values of revolutionary action were consummately realized. "Outstanding among the councils' common characteristics," states Arendt, was "the spontaneity of their coming into being." They represent in her view authentic "spaces of freedom."[22]

However, many commentators have found Arendt's support for council communism contradictory. For one, the councils themselves emerged directly from the European labor movement, the domain of the "life-process." As such, their concerns were both political and social. Yet it was precisely the social element, associated with the sphere of production, that Arendt always strove to keep at a distance from the political sphere.

Arendt's embrace of the direct democracy of council communism goes hand in hand with her critique of party politics. Ultimately, this critique develops into a denigration of representative democracy as such. According to Arendt, only interests can be "represented," never action. In order to be meaningful, action must be enacted directly by the actor, not by someone standing in for or representing him. Such thinking pushes Arendt toward the conclusion that representative democracy or the party system as such is constitutionally in-authentic on the basis of its ties to "society" or the sphere of "interests"— which in the last analysis are what is "represented." Thus, the domination of interests in a parliamentary setting is merely the reverse side of the wholesale inattention to action in Arendt's sense.

Lastly, the councils were fundamentally populist and egalitarian institu-tions, a fact difficult to reconcile with the elitist-aristocratic conception of action that Arendt elsewhere endorses so vigorously.

III

If we return to the concluding pages of *On Revolution*, the fundamentally aristocratic nature of Arendt's political predilections comes starkly into view. "The political way of life never has been and never will be the way of the many," she declares. The fallacy of the "democratic mentality of an egalitarian society," she continues, is that "it tends to deny the obvious inability and conspicuous lack of interest of large parts of the population in political matters as such."[23] The crisis of modern democracy cannot be explained by the fact that opportunities for participation and decision-making have been monopo-lized by a professional elite. It is not its oligarchical character per se—the fact that the many are ruled by a few—to which she objects. Instead, the dilemma of modern democracy may be attributed to the absence of public spaces "from which an elite could be selected, or rather, from which it could select itself."[24] Thus, in Arendt's view, contemporary democratic practice merely suffers from the fact that it is an "administrative elite" rather than a "glorious elite"—men and women capable of truly distinguishing themselves—that dominates. To-day, "authentically political talents can assert themselves only in rare cases," laments Arendt.[25]

In retrospect, then, council communism's chief merit was not that it was democratic, participatory, or truly egalitarian. Its real virtue lay in the fact that it proved an effective mechanism of selecting political elites—men and women capable of acting with distinction. The councils provided a space—a Heideg-gerian "Lichtung"—in which such leaders were able to emerge.

Such aperçus suggest that Arendt was a democrat only in a highly qualified sense of the term. Democracy's major advantage is that it offers a space where authentic political natures can attain their rightful positions of rule over the many—that is, over the greater mass of men and women who are politically "unmusical." The avowedly elitist character of Arendt's view of democracy are well captured in the following remarks from *On Revolution*. With the rule of a self-selected political elite, observes Arendt,

> the joys of public happiness and the responsibilities for public business would then become the share of those few from all walks of life who have a taste for public freedom and cannot be "happy" without it. Politically, they are the best, and it is the task of good government and the sign of a well-ordered republic to assure them of their rightful place in the public realm. To be sure, such an "aristocratic" form of government would spell the end of general suffrage as we understand it today; for only those who as voluntary members of an "elementary republic" have demonstrated that they care for more than their private happiness and are concerned about the state of the world would have the right to be heard in the conduct of business of the republic.

The exclusion of the many from politics, Arendt continues, would "give substance and reality to one of the most important negative liberties we have enjoyed since the end of the ancient world, namely, freedom from politics."[26]

We know that one of the keywords of Arendt's political lexicon is human plurality. Her use of this term derives from a democratic re-reading of Heideggerian "Being-with" (*Mitsein*) which, in *Being and Time*, tends to be discounted as pertaining to the sphere of the "they"; that is, the sphere of everydayness or inauthenticity.

Yet, as with Heidegger, for Arendt true human plurality ultimately applies solely to an elect: to those individuals who are capable of extraordinary or distinctive forms of political self-expression. Only such an elect proves capable of attaining the higher ontological plane of authentic human intersubjectivity or Being-with. Conversely, those who are politically less able and who remain absorbed in the mass, become ontologically deprived: in their separation from politics as sphere of authentic human action, they suffer in a highly literal sense from a "reality deficit"; they are atomized in a way that Arendt, following Tocqueville, claims is conducive to tyranny or, under modern conditions, totalitarianism. As Canovan has remarked: "Those who live their lives in this shadowy way without ever fully affirming their identity seem to include the vast majority of the human race."[27] Among their number Arendt explicitly includes, "the slave, the foreigner, and the barbarian in antiquity . . . the laborer, or craftsman prior to the modern age, the jobholder or businessman in our world."[28]

The risk entailed by Arendt's aristocratic doctrine of action is clear: that of regressing behind the fundamental precepts of modern egalitarianism, such as Kant's invaluable axiom concerning the intrinsic worth of all rational natures. With an aristocratic doctrine of human nature such as Arendt's, there is no way of avoiding the fact that certain natures are more worthy than others. Arendt remains a liberal as far as judicial or civil rights are concerned. She remains a believer in the virtues of rule of law, civil liberties, the constitutional state, and so forth. But as far as the rights of active citizenship or the question of political participation are concerned, her orientation proves to be frankly and disappointingly paternalistic.

IV

The Nietzschean, heroic-aristocratic basis of Arendt's theory of action becomes even more pronounced if we turn to an unpublished text from the early 1950s, "Karl Marx and the Tradition of Western Political Thought," one of the first sketches for *The Human Condition*. What is noteworthy about this work, delivered as a series of lectures at Princeton in 1953, is that it is not Periclean Athens that Arendt relies on for her model of action, but the Homeric age—the same era that Nietzsche in *The Genealogy of Morals* counterposes to the "Socratic decadence" of fourth-century Athens.

In Arendt's unpublished lecture, "action" emerges not with the polis, but with the Achaean institution of kingship that is celebrated in the Homeric epics. Homer's heroes, deprived of an afterlife, were driven by a quest for immortality or eternal glory in this life. Of course, their site of distinction was not political activity per se, but the accomplishment of great deeds in war. As Arendt observes critically with reference to fifth-century Athens: "pure action no longer had much place in the polis except in times of war."[29]

The last remark is surprising insofar as elsewhere Arendt denigrates violence as (1) destructive of both the public sphere and human plurality, the two essential preconditions of political life; and (2) the political equivalent of instrumental reason; hence, a form of "production" rather than "action," since violence usually aims at some concrete end or effect. But upon reviewing her text of 1953, we see that Arendt did not always hold such views. There she emphasizes that violence often plays an indispensable and positive role in the act of political founding, as one sees in the two myths associated with the founding of Rome: Romulus's slaying of Remus and Aeneas's conquest of the Italian tribes. In *On Revolution*, she also speaks positively about the constitutive role of violence in acts of political founding: "Only where change occurs in the sense of a new beginning, where violence is used to constitute an altogether different form of government, to bring about the formation of a new body politic, where the liberation from oppression aims at least at the constitution of freedom can we speak of revolution."[30]

The conclusion she arrives at in "Karl Marx and the Tradition of Western Political Thought" is that in the fifth century the Greek polis was already overpreoccupied with "social" concerns: with the biological sphere of "mere life" as contrasted with the "good life." Already, the focal point of Greek life had become the *oikos* rather than the *agora:* ruling slaves, the art of making money (*chrēmatistikē*), or the mundane tasks of political administration as a pendant to managing the *oikos*. Thus, Arendt concludes, in the polis action, in the sense of Homeric glory, played a negligible role: "The polis is where people *live* together, not act [*sic*]," observes Arendt. "This is the reason why action plays such a minor role in ancient philosophy which speaks out of the polis-experience."[31] And she goes on to lament the degeneration of heroic "deed" to "word" (the transition from Homer to Pericles, as it were) in the following terms: "*doxa* . . . becomes more and more an opinion by which the citizen distinguishes himself in the constant activity of *politeuesthai* [acting politically] and less the shining glory of immortal fame which may follow the great deed."[32] In the same manuscript, she bemoans the fact that, in ancient Athens, action was no longer equated with the doing of great deeds. Instead, it had decayed into the more ephemeral and transitory form of language or speech.

V

Some concluding remarks concerning the serviceability of Arendt's concept of action are in order. The paradigm of agon on which Arendt relies is devoid of altruism or fellow feeling. It seems incompatible with the values of solidarity that are essential to the normative concept of democratic citizenship. As one critic has noted, her dramaturgical model promotes a "politics of actors rather than citizens . . . agonistic rather than participatory, [it encourages] men to stand out rather than to take part in, to share."[33]

Her elitist denigration of the social too readily accepts the then fashionable Nietzschean-aristocratic criticism of "mass society." It thereby neglects one of the fundamental lessons of the study of social history: meaningful instances of expression, distinction, and even action are to be found on the level of everyday life in the nonpolitical spheres of culture, intimacy, and the workworld. Such instances should not be dismissed out of hand by virtue of a series of neoclassical conceptual prejudices that exalt the political and disparage the social.

Though one would like to enlist Arendt's support for the cause of modern democratic reform, her conception of democratic practice ultimately proves to be self-defeating. Since hers is a normative rather than an immanent critique of modern politics, the philhellenic value-orientation she employs to condemn the deficiencies of modern democracy is destined to remain without historical efficacy or impact. It is intellectually illuminating but politically inconsequential. Arendt defines the normative prerequisites of democratic practice so selectively and in such antiquarian fashion as virtually to rule out the prospect of their realization.

The contradictory nature of Arendt's conception of democracy is apparent both in her exclusion of all social concerns from modern politics (a neo-Aristotelian prejudice that remains significantly at odds with the structure of modern class societies) as well as her belated embrace of the council movement. Movements can only be institutionalized on pain of routinization, at which point they ipso facto leave behind their vitality.

Needless to say, there is still much one can learn from Arendt's rich and fascinating critique of modern society and its "action deficits." At the same time one must take into account the fact that our capacity to learn from her framework is circumscribed by definite limits. In many ways the limitations of her worldview are those of her generation: the Central European intelligentsia that came of age during the interwar period. The systematic misapprehension of the egalitarian demands of political modernity afflicts the outlook of an entire generation of intellectual peers: figures such as Carl Schmitt, Eric Voegelin, and Leo Strauss.

In sum: only once we begin to appreciate the analytical shortfalls of Arendt's political thought can we begin to do justice to the otherwise profound insights in her work that, as so many commentators have shown, are eminently worthy of redemption.

ANTIHUMANISM IN
THE DISCOURSE OF FRENCH
POSTWAR THEORY

Whether conducted in the name of a radiant future or a traditionalist reaction, the total critique of the modern world, because it is necessarily an antihumanism that leads inevitably to seeing in the democratic project, for example in human rights, the prototype of ideology or of metaphysical illusion, is structurally incapable of taking up . . . the promises that are also those of modernity.—L. Ferry and A. Renaut, *French Philosophy of the Sixties*

The War Has Taken Place

In a recent book on French intellectuals of the postwar period, the historian Tony Judt remarks on a long-standing "vacuum at the heart of public ethics in France," on "the marked absence of a concern with public ethics or political morality" characteristic of the French intelligentsia in our century.[1] Judt attempts to account for this ethical vacuum in terms of a French ambivalence vis-à-vis the values of liberal democracy; an ambivalence that culminated in the 1930s, when the Third Republic found itself under increasingly vigorous attack by those on both the left and the right, with few enthusiasts of republican values capable of holding the center together. After all, this was a regime that had endured sensational financial scandals, the shame of Munich, and that in 1936–37 had refused to aid the Republican cause in Spain. With the fall of France in 1940, many French men and women came to perceive Vichy as a welcome opportunity for a much-needed national renewal. It is important to recognize that for intellectuals on both the left and the right, the empirical shortcomings of the beleaguered French republic were treated as compelling evidence of the failure of democracy in principle. Moreover, this antidemocratic sentiment was not merely an ephemeral trend, but a defining feature of twentieth-century French political culture. In fact, the conviction among those on the left in France that democratic regimes are prone to dishonesty and betrayal has a pedigree of long standing: it harks back to the values of the French revolutionary tradition (1789, 1848, 1871) and the belief that prospects for a total, social revolution were on each occasion sold short by the bourgeois class. Thus, until quite recently one might say that democratic institutions bore the indelible taint of their bourgeois origins.

Judt's analysis is for the most part confined to the Stalinist misadventures of the existentialist thinkers who ruled the left bank of Paris in the decade and a half following World War II. Recently, some have suggested that an analogous ethical shortfall haunts the discourse of the critics of humanism who, in the 1960s and 1970s, succeeded the existentialists in the Parisian intellectual lime-light. Among their number, one would include structuralists such as Roland Barthes, Claude Lévi-Strauss, and Louis Althusser, the psychoanalyst Jacques Lacan, as well as their poststructuralist successors, Jacques Derrida, Michel Foucault, and Jean-François Lyotard. As Raymond Aron has observed: "the god of the intellectuals of the sixties was no longer the Sartre who had domi-nated the postwar period but a mixture of Lévi-Strauss, Foucault, Althusser, and Lacan."[2]

The Achilles heel of this later generation of French thinkers would not be an uncritical infatuation with Communism. These luminaries, perhaps having learned the unfortunate lesson of their predecessors, have (with the important exception of Foucault) tended to shy away from public political involvement or commentary. Nevertheless, it would be worth inquiring as to whether the aforementioned "vacuum at the heart of public ethics in France," which Judt perceives as endemic to the French political left, lives on today in the theoret-ically sublimated guise of philosophical antihumanism.

To be sure, antihumanism, as it came to prominence in French intellectual life in the 1950s and 1960s, had an ethical agenda to purvey. It sought to highlight the hypocrisy of traditional humanism, which, in the era of decolo-nization (Vietnam, Algeria, etc.), appeared to serve as the ideological window-dressing for the corruptions of the imperialist West. In fact, the true origins of antihumanist sentiment may be traced to an earlier point in French cultural life: to the surrealists, who enact a deconstruction *avant la lettre* of "man," subjectivity, reason, and so forth.[3] In its valorization of unconscious rather than conscious mental functioning, in Breton's original definition of surrealism as "pure psychic automatism . . . , the dictation of thought in the absence of any control exercised by reason,"[4] in its revolutionary iconographic emphasis on bodily *membra disjecta* (often quite sexist), surrealism sought to expose and renounce the inadequacy of the post-Enlightenment conception of "man." The case of surrealism demonstrates quite effectively the impact that the traumas of the Great War had upon the self-confidence of European humanity.

By the 1960s, the embrace of "philosophical antihumanism" had become a type of litmus test for the post-Marxist French left. Yet, as pertinent and cogent as this rejection of humanism may have seemed at the time, in ensuing decades, some of the limitations of this obligatory gesture of intellectual radicalism came into view. Ironically, by the 1970s it seemed that the critique of humanism had itself become ideological. Owing to the worldwide persistence of totalitarian regimes on both the left and the right, torture, and the systematic violation of human rights, a recovery of "humanism"—the belief in the intrinsic, inviolable worth of all persons—in some form appeared indispensable. Increasingly, there seemed to be an unbridgeable gap between the imperative political needs of the day, which revolved around a civil libertarian politics of human rights, and the standpoint of philosophical antihumanism.

After all, this was a decade that had witnessed the signing of the Helsinki accords, the coming to world prominence of Amnesty International, and the devastating revelations of Solzhenitsyn's *Gulag Archipelago*. The "imperialists" had been defeated in Southeast Asia. But the tyrannical nature of those communist regimes that had supplanted the pro-Western puppet governments was undeniable. Fearing communist reprisals, refugees, euphemistically known as "boat people," pitifully poured forth from the coasts of Vietnam. And the Khmer Rouge, led by a coterie of homicidal Maoists (who had, not coincidentally, been educated at the finest Parisian universities), visited a holocaust upon some two million of the "politically incorrect" among their own people. Once again, the world's heart bled for the—newly communized—inhabitants of Southeast Asia. As a fitting end to a decade of communist excess, the world's oldest and most powerful Marxist regime summarily invaded a near defenseless Afghanistan.

The ethical implications of this sorry train of events seemed clear: a revival of humanistic discourse became an unequivocal political imperative. Hence, when viewed in terms of the foregoing historical chronology, the radical critique of humanism—a unifying theme of the French intellectual avant-garde of the 1950s and 1960s—could not but seem excessive. At the very least, it seemed out of place given the changed political temperament of the late 1970s and early 1980s. It was as though French cultural radicalism, in its rush to condemn the sins at home, had rashly overshot the object of its criticism.

One of the few genuinely political corollaries of the antihumanist position had been a militant third-worldism. Third World revolutions—in China, Cuba, Africa, South America, and even Iran—were romantically viewed as the "other" of the exploitative capitalist metropoles.[5] Yet, by the end of the 1970s, the force of historical circumstances proved that this position, too, was untenable. In view of the retrograde state of civil rights and liberties in the revolutionary regimes, many came to view Eurocentric standards of justice with considerably less cynicism.

In what follows, I shall be more concerned with the intellectual history of postwar France than with its political history. I have begun with a brief sketch of the latter since it forms the indispensable subtext for understanding the twists and turns of French theory in the postwar years. However, what is, in a Foucauldian spirit, really needed is a "genealogy" of French intellectual politics of the period; a genealogy that can account for why philosophical antihumanism could present itself as a redoubtable theoretical option—to the point where, in the course of a decade (1955–65), it was able to vanquish the other dominant positions from the intellectual field.[6]

To explain these developments, one must address a peculiar confluence of philosophical positions that, beginning in the mid-1950s, united to overthrow the reigning intellectual paradigm of the preceding decade: the paradigm of existential Marxism, which claimed to be the rightful heir to the legacy of Western humanism in the same way that Marx and Engels had spoken of the proletariat as the heir to German classical philosophy. What one discovers is that the influences of (1) the later Heidegger, (2) structuralism and structural anthropology, (3) semiology and linguistics and, later, (4) poststructuralism had combined to form, as it were, an epistemological united front whose main object was to have quit with "man," the subject of traditional humanism.

The specific goal of my inquiry, therefore, is to account for a peculiar conjuncture in French intellectual life whereby three theoretical currents—Heideggerianism, structuralism, and poststructuralism—enter into alliance to render antihumanism the culturally dominant intellectual paradigm for a period of nearly two decades.

The French Heidegger Revival

Certainly one of the more baffling developments of modern European intellectual history concerns the rebirth of Heideggerianism in postwar France, at a time when the philosopher's career in Germany had reached its nadir. In 1946 Heidegger was dismissed from his position at the University of Freiburg for having, in the words of a university denazification commission, "in the fateful year of 1933 consciously placed the great prestige of his scholarly reputation . . . in the service of the National Socialist Revolution, thereby [making] an essential contribution to the legitimation of this revolution in the eyes of educated Germans."[7] In the aftermath of the university commission's stern findings, Heidegger suffered a nervous breakdown that required two months of hospitalization. He was only reinstated some five years later, at a time when the political situation in Germany had stabilized.

We now know that, in the aftermath of this setback, Heidegger consciously set out to find among a French philosophical public the vindication that had been denied him in his own country. The first gambit in this strategy of rehabilitation was the publication of his 1947 "Letter on Humanism." This text was a fifty-page response to an epistolary inquiry by the French philosopher Jean Beaufret. Beaufret's two essential questions concerned: (1) a clarification of the relationship between fundamental ontology and "ethics"; and (2) the contemporary prospects for revivifying the concept of "humanism."[8]

Heidegger, refusing to deviate from the position he had established at the time of the publication of *Being and Time* (1927), argued that ontology—the "question of Being"—had rendered an independent ethical theory superfluous. Every attempt to formulate an ethics, he explained, risked "elevating man to the center of beings."[9] In this respect, such attempts courted the dangers of a relapse into an anthropocentric mode of philosophical questioning. For Heidegger, such subject-centered approaches to philosophy represented the essence of the traditional metaphysics from which the Freiburg sage had desperately sought to free himself (especially in the later philosophy; and here, the "Letter" constitutes an ideal instance).

To Beaufret's other query concerning the contemporary status of "humanism"—How can we restore meaning to the word "humanism"?—Heidegger responds: "I wonder whether that is necessary." A restoration of humanism similarly risked succumbing to the fatal lures of "metaphysical subjectivism."

In his response to this question, Heidegger also took the occasion to differentiate his philosophy of Being from the existentialism of Jean-Paul Sartre. This move was a strategic imperative given the considerable prominence Sartrean existentialism had come to enjoy after the war. Moreover, Sartre had just come out with the short, but highly influential, existentialist primer, "Existentialism is a Humanism."[10] The painstaking detail of Heidegger's "Letter" allowed him to put to rest all doubts that there might exist significant affinities between the two variants of *Existenzphilosophie*.

In "Existentialism is a Humanism," Sartre had maintained: "We are precisely in a situation where there are only human beings"; a statement that in many ways merely echoed his well-known characterization of existentialism in terms of the priority of "existence" over "essence." In the "Letter on Humanism," conversely, Heidegger claims the direct obverse: "We are precisely in a situation where principally there is Being."[11]

To be sure, the reversal (*Kehre*) of the relationship between "Being" and "human being" that Heidegger sought to effect was critically motivated. Heidegger himself had become convinced that the "planetary" devastation of the Second World War was of metaphysical provenance: it was a direct result of the philosophical paradigm of "metaphysical subjectivism" or the "will to will," which, from Descartes to Nietzsche, had singularly determined the manner in which "man" allows "beings" to "come to presence" in the modern world. The terrible consequence of this mode of disclosing the world, according to Heidegger, was a frenzy of technological nihilism, whose catastrophic results were transparent for all to see. Thus, to criticize this paradigm, to advocate its reversal, was crucial in reestablishing a radically different, more harmonious relationship between "man" and "Being."

There are other fascinating "strategic" aspects of Heidegger's text. Although to discuss them fully would take us far afield from the inquiry at hand, it should at least be noted that the "Letter" includes uncharacteristically rhapsodic discussions of both Marxism and the Soviet Union. With reference to the author of *Das Kapital,* Heidegger at one point observes: "Because Marx by experiencing estrangement attains an essential dimension of history, the Marxist view of history is superior to that of other historical accounts." The "inferior" views of history he goes on to reject are those of Husserl and Sartre, neither of which, according to Heidegger, "recognizes the importance of the historical in Being."[12] With respect to the "doctrines of Communism," Heidegger goes out of his way to note: "from the point of view of the history of Being it is certain that an elemental experience of what is world-historical speaks out in it."[13]

These peculiar asides can be explained in terms of the precariousness of the current world-political situation. The cold war had begun, but at this point no one knew which camp would triumph. Heidegger had already been mistreated by the occupying French troops: classifying him as a "Nazi-typique," they had proceeded to confiscate his house as well as his invaluable personal library. Clearly, Heidegger did not wish to burn his bridges to the other side, just in case.[14] Moreover, as Anson Rabinbach has pointed out, the precise fate of Heidegger's two sons, who were reported as "missing" on the eastern front, was still very much uncertain.[15] The favorable allusions to Marxism and Communism in this dense philosophical text, therefore, can only be explained as a result of a number of pressing circumstantial concerns.

Yet, because in the "Letter" the relationship between the ends of "humanity" and those of "Being" are so prejudicially formulated, a fatal precedent was established for postwar French thought. It is safe to say that Heidegger drew the wrong conclusions from his involvement with Nazism in the 1930s. Instead of rejecting a specific type of politics—namely, the politics of totalitarianism that had led to the "German catastrophe" of 1933–45—the later Heidegger appeared to reject human "praxis" in toto. From the ethereal standpoint of his later philosophy of Being, there were no "essential" differences between Communism, fascism, and world democracy. All three were "essentially" equivalent insofar as all three represented instances of technological nihilism. As he remarks in 1945: "Today everything stands under this reality, whether it is called Communism, fascism, or world democracy."[16]

In the philosophy of the early Heidegger, *Dasein* or human reality played an essential role in the disclosure of Being. As he remarks in *Being and Time:* "Only so long as *Dasein is*—that is, the ontic possibility of the understanding of Being—'is there' Being."[17] In the later Heidegger, however, it is as if humanity itself comes to represent little more than an impediment to the quasi-holy "sendings" (*Schickungen*) of Being. And thus, in the Nietzsche lectures, Heidegger affirms that the "essence of nihilism is not at all the affair of man, but a matter of Being itself";[18] and that "The History of Being is neither the history of man and of humanity, nor the history of human relation to beings and to Being. The history of Being is Being itself, and only Being."[19] In "Overcoming Metaphysics" (1946), Heidegger delivers, as it were, a final indictment of the possibilities of meaningful human action in the world: "No mere action will change the state of the world, because Being as effectiveness and effecting [*Wirksamkeit und Wirken*] closes all beings off in the face of the Event [*das Ereignis*]."[20] And if we return to the 1947 "Letter on Humanism," we find the following specification of the relationship between "Being" and "man": "Man does not decide whether and how beings appear, whether and how God and the gods or history and nature come forward into the lighting of Being, come to presence and depart. *The advent of beings lies in the destiny of Being. . . .* Man is the shepherd of Being."[21]

The foregoing depictions of the possibilities for human action in the world come to a point in Heidegger's 1966 *Spiegel* interview. In Heidegger's view, so forlorn and remote are the prospects of human betterment in the here and now that "only a god can save us!"[22]

The full story of the reception of Heidegger's thought in postwar France merits independent treatment. In the context at hand (that is, with a view to understanding its impact on French antihumanism) I provide only the main outlines. It is important to note that Heidegger's main champion in France, Jean Beaufret—the addressee of the "Letter"—was both an ex-*résistant* and a Marxist. For Heidegger, it was Beaufret's status as a *résistant* that was crucial: it functioned as an important prophylactic against attempts to link him or his thought in the *après guerre* with Nazism. At the same time, it is less obvious what Beaufret the Marxist, saw of value in the later Heidegger's philosophy of Being.

The answer pertains to the intellectual politics of the period. This was the era of existentialism's great vogue. The names of Sartre, de Beauvoir, Merleau-Ponty, and Camus (who in the late 1940s had not yet broken with Sartre) were on everyone's lips. With his novellas and short stories of the prewar period (e.g., *Nausea* and "The Wall") Sartre had established himself as a littérateur of the highest order. Yet, by the *après guerre*, he had risen to become France's most celebrated philosopher, one of the nation's leading dramatists and political commentators, as well as the founding editor of one of the world's most prestigious intellectual organs, *Les Temps modernes*.[23] One of the primary tasks of the *marxisant* intellectuals of the period, therefore, was to put a damper on this rising tide of existential humanism as purveyed by Sartre and company, which was viewed as a direct philosophical challenge to the worldview of dialectical materialism.

Enter Beaufret as champion of the later Heidegger. Insofar as the ex-*résistant* was able to show that, as a philosopher of existentialism, Sartre was essentially an impostor—that is, that his "existential humanism" had virtually nothing to do with the real item—Beaufret believed he possessed the theoretical leverage necessary to disqualify the formidable humanistic challenge to Communism posed by Sartre and his disciples. Thus, Beaufret was able to invoke Heidegger's "Letter" (which, as we have seen, amounted to an extensive denigration of Sartre's position on the relation between humanism and existentialism) as evidence to unmask the inauthenticity of Sartre's philosophical credentials.

Moreover, as Rabinbach points out, "what led Beaufret to Heidegger [was] his essentially correct intuition that the perspective of a history of Being *ipso facto* sanctions not merely violence and 'resolve' in the face of 'nihilism,' but Marxism's account of the violence of human history."[24] That is, there existed significant intellectual affinities between Marxism and the Heideggerian "history of Being" insofar as both doctrines displayed an a priori mistrust of Western humanism. The thinking of Marx and Heidegger thus converged in the conviction that humanism merely provided a veil of ideological respectability for the exploitation and mass conformity characteristic of bourgeois society. By virtue of the calculated paeans to the virtues of Marxism that Heidegger sprinkled throughout his influential 1947 "epistle," he had managed to meet Beaufret halfway, as it were. Even though Heidegger himself remained a virulent anti-Communist after the war,[25] his remarks about Marx in the "Letter," coupled with his devastating critique of the "planetary" dominance of modern technology (*das Gestell*), made his thought *salonfähig* for an entire generation of French left-wing intellectuals—to the point where one would be justified in speaking of a "left Heideggerianism."

Heidegger's "Letter" became one of the foundational texts for French postwar theoretical discourse. In a large measure it came to occupy this niche of honor owing to its exemplary articulation of the position of philosophical antihumanism. As Vincent Descombes remarks, "After Heidegger's intervention [in the "Letter on Humanism"], the word 'humanism' ceased to be the flag which it had been such a point of honor to defend." He continues: "Marxists condemning the bourgeois ideology of 'Man'; Nietzscheans despising the doctrine of resentment born in the spent intelligence of the 'last man'; structuralists of a purist persuasion announcing with Lévi-Strauss the program of the 'dissolution of man'—all these contended with one another in their antihumanism. 'Humanist' became a term of ridicule, an abusive epithet to be entered among the collection of derided 'isms' (vitalism, spiritualism, etc.)."[26]

Yet, the question remains: can one recoup a notion of moral responsibility once the capacities of human agency are so thoroughly denigrated as a species of "metaphysical illusion"?

Lacan and Lévi-Strauss

Freud had taken pride in the fact that, following Copernicus and Darwin, psychoanalysis had delivered a third major blow to the delusions of human narcissism. The theory of the unconscious demonstrated that "man" was not even master in his own house, the human psyche. Thus, one could understand conscious thought as an expression of "symptom formation," as something that was fully determined rather than determining. The surrealists treated his emphasis on the unconscious and dreams as breakthroughs of landmark intellectual significance—though Freud himself pointedly failed to reciprocate their admiration for his work.[27] For them, this emphasis signified a crucial displacement of the premium modern civilization had placed on the values of rational subjectivity. All in all, Freud's discovery of the unconscious would be vital for the temperament of French intellectual life in the post–World War II period. It harmonized well with the anti-Cartesian spirit, with the structuralist distinction between manifest and latent elements, and, more generally, with the idea that mental phenomena were constituted rather than constituting.

In the domain of psychoanalytic theory proper, it was Jacques Lacan who would draw the radical consequences of the Freudian theory of the unconscious. Despite Lacan's own self-understanding as someone intent on facilitating a "return to Freud," it was a "return" that would render a number of Freud's original intentions unrecognizable.[28] Freud, as a proponent of self-enlightenment, argued that the goal of analysis was to "transform what had become unconscious, what had been repressed, into preconsciousness in order to return it to the Ego"; or, in a famous definition of the analytic method, "where id was, there ego shall be."[29] It is precisely this moment of a "return to the ego," which had been gaining ascendance in both the French and American interpretations of Freud, that Lacan vigorously contested.[30]

Lacan would combine (1) the Heideggerian critique of the transcendental ego, (2) the structuralist doctrine of the relation of *langue* and *parole*, and (3) the Freudian critique of consciousness. He viewed Heidegger and Freud as complementary: both had insisted that the "I" was first and foremost an embodied "I"; the "subject" possessed an elaborate somatic-ontogenetic history before it emerged as a self in its own right. That which appeared primary according to the tradition of post-Cartesian metaphysics—*res cogitans* or thinking substance—was in fact entirely derivative.

But at least as important for Lacan's enormously influential recasting of psychoanalytic theory was his encounter with the semiology of Ferdinand de Saussure. In his *Course in General Linguistics* Saussure had coined the famous distinction between *langue* and *parole*. It was an opposition that would become a signature for all subsequent structural analysis, from Barthes, to Lévi-Strauss, and even for the "episteme" of Foucault. The notion of *langue* emphasized the importance of language as a differential system. Language may be described as a differential system inasmuch as words stand in relation to each other by virtue of their differences. That in language words refer primarily to other words rather than to things in the world may be treated as one of Saussure's revolutionary contributions to linguistic theory. Moreover, though Saussure himself harbored few metaphysical aspirations, the philosophical import of such claims was potentially enormous. His observations tended to minimize the importance of the manifest dimension of speech or utterances—that of *parole*—and stress the priority of language qua system or *langue*. This meant that even first philosophy could be subjected to a structural linguistic analysis, implying that its claims to primacy, its self-understanding as a *fundamentum inconcussum*, were inherently dubious. The latent character of language as differential system thereby took precedence over the manifest content of utterances—even philosophical utterances. Because language was the medium of metaphysics, the latter was subject to all the vicissitudes and constraints of language.

The claim that, within language, words refer primarily to other words rather than to things in the world was of far-ranging philosophical significance. It virtually spelled the death of all claims to metaphysical realism. If the alleged purity of language's referential or denominative function were called into question, then in what way could philosophy or science be said to provide us with truthful statements about the world? Moreover, one of Saussure's best-known claims concerns the *arbitrariness of the sign*, which serves to highlight the wholly contingent, non-necessary relation between the signifiers we employ and the objects they are intended to designate. Both Western science and metaphysics were predicated on a correspondence theory of truth, on an *adaequatio intellectus et rei*. But structural linguistics, as elaborated by Saussure and others, dealt a serious blow to the very possibility of a correspondence theory of knowledge as it had been traditionally formulated. It would be a very short step from Saussure's view of language as differential system to the critique of metaphysics embodied in Derridean *différance*.

Lacan came to view Saussure as an essential ally in the struggle initiated by Freud to decenter the idea of a consciousness fully present to itself. From Saussure he would derive the idea that "the unconscious is structured like a language"; that is, distinguished by the same order of differential signification characteristic of Saussure's *langue*. Here, Lacan explicitly followed the lead of Lévi-Strauss who, in *The Elementary Structures of Kinship* (1949), had put the precepts of structural linguistics to such productive use in his analysis of kinship and myth. Lacan's notion of the "symbolic," which designates the passage of the narcissistic, presocialized ego to the realm of language, also constitutes an essential Saussurian inheritance. Yet, the order of language that Lacan invokes is neither a realm of intentional linguistic expression, nor is it "hermeneutic." Instead, it is a structural order in which the intentionality of linguistic meaning has been fully displaced by a more primordial order of signification—language as differential system—that precedes the operations of conscious thought.

In Lacan's view of mental topography, prior to the symbolic sphere there exists the realm of the imaginary. It is through the use of this concept that Lacan effects his assault on the prejudices of ego-psychology—and, by association, those of the philosophy of consciousness in general. Insofar as it is a product of the imaginary, the self as ego is a necessary fiction or illusion: "The ego we are discussing is absolutely impossible to distinguish from the imaginary inveiglings that constitute it from head to foot," remarks Lacan.[31] If the unconscious is structured like a language, then the self is essentially an effect of language, an epiphenomenal result of the play of signification. Under the twin influences of Lévi-Strauss's structural anthropology and semiotic linguistics,

Lacan's research program would undergo a major shift. Circa 1953 he would abandon the quasi-existential humanist vocabulary of his earlier writings. Instead, the new emphasis on his thought would be "on the extent to which the human subject is irredeemably fractured, decentered, condemned to a permanent dispossession of self."[32] In his 1953–54 seminar on the ego he has recourse to Rimbaud's famous bon mot, "Je est un autre" ("I is another"—"poets, as is well known, don't know what they're saying, yet they still manage to say things before anyone else") to dramatize the radical displacement of the I he is seeking to effect.[33]

Lacan's characterization of the ego as indistinguishable from the imaginary carries with it profound prescriptive as well descriptive implications. And from this perspective one can easily see how central are his contributions to the poststructuralist critique of subjectivity, consciousness, "man," and so forth. Insofar as the coherent self, as artificial construct of the imaginary, is an illusion, it also proves distortional vis-à-vis more fundamental, tenebrous aspects of the self that have been repressed for the sake attaining this condition of spurious unity. Fundamentally, it has amputated everything that is nonego: the unconscious, the body, and the id. In Lacan's view, the self as dominated by the ego is essentially a reification; it has turned into something inflexible and rigid, a thing. In his seminar on the ego, he goes so far as to refer it as "the human symptom par excellence."[34] The goal of analysis, therefore, cannot be to strengthen the ego at the expense of the other components of mental functioning, the superego and the id, as Freud seems to recommend. Instead, analysis must attempt, as it were, to *deconstruct* the ego, to weaken its tyrannical sovereignty, in order to allow those repressed aspects of psychic existence to undo the repressions they have endured since the onset of the "mirror stage," when the "imaginary" first takes hold.[35] What Lacan accomplished in a French intellectual context was to have turned Freud's discovery of the unconscious against the master, thereby making him one of the foremost critics of humanism.

Thus, for Lacan, "The unconscious completely eludes the circle of certainties by which man constitutes himself as ego."[36] This claim has major repercussions for a theory of the subjectivity. Once the ego is radically displaced—for Lacan it appears as figment of alienation *simpliciter* and, as such, needs to be unmade or undone—it is the unconscious that stands revealed as the "true" subject.

One of the fundamental premises of modern humanism that Lacan radically calls into question is that individuals have the capacity to function as the subjects or authors of their own acts. He observes that, "The subject does not know what he is saying, and for the best reasons—because he does not know what he is."[37] In Lacan's view, whereas Hegel's thought and that of his French heirs remain mired in anthropology, the discourse of "man," "Freud has gone beyond it. His discovery is that man is not entirely within man; Freud is not a humanist."[38] Since the self can never be anything other than a patchwork of artificial, linguistic constructs that serve to cover up and distort the unconscious (for Lacan, the "true" subject, which is unattainable as such; any attempt to reach it is of necessity mediated by language qua falsifying medium of representation), the scientifically honest approach to subjectivity would be to embrace its primordial fragmentation. According to Whitebook, in Lacan, "The standpoint of the ego is not simply a 'mistake' or a 'partial point of view' which can be corrected or expanded, but must be circumvented or abandoned in toto if the truth of the unconscious subject (whatever that might mean) is to be attained."[39] In Lacan's view, the ego is purely and simply the equivalent of *méconnaissance*, a failure to recognize. "What Freud introduced from 1920 [*Beyond the Pleasure Principle*] on are additional notions which were at that time necessary to maintain the principle of the decentering of the subject."[40] It is of course in *Beyond the Pleasure Principle* that Freud introduces the death instinct, a notion that Lacan views as absolutely incompatible with the superficial claims concerning the transparency of the I advanced by ego psychology.

Nevertheless, one can easily reverse the terms on Lacan and say that he has merely substituted a substantialist concept of the unconscious (the "true subject") in place of the substantialist view of the ego he is trying to surmount.

A decade later, poststructuralism would, in vintage Heideggerianism fashion, make provocative use of the Lacanian critique of the subject by linking its reign to the dominion of a technological nihilism that stifles the proliferation of otherness, heterogeneity, and "free play." According to this reading, the tragedy of Western culture lies in the predominance of a rational consciousness that is intrinsically hostile to difference. In this way poststructuralism would seek to thematize the integral relation between "violence" and "metaphysics" that is key to the work of Emmanuel Levinas.[41] In this view, metaphysics cannot but enframe the world in other than "violent" fashion, insofar as objects can only become meaningful to it as raw material for a imperious and manipulative (Cartesian) subject; that is to say (to return to Lacan), *narcissistically:* "When the narcissistic ego constitutes the object in its own image—'egomorphically'— its orthopedic rigidity is conferred on the object; this reified object becomes an object of possible technical manipulation."[42]

Another major blow to the status of humanism was delivered by the structural anthropology of Claude Lévi-Strauss. By replacing the categories of historical agency and transcendental subjectivity with the concept of "structure," Lévi-

Strauss succeeded in displacing "man" from the center of the human sciences. As a result, philosophers came to applaud his work as an essential social scientific complement to Heidegger's antihumanism.[43]

Like all French structuralists, Lévi-Strauss builds on the linguistic insights of Saussure.[44] Here, Saussure's insistence on the priority of *langue* over *parole*— the view of language as a predefined network of structural coordinates that for their part determine individual utterances—would prove central. Lévi-Strauss takes over directly Saussure's emphasis on the primacy of *langue* as "code" and attempts to establish structural anthropology on this basis. In structural linguistics as well as structural anthropology, the code performs essentially the same function: "it is the rule that must be obeyed if messages are to be produced or received."[45] The code becomes a type of transcendental ground of signification, the "condition of possibility" for the circulation of meaning. In this respect, structuralism purveys something like a "Kantianism without a transcendental subject."[46]

With the structural anthropology of Lévi-Strauss, the science of "man" has been dehistoricized. He rigorously turns his back on the premises of both nineteenth-century historicism and evolutionary theory. "Man" ceases to be the "subject" of his own history and historical change is deemed the realm of the ephemeral, the epiphenomenal. Instead, amid the diversity of historical flux, anthropology's task is to seek out those structural invariants—the "universal code"—that define human culture wherever and whenever it is to be found. In Lévi-Strauss's words: "The analysis of different aspects of social life will have to be pursued until it . . . elaborates a kind of universal code capable of expressing the properties common to the specific structures arising from each aspect."[47] He thereby suggests that "all forms of social life are substantially of the same nature"; "they consist of systems of behavior that represent the projection, on the level of conscious and socialized thought, of universal laws which regulate the unconscious activities of the mind."[48]

It is not difficult to appreciate the polemical relation in which Lévi-Strauss's theories stand vis-à-vis the previously dominant intellectual paradigm, existential humanism. By virtue of his avowal that "structures," rather than human will and consciousness, are the fundamental determinants of cultural life, his thought became one of the linchpins of theoretical antihumanism. More than any other approach, structural anthropology appeared to deliver the coup de grâce to the narcissism of the Sartrean "Pour-Soi"; above all, to its delusions of unconditional, transcendental freedom.

Moreover, Sartre's subsequent attempt to combine existentialism with Marxism aimed at nothing less, it seemed, than a *humanization* of human history writ large. In his desire to subjugate the laws of history to the laws of human freedom, he sought, as it were, to subsume the phenomenal under the noumenal, and thereby to effectuate a *Kantianization* of history.

It was the work of Lévi-Strauss that, more than any other, challenged the influence of this humanist paradigm of self-realizing subjectivity. It represented another essential moment in the process whereby the autonomy of philosophy (the legacy of Descartes, as it were) was challenged by the empirical findings from the human sciences. As Lévi-Strauss remarks in his critique of Sartre's existential Marxism: "Sartre in fact becomes a prisoner of his Cogito: Descartes made it possible to attain universality, but conditionally on remaining psychological and individual; by sociologizing the Cogito, Sartre merely exchanges one prison for another."[49]

In his celebrated scientific autobiography, *Tristes Tropiques* (1955), Lévi-Strauss provided an influential narrative concerning his youthful frustrations with the aridity of philosophical study. Commenting on the disproportionate emphasis on "method" in French philosophy, he remarked: "I was confident that, at ten minutes' notice, I could knock together an hour's lecture with a sound dialectical framework on the respective superiority of buses and trams. Not only does this method provide a key to open any lock; it also leads one to suppose that the rich possibilities of thought can be reduced to a single, always identical pattern, at the cost of a few rudimentary adjustments." In sum: "our philosophical training exercised the intelligence but had a desiccating effect on the mind [*l'esprit*]."[50]

His comments concerning Sartrian existentialism are predictably harsh:

As for the intellectual movement which was to reach its peak in existentialism, it seemed to me to be anything but a legitimate form of reflection, because of its overindulgent attitude towards the illusions of subjectivity. The raising of personal preoccupations to the dignity of philosophical problems is far too likely to lead to a sort of shop-girl metaphysics, which may be pardonable as a didactic method but is extremely dangerous if it allows people to play fast-and-loose with the mission incumbent on philosophy until science becomes strong enough to replace it: that is, to understand being in relationship to itself and not in relationship to myself. Instead of doing away with metaphysics, phenomenology and existentialism introduced two methods of providing it with alibis.[51]

From a structuralist perspective, existential Marxism, as an ideology of social change, was little more than a species of modern mythology. Nor, according to Lévi-Strauss's strict antievolutionism, was modern science more intel-

lectually sophisticated or complex than so-called primitive systems of classification. In his view: "This thirst for objective knowledge is one of the most
neglected aspects of the thought of people we call 'primitive.' Even if it is rarely
directed towards facts of the same level as those with which modern science is
concerned, it implies comparable intellectual application and methods of observation. . . . Every civilization tends to overestimate the objective orientation
of its thought."[52]

Thus, in his discussion of Sartre's *Critique of Dialectical Reason*, Lévi-
Strauss contends that the philosopher's treatment of the "practico-inert"
(brute matter that proves unassimilable to the syntheses of socialized humanity) merely represents the "language of animism" redivivus. There is little
difference, he observes, between the conceptual oppositions in Sartre's work
and those "formulated by a Melanesian savage." In essence, "Sartre's view of
the world and man has the narrowness which has been traditionally credited to
closed societies." Insofar as "all these aspects of the savage mind can be discovered in Sartre's philosophy, that the latter is in my view unqualified to pass
judgment on it: he is prevented from doing so by the very fact of furnishing its
equivalent. To the anthropologist, on the contrary, this philosophy (like all the
others) affords a first-class ethnographic document, the study of which is
essential to an understanding of the mythology of our own time."[53] According
to the precepts of structural analysis, therefore, whereas the *manifest content* of
systems of cultural belief (in semiotic terms, the dimension of the *signified*) vary
historically, the *latent content,* as defined by a universal cultural code, remains
essentially the same. Hence, in the last analysis, "dialectics" proves to be
merely another mechanism of cultural classification; one that possesses no
greater claim to "rationality" than any of the systems that have preceded it.
The object of Marxist humanism, the rational totalization of human history, is
in Lévi-Strauss's view chimerical; "a conscious being aware of itself as such
poses a problem to which it provides no solution."[54] Or, to paraphrase a similar
insight of modern hermeneutics (which is also suspicious of the totalizing
claims of human reason): "historically effective consciousness is always more
being than consciousness."[55]

The paradigm of existential humanism neglects a fundamental fact of human cultural life: that "[man's] discourse never was and never will be the result
of a conscious totalization of linguistic laws." Indeed, the fundamental laws of
semiotics—the priority of the signifier over the signified, of *langue* over *parole,*
of synchrony over diachrony—ensure that this will be true throughout the
whole of human history. Thus, as Lévi-Strauss concludes: "Linguistics thus
presents us with a dialectical and totalizing entity but one outside (or beneath)

consciousness and will. Language, an unreflecting totalization, is human reason which has its reasons and of which man knows nothing."[56]

Of course, to concede that Lévi-Strauss had succeeded in exposing many of the weaknesses of Sartre's position does not mean that the structuralist understanding of human culture is unimpugnable. The unyielding emphasis on "synchrony" over "diachrony"—an inheritance of structural linguistics—allows Lévi-Strauss summarily to write off the domain of history as a realm of epiphenomenal and inessential *événements*. If structural relations are, as he contends, all-determining and "universal," then the events of world history can never be more than "a tale told by an idiot," akin to the shadows on the wall of Plato's cave.

In sum, if Sartre systematically overvalues the categories of human intentionality, consciousness, and will (a phenomenological inheritance), Lévi-Strauss, conversely, consistently underestimates their importance. In this respect the contentious debate between Lévi-Strauss and Sartre over the respective merits of "history" and "structure" is representative of the methodological antinomies afflicting French intellectual life in the postwar era. Above all it indicates the widening gulf between philosophy and the human sciences. Neither approach taken by itself offers an adequate (i.e., balanced) portrait of the interplay between freedom and necessity in history. One characterizes humanity's lot deterministically as totally conditioned. The other characterizes it voluntaristically as open to total change by the powers of human will. Neither understands that history is the realm in which the weight of the past establishes specific parameters—which should not be confused with insuperable ontological limits—in which freedom or meaningful historical change can be actualized. To paraphrase Theodor Adorno: the two positions represent "torn halves of an integral freedom to which, however, they do not add up."[57]

The fundamental shortcoming of structural anthropology (and, implicitly, *all* structuralism) is that it systematically denigrates both the possibility and reality of meaningful historical change. Feudalism or parliamentarianism, Kwaikutl religion or modern science, Communism or capitalism—when viewed structurally, the foregoing pairs are essentially the same. The valorization of synchrony at the expense of diachrony ultimately proves prejudicial: the structuralist's antihistoricism is so pronounced that all prospects of incremental human betterment are a priori ruled out. According to this interpretive schema, the most one can hope for is an extremely modest piece of self-knowledge. Thus, in the words of Lévi-Strauss: "man will have gained all he can reasonably hope for if, on the sole condition of bowing to this contingent law [of structural causality], he succeeds in determining his form of conduct and in placing all else in the realm of the intelligible."[58] As for the later Hegel, for Lévi-Strauss, "freedom," resignedly, means ceding to the ontological primacy of necessity.

Because of their aversion to categories of human meaning and historicity, structuralism and poststructuralism have often met with the charge of nihilism. Of course, it is their claim that it is the old rhetoric of humanism that is itself nihilistic; that the legacy of disaster wrought by twentieth-century European history is directly traceable to an inflated, uncritical celebration of occidental humanity; an attitude, that moreover, is inherently insensitive vis-à-vis the cultural specificity of nonoccidental peoples. These are premises worthy of investigation. But they cannot be merely assumed. They would have to be verified or substantiated empirically. They cannot have the status (as often seems the case, for example, with Heidegger) of a "transcendental deduction," whereby metaphysics, humanism, technology, and nihilism become a priori mutually exchangeable terms.[59]

Moreover, the criticism of "nihilism" cannot simply be parried à la Nietzsche by variants of tu quoque reasoning ("it is the humanists who are the true nihilists, not us"). Instead, it must be convincingly disproved. Otherwise, the thoroughgoing critique of agency, "man," and history will appear unable to escape the charge that, in justifiably trying to counter the naiveté with which such concepts have in the past been employed, too much ground has been surrendered; and that, consequently, the antiepistemologies of posthumanism would be unable to recoup the normative potentials pertaining to "meaning," "truth," and "human agency" that have been surrendered. For example, the suspicions of one critic proceed along the following lines: "Anti-humanism amounts to a denial of the role of individual will or agency in history. Since to be an agent means to be capable of framing intentional aims and projects by the light of an independent intelligence, to eliminate agency is to eliminate man and any teleological conception of human nature. The elimination of any substantive ground for free action constitutes the core of the doctrine of scientific structuralism."[60] For the author, the wholesale abandonment of such terms raises the specter of nihilism. If, therefore, history is to be thought of antiteleologically, as devoid of intrinsic meaning, why should we surrender joyfully (again, à la Nietzsche) to an *amor fati* or a doctrine of eternal recurrence—the conclusion toward which structuralism's antihistoricism *nolens volens* drives us?

The emphasis on structure over history has ironically given the structuralist movement a profoundly conservative cast. When all is said and done, it seeks to emphasize the prerogatives of science, stability, order, and pattern maintenance in a way not that dissimilar from structural-functionalist sociology (e.g., Parsons and his school). As a theory of historical explanation, structuralism threatens to subsume the phenomena it is dealing with under a set of a priori categories instead of meeting them halfway or addressing them "on their own terms." As a method, it is staunchly antiphenomenological in the Husserlian–Heideggerian sense of unveiling "things themselves." While its value in unearthing fundamental underlying features of human societies is incontestable, aspects of those societies that prove irreducible to the methods of structural analysis (e.g., characteristics of everyday life that can be shown to have little to do with significant structures per se) tend to be accorded short shrift or relegated to the domain of the inessential.

One of the most influential and legitimate aspects of Lévi-Strauss's thought has been his unmasking of the ethnocentric prejudices of evolutionary approaches to the study of culture. Western eyes have often viewed non-Western societies either as devoid of history or as developmentally immature. As a result, social scientists have failed to see that these cultures are intrinsically meaningful on their own terms. Moreover, under the influence of Montaigne and Rousseau, Lévi-Strauss was able to use his insights into these societies' proximity to nature to proffer a powerful indictment of a disjointed and catastrophe-ridden modern West. In *Tristes Tropiques*, a work that catapulted Lévi-Strauss to the status of an international cultural hero, he reflects, in terms that are far from "value-free," on what has gone wrong with the civilization he, as ethnographer, has elected to distance himself from:

A proliferating and overexcited civilization has broken the silence of the seas once and for all. The perfumes of the tropics and the pristine freshness of human beings have been corrupted by a busyness with dubious implications, which mortifies our desires and dooms us to acquire only contaminated memories.

Our great Western civilization, which has created the marvels we now enjoy, has only succeeded in producing them at the cost of corresponding ills. The order and harmony of the Western world, its most famous achievement . . . demand the elimination of a prodigious mass of noxious byproducts which now contaminate the globe. The first thing we see as we travel around the globe is our own filth, thrown into the face of mankind.

Mankind has opted for monoculture; it is in the process of creating a mass civilization, as beetroot is grown in the mass. Henceforth, man's daily bill of fare will consist only of this one item.[61]

Yet, while Lévi-Strauss's attentiveness to the values of cultural difference has been of inestimable importance for enhancing both our sense of the worth of other cultures as well as of the limitations of our own, it is difficult to see how from his point of view one could evaluate cultural differences. In point of fact, one could not. One is left with an avowed cultural relativism that is merely the flip-side of ethnocentrism—ethnocentrism in the plural, as it were. Thus, in his 1953 UNESCO paper, "Race and History," Lévi-Strauss favorably counterposes ethnocentrism to racism.[62] The former, he claims, helps preserve the essential diversity of cultures that threatens to disappear amid the omnipresent monoculture of the capitalist West. However, he fails to realize that ethnocentrism, as tribalism, is a necessary component of full-blown racism (and, as contemporary Balkan history testifies, often no less poisonous). Lévi-Strauss legitimizes ethnocentrism by naturalizing it as a bedrock of healthy functionalist prejudices. Attempts to mediate constructively between cultures must be rejected. It is precisely such cross-cultural contacts, as they have proliferated since the age of discovery, that have tended to efface entrenched cultural differences. His unflinching rejection of cosmopolitanism induces him unreflectively to embrace the opposite extreme: sheer particularism. His perspective on cross-cultural study, which has been so enormously influential, leaves us with a dilemma: there is no middle ground. He fails to understand that, in the words of Tzvetan Todorov, "If I wish to communicate successfully with others, I [must] presuppose a frame of reference which encompasses both my universe and theirs."[63] Because Lévi-Strauss assumes ethnocentrism as the irreducible sine qua non of all intercultural contact, the idea that, to understand the other we must be capable of suspending our own prejudices in order to take her standpoint, does not occur to him.

For Lévi-Strauss, cultures are of equal value insofar as they are equally *meaningful*—a distinctly functionalist residuum. In his thought, the philosophical distinction between meaning and validity thus falls out of account. To judge questions of meaning according to terms of validity would be to pretend to some sort of judgmental objectivity. It is to risk importing the standards of one culture (which, by definition, are ethnocentric) to judge another. As he remarks at one point: "beyond the rational there exists a more important and valid category—that of the meaningful, which is the highest mode of being of the rational."[64]

But, here, he abandons too quickly the spirit of cosmopolitanism that attempts to sketch valid, cross-cultural norms of international behavior and citizens' rights. In this sense, a culture that willfully violates the sovereignty of its neighbors or that systematically infringes the rights of its citizens must be held to a concept of justice that is higher than local standards. Otherwise, there are de facto no grounds on which the tribunal of world opinion might *justifiably* (i.e., nonarbitrarily) condemn Nazi racism, South African apartheid, or the stultifying domestic repression of the former communist states. The key is to be able to formulate cross-cultural standards of justice that can in principle genuinely be agreed on by all (with the exception of the offending parties) and that therefore cannot be commandeered as a pretext for the most powerful nations to assert their self-interest on the world stage (the 1991 Persian Gulf war being a fascinating case in point in which the two sides of the equation—justice and self-interest—were palpably combined).

In the last analysis, one must seriously inquire as to whether structuralism, by so persistently devaluing the categories of human consciousness and will, remains capable of recouping a serviceable concept of the ethical subject. If structures really function as the subterranean determinants of historical practice, does there remain any room for the notion of moral accountability? Or is this concept, too, to be relegated to the antiquarian closet of humanist shibboleths? In a century in which crimes against humanity have become a virtual norm, to relinquish the normative commitments of traditional humanism risks meeting the forces of tyranny halfway.

Derrida

The critique of "man" that was forcefully elaborated in the thought of Heidegger, Lacan, and Lévi-Strauss provided the ensuing wave of antihumanist discourse—so-called poststructuralism—with a firm foundation on which to build.

Derrida is the true poststructuralist. In one of the foundational texts of deconstruction, "Structure, Sign, and Play in the Discourse of the Human Sciences," he directly challenges Lévi-Strauss's notion that "structure" would be capable of controlling the totality of signification in a given field. For Derrida, the centered totality of structuralism is "always already" undermined by the play of linguistic indeterminacy. Thus, (to cite Yeats) "the center will not hold." Structuralism is merely a contemporary variant of metaphysics, a modern incarnation of what Heidegger denounced as "onto-theology." Like all metaphysics, it, too, aims at limiting the free play of signification, by subsuming this "play" according to a set of structurally predetermined, binary oppositions: "nature" versus "culture," "sacred" versus "profane," and so forth.

As a species of metaphysics, structuralism, to its own detriment, partakes of the kinship between "metaphysics" and "violence."[65] In a way that is different from and yet akin to Foucault, the relationship between "knowledge" and "power" also occupies center stage in Derrida's reflections on the legacy of Western metaphysics. Thus, in a philosophical spirit that stands in close proximity to Heidegger, the quasi-ontological judgments Derrida passes on meta-physics implicitly contain a series of ethical judgments. Metaphysics is "vio-lent" insofar as it seeks to establish a "limit" to "dissemination," to the inherent polysemy of signifying practice. It seeks to master and subdue that which would otherwise escape its control. For Derrida, the quest for philosophical certitude is motivated by a type of metaphysical angst: a fear of those elements of language that might escape the predominant mandates of cultural control. In an attempt to alleviate this Angst, metaphysics provides a semblance of reassurance; but such reassurances—which, when traced throughout the long history of Western thought, signify a type of philosophical "compulsion to repeat"—always occur at the expense of other terms and possibilities, which are thereby occluded and accursed: terms whose nature is suggested by the con-cepts of "otherness," "heterogeneity," and "difference."

It is in precisely this vein that Derrida issues the following antimetaphysical injunction against the "metaphysical structuralism" of Lévi-Strauss: "The concept of centered structure is in fact the concept of a play based on a fundamental ground, a play constituted on the basis of a fundamental immo-bility and a reassuring certitude, which itself is beyond the reach of play. And on the basis of this certitude anxiety can be mastered."[66]

Structuralism remains onto-theological insofar as the divine attributes of consummate intellectual mastery that were attributed by theology to God and then, with Descartes, to the creaturely "I think," have merely been sublated by "structure": the new scientific, first unmoved mover. As Manfred Frank puts it: "Derrida, following in Heidegger's footsteps, considers as 'metaphysical' every interpretation of being as such and as a whole that wants to ground its *meaning* on a principle that is superior to, indeed, removed from that being itself."[67]

Frank's insight describes the essential philosophical difference between structuralism and poststructuralism: one believes in the possibility and desir-ability of a stable center of meaning, whereas the other gainsays this pos-sibility/desirability. Derrida's critique of structuralism as metaphysics would also apply to Foucauldian archaeology as a quasi-structuralism. It, too, strives to produce a seamless, hence, totalizing understanding of "the order of things," with the "episteme" as the organizing principle. Yet, according to Derrida, such an understanding belies the manifold slippages of time, play, signification, and, ultimately, *différance:* "This is why one perhaps could say that the move-ment of any archaeology, like that of any eschatology, is an accomplice of this reduction of the structurality of structure and always attempts to conceive of structure on the basis of a full presence which is beyond play."[68]

It is clear that, in one respect at least (and, at that, a far from trivial one), Derrida is one of Heidegger's most faithful disciples. The centerpiece of deconstruction (the very word, after all, is derived from Heidegger's *Destruktion*), the critique of "logocentrism," would be unthinkable apart from the critique of reason elaborated in Heidegger's 1947 "Letter" and other texts.

But for Derrida, even Heidegger's thought remains excessively metaphysical. The "question of Being" with which Heidegger is so concerned is, for Derrida, much too substantive, too redolent of a traditional "metaphysics of presence." For Derrida the very metaphorics of Heideggerian discourse, which emphasize the values of home, place, and "nearness" to Being, betray the metaphysical illusion that Being in its plenitude might somehow be captured and reproduced in discourse. But this prospect is a sheer non sequitur for Derrida. The strictures of what Derrida calls "archiwriting," that is, of the grammatological "nonconcepts" such as the "trace," "spacing," "hymen," "supplement," and, of course, *différance,* ensure that "meaning" in the sense of "presence" remains a philosophical impossibility. Once it is subjected to the vagaries of "representation," once it is articulated in "writing" or *écriture* (which, for Derrida, is more original than "speech"), meaning (to paraphrase Wittgenstein) goes on a holiday. It is "always already" irretrievably marred by the figurations of language such as spacing, deferral, and difference, by the instability of the domain of signification via which alone meaning can be conveyed.

Derrida's point is that meanings, whose domain is that of the "signified," never materialize of their own accord, that is, "in and of themselves." Instead, they are inevitably conveyed via the medium of linguistic signification; and, as we have known at least since Saussure, signifiers, the linguistic purveyors of "meaning," are inherently arbitrary and unstable.

Derrida's own version of antihumanism follows directly from his position as a philosopher of language who has been profoundly influenced by the Heideggerian critique of metaphysics. He seeks to extend the critique of logocentrism to the "transcendental subject" of modern philosophy, which, in a posttheological era, has been the traditional guarantor of epistemological certainty.

However, one cannot but ask whether the critique of humanism, in its radicality, does not consume too much in its wake. The potential shortfalls of the discourse of antihumanism become evident in its attempts to address the question of human rights. The doctrine of modern natural right, whence stems the contemporary theory of human rights, is fully indebted to metaphysical nostrums. In the tradition of modern political theory (Hobbes, Locke, Rousseau, etc.), natural rights are the moral equivalent of "innate ideas" or "ideas of reason."[69] Derrida consequently has avowed that a politics of human rights must be rejected owing to its "logocentric" origins: it is part and parcel of a discourse of "metaphysical voluntarism" that must be rejected wholesale.[70] But not only is such a rejection in and of itself questionable; one is also left to wonder, What would become of a politics of human rights when it is divested of the philosophical substructure that, traditionally, has served as its intellectual grounds of support?

In his attempts to carve out a position on world politics, Derrida seems at times hamstrung by the rigidity of his own antimetaphysical convictions. In this context, the epistemological negation of humanism seems an especial liability. In his essay on racism in South Africa, for example, he claims that apartheid must be attributed to a characteristic European discourse, the discourse of "race."

However, for Derrida, there is of course much more at stake in such a verdict on the European origins of South African racism. For in his thinking, "Europe" is not only the home of Western metaphysics; the very idea of Europe and what is European is in truth inconceivable without metaphysics.[71] "Europe," therefore, is something that has been, as it were, *predicated* by metaphysics. Thus, by virtue of his characterization of the European origins of non-European racism, Derrida seeks to make a philosophical point: that it is ultimately *the discourse of Western metaphysics* that is the irreducible progenitor and origin of apartheid.

However, the intellectual origins of racism are not so straightforward as Derrida suggests. They are not, as Derrida contends, traceable to a metaphysical discourse per se. In fact, modern racism first emerges in nineteenth-century Europe among the theorists of counterrevolution. It was Count Arthur de Gobineau's *Essai sur l'Inégalité des Races Humaines* (1854) that would, according to Hannah Arendt, become "the standard work for race theories in history."[72] Thus, instead of being "metaphysical," theories of European racism are part and parcel of an anti-Enlightenment, anticosmopolitan discourse. They represent, moreover, an avowedly particularistic idiom, one that seeks to dismantle both the cosmopolitanism of the Enlightenment as well as the democratic heritage of 1789. As Arendt observes: "What Gobineau was actually looking for in politics was the definition and creation of an 'elite' to replace the aristocracy. Instead of princes, he proposed a 'race of princes,' the Aryans, who he said were in danger of being submerged by the non-Aryan lower classes through democracy."[73] Hence, as an integral part of counterrevolutionary ideology, European racism sought to reverse the trend whereby a society of orders, based on the privileges of birth, was destroyed in favor of a society whose animating precept was "equality before the law." In such a society alien races—such as the Jews—could legally accede to political authority and influence.

To claim that the intellectual origins of apartheid are European is correct; yet, as such, this claim lacks specificity. To become meaningful, it must be historicized and contextualized. Only then can one gain a concrete sense of what the discourse of European racism stands for as well as the specific political culture (that of the Enlightenment) it strives to combat. Hence, as an interpretive strategy, to condemn racism as "European," hence, "metaphysical," proceeds at too high a plane of abstraction. It threatens to "explain away." In the last analysis, it places a burden of historical explanation on the concept of metaphysics that the concept is unable to bear.

In "Racism's Last Word" (1985) Derrida laments the fact that "the customary discourse on man, humanism and human rights, has encountered its effective and unthought limit, the limit of a whole system in which it acquires meaning."[74] He goes on to condemn the sterility of a "discourse" that can only "draw up contracts, dialecticize itself, [and thus] let itself be reappropriated again" by the powers that be.

Ten years after these words were written, the systems of political oppression Derrida describes are in the process of being dismantled, in no small measure owing to the productive intransigence of a politics of human rights. Under these circumstances it would be self-defeating to maintain an attitude of cynicism toward "the customary discourse on man, humanism and human rights."

Moreover, the category that Derrida invokes to counter the Eleatic tyrannies of logocentric thought—"difference"—is unable to bear the ethico-political weight he and his followers have placed on it. Unless it is incorporated within an overarching civil libertarian framework emphasizing the eminently universalistic values of tolerance and cosmopolitanism, to glorify difference can be as chauvinistic as the perspectives it is meant to offset. To celebrate differences at the expense of sameness or unity threatens to belittle our common humanity. Thus the passing of humanism should not be unequivocally celebrated. Otherness should be embraced, as Derrida suggests, but not extolled. Otherwise, what one finds is that various groups begin to differentiate themselves according the neo-ontological determinants of race, class, ethnicity, and gender. That is, they segregate themselves solely on the basis of their own particularity, and the politics of difference threatens to turn into a new essentialism. Such an approach is part and parcel of the new "identity politics," where groups speak from the standpoint of entrenched "subject-positions." However, identity politics can all too easily turn into a recipe for warring *ethnoi*, a new tribalism.[75] Far from being a solution to the age-old philosophical dilemma of the one and the many as deconstruction would have it, it proceeds by unreflectively apotheosizing the second term—albeit, in opposition to a universalism (Lévi-Strauss's Orwellian "monoculture") that is perceived as increasingly insensitive to local specificity.

In fact, today's new European racism goes by the name of "differentialist racism."[76] It is an ideology that seeks to legitimate the separation of the races on the basis of their intrinsic differences. It is a "nonessentialist" racism insofar as the emphasis on cultural and ethnic difference steers clear of earlier attempts to justify racial superiority on the basis of genetics or biology. It may be described as a *postmodern racism:* it no longer wishes, like nineteenth-century racism, to develop a theory of racial hierarchy that would, for example, serve to legitimate the conquest of one race by another. Here, there are no "master" and "inferior" races, only cultural differences that, it is argued, should be respected at all costs. Translated into concrete terms, the new racism means airtight immigration policies and expulsion of all non-nationals. "France for the French and North Africa for the North Africans"—so goes the new slogan. The European Union (Maastricht) is vigorously criticized as a cosmopolitan gambit that threatens to dilute difference qua national particularity. The latter, it is claimed, represents a type of authentic diversity and heterogeneity that stands as a bulwark against the leveling precepts of a united Europe.

Only a theory that makes room for differences under the auspices of a common humanity or a renewed cosmopolitanism can prevent the misuse of the ideology of difference for the ends of differential racism.[77] It has become increasingly apparent that unless a politics of difference simultaneously embraces a normative standpoint that is both civil libertarian and democratic (traditions formerly tabooed as "logocentric") it can just as easily become a politics of xenophobia. Julia Kristeva has recognized this dilemma when she observes:

> In years to come it is likely that we could witness a loss of concern for personal freedom, which was one of the essential assets in the *Declaration of the Rights of Man and Citizen,* to the advantage of subjective, sexual, nationalist and religious protectionism that will freeze evolutionary potentialities of men and women, reducing them to the identification needs of their originary groups. . . . Beyond the *origins* that have assigned to us biological identity papers and a linguistic, religious, social, political, historical place, the freedom of contemporary individuals may be gauged according to their ability to *choose* their membership, while the democratic capability of a nation and social group is revealed by the right it affords

individuals to exercise that choice. Thus when I say that I have chosen cosmopolitanism, this means that I have, against origins and starting from them, chosen a transnational or international position situated at the crossing of boundaries.[78]

French Philosophy of the 1980s

If one scans the writings of the Parisian intellectual avant-garde since the 1960s, one discovers what might be termed an "illiberal cultural politics" that gives credence to Judt's apprehensions concerning "a vacuum at the heart of public ethics in modern France."[79] The literary theorist Thomas Pavel observes a similar phenomenon. In the postwar period one sees "the rise of discretionary intellectual behavior with its conspicuous disregard for the moral premises or the consequences of theories."[80] In essence, the political radicalism of an earlier generation of existential Marxists—the *résistantialistes*—was transmuted along the lines of an uncompromising cultural radicalism. As befits a culture that exalts the status of the written word, this novel genre of *Kulturkritik*, instead of denouncing the sins of capitalism, addressed the predominance of "binary oppositions," "logocentrism," "consensus," the "code," "discursive regimes," and so forth.

By a strange twist, a traditional left-wing hostility to the values of political liberalism was preserved in a sublimated, cultural guise. The spirit of philosophical anarchism emanating from Paris had internalized the anti-authoritarian ethos of May 1968. It had, however, stopped short of assimilating one of the basic political lessons of the critique of totalitarianism: a renewed appreciation of the civil libertarian and democratic traditions. As a result of the ostensible moral deficits proper to French philosophy of the 1960s, suspicions grew as to whether poststructuralism was adequate to the ethical challenges of a post-totalitarian era.[81]

The 1970s had been a decade noted for an effective unmasking of all pretensions to political and cultural radicalism. Maoists of yore, properly chastened, became "new philosophers," railing against the *naïveté gauchiste* of an entire generation. Criticisms of the "master thinkers," though philosophically shallow, well captured the intellectual temperament of the era: a distaste for grand theorizing and all varieties of intellectual pretense, coupled with a refreshingly modest political vision oriented toward *droits de l'homme*.[82] That venerable premature anti-Communist, Albert Camus, was rediscovered and celebrated as a twentieth-century Dante, railing against a new "trahison des clercs," perpetrated by apologetic *marxisant* intellectuals.

It was also the decade that witnessed a tearless farewell to the French revolutionary tradition: that is, a break with the glorification of revolutionary dictatorship that had been a distinguishing feature of French Marxism.[83] The clarion call was sounded by François Furet, who, in the opening chapter of *Penser la Révolution Française,* proclaimed with elegant simplicity: "The French Revolution is over."[84] When coupled with the ongoing unmasking of "really existing socialism," Furet's powerful indictment of the pieties of revolutionary vanguardism helped set the stage for the emergence of a novel and vigorous humanist sensibility, which the philosopher Alain Finkielkraut has dubbed "French thought of the eighties": a new "rationalist-democratic consensus, the most striking feature of which [was] the simultaneous growth of a liberal . . . school of political thought and a rationalist left."[85]

An additional blow to the intellectual currency of antihumanist thought was struck with the Heidegger affair of the late 1980s. In the wake of this debate, it became undeniable that the man whose thought had provided the philosophical inspiration for the critique of humanism was himself irretrievably tainted by an association with Nazism. Ultimately, the link between the antihumanism of the genocidal Nazi dictatorship and that of the philosopher whose influence had overshadowed Parisian intellectual life in the postwar period would prove insurmountable. In the 1980s, therefore, Heidegger's doctrines were exposed to the same fate as had been those of Marx in the 1970s: they ceased to enjoy their customary *effet d'évidence* and instead were subjected to unsparing reexamination and critique.[86]

The 1980s were the years in which France at long last began to confront in earnest the complicities of Vichy.[87] In 1987, the nation stood mesmerized as the notorious "butcher of Lyon," Klaus Barbie, was brought to trial and convicted of "crimes against humanity."[88] The cultural event of the decade was Claude Lanzmann's magisterial film on the politics of genocide, *Shoah* (1985). And with the stunning electoral showings of Le Pen's National Front, the specter of neofascism took on an ominous contemporary relevance.[89] Amid this political climate, in which the necessities of "coming to terms with the past" had become the order of the day, attempts to make light of Heidegger's commitment to Nazism played rather poorly.

Nevertheless, among the French Heideggerians Philippe Lacoue-Labarthe took up the challenge of defending Heidegger in *La Fiction du politique.* However, in order to preserve the antihumanist position from the taint of Nazism, he was forced to pursue a line of reasoning that was highly counterintuitive: he had to claim that it was, in truth, a *surfeit* of humanism, rather than a dearth, that seduced Heidegger into embracing Hitler in the 1930s. In Lacoue-

Labarthe's words: "Nazism is a humanism insofar as it rests upon a determination of *humanitas* which is, in its view, more powerful—i.e., more effective—than any other. The subject of absolute self-creation . . . it transcends all the determinations of the modern subject, brings together and concretizes these same determinations (as also does Stalinism with the subject of absolute self-production) and constitutes itself as *the* subject, in absolute terms."[90]

Lacoue-Labarthe's equation of Nazism with humanism represents an orthodox Heideggerian understanding of the origins of Nazism. National Socialism is viewed as the logical consummation of the development of Western rationalism; a consummation, moreover, that is on a par with other species of technological nihilism, such as "Communism" and "Americanism."[91] In the last analysis, the Third Reich is perceived as merely one more manifestation of the way in which Western thought elevates the metaphysical subject—the "man" of humanism—to a position of unchallenged preeminence.

But this somewhat strained attempt to view the Third Reich as a type of "humanism writ large" proved relatively easy to counter. As one critic wryly observed with reference to the attempts to regard Heidegger's antihumanism as a potential bulwark against Nazism: "Isn't it rather fortunate that half a century ago the adversaries of Nazi Germany had other weapons to rely upon?"[92] Pierre Bourdieu simply throws up his hands in dismay: "When I hear people say that Heidegger alone makes it possible for us to think the Holocaust . . . I think I must be dreaming."[93] And as Robert Holub has appropriately observed concerning Lacoue-Labarthe's curious defense of Heidegger's antihumanism:

> Lacoue-Labarthe would have us believe that the person who proudly wore his party pin in 1936 . . . , who never publicly or privately renounced National Socialism and his involvement with it, and who never in the postwar period reflected directly on the most horrific consequences of Germany's fascist regime is the only reliable source for a comprehension of his own involvement with Nazism and of Nazism as a European phenomenon. Such a conclusion can be maintained only by someone who has already and without critical questioning accepted the major propositions of the very philosophy which Heidegger's fascist proclivities should compel us to rethink.[94]

A significant confusion lurks at the heart of this debate over the legacy and status of Western humanism. Each camp—liberal humanists, on the one side, Heideggerian antihumanists, on the other—relies on conflicting conceptions of the meaning of humanism. The liberals seek to defend a *political* definition of humanism that makes possible a politics of human rights. As they see it, to credit the legacy of Western humanism with direct responsibility for the misfortunes and disasters of twentieth-century history is a gross oversimplification of history. After, all the regimes primarily responsible for those disasters—Nazi Germany, Stalin's Soviet Union, Pol Pot's Cambodia—were staunchly anti-Western, anti-liberal regimes. According to the defenders of the liberal perspective, a preservation of the values of humanism and subjectivity is indispensable to the perpetuation of the democratic project worldwide.

The Heideggerians, conversely, rely on an *epistemological* definition of humanism that harks back to the "subjectum" of modern metaphysics from Descartes to Husserl. To them the liberal approach seems complacent and naive vis-à-vis the historical failings of modern democratic societies. For example, rights-oriented approaches to political affairs have typically been unable to certify the traditional values of human solidarity and community. Historically speaking, societies in which the epistemological paradigm of self-positing subjectivity has reigned have been in league with the hubristic delusions of a technologically empowered *homo faber*. World conquest, widespread alienation, environmental devastation, "exterminism" (E. P. Thompson) have been the result. Yet, this account of the logic of modernity threatens to become a type of reverse teleology—an inverted metanarrative—characterized by increasing enslavement rather than Hegel's "progress in the consciousness of freedom." It is an account that risks becoming excessively one-dimensional: one is left with an understanding of modernity, from Descartes on, that perceives a unilateral reign of "technology," "nihilism," "subjectivism," and "metaphysics." All countervailing tendencies in the realms of art, politics, philosophy, and everyday life are, it seems, a priori disqualified on the basis of their participation in this Heideggerian era of *Seinsverlassenheit* (abandonment by Being).

The French debate over the merits of humanism versus antihumanism represents a cultural referendum on the legacy of modernity. The partisans of antihumanism opt for what one might call an attitude of "total critique." According to this standpoint, there remain very few normative potentials of modernity worthy of redemption. As with the later Heidegger, modernity and subjectivity are the twin linchpins of an omnipresent reign of "technological nihilism." One cannot but wonder, however, whether this position, in its critical zeal, rejects too much. Democratic ideals are unthinkable unless they are to some extent based on the principles of subjective autonomy and individual freedom that the modern era, for all its shortcomings, has allowed to flourish. Hence, the relevance of Tzvetan Todorov's observation: "It may be difficult to be sure whether one is for or against rationality; things become a little clearer when one understands that the decision is also a choice for or against democracy."[95] Thus, as it became increasingly evident how difficult it was to reconcile philosophical antihumanism with a viable notion of democratic practice, dissatisfaction with the epistemologies of poststructuralism intensified.

Left Heideggerianism became the authentic heir to the critique of bourgeois society formerly purveyed by a (since the 1970s no longer viable) French Marxism. It was French Heideggerianism that took up the gauntlet of radical *Kulturkritik,* condemning the ideology of "man" in all its forms: liberalism, democracy, individualism, constitutionalism, and human rights.

And yet, this theoretical stance preserved the trappings of cultural radicalism at the expense of being able to intervene effectively in the politics of the modern world. It became exceedingly difficult to reconcile the epistemological politics of poststructuralism with a new post-totalitarian sensibility; a sensibility for which the values of "humanism"—a defense of the integrity of persons, human rights, civil liberties, etc.—had once again become central.

In the 1950s, Sartre felt comfortable defining Marxism as the "unsurpassable philosophy of our time."[96] But the historical experiences of our century strongly suggest that, instead, it is the concept of human rights that has become unsurpassable. In a post-totalitarian world, a respect for basic civil liberties and the integrity of all persons has become the necessary—if not the sufficient—condition for humane politics. Hence, the renewed relevance of the concept of "humanism" in the contemporary world. One of liberalism's advantages is that, as a theory of justice, it is formal: it does not presume to judge the validity of different worldviews, private opinions, or other substantive claims. In principle it can be reconciled with a variety of regional customs, local value-systems, and, to use Wittgenstein's phrase, "forms of life."

Though "unsurpassable," the idea of human rights does not represent a sufficient condition for contemporary democratic politics because it is essentially defensive. Taking its cue from traditional political liberalism, it valorizes the ideal of *negative freedom:* it seeks to underwrite a series of formal legal guarantees whose aim it is to secure an inviolable sphere of individual autonomy. However, this sphere of personal freedom represents merely the basic precondition for the realm of politics proper, which instead must be conceived of along the lines of "active citizenship": that is, as a sphere of political participation. For this reason, the traditional liberal definition of politics, with its exclusive emphasis on the preservation of rights, proves too thin for the purposes of adequately grounding the idea of democratic political practice.

There is a fundamental tension in the conduct of modern democratic life. Under the conditions of modern democracy, liberalism has functioned not so much as the necessary precondition for democratic politics, but, often enough, as its antipode.[97] Thus, in modern democratic societies, liberalism, in keeping with the ideology of negative freedom, has often served as a justification of freedom *from* politics. It has consistently emphasized values other than those of political participation: the values of privatism (family, home, personal health and fitness, consumerism, etc.), bourgeois intimacy, economic accumulation, rugged individualism, and so forth.[98] Too often, these values are explicitly defined in opposition to those of civic virtue or the active participation in public life.

Liberalism has de facto monopolized the discourse of modern humanism. However, liberalism's understanding of humanism remains both exceedingly thin and in too great a proximity to the hedonistic values of economic liberalism or possessive individualism. Hence, to its own detriment, the modern concept of humanism has been effectively shorn of the values of self-cultivation and civic virtue that were still so prominent for the Renaissance ideal of *humanitas*.[99] Nor have the ideals of liberalism provided an adequate bulwark against a characteristic Eurocentric insensitivity to the integrity of non-European lifeforms. It is little wonder, therefore, that these ideals provoked such vigorous opposition among the post-1960s left-wing intelligentsia.

Earlier I made reference to a new humanistic temperament—a "French thought of the 1980s"—in which the ideals of humanity have once again received their due. As an intellectual movement, this temperament emerged in polemical contrast to the antihumanist debunking of the precepts of democracy and political liberalism.

As represented by thinkers such as Luc Ferry, Alain Finkielkraut, and Alain Renaut—all of whom are in many respects direct heirs of the *nouveaux philosophes* of the 1970s—French thought of the 1980s has assumed the guise of a neoliberalism.[100] As such, it abandoned too readily the emancipatory dreams of the *soixant-huitards* ('68ers). Many of its contributions to the French culture wars of the 1970s and 1980s have been salutary. However, when viewed from the standpoint of the history of political thought, it has done little more than reinvent the wheel. A more charitable estimation of its goals might suggest that it attempted to provide the theoretical grounding for the philosophy of liberalism that France never had. Yet, in the 1980s, it functioned as an intellectual corollary to the politics of "modernization" effected by the French Socialists in their "postideological" phase (that is, following the break with the Communists in 1983). However, as a party of modernization, the Socialists failed to distinguish themselves substantially from the contemporaneous neoconservative regimes in England, the United States, and elsewhere.

The neoliberal attempts to base democratic politics on the rights of "man," separation of powers, and individualism, have, in truth, added very little to the time-honored catalogue of liberal nostrums. Moreover, such attempts have made even less headway in remedying the traditional debilities of political liberalism that revolve around the defensive concept of *passive citizenship*. According to this model, civic duty is de facto limited to voting. The result is (1) a considerable depoliticization of public life and (2) the birth of an "expertocracy"; that is, rule by professional politicians in combination with a technocratic elite.

On the epistemological front, the neoliberals have sought to renew a philosophy of the subject. Here, too, however, the results have been less than satisfactory. On the one hand, they have claimed that, "On the philosophical level it is impossible to return, after Marx, Nietzsche, Freud, and Heidegger, to the idea that man is the master and possessor of the totality of his actions and ideas."[101] But in their meditations on the question of the subject, they have invoked the most traditional theories of subjectivity *tel quel*, from Leibnizian monadology to Kant's transcendentalism to Fichte's "philosophy of reflection."[102] Their attempts to rethink the question of the subject, therefore, have been oriented entirely toward the "classical" discussions of the concept. Consequently, their reflections on these matters have been static and have assumed the form of an uncritical "restoration" rather than a "renewal." They have shown little sensitivity to the problematics of those thinkers who have legitimately called into question the viability of the traditional philosophical conception of the subject from the standpoint of contemporary intellectual and cultural needs.

The French critics of subjectivity have justifiably sought to highlight the manner in which traditional bourgeois ideals have become lifeless and rigidified. These ideals live on in merely nominal fashion, ghostlike, functioning nevertheless as the ideological cornerstones of a civilization in which both inner and outer nature are systematically repressed. It is a society that is excessively utilitarian, predicated on the logic of production for production's sake, one that has effectively banished affective solidarity, and in which libidinal satisfaction is increasingly tied to the administered spheres of advertising and consumption; in such a society, the precepts of "man" and the "individual" have become self-caricatural. To deconstruct them, therefore, in the name of otherness, difference, and the claims of experiential immediacy became, in an *esprit soixant-huitard*, an urgent cultural-political as well as philosophical task.

Already in the 1940s, Horkheimer and Adorno suggested that the ideas of "man," "the individual," "subjectivity," and so forth had been robbed of their substance and served as hollow testimonials to the bourgeois ethos of self-preservation.[103] Yet the intellectual differences between the critical theorists and the poststructuralists are important. Whereas the French critics of reason believe that the old bourgeois-metaphysical nostrums should be rejected outright, the Frankfurt School maintained that the ideals themselves possessed an important kernel of truth that was worthy of redemption. In their eyes, what called for criticism was not the ideals as such, but the fact that, by the mid-twentieth century, their truth-content had receded into the distance, rendering them merely ideological: one paid them constant lip-service, but increasingly they came to serve as rationalizations, as the normative window-dressing for a society that had long ceased to honor their original libertarian thrust.

The neoliberals have had difficulty in acknowledging one of the fundamental normative determinants of late capitalist societies: that there exists an essential tension between ideal and reality. Their standpoint is often perceived as inadequate insofar as they act as though the ideals were fully embodied in the institutional life of these societies, which is far from true. As a result, their thought has taken on apologetic overtones. It risks conflating the real with the rational, what is socially given with the just.

From a philosophical standpoint their theories have suffered from a failure to take into account contemporary developments that have sought to reestablish the rights of subjectivity via the mediations of otherness (e.g., neopragmatism and theories of intersubjectivity). In the philosophy of reflection, from Descartes to Kant and Fichte, the claims of the subject as isolated "I think" have been deduced monologically. More recently, however, philosophers have relied on the symbolic interactionism of George Herbert Mead to revitalize a concept of subjectivity that would no longer be identical with the claims of a philosophy of consciousness. In the new theories of intersubjectivity, the claims of first philosophy have been augmented by insights drawn from theories of socialization. According to these findings, "subjects" or "selves" do not exist, as in the metaphysics of old, a priori; instead, they first originate as the result of *social interaction*. According to Mead, the self is first and foremost a "social object." The "I" only emerges upon becoming a "me": the image I have of myself ineluctably develops out of the way others see me. In this respect alone does it make sense to speak of "subjective experiences," which, by definition, are therefore *intersubjectively* mediated. As Mead observes, "The 'I' reacts to the self which arises through the taking of the attitudes of others. Through taking those attitudes we have introduced the 'me' and we react to it as an 'I.' "[104] There is, therefore, no autonomous subject that would predate social interaction. Insofar as the self is simultaneously subject and object, autonomy is something it attains via the medium of interaction. In this respect at least, one can agree with the poststructuralist claim concerning the decentered subject. Following Mead, one might say that the self is "always already" a decentered self: "The growth of the self arises out of a partial disintegration—the appearance of the different interests in the forum of reflection, the reconstruction of the social world, and the consequent appearance of the new self that answers to the new object."[105]

In this sense, one might say that difference and a relation to otherness prove to be constitutive aspects of the self, which is formed via the internalization of others' expectations and, more generally, social norms. Though "decentered," this self is a far cry from the centerless, fragmented self of Lacanian psychoanalysis and poststructuralism. Instead, as social differentiation increases and, along with it, the extent and scope of intersubjective expectations, the subject becomes less particularized and more universal: its level of tolerance (vis-à-vis selves that are different than it) is enhanced. The imperatives of socialization have made it necessarily more adept at "taking the role of the other." In all of these respects the identity of the self is grounded in difference.

The situation in contemporary French philosophy is paradoxical, and far from intellectually fruitful. In the less academic and more engaged texts of antihumanism (e.g., Gilles Deleuze and Félix Guattari's *Anti-Oedipus* and *A Thousand Plateaus*), one finds an unnuanced celebration of decentered subjectivity. The self of modernity is supplanted by "desiring machines." Their main virtue, it seems, is to glorify the ongoing fragmentation of individuality characteristic of late capitalist society; that is, the progressive negation of autonomous subjectivity by large-scale organizations and the new technologies of the culture industry. Here, catastrophe is confused with emancipation.

On the neoliberal side, conversely, as we have just seen, one observes an uncritical revival of a series of concepts and categories—individualism, subjectivity, "man," and so forth—whose cogency had been properly challenged by the preceding two decades of French thought. *Les extrêmes ne se touchent pas.* As a French philosopher I spoke with recently lamented, "Au moment la philosophie française est totalement bloquée." One can understand—if not pardon— this situation of extreme intellectual polarization when one realizes how deep-seated and overdetermined are the historical, political, and epistemological stakes involved in the debate over the legacy of humanism in postwar France. Only in France (as opposed, for example, to Germany and the United States) did the Heidegger debate of 1987–88 produce such a veritable media frenzy (from major exposés in every major Parisian daily to television debates). As should be clear by now, at issue was the entire self-understanding of postwar French intellectual culture as a theoretical antihumanism.

DECONSTRUCTION AT AUSCHWITZ: HEIDEGGER, DE MAN, AND THE NEW REVISIONISM

The Triumph of Life warns us that nothing, whether deed, word, thought, or text, ever happens in relation, positive or negative, to anything that precedes, follows or exists elsewhere, but only as a random event whose power, like the power of death, is due to the randomness of its occurrence.—Paul de Man, *The Rhetoric of Romanticism*

Deconstruction's viability as a method of criticism has of late suffered from a preponderance of damning circumstantial evidence. This evidence pertains to its relation, or nonrelation, to the greatest crime of the modern era, the Holocaust. In the aftermath of the Heidegger and de Man scandals, deconstruction's evasions, equivocations, and denials with regard to this theme have caused its standing to plummet—perhaps not so much among true believers, but among an open-minded public prepared to judge *sine ira ac studio,* without hatred or passion. The widespread controversies over the repressed pasts of Heidegger and de Man have had the effect of exposing deconstruction to an unprecedented public scrutiny. To be sure, some of this scrutiny has been prejudicially motivated. But some has also been genuine. What has been of positive value about these recent debates is that they have forced deconstruction, as never before, to take a position on matters of great historical importance: on questions of fascism, collaboration, anti–Semitism, and the repression of sordid biographical pasts. The esteem in which both Heidegger and de Man were held has fallen insofar as both men proved inauthentic (here, I choose my words carefully) in failing to own up to their far from trifling youthful transgressions.

As any lawyer knows, circumstantial evidence will not always suffice to gain a conviction. Moreover, it would be wholly irresponsible to condemn deconstruction on the basis of a type of intellectual guilt-by-association: the idea that, because a number of its theoretical forbears or exponents were for a time avowed fascists (Heidegger, de Man, and, to a lesser extent, Maurice Blanchot),[1] deconstruction, too, would somehow be contaminated. I suggest quite forcefully that the attempt to read these recent academic scandals as somehow implicating deconstruction in real historical crimes is patently off-base. Moreover, such attempts serve as a disingenuous mechanism to close off debate prematurely. After all, if a method of criticism can be qualified as "fascist" or convicted of "intellectual collaboration" then it would appear that there is not much more to discuss. Those who believe that there are "grounds for viewing the whole of deconstruction as a vast amnesty project for the politics of collaboration in France during World War II" surely have jumped the gun.[2] It is not along this route that the true intellectual stakes of the Heidegger and de Man affairs are to be found.

I propose instead that these contentious recent debates be treated as a symptomatology: once they are divested of their polemical surcharge, they provide real insight into the possible weaknesses of deconstruction as a method of political analysis.[3] They show that textual analysis and historical analysis are far from the same thing; that, to paraphrase Derrida, "Il y a *bien* de hors texte"; and that when the "hors texte" of history is systematically kept at a distance, it will ultimately wreak revenge on the methodology that chooses to ignore it. The debate over the heritage of fascism (or, metaphorically expressed, over the historical significance of Auschwitz) may be treated as a litmus test of a given critical school's judgmental capacities. For better or for worse, our century's moral sensibility, the reigning *sensus communis*, has been constructed upon the ruins of the totalitarian experience. It has, as it were, been "indexed" in relation to the horrors of the Holocaust. We may not know how to define the true, the right, and the good per se; but we do know that an event such as Auschwitz stands as an important *negative index* as to how we might go about seeking them. Habermas once remarked that "we can if needs be distinguish theories according to whether or not they are structurally related to possible emancipation."[4] In light of deconstruction's weak showing in the aftermath of the Heidegger and de Man controversies, its serviceability for the ends of possible emancipation has been called into question.

Paul de Man's wartime journalism has been discussed ad nauseum. The *Schadenfreude* cum unmitigated glee of deconstruction's detractors has been palpable and can in no way serve as a reliable guide to what is truly at stake. Here, I restrict myself to a number of essential points that, amid the clamorous array of accusations and counteraccusations, have fallen out of account. My concerns will be threefold: (1) the line of defense established by de Man's defenders; (2) the historical status of de Man's collaborationist writings; and

(3) the possible relation between those writings and (as aficionados might say) "so-called deconstruction."

Deconstruction has been purveyed as a form of radical criticism: in its own view, it is the most radical. In a Heideggerian mode it seeks to ferret out and unmask all instances of "presence": specious, metaphysical claims to totality, wholeness, or Being-in-Itself; claims that are part and parcel of the onto-theological biases of Western metaphysics—a preference for substance over accidents, necessity over contingency, essence over appearance. Of course, there are many intellectual trends that have also sought to call such onto-theological prejudices into question: sophism, nominalism, skepticism, in addition to a variety of antinomian movements. In this respect, deconstruction hardly comes down to us without precursors and precedents.

It is all the more astonishing, therefore, to view the initial reactions among the deconstructionist faithful to the unflattering revelations concerning Paul de Man. Suddenly, the unsparing critical sensibility for which deconstruction had become known was placed on indefinite hold. The interventions of its leading practitioners, J. Hillis Miller and Derrida himself, immediately gave notice that the critical spirit stops at home: it was not so much de Man's youthful misdeeds that should be exposed and denounced, but the cabal of academicians and journalists who had dared to unmask him. From the beginning Derrida has always insisted that "deconstruction . . . is not *neutral*. It *intervenes.*"[5] Yet, where the institutional status of deconstruction itself is at stake, intervention must be suspended; one circles the wagons. Deconstruction has become a massive institutional force in the American academy, with conferences, journals, and entire departments dedicated to disseminating its virtues. To all intents and purposes, its response to the de Man affair was consistent with the most typical and predictable academic corporatism: a defense of considerable, vested institutional interests. All of this suggests that deconstruction, its critical pretensions notwithstanding, has itself become a form of "presence," that its anti-institutional pretensions have been undermined by its own success. Or, as one critical observer has remarked: "an entire theory industry has grown up around literature departments in the past twenty years, and with this industry has come the increasingly specialized professionalization of interpretation."[6] As Harold Fromm observes in *Academic Capitalism and Literary Value*, "The radical academic exhibits the verbal trappings and forms of Marxist renunciation while acting as paradigmatic acquisitive capitalist."[7] In an era marked by the death of the "subject," Derrida has become an intellectual mega-subject and deconstruction an academic growth industry. Ironically, many critics of subjectivity felt obliged to preserve the veritable cult of personality that Paul de Man had engendered at Yale.[8]

But let's dispense with generalities and enter into specifics. Taking Hillis Miller's several contributions to the affair as a point of departure, ironies begin to multiply. Miller chastises Jon Wiener, the professor-journalist who broke the de Man story in *The Nation,* for failing to base his judgments on "an accurate identification of the facts . . . and on a careful reading of the documents."[9] Prima facie, there is nothing wrong with this claim. But deconstruction, if it has taught us anything, suggests that "documents" and "facts" per se do not exist; instead, they are the "effects" of textuality, rhetorically constituted, a priori embedded in value-laden narrative frameworks. Why in this case might a (precritical) appeal to the integrity of facts resolve the dilemmas at issue? After all, does not a reliance on so-called facts invoke precisely those delusions of "presence" and absolute knowledge that deconstruction has always called into question? For a deconstructionist to suggest such a naive appeal to evidentiary sources as a way of settling a disagreement cannot but raise our suspicions.[10]

Miller opens another contribution to the debate with the following words: "The violence of the reaction in the United States and in Europe to the discovery of Paul de Man's writings of 1941–42 marks a new moment in the collaboration between the university and the mass media."[11] What are the implications of these remarks? Miller denies that it is Paul de Man who was a collaborator or a perpetrator. Although he admits that certain of his articles may be so interpreted, he, like Derrida, goes on to perform a classical deconstructive reading which shows that de Man's purportedly collaborationist texts are in fact rhetorically self-undermining, that his appeals for collaboration turn out to mean the opposite of what they say. Hence, de Man is merely a pseudocollaborator. Miller even goes so far as to muster hearsay, defying massive textual evidence to the contrary, to the effect that de Man was a closet *résistant.* Conversely, if we return to the remarks just quoted, we discover who the *real* collaborators are: the mass media and professors who have conspired at home and abroad to sully de Man's reputation—and, by implication, that of deconstruction: "The real target is not de Man himself. . . . The real aim is to discredit that form of interpretation called 'deconstruction,' to obliterate it as far as possible from the curriculum, to dissuade students of literature, philosophy and culture from reading de Man's work or that of his associates, to put a stop to the 'influence' of 'deconstruction.' "[12]

Let us be clear about the intentions and effects of Miller's deconstructive strategy, his "overturning" and "reinscription" of the inherited binary opposition between collaboration and noncollaboration. It was, after all, de Man who disingenuously praised the "decency, justice, and humanity" of the Nazi occupation forces and urged his fellow Belgians to cooperate with them to the utmost;[13] who in 1941 claimed that "the future of Europe can be envisioned only in the frame of the needs and possibilities of the German spirit. It was not a matter only of a series of reforms but of the definitive emancipation of a [German] *Volk* which finds itself called upon to exercise, in its turn, a hegemony in Europe";[14] who asserted that "the necessity of action which is present in the form of immediate collaboration is obvious to every objective mind";[15] who contrasted the "stirring poetic intuition" of Germanic literature favorably with "Latin intelligence and reasoning";[16] and who eulogized the "very beautiful and original poetry" that prospers "in the fascist climate of contemporary Italy."[17] It is this de Man whose collaboration is seriously called into question by Miller. Instead, in Miller's reading, it is the international cabal of professors and journalists who become the true collaborators. Lest this point be missed, in the same article Miller goes out of his way to emphasize that it is not Paul de Man, but in fact his critics, who display the real affinities with the totalitarian mentality. According to Miller, their argument against de Man "repeats the well-known totalitarian procedures of vilification it pretends to deplore. It repeats the crime it would condemn."[18] One fears that amid this sorry confusion of actual historical collaboration with those who, some fifty years later, have merely reported the events, the reality principle has been left far behind. At issue in this sad tale of misguided youth are the horrors of war, occupation, collaboration, anti-Semitism, and deportation. Miller's foremost concern seems to be that, owing to the damning revelations concerning de Man, in the future, a few students might be deterred from reading his books.

Derrida's own apologetics fare little better than Miller's. Like Miller, he sees a definite parallel between the "gestures of simplification and the expedited verdicts" contained in the journalistic coverage of the de Man affair and the realities of European fascism—"what happened around 1940–42 . . . in Europe and elsewhere."[19] One is impelled to point out that under the conditions of democratic publicity, at least Derrida and his colleagues have the right to a public response when they feel their interests have been misrepresented; a right that was systematically denied to the opponents of fascism living under the German occupation. To insinuate that those with whom one bitterly disagrees are in essence fascist, or are behaving fascistically, does nothing to raise the level of debate. Moreover, the analogical conflation of shoddy journalism with historical fascism is purely inflammatory, a historical parallel that is by any standards specious and inapt. With reference to Jon Wiener's contributions to the de Man affair, Derrida observes: "It is frightening to think that its author teaches history at a university."[20] Derrida is of course entitled to his opinion. But what makes this instance of character defamation any more acceptable than the famous case of the Yale philosophy professor who, in a letter to the French minister of culture, urged that Derrida be forbidden from calling himself a philosopher during his sojourns abroad, since deconstruction has nothing to do with philosophy?

In his analysis of de Man's collaborationist writings, Derrida employs the method of textual analysis—"so-called deconstruction"—he has refined over a period of thirty years. De Man's wartime journalism, he tells us, is afflicted with the same textual fissures and cleavages that characterize all *écriture:* it is "constantly split, disjointed, engaged in incessant conflicts." Or, as he goes on to inform us in a classically deconstructionist mode: "all [de Man's] propositions carry within themselves a counterposition"; all are marked by a "*double edge* and a *double bind.*"[21] As a result, they become fodder for the by now familiar deconstructionist technique of a double reading: of a *double séance* or a *double lecture.*

One can, I think, concede Derrida's rhetorical caveats while disagreeing with the material conclusions to which they ineluctably propel him: that texts which at first glance appeared collaborationist prove in fact not to be so once subjected to the procedure of the *double lecture,* which increasingly becomes a type of hermeneutical universal solvent. Moreover, as a result of this classical deconstructionist gesture, a new leitmotif in the de Man texts becomes apparent: Derrida shows them to contain a veiled protest against the Occupation and its consequences for European cultural life.

The boldness of Derrida's strategy is unquestionable. He undertakes a deconstruction of de Man's most blatantly anti-Semitic text, "The Jews in Contemporary Literature," to show how an article that concludes by recommending "the creation of a Jewish colony isolated from Europe" as a "solution to the Jewish problem"[22] masks instead the sentiments of a conscience-ridden *résistant.* However, according to the historian Raul Hilberg, author of *The Destruction of the European Jews,* at this point the deportations in Belgium had reached such an extreme that it was impossible to remain unaware of the insidious fate awaiting the Jews. As Hilberg observes, "Almost all educated Belgians knew by 1941 or at the latest, 1942, that Jews were being sent eastward to be exterminated."[23] Even if de Man remained unaware of the fate awaiting Belgium's deported Jews, there could be little doubt concerning the massive, everyday persecution they endured at the hands of the Nazi occupiers and their Belgian henchmen: a 1940 decree had already banned Jews from the civil service, the press, the practice of law, and education. In the summer of 1941, Jewish businesses were confiscated; a few months later, a curfew was imposed on Jews. In the words of historian Michael Marrus: "One would have had to live in a plastic bubble to be oblivious to the massive, open, intense persecution of the Jews then under way, which was perfectly evident to someone in de Man's position."[24] But Derrida characteristically shows little interest in historical context. He is exclusively interested in *rhetorical* context, which he proceeds autocratically to define. Yes, he at first concedes, such remarks would seem to reflect poorly on the young de Man. Nevertheless, he counters, "one must have the courage to answer injustice with justice"—that is, "justice" for de Man.

The linchpin of Derrida's double reading concerns de Man's by now well-known critique of "vulgar anti-Semitism," an ideology that perceives the entirety of interwar European literature as "degenerate" insofar as it has been "enjuivé." De Man comes to the defense of European modernism of the 1920s and 1930s in order to deny that, as the so-called vulgar anti-Semites would have it, Jews have played a dominant role. "It would be a rather unflattering appreciation of Western writers to reduce them to being mere imitators of a Jewish culture that is foreign to them," he observes. Moreover, de Man tells us, it is the Jews themselves who are guilty of having disseminated this myth: "Often, they have glorified themselves as the leaders of literary movements that characterize our age. But the error has, in fact, a deeper cause. At the origin of the thesis of a Jewish takeover is the very widespread belief according to which the modern novel and modern poetry are nothing but a kind of monstrous outgrowth of the world war. Since the Jews have, in fact, played an important role in the phony and disordered existence of Europe since 1920, a novel born in this atmosphere would deserve, up to a certain extent, the qualification of *enjuivé*."[25]

The so-called vulgar anti-Semites thus commit the additional sin of succumbing to Jewish propaganda. De Man in no way contests the fact that, to repeat, "the Jews have . . . played an important role in the phony and disordered existence of Europe since 1920." He merely wishes to point out, in a manner consistent with his general position on modern art and literature, that the sanctum of twentieth-century modernism has fortunately largely remained uncontaminated by pernicious Jewish influence.

Now, for Derrida, de Man's equivocations concerning "vulgar anti-Semitism" suggest an interpretation of the foregoing passages that is remarkably free of slippages and ambiguities.[26] Instead, it would seem they make for an open-and-shut case in de Man's favor. Here are Derrida's conclusions: "To scoff at vulgar anti-Semitism, is that not also to scoff at or mock the vulgarity of anti-Semitism? . . . To condemn vulgar anti-Semitism may leave one to understand that there is a distinguished anti-Semitism in whose name the vulgar variety is put down. De Man never says such a thing, even though one may condemn his silence. But the phrase can also mean something else, and this reading can always contaminate the other in a clandestine fashion: to condemn 'vulgar anti-Semitism,' especially if one makes no mention of the other kind, is to condemn anti-Semitism itself *inasmuch* as it is vulgar, always and essentially vulgar."

This is a conclusion that, shortly thereafter, Derrida considers worthy of re-emphasizing: "The logic of these first two paragraphs controls everything that follows; it is a matter of condemning anti-Semitism *inasmuch as it is vulgar* . . . and of condemning this anti-Semitism *as regards literature:* its history, its own laws, its relations to history in general."[27] Consequently, Derrida believes that as a result of de Man's forthright denunciation of "vulgar anti-Semitism," "The Jews in Contemporary Literature" represents a "nonconformist" text ("as Paul de Man, as also his uncle, always was [nonconformist]").[28]

But, contra Derrida, in the article in question de Man's discussion of vulgar anti-Semitism does not blossom into a critique of anti-Semitism in general; or even, as Derrida contends, of all "anti-Semitism inasmuch as it is vulgar." Instead, the reference is decidedly localized and specific, referring only to those who employ anti-Semitism in order to denigrate modern art and literature. Moreover, there exists a third possibility—very likely, the most plausible—that Derrida strangely fails to contemplate: that in the text in question, vulgar anti-Semitism stands for a type of traditional European cultural anti-Semitism, to which a modern doctrinaire and systematic anti-Semitism stands in opposition. Cultural anti-Semitism rests content with attributing to Jews primary responsibility for a vast array of social ills, such as excessive economic, professional, and cultural influence. Conversely, scientific anti-Semitism understands Jewish influences in terms of their unexpungeable hereditary bases. In fact, one of the distinguishing features of National Socialist racism is that it presented an insidious and methodical alternative to customary European anti-Semitism. Under the old anti-Semitism, which was religiously based, Jews at least had the option of conversion to spare themselves from proscriptions, persecutions, and the inquisitor's auto-da-fé. According to Nazism's biological anti-Semitism, conversely, there was no possibility of escaping the strictures of blood and race.

De Man's recommendation concerning "the creation of a Jewish colony isolated from Europe" is of course far from innocent. Instead, it corresponds to the so-called Madagascar solution to the Jewish question openly entertained by Nazi officials during the 1930s, which envisioned a massive resettlement of Jews on the African island. The plan was scrapped once the Nazis realized that it was something that the British, who controlled vital Atlantic shipping lanes, would never permit. Once abandoned, it was replaced by the better known

Final Solution. Nevertheless, in a 1937 Nazi publication, one finds the following ominous reference to its currency in a Francophone context: "The Madagascar solution has also found its partisans in France; we would like to quote as proof this phrase that has been seen written by us a number of times in French newspapers: 'Madagassez les Juifs.' "[29]

Finally, as the historian Zeev Sternhell points out, "The men in charge of German propaganda . . . had a wonderful knowledge of the mentality of the French-speaking intelligentsia. They grasped that a coarse, low-level anti-Semitism could be counterproductive, that they needed something [more] subtle"—such as the more refined racism purveyed by de Man.

The editors of de Man's wartime journalism do their readership a potential disservice by characterizing the articles as "texts, chiefly on literary and cultural topics, [which] at times take up the themes and idiom of the discourse promulgated during the Occupation by the Nazis and their collaborators."[30] That de Man's contributions to *Le Soir* in the main concerned "literary and cultural topics" makes them no less collaborationist. As anyone familiar with the terms of the Occupation should know, an essential part of the Nazi program consisted of a battle for the hearts and minds of the civilian population. The more the Nazis could present their conquests as a palatable or legitimate alternative to the status quo ante, the less they would have to squander their resources via more forceful means. Once their military conquests proved successful, their struggle for European cultural hegemony began. Prominent journalists and intellectuals who urged cooperation with the Nazis on cultural grounds often facilitated their success as much as those engaged in more direct forms of collaboration. De Man plays into the hands of the Nazi conquerors in precisely this vein when he urges his readers not to view the German victory as a Belgian defeat, but as "the beginning of a revolution that seeks to organize European society in a more equitable manner."[31] In quite a few cases (e.g., that of French fascist littérateur Robert Brasillach) ideological collaborators were in fact tried and executed for their acts. In order to avoid a similar fate, Brasillach's fellow fascist scribe and collaborator, Drieu la Rochelle, committed suicide in 1945. The following year, the wartime editor of *Le Soir*, Raymond de Becker, was convicted of war crimes and sentenced to death (though the sentence was later commuted). Finally, one of de Man's *Le Soir* colleagues, Louis Fonsny, who, like de Man, was a regular contributor to the paper's feuilleton section, was assassinated by the Belgian Resistance in January 1943.[32]

The article on "The Jews in Contemporary Literature" notwithstanding, anti-Semitism did not play a large role in the collaborationist worldview of the young Paul de Man. Moreover, a cursory reading of his wartime writings reveals that, although de Man may have been a Nazi sympathizer, he was anything but a Nazi. Instead, he was what one might call a "normal fascist"—a term that merits further scrutiny if one is to fathom the rationale behind de Man's commitment to the occupationist cause. What stands out about de Man's collaborationist writings is that they are entirely unexceptional; which makes the voluminous and immense interpretive energies that have been devoted to deciphering their hidden meanings all the more curious. Thus, according to Sternhell, "Considered in their context, de Man's youthful writings appear to be extremely banal."[33] Alice Kaplan expresses a remarkably similar insight: "De Man's work in *Le Soir* is at once a brilliant and banal example of all clichés of fascist nationalism: brilliant for the way he argues his position, for the logic he brings to bear, and banal because a thousand other intellectuals claimed the same high ground, reached the same conclusions, had essentially the same effect."[34]

In his youth, de Man participated in a European-wide movement to have quit with the values of liberalism, republicanism, humanism, individualism, *les droits de l'homme;* in short, to put an end to the so-called ideas of 1789 that had been ushered into European political culture by the French Revolution. The European fascist movements varied from country to country. The German variant was fanatically anti-Semitic; in Italian fascism, conversely, racial animus toward the Jews played no role. French fascism, closer to the Italian model in many respects, stood somewhere between the two. However, if one peruses de Man's wartime articles, one finds that all the essential concepts and categories of the generic fascist *Weltanschauung* are unmistakably present: an endorsement of the values of leadership, virility, authority, hierarchy, corporatism, and race—all of which stand as antitheses to the heritage of European liberalism and represent the necessary preconditions for a sweeping national and cultural renewal.

The fascist worldview of which de Man partakes did not emerge suddenly or ex nihilo. In France it was a logical outgrowth of the counterrevolutionary ideology of the Third Republic, which gained political credibility and coherence in the aftermath of the Boulanger and Dreyfus affairs. Dreyfus's case revealed dramatically (and well in advance of conditions in central Europe) the tremendous amount of political capital that anti-Republican forces stood to reap from playing the anti-Semitic card. In the mid-1920s, Georges Valois's Faisceau gave France its first (if short-lived) bona fide fascist party. By the 1930s the political stock of the Third Republic had fallen so low that the cry of many intellectuals—both on the left and on the right—had become: "Better Hitler than Blum." For many, a German victory offered the prospect of abandoning a moribund bourgeois democracy and supplanting it with "a superior political culture, based on the primacy of the collectivity, on the sense of duty and sacrifice, on hierarchy and discipline."[35] In July 1936, Maurice Blanchot, writing in the protofascist journal *Combat,* would openly polemicize against "the detestable character of what is called with solemnity the Blum experiment" (i.e., the Popular Front government), which he characterizes as, "A splendid union, a holy alliance, this conglomerate of Soviet, Jewish, and capitalist interests."[36] A year earlier, Georges Bataille, in "The Psychological Structure of Fascism," had openly sung the praises of the European fascist leaders: "Opposed to democratic politicians, who represent in different countries the platitude inherent to *homogeneous* society, Mussolini and Hitler immediately stand out as something *other.*"[37]

In de Man's case the influence of his uncle Henri—convicted of treason in absentia by a Belgian military tribunal following the war—would play a determinative role in the nephew's political formation. The elder de Man, president of the Belgian Workers' Party and a leading figure in international socialism during the interwar years, was largely responsible for convincing King Leopold III, whom he served as adviser, to capitulate following the German invasion. By 1940 he was convinced that "the war has led to the debacle of the parliamentary regime and of the capitalist plutocracy in the so-called democracies. For the working class and for socialism, this collapse of a decrepit world, far from being a disaster, is a deliverance." His conclusion, expressed a few weeks later: "Henceforth, democracy and socialism will be authoritarian or they will not exist at all."[38]

All of de Man's defenders—Miller, Derrida, Geoffrey Hartman, and many others—who declare that the articles published in *Le Soir* in 1941 and 1942 were far from the work of a die-hard National Socialist are right. At the same time, their observations are entirely beside the point. In the years 1940–44 one need not have been a convinced Nazi to have been an extremely valuable collaborator. In fact, often the opposite was true. After all, despite its brutality toward Communists, Jews, *résistants,* and other undesirables, the Nazi Occupation of Western Europe was not on a par with what was occurring simultaneously in the East. With the exception of historically disputed Alsace-Lorraine, there were no large-scale annexations in the West. Nor did there occur, as in the East, mass deportations of slave laborers. During 1940–42, one-third of France remained unoccupied and, under Pétain and Vichy, was allowed a semblance of self-rule. All of which is to say that in Western Europe, including Belgium, the Nazis put on a very different face from the one they wore in Poland, Czechoslovakia, and the Baltic states. In France and Belgium they were at great pains to present themselves as conquerors who were also liberators: as victors who purportedly had the best interest of the vanquished peoples in mind; as occupiers who sought to free those they had conquered from the political morass of a decadent democratic culture and thereby to pave the way for the establishment of indigenous corporative-authoritarian political regimes, such as Vichy. To this end, and strange as it may sound to American ears, the Nazis systematically strove to pass themselves off as the guarantors of European civilization: a civilization whose greatness was threatened by the values of corrupt, plutocratic, and materialistic democratic regimes. They wanted the occupied countries to view the war against England and the United States (not to mention the Soviet Union) as a heroic struggle against an ignoble materialist culture—against the spirit of "Manchester"—that was alien to the good European traditions that the Nazis claimed to defend. After all, didn't France's "strange defeat" of June 1940 serve as an undeniable historical confirmation that those governments who represented the "ideas of 1789" had failed to measure up to the might and vigor of Europe's youthful fascist regimes? Hence, the German occupiers were not so much desirous of propaganda that would reflect Nazi values per se. They actively sought to mask the true brutality of those values. Instead, in the West they wanted the ideology of fascism to conjure visions of postdemocratic European cultural renewal. In this context de Man's contributions to *Le Soir* fit like a glove.

One theme over which de Man's advocates have pondered concerns his stalwart defense of literary modernism. To take one instance: in the article "Jews in Contemporary Literature," he singles out Gide, Lawrence, Hemingway, and Kafka for praise. Surely, this is a stance that is not only unreconcilable with the Nazi position on art—according to which modernism was summarily dismissed as "entartete Kunst" (degenerate art)—it must represent a form of covert criticism of or resistance to the heroic realism of National Socialist aesthetics. Indeed, this is the conclusion explicitly reached by Derrida:

> In 1941, under the German occupation, and first of all in the context of this newspaper, the *presentation* of such a thesis [in defense of aesthetic formalism] . . . goes rather against the current. One can at least read it as an anticonformist attack. Its insolence can take aim at and strike all those who were then . . . undertaking to judge literature and its history, indeed to administer, control, censor them in function of the dominant ideology of the war. . . . The examples chosen . . . represent everything that Nazism or the right-wing revolutions would have liked to extirpate from history and the great nation.[39]

Derrida's argument would be plausible were it not for two caveats. First, as already indicated, in France and Belgium Nazi censorship was, within certain limits, much less inflexible than Derrida believes. This semblance of tolerance, moreover, was instrumental in allowing the occupiers to pass themselves off, at least in the eyes of those who chose to look the other way, as humanitarian and cultured. As we have seen, de Man's defense of the Occupation and of the "decency, justice, and humanity" of the occupiers may be squarely situated within such an ideological position.

Second, and at least as important, Derrida's defense of de Man presupposes an untenable opposition between modernism and fascism; that is, it implies that one cannot be both a modernist and a defender of fascism. Not only is such a contention unsound; it flies in the face of the many historical instances where partisans of fascism and aesthetic modernism made common cause. The locus classicus of this seemingly strange alliance was of course Mussolini's Italy, where the fascist literati included Gabriele d'Annunzio, Ezra Pound, and Filippo Marinetti. One might look at the case of the British writer Wyndham Lewis, whose embrace of both fascism and literary modernism has been ably analyzed by Fredric Jameson.[40] On occasion, profascist themes made their way into the work of both Lawrence and Yeats.[41] Finally, one might consider the example of the German fascist modernist Ernst Jünger, whom de Man goes out of his way to praise as "the greatest German man of letters of the moment" as well as "the author of a most remarkable sociological study, *Der Arbeiter.*"[42] The latter treatise is an unadulterated fascist encomium that gained widespread influence in the years immediately prior to Hitler's seizure of power.

In his wartime journalism, de Man on several occasions reserves special praise for cultural developments in contemporary Italy. During the interwar years Mussolini's Italy had gained a reputation as a state in which not only would artists play a leading role, but, in particular, those who inclined toward aesthetic modernism. As one observer has remarked: "The young Paul de Man was not torn between fascism and a commitment to modern art; he identified them. And just as important, this is not an idiosyncratic notion on his part. He was in a coherent intellectual tradition when he looked to Italian fascism as a model of a state that gave birth to modern art and gave a role to artists. Seeing de Man in that tradition, as that type of fascist intellectual—different from the Nazis but no less fascist for all that—makes much in the wartime journalism clearer."[43]

The marriage of convenience between fascism and aesthetic modernism, therefore, is not so strange as it may at first sound. After all, literary modernism was often implicitly critical of the unexalted, pedestrian, and utilitarian orientation of modern bourgeois society. Some of its representatives, such as the surrealists and Joyce, chose to align themselves with the political left. Others, such as Pound, the Futurists, and Céline believed that the optimal political means for overcoming the degraded reality of bourgeois liberalism lay with the young fascist regimes. Moreover, the proponents of fascist modernism believed that art had an essential role to play in the process of European cultural renewal. Modernist works, be they poetic, architectural, or literary, were to have a demonstrable *effect* on the reader or viewer. "No longer an autonomous object of beauty to be contemplated by a passive recipient, [they] were designed to transform the status of the recipient in order to reunite him or her with the primal order of race and the permanence of unquestionable values."[44] For de Man, conversely, literary modernism was not immediately practical. It was, nevertheless, a primary manifestation of a cultural health.

There is a final line of defense concerning de Man that also bears scrutiny. It concerns the claim, perhaps most eloquently articulated by Geoffrey Hartman, that de Man's later critical writings represent "a belated, but still powerful, act of conscience"; they constitute "a generalized reflection on rhetoric spurred by the experience of totalitarianism. . . . [H]is turn from the politics of culture to the language of art was not, I think, an escape into but an escape from aestheticism: a disenchantment with that fatal aestheticizing of politics . . . that gave fascism its brilliance."[45]

This point has also been forcefully made by Hillis Miller, who claims the relation between de Man's early and later work is one of "reversal":

The special targets of his radical questioning of received opinions about particular authors, about literary history, and about the relation of literature to history in his later work were just those ideas about these topics that recur in the articles he wrote for *Le Soir:* notions about specific national and racial character and about the uniqueness of each national literature, notions about the independent and autonomous development of literature according to its own intrinsic laws and according to a model of organic development, that is, according to what he called in his latest essays "aesthetic ideology."

According to Miller, de Man's later critique of aesthetic ideology expresses the political pedigree of deconstruction: "Deconstruction is in all its many forms a contribution to knowledge by being a contribution to good and accurate reading of 'social and political reality' as well as of literary and philosophical texts and of the relation between the former and the latter."[46]

In the lexicon of de Man and others (e.g., Philippe Lacoue-Labarthe and

Jean-Luc Nancy in *The Literary Absolute*) aesthetic ideology refers to a longing for wholeness, reconciliation, and formal integrity. It represents a modernist impulsion that one can trace back to romanticism in the programs of "aesthetic education" one finds in the theoretical writings of Schiller and Kleist.[47] It promotes delusions of aesthetic totalization which played a crucial role in the self-understanding of the fascist states. In its reconciliation of antagonisms and its suppression of difference, the drive toward aesthetic totalization, whether in politics or in art, betrays an essential violence. Jonathan Culler picks up where Miller leaves off: "De Man's critique of the aesthetic ideology now resonates also as a critique of the fascist tendencies he had known. . . . The fact that de Man's wartime juvenilia had themselves on occasion exhibited an inclination to idealize the emergence of the German nation in aesthetic terms gives special pertinence to his demonstration that the most insightful literary and philosophical texts of the tradition expose the unwarranted violence required to fuse form and idea, cognition and performance."[48] In the same spirit, Shoshana Felman declares that "de Man's entire work and his later theories bear implicit witness to the Holocaust."[49] To be sure, such witness could hardly be explicit, since the word "Holocaust" itself does not appear *once* in the course of de Man's voluminous writings.

In response I merely pose some questions concerning the viability of the critique of aesthetic ideology as a point of departure for the critique of fascism.

I begin by recalling Thomas Pavel's: "Isn't it rather fortunate that half a century ago the adversaries of Nazi Germany had other weapons to rely on?"[50] Not only is the critique of aesthetic ideology remarkably free of social, historical, or political points of reference; de Man positively cautions against the employment of such references. As he remarks in *Blindness and Insight:* "The bases of historical knowledge are not empirical facts but written texts, even if these texts masquerade in the guise of wars or revolutions"; "Considerations of the actual historical existence of writers are a waste of time from a critical viewpoint"; "Instead of containing or reflecting experience, language constitutes it."[51] The emphasis on the autonomy of texts, on the irreducible rhetoricity of texts, the confusion of "texts" and historical "events" (a classically structuralist confusion, one might add) threatens to make this critical approach virtually *Wirklichkeitsfremd* (alienated from reality). The concern with the rhetorical determinants of textuality is perfectly justifiable; the exclusivity of emphasis, however, is not.

De Man's approach explicitly shuns the idea of historical experience as touchstone or referent. It concentrates single-mindedly on the rhetorical dimension of texts. While the rhetorical approach might excel at accounting for the figurative dimensions of literary texts—metaphor, metonymy, catachresis, and so forth—there would seem to be very little room for another series of concepts and categories manifestly more relevant to the analysis of historical study: categories such as class, economic crisis, modernization, sovereignty, and so forth, many of which would be central for an account of fascism's historical viability and situatedness.[52] Historical events are most often codetermined via forces of "agency" (the intentionality of actors) and "structure" (preexisting institutional factors); they cannot be exclusively understood according to a textual model. Deconstructionists who claim that "every human act whatsoever" is a variant of "reading" risk confusing the issue by inflating the textualist approach to the point where it threatens to become a metaphysical first principle instead of a "practice."[53]

Caveats such as these point to the limitations of invoking de Man's thought as a prototype of antitotalitarian criticism. In the interpretation proffered by Miller, Culler, and others, the emphasis on fascism as a variant of "aesthetic ideology" is drastically overblown.[54] The "aestheticization of politics" (W. Benjamin) is a prominent moment of fascism. It is doubtful, however, whether it is the most important aspect or even one of the most important. It is an approach that certainly recommends itself to those versed in literary or aesthetic theory. But it makes precious little effort to account for other prominent aspects of the fascist experience: the ideology of anti-Semitism, the pitfalls of the German *Sonderweg*, the leadership cult, Germany's belated nationhood, or its crisis of modernization circa 1871–1929. None of these factors can be explained exclusively in semiological terms. Their origins are to be found in nonrhetorical components of German history whose crucial dates are 1806, 1848, 1871, and 1914.

One cannot escape the suspicion that the attempt to endow the later de Man with the credentials of a militant, literary critical antifascist is a post hoc construct, the stuff of apologetic convenience. What raises suspicions, moreover, is that efforts to portray de Man in this vein occurred only after the existence of the *Le Soir* articles was first disclosed, not a day before. Contra the insinuations of Culler and Miller, what strikes one about de Man's literary essays is how remarkably free they are of references to political and social concerns. To paraphrase Hartman, if the later de Man's writings were not quite an escape into aestheticism, neither do they appear as an unmitigated triumph over aestheticism. The emphasis on the autonomy of literature (albeit, a rhetorically fissured autonomy), on the nonrelation between the rhetoricity of texts and their historicity, unambiguously parallels the repeated claims concerning the autonomy of literary modernism in the wartime journalism.

The deconstructive gesture contending that the purported stability of meaning in texts is constantly undermined by their rhetorical dimension risks congealing into an inflexible methodological imperative. Like all fixed ideas, it tends to produce results that are predictable and familiar. As Terry Eagleton has remarked, "The (anti-)epistemology of poststructuralism focuses recurrently on impasse, failure, error, missing the mark, not quite-ness, to the point where insistence that something in a text does not quite come off, has always already failed, is even now not quite failing to deviate from what never exactly already was, has hardened into the sheerest conventional gesture."[55] The irony here, of course, is that once semantic instability or "difference" become sanctified theoretical watchwords, they acquire a "foundational" status that is rhetorically at odds with their intended meaning. In this way deconstructive readings themselves ironically threaten to become not only predetermined, but totalizing: every new reading becomes grist for the mill of Derridean "undecidability" or "différance." As M. H. Abrams once noted: "The deconstructive method works because it can't help working; it is a can't-fail enterprise; there is no complex passage of verse or prose which could possibly serve as a counterinstance to test its validity or limits."[56] Nor have such limitations redounded to the credit of deconstruction as a method of political criticism. As one critic has remarked, "Derrida's insistence that deconstruction's 'work' must be limited to a rigorously elucidated analysis of the conditions of discourse"—that is, his well-nigh exclusive focus on the transcendental-grammatological preconditions of writing or *écriture*—"has continued to mark the limits of its usefulness for political critique."[57]

Under these circumstances it is hardly surprising that talk of the "death of deconstruction" is rife. As Jeffrey Nealon observes in *Double Reading:*

> Deconstruction, it seems, is dead in literature departments today. There is still plenty of discourse being produced concerning deconstruction, but deconstruction's heyday has clearly passed. Precious few critics would identify themselves any longer as "deconstructionists." . . . Deconstruction's death is usually attributed either to suicide, that deconstruction fell back into dead-end formalism it was supposed to remedy, or to murder at the hands of the new historicists, whose calls for rehistoricizing and contextualizing the study of literature have successfully challenged the supposed self-canceling textualism of the deconstructionists.[58]

For the moment I leave aside the more general question concerning deconstruction's possible afterlife and fate. Instead, I conclude by taking a brief look at another representative instance in which poststructuralism's interpretation of fascism figures prominently. Since the debate was provoked by the leading practitioner of poststructuralist historiography, Hayden White, many of the questions concerning deconstruction's understanding of the legacy of fascism appear in a less theoretically sublimated, more clarifying light.

The debate in question was occasioned by White's article on "The Politics of Historical Interpretation," later anthologized in *The Content of the Form*.[59] Much of the article represents a clarification and extrapolation of a position White first developed in *Metahistory* concerning the irreducible discursive-rhetorical constitution of historical knowledge. According to White, there is no such thing as "history in itself," an autonomous body of facts or events that would exist prior to or independently of discourse. Instead, our knowledge of historical events is unavoidably predetermined by the narrative frameworks and rhetorical figures we adopt to situate them. Correspondingly, there can be no such thing as an objective or value-free historical text. Since all attempts at historical understanding are willy-nilly governed by such theoretical para-digms or frameworks, all are inevitably acts of interpretation. This is only another way of saying that all historical interpretations are "political": they entail an often concealed, though, in the last instance, determinative series of ethical choices, value-preferences, and networks of exclusion. One can see clearly how White's reliance on the deconstructive notion of the essentially rhetorical and figurative constitution of texts (an indebtedness he has never denied) plays a key role in his attempt to radically recast the presuppositions of traditional historiography.[60]

In "The Politics of Historical Interpretation" White makes a number of disparaging remarks, inspired in part by Foucault, about history as a profession or "discipline." For White, the professionalization of historical study over the last two centuries, governed as it has been by affirmative, Eurocentric narra-tives of "progress," has been marked and marred by a banishment of utopian prospects. Thus, according to the requirements of history as "discipline," utopian narratives, which defy the accepted standards of scientificity and ob-jectivity, have been expelled insofar as they ipso facto contravene the estab-lished reality-principle.

There are many valuable insights that derive from White's attempt to coun-terbalance the tendential conservatism characteristic of historical study. Still, his critique underestimates the reality and potential for countervailing tenden-cies. To wit: much of the "social history from below" that has been written since the 1960s embraces the utopian goal of restoring key aspects of the past to its victims; moreover, it does so in a spirit of Benjaminian remembrance oriented toward an emancipatory future. As a result, White's own choice of narrative frameworks becomes monolithic: the portrait he paints is one of absolutes in which it is difficult for mediating tendencies or prospects to emerge. On the one hand, there is the wholly depraved field of professional historiography; on the other hand, there is an elusive panacea of utopian history-writing. And it is precisely at the point where White tries to specify what the latter has to offer qua "other" or "heterological" that his position frankly begins to unravel. Not coincidentally, this is also the point where poststructuralism's relation to the tradition of European fascism is thematized.

To begin with, if history-writing can no longer be construed as the representation of the "real," then the traditional historicist criterion of writing history "the way it really was"—correspondence to the "facts"—also falls by the wayside. But insofar as all objective standards have also been eliminated, and since all history-writing is deemed discursive-rhetorical, the question arises as to how we are to go about choosing and evaluating among the various discursive positions available to us. As White confesses: "One must face the fact that when it comes to apprehending the historical record, there are no grounds, to be found in the historical record itself for preferring one way of construing its meaning over another."[61]

But this methodological cul-de-sac results in White's adoption of some rather tenuous positions, as when he grapples with the phenomenon of so-called Holocaust revisionists or deniers. In lieu of any normative grounds to differentiate between interpretations we might embrace and those we ought to reject (such as the deniers), White leaves us with "effectiveness" as the sole criterion of truth. Thus, comparing Israeli and Palestinian interpretations of the Holocaust, he comes to a conclusion that seems to verge on moral bankruptcy: "the effort of the Palestinian people to mount a politically effective response to Israeli policies entails the production of a similarly *effective ideology* [concerning the Holocaust], complete with an interpretation of their history capable of endowing it with meaning."[62] In other words (and there are additional passages in which White admits this verbatim), if a standpoint proves "functional" for a given community—as Holocaust denial might be for Europe's neofascists—it would qualify as "true" in White's terms. The Israelis have an interpretation of the Holocaust that is "functionally effective" for their nation, just as the Palestinians have their interpretation. That a critical historiography, constituted by responsible practitioners, might be able to lay bare the ideological (hence, inaccurate and unjust) aspects of *both* positions is an option that never occurs to White, in part, due to his a priori rejection of history as "discipline." In such passages, it becomes clear that "truth as effectiveness" is all that remains in White's rigid endorsement of a neo-Nietzschean, perspectival morality/epistemology. But as Carlo Ginsburg warns in this connection: "We can conclude that if [Holocaust denier Robert] Faurisson's narrative were ever to prove *effective*, it would be regarded by White as true as well."[63] Similar objections to White's functionalist interpretation of historical narrative have been voiced by Saul Friedlander: "White's theses . . . appear untenable when their corollaries are considered within the present context. For instance, what would have happened if the Nazis had won the war? . . . How in this case would White (who clearly rejects any revisionist version of the Holocaust) define an epistemological criterion for . . . these events, without using any reference to 'political effectiveness.' "[64]

This brings us to the aspect of White's argument that is explicitly concerned with the fascist tradition. If functional truth is all there is, then the standpoint of metahistory would be able to increase our self-awareness, but would bear little relation to the project of freeing us from the constraints of domination. From this perspective, one truth would be as good as another. Those aware of this situation would merely possess a greater degree of self-knowledge. White attempts to remedy the quietistic implications of this position by identifying metahistory with a historiography of the "sublime," while accusing conventional historiography of rhetorically privileging the "beautiful." In doing so, it seems that White has borrowed a page from Jean-François Lyotard's *The Postmodern Condition*. There, too, the sublime, as reappropriated by postmodernism, serves as a cure for the modernist/aestheticist celebration of beauty.

The problem with historical narratives that rhetorically favor beauty is that they are oriented toward the values of "totality," "unity," and "coherence." In other words, they are at cross-purposes with the poststructuralist values White seeks to promote, which champion rupture, fragmentation, and difference. The "beautiful" narratives of conventional historiography promote Enlightenment visions of seamless progress and wholeness, and all their attendant ills. White's partisanship for the sublime seeks to undercut these tendencies and thereby to restore a deconstructionist-utopian dimension to history-writing that has been marginalized by a canonical modernism. White refers to this poststructuralist utopia as a "visionary politics."

But what would this historiography of the sublime look like? From where would it take its bearings and models? What exactly would it pose as an alternative to the much-maligned modernist historiography of the beautiful?

At long last, White sets his cards down on the table for all to see. The choice we are offered couldn't be more stark—or more alarming. As White confesses: "the kind of perspective on history that I have been implicitly praising is conventionally associated with the ideologies of fascist regimes. Something like

Schiller's notion of the historical sublime or Nietzsche's version of it is certainly present in the thought of such philosophers as Heidegger and Gentile and in the intuitions of Hitler and Mussolini. But having assumed as much, we must guard against a sentimentalism [*sic*] that would lead us to write off such a conception of history simply because it has been associated with fascist ideologies."

In sum: "fascist politics is in part the price paid for the very domestication of historical consciousness that is supposed to stand against it."[65]

White's embrace of a fascist sublime as an antidote to the purportedly beautiful narratives of modernist historiography is especially intriguing in light of the "critique of aesthetic ideology" defense that has been proffered on de Man's behalf. That defense claimed that de Man's critique of the aestheticist longing for wholeness, totality, and beauty was in principle antitotalitarian. But White's position has the merit of showing us that the intellectual stakes involved in an ethos that celebrates the transgressive sublime are more complex; that a "visionary politics" of gratuitous rupture embraced by poststructuralism also bears affinities with aestheticizing tendencies proper to the fascist sublime.

Mussolini's son-in-law and foreign minister Galeazzo Ciano clarified the issue with his notorious comparison of the aerial bombs exploding among defenseless Ethiopians with flowers bursting into bloom. The aesthetics of violence characteristic of the fascist sensibility harbors its own "critique of aesthetic ideology." It seeks to replace the totality-oriented aesthetics of beauty that is proper to bourgeois culture with sublime acts of transgression—not in the sphere of autonomous art, but in life itself.

AFTERWORD:

DERRIDA ON MARX, OR THE PERILS

OF LEFT HEIDEGGERIANISM

The question of deconstruction's relationship to contemporary politics has always been a sore point. The criticisms that have been leveled against it for its deficiencies in this regard are by now quite familiar. Most of these critiques have centered on the issue of deconstruction's inordinate focus on questions of textuality and reading—an issue best dramatized perhaps by Derrida's oft-cited and controversial maxim: "there is nothing outside the text."[1] Derrida's detractors have alleged that this well-nigh exclusive preoccupation with semiotic themes, with the figuration of texts, has functioned at the expense of more worldly and practical concerns. The world might be crumbling all around us, they charge, but Derrida is more interested in the contingencies of this or that phoneme: for example, the amusing fact that in French, Hegel's name is a homophone for the word for eagle ("aigle"). As those familiar with Derrida's work know, this chance homophonic equivalence gave rise to a rumination of some three hundred pages concerned with analogous linguistic slippages and fissures in the (some would say) appropriately titled *Glas*.[2]

One of the first to raise such charges of practical-political irrelevance against Derrida's negative semiotics of reading was none other than Michel Foucault. In his response to Derrida's unsparing critique of *Madness and Civilization*, Foucault lambasts deconstruction as nothing more than a (negative) variant of the classically French method of "éxplication du texte." According to Foucault, it practices a "historically determined little pedagogy" which is characterized by "the reduction of discursive practices [which are for Foucault at the origins of "power"—R.W.] to textual traces: the elision of the events produced therein and the retention only of marks for a reading; the invention of voices behind texts to avoid having to analyze the modes of implication of the subject in discourses; the assigning of the originary as said and unsaid in the text to avoid replacing discursive practices in the field of transformations where they are carried out." Thus, according to Foucault, Derrida offers us a pedagogy "which teaches the pupil that there is nothing outside the text" and "which conversely gives to the master's voice the limitless sovereignty which allows it to restate the text indefinitely."[3]

Nor is Foucault the only critic to have challenged Derrida in this way. Edward Said contends that Derrida's highly formalized obsession with the abstruse terms of "archewriting"—that is, with avowed "non-concepts" such as the trace, grammatology, supplement, différance, dissemination, and so forth—ends up by "muddling . . . thought beyond the possibility of usefulness." Said continues: "The effect of [deconstructionist] logic (the *mise en abime*) is to reduce everything that we think of as having some extratextual leverage in the text to a textual function. . . . Derrida's key words . . . are unregenerate signs: he says that they cannot be made more significant than signifiers are. In some quite urgent way, then, there is something frivolous about them, as all words that cannot be accommodated to a philosophy of serious need or utility are futile or unserious."[4]

Indeed, other critics on the Left have accused deconstruction of representing a linguistically sublimated version of 1960s radicalism. In their eyes it embodies a form of ersatz praxis, which promotes a type of displaced or pseudo-radicalism: instead of unmasking the ills of contemporary society, one exposes the traces of "metaphysics" or "presence" in the theoretical texts of Plato, Lévi-Strauss, Rousseau, Husserl, Levinas, Austin, and so forth. Nor has Derrida's well-nigh exclusive orientation toward the texts of Dead White European Males endeared him among proponents of contemporary multiculturalism.[5] Even former wholehearted supporters, such as Gayatri Spivak, have on occasion railed volubly against deconstruction's long-standing refusal "to open onto an 'outside' constituted by ethico-political contingencies."[6]

Needless to say, Derrida has not taken well to such criticisms. He believes that, apart from a loyal coterie of initiates, the political implications of his work have been seriously misunderstood. Here, however, one might inquire as to how one could, from a strictly deconstructionist standpoint, actually distinguish instances of misunderstanding from understanding in general. After all, when a theory is predicated on the maxims of dissemination, translation, and "iterability," on the claim that "all understanding is merely a species of misunderstanding," one would like to know on what basis the founder of deconstruction can plausibly claim to have been "misunderstood." In an era in which the claims to authorship as well as other so-called transcendental signifieds and signifiers have been so thoroughly deconstructed, and in which the Derridean maxim about understanding as a species of misunderstanding has become a commonplace, how exactly can an author rightfully claim to be misinterpreted?

It would be more fruitful, I believe, to inquire why it is that Derrida's texts have been so consistently read—or as he would have it, "misread"—along the lines of the aforementioned criticisms.

Nevertheless, in his own defense Derrida has always insisted that "discourses on double affirmation, the gift beyond exchange and distribution, the undecidable, the incommensurable or the incalculable, or on singularity, difference and heterogeneity are also, through and through, at least obliquely discourses on justice, [ethics and politics]."[7] And in response to one critic's accusation that "deconstruction is so obsessed with the play of difference that it ultimately ends up indifferent to everything," Derrida insists that "deconstruction is not an enclosure in nothingness but an openness towards the other"; in this openness it seeks to "reevaluate the indispensable notion of responsibility" in ways that are fraught with ethical and political consequences.[8] Elsewhere he does not shy away from immodestly insisting: "Deconstruction is justice. . . . I know nothing more just than what I call deconstruction." And further: "Deconstruction is mad about this kind of justice. Mad about the desire for justice."[9]

From his very first texts, Derrida has always emphasized the positional or contextual nature of deconstruction. His recent preoccupation with Marx is no exception. Undeniably, since the mid-1980s Derrida has sought to reposition his thought in order to counter the charges of ethical indifference and apoliticism, the suspicion that deconstruction is interested in little more than the arbitrary "free play of signification." Nevertheless, many of these efforts have failed to go beyond a few rather abstract and perfunctory invocations of "responsibility" and "openness toward the other" as in the remarks just cited. In lieu of a more concrete specification of the meaning of otherness and openness, of which "others" we should open ourselves toward, of how precisely we should open ourselves to the other and why, and of the ways we might translate the ethical maxim of openness into forms of practical life conduct or everyday institutional settings, we are left with a directive that in its generality and imprecision seems more frustrating than illuminating.

In certain respects, the problematic of otherness as raised by Derrida raises more questions than it is able to solve. One can for example think of "others"—neo-Nazis, white supremacists, racists—who for compelling reasons have forfeited their right to my openness. Should or must I remain open to *all* others in precisely the same way—my wife, colleagues, friends, perfect strangers, enemies? Freud tried to address some of these dilemmas in *Civilization and Its Discontents* when he forcefully called into question the biblical commandment, "love the other as thyself." For him this maxim represented merely one in a series of unattainable ideals erected by civilization. Such commandments, which emanate from the social super ego, are a primary source of a neurotic discomfort with civilization, Freud would contend. "My love is something valuable to me which I ought not to throw away without reflection," he remarks. "On closer inspection . . . not merely is [the] stranger in general unworthy of my love; I must honestly confess that he has more claim to my hostility and even my hatred."[10]

In the Introduction I spoke of a peculiar development in the history of ideas whereby a critique of "the West" formerly purveyed by thinkers on the German Right during the 1920s became popular among the French intellectual Left in the 1960s. In Germany this critique, as set forth by conservative revolutionary theorists such as Oswald Spengler, Ernst Jünger, and Carl Schmitt, took aim at a decadent and materialistic bourgeois civilization. They sought to replace the latter with a new form of Gemeinschaft or community that would nevertheless prove capable of meeting the challenges of modern technological society—especially with reference to the realm of international politics and the ultimate instance of war. The tenor of their views, which often crystallized around the latently totalitarian notion of the "total state," was distinctly fascistic.[11]

In postwar France this critique of civilization took hold via the influence of the German philosopher Martin Heidegger. In the years preceding Hitler's seizure of power, Heidegger had allied himself intellectually and politically with conservative revolutionaries such as Schmitt and Jünger.[12] And of course in the fateful year of 1933, he committed himself wholesale to the Nazi revolution. As he remarked on one occasion: "Let not doctrines and ideas be the rules of your Being. The Fuhrer alone is the present and future German reality and its law."[13] Insofar as Heidegger's reception in France was primarily philosophical and highly decontextualized, the profoundly ideological implications of his thought remained largely unremarked.[14] Nevertheless, Heidegger's doctrine of philosophical antihumanism, as mediated through indigenous French traditions such as Lévi-Strauss's structural anthropology and Lacanian psychoanalysis, became during the 1960s an obligatory right of passage for a vast array of significant figures on the French intellectual Left. Here, one would have to add the names of Barthes, Foucault, and Lyotard, as well as, of course, Jacques Derrida. This transplantation of the conservative revolutionary critique of modernity from Germany to France gave rise to a phenomenon that might aptly be described as a "Left Heideggerianism." In the end, a critique of reason, democracy, civilization, and humanism that originated on the German Right during the 1920s was wholly internalized by the French Left. These members of the French philosophical New Left were avowed "post-Marxists," insofar as, in their eyes, Marxism remained overly beholden to the predominant Western theoretical paradigm of self-positing subjectivity.[15]

Derrida's appropriation of Marx may be read in part as a strategic gesture: in an era marked by the collapse of communism and the apparent worldwide triumph of capitalism (yet, one sees that as a result of recent elections in Eastern Europe where the former communists have made significant gains, such claims need to be seriously qualified), we find ourselves at a point where, for the first time in nearly two centuries, bourgeois society is without a major ideological competitor. By underlining the continued relevance of certain aspects of the Marxist tradition, Derrida is trying to remark or reinscribe the events surrounding the fall of communism in a manner that leaves room for political alternatives. But there is another motivation at issue, which allows Derrida, as it were, to reposition himself vis-à-vis his primary constituency, the Anglo-American literary Left. A book on Marx permits him to recertify his left-wing credentials at a time when not only have deconstruction's adequacy for political purposes been called into question, but when Derrida's popularity has been displaced in literature departments by the Foucault-inspired paradigm of the "new historicism."

There are some ironies involved in Derrida's late confrontation with Marx. Forty years ago Derrida's intellectual bête noire, Jean-Paul Sartre, claimed that "Marxism is the unsurpassable horizon of our time."[16] Derrida at last seems to agree. No thinker, he tells us, "seems as lucid concerning the way in which the political is becoming worldwide, concerning the irreducibility of the technical and the media"; few thinkers "have shed so much light on law, international law, and nationalism," and so forth.[17]

The problems that beset Derrida's attempt to come to grips with Marx are the same as those that afflict his efforts to address questions of justice. The title of Derrida's reflections, *Spectres of Marx,* plays on the oft-cited first sentence of the *Communist Manifesto:* "A specter is haunting Europe—the specter of communism." In keeping with this preferred imagery of phantoms and specters, Derrida would like to read Marx and all that his doctrines signify—the critique of capitalism, of modern technology, of the nation-state, and so forth—as a ghostly presence whose theories continue to "haunt" modern bourgeois society and all its multifarious inadequacies, despite the collapse of "really existing socialism." Herein lies the initial plausibility of his argument: now that state socialism has, to continue Derrida's metaphorics, given up the ghost, the specter of the Marxist critique of capitalist society has become more necessary than ever. Otherwise, world capitalism threatens to become an all-consuming mono-lith, devoid of countervailing tendencies and otherness.

But the terms in which Derrida understands contemporary society are semi-apocalyptical. In fact they rely on aspects of the Marxist tradition that in many ways have proved the most problematical and the least serviceable for the purposes of radical criticism. The deficiencies of Marxist thought pertain to a metatheoretical framework that stressed: (1) a nonfalsifiable philosophy of history; (2) a neo-Hegelian (hence, metaphysical) conception of the proletariat as the "universal class"; (3) a naiveté concerning the bureaucratic conse-quences related to the goal of socializing the means of production. Moreover, in Marx's theory one finds a debilitating conflation of the values of economic and political liberalism. In practice, he often cynically assumed that liberal princi-ples were little more than ideological window-dressing for mechanisms of bourgeois class domination. Often, however, liberal-humanitarian impulses served as the basis for the progressive reform of inhuman levels of exploitation that existed under early capitalism. For such conditions existed in blatant contradiction to the universalistic sentiments espoused by the intellectuals and philosophers who had laid the groundwork for the transition from feudal to modern democratic society.

As part of the attempt to compensate for the manifest normative deficits of traditional Marxism, in the last ten years a major effort has been undertaken in order to develop a critical theory of democracy. In principle such a theory would preserve Marx's original critique of the excrescences of capitalist de-velopment with a greater attention to the requirements for justice, fairness, and equity embodied in the modern democratic idea.[18] It is worth noting that Derrida takes virtually no interest in these developments. He situates himself *au delà* or beyond contemporary debates concerning democratic theory. But this is hardly an accident. He adopts this position in part for reasons of theoret-ical consistency: according to the precepts of deconstruction, normative ques-tions are, strictly speaking, "undecidable." Were deconstruction to condescend to debate in the idiom and terms of normative political theory, it would suc-cumb to an entire train of logocentric biases and illusions that, for decades, it has been at pains to combat.

Instead, in *Spectres of Marx,* as in "The Force of Law," we are presented with a set of Manichean extremes: on the one hand there is the degraded phenome-non of what Derrida characterizes as "world capitalism"; on the other, a myste-rious appeal to a messianic condition *à venir.* As Derrida avows at one point: it is a "matter of thinking another historicity—not a new history or still less a 'new historicism,' but another opening of event-ness as historicity that permitted one not to renounce, but on the contrary *to open up access to an affirmative thinking of the messianic.* . . ."[19] The Marxist critique of capitalism, we are told, points in the direction of this messianic future, this specter or ghost of a utopia "to come." Yet, what hinders Derrida's presentation is a dearth of mediating elements: concepts or terms that would be able to bridge the gap between the two extremes he has set forth. In lieu of such mediating elements or tendencies, one is left, in the tradition of *Heilsgeschichte,* with a stark opposition between the absolute perdition of the historical present and the sublimity of the messianic era to come. As one critic has pointed out: "in order to identify himself with a 'certain spirit of Marx' Derrida must not only strip Marxism of all its political practices and philosophical traditions but also then recoup it only in the indeterminacy of a . . . 'messianic-eschatological' mode."[20] The later Heidegger once famously observed that so utterly forlorn and hopeless were conditions in the modern world that, "Only a god can save us."[21] By relying on the idiom of messianism and negative theology to ground social critique, Derrida—true to the Left Heideggerian legacy—follows closely in the master's footsteps.

Thus, in the book on Marx, and in keeping with the tradition of Left Heideggerianism, Derrida succumbs to the temptation of reducing democracy and liberalism essentially to forms of capitalist rule. He rails against those "who find the means to puff out their chests with the good conscience of capitalism, liberalism, and the virtues of parliamentary democracy"—as if the conceptual bases of all three phenomena were in essence the same.[22] Historically, the normative precepts of liberalism and democracy have often entered into sharp conflict with the capitalist ethos of profit maximization—as one has seen in the history of the labor, women's, and ecology movements. In the interstices of these various social spheres, with their conflicting normative claims, lies a potential for protest and social reform that Derrida excludes by virtue of the apocalyptical theoretical framework he adopts.

In an earlier work Derrida, in neo–Heideggerian fashion, condemned the social sciences as a species of "techno-science"—that is, for being in essence logocentric: "The term techno-science has to be accepted," observes Derrida, "and its acceptance confirms the fact that an essential affinity ties together objective knowledge, the principle of reason, and a certain metaphysical determination of the relation to truth."[23] As a result of this condemnation, his understanding of late capitalist society seems empirically impoverished. Throughout his text one finds tantalizing yet superficial allusions to new social tendencies that are threatening to break through. In the last analysis, though, these innuendoes possess a merely gestural or rhetorical function. They are lacking in substance, in the type of empirical grounding that would provide them with the requisite cogency. As one reviewer has observed, Derrida's text displays a "systematic . . . failure to engage genuinely with any of the social forces which he is concerned to regulate through revised, 'inspired' laws."[24] Ultimately, the inspired rhetoricity of his text threatens to collapse amid the weight of platitudes and clichés. "At a time when a new world disorder attempts to install its neocapitalism and neoliberalism," remarks Derrida, ". . . hegemony still organizes the repression and thus the confirmation of a haunting." "No one, it seems to me, can *contest* the fact," he continues, "that a dogmatics is attempting to install its worldwide hegemony. . . ."[25]

Derrida polemicizes ineffectually against the triumph of "tele-technics," which he defines as "communications and interpretations, selective and hierarchized production of 'information' through channels whose power has grown in an absolutely unheard of fashion. . . ." The techno-mediatic frenzy is supported, in Derrida's words, by the proliferation of a "scholarly or academic culture, notably that of historians, sociologists and politologists, theoreticians of literature, anthropologists, philosophers, in particular political philosophers, whose discourse itself is relayed by the academic and commercial press, but also by the media in general."[26] Strangely yet conveniently, the one academic subculture that has been exempted from the foregoing list is deconstruction itself.

The "techno-mediatic power," as well as its "*spectral* effects," must be analyzed, claims Derrida, in terms of its "new speed of *apparition*": that is, in terms of "the simulacrum, the synthetic or prosthetic image, the virtual event, cyberspace and surveillance," as well as "the speculations that today deploy unheard-of powers."[27] The aforementioned list—"simulacrum," "prosthetic image," "surveillance—reads like a litany of *gauchiste* buzzwords made familiar to us over the last three decades via the writings of Baudrillard, Foucault, and the late Guy Debord. We find ourselves, as it were, in the middle of a William Gibson novel that has been ghost written by Jacques Derrida. At one point Derrida gratuitously lapses into a few choice Althusserianisms: "In a given situation . . . a hegemonic force always seems to be represented by a dominant rhetoric and ideology, whatever may be the conflicts between forces, the principal contradiction or the secondary contradictions, the overdeterminations and the relays that may later complicate this schema. . . ."[28]

I have assembled these citations at some length in order to make a point. One would have hoped that Derrida, in returning to Marx, would have broken some new ground; that, at the very least, he would have pointed to a new way of understanding Marxism that would free us of some of its more dogmatic encumbrances. Instead, what we are provided with essentially is a Heideggerianized Marx, which is far from an improvement. Like Heidegger's later doctrine of technology, of an all-encompassing logic of "enframing" or *das Gestell*, Derrida's discussion of capitalism in an age of media technics suffers from an impoverishment of action categories. In his analysis surveillance, the prosthetic image, and the simulacrum function as omnipotent unmoved movers. There is no discussion of logics of socialization, of the complex process via which norms are internalized by social actors. The ontological prejudices of philosophical antihumanism, a Heideggerian inheritance, categorically rule out such terms of social analysis. In Derrida's portrayal of information-era capitalism, there are no actors left to speak of; they have been deconstructed along with the "subject"—thus, only ghosts and phantoms remain.

Here, the debilities of the analytical framework correspond to those of arche-writing in general. As a philosophy of language that is predicated on the logics of dissemination and the trace, Derridean grammatology is unable to account for mutual solidarity among actors. The process whereby norms are criticized or accepted by individuals is not merely a product of "iterability," nor is it merely an epiphenomenal blip set against the omnipotent backdrop of Derridean negative semiotics. It is rather the outcome of an intricate interweaving of ontogenesis and socialization. It is a process whereby persons become "social selves" via the internalization of societal roles, values, and norms. Yet, such mechanisms of social integration are always contingent on a moment of individual autonomy: on the capacity of social actors to assent to or to reject communally transmitted norms. Only a theory of socialization that is able to account for this capacity for refusal, for a moment of autonomous individuation, can simultaneously explain the capacity of social actors to resist inherited constellations of power. For want of such perspectives, Derrida's negative hermeneutics of reading threatens to become merely a literary critical version of systems theory: trace, supplement, and différance become the prime movers; the convictions of social actors are merely their effects, something merely inscribed by the endlessly churning, infernal machine of Derridean archewriting.

Following the lead of Debord and Baudrillard, there is a certain plausibility in trying to understand deconstruction as a form of theory appropriate to a neo-Orwellian age of semio-technics: an era in which a surfeit of signification simply overwhelms the subject, leaving in its wake a substratum that is heteronomously fabricated rather than, as with the old liberal ideal, autonomous and self-positing. But this would mean the realization of a brave new world in which no contestation or oppositional praxis could take place, the potential addressees of the theory having been long cyberneticized out of existence.

NOTES

Introduction

1 Lutz Niethammer, *Posthistoire: Has History Come to an End?* trans. P. Camiller (London: Verso, 1992). For Niethammer's discussion of Benjamin in contrast with the theorists of *posthistoire,* see chapter 4, "The Blown-Away Angel: On the Posthistory of a Historical Epistemology of Danger," 101–34. I discuss the postmodernist appropriation of Benjamin in Chapter 4.

Many aspects of the German young conservative, quasi-apocalyptic diagnosis of the times indeed found their way into Benjamin's own historiographical prescriptions, though with an important shift of emphasis: through his metaphor of the "angel of history," Benjamin urges the materialist critic to "brush history against the grain." In this way alone might the passivity of historicism—its tendency to rest content with merely registering and reflecting historical decline—be surmounted. Conversely, Benjamin summons a dialectical historiography to relate the past to the present as a "now-time" (*Jetztzeit*), a moment of "messianic cessation of happening." Instead of prostrating himself before the historicist injunction to record history "the way it really was," the materialist critic must treat the "past [as] charged with the time of the now [in order to] blast it out of the continuum of history." In this way he avoids the perils of the end of history, history perceived as incessant catastrophe or ruin. See Walter Benjamin, "Theses on the Concept of History," in *Illuminations,* ed. Hannah Arendt, trans. H. Zohn (New York: Schocken, 1968), 261.

2 Manfred Frank, "Two Centuries of Philosophical Critique of Reason," in *Reason and Its Other: Rationality in Modern German Philosophy and Culture,* ed. Dieter Freundlieb and Wayne Hudson (Oxford: Berg, 1994), 71. For a discussion of Baeumbler, see Hans Sluga, *Heidegger's Crisis* (Cambridge: Harvard University Press, 1993). For a conventional poststructuralist understanding of Nietzsche as an *avant la lettre* deconstructionist, see Giovanni Vattimo, *The End of Modernity,* trans. J. Snyder (Baltimore: Johns Hopkins University Press, 1988) and *The Adventure of Difference: Philosophy after Nietzsche and Heidegger* (Cambridge: Polity Press, 1993).

3 Frank, *Der kommende Gott: Vorlesungen über die Neue Mythologie* (Frankfurt: Suhrkamp, 1982), 33. For an extensive survey of the French Nouvelle Droite, see Pierre-André Taguieff, *Sur la Nouvelle Droite* (Paris: Descartes et Compagnie, 1994). Of late, the French New Right has entered into a peculiar (though far from unprecedented) devil's pact with certain remnants of French *gauchisme.* On this point, see the interview with Taguieff in *Sur la Nouvelle Droite,* 9–64.

4   See Gitlin, "The Limits of Identity Politics," *Dissent* (Spring 1993): 172–77: "The specialists in difference may do their best to deny the fact that for a quarter of a century, they have been fighting over the English department while the right held the White House as its private fiefdom."

5   See Thomas Sheehan, "Heidegger and Hitler," *New York Review of Books* January 15, 1993, 30–35. See also my letter to the editor of March 25, 1993, as well as Derrida's response of April 22, 1993 (it was in this issue that the letter-petition appeared). The episode has been discussed in Reed Way Dasenbrock, "Taking It Personally: Reading Derrida's Responses," *College English,* 56, no. 3 (March 1994): 261–79. See also the excellent discussion in Ingrid Harris, "*L'affaire derrida:* Business or Pleasure?" *Philosophy and Social Criticism* 19, nos. 3–4 (1994): 216–42. In my introduction to *The Heidegger Controversy: A Critical Reader,* ed. R. Wolin (Cambridge: MIT Press, 1993), I offer some general reflections on why Derrida might be interested in suppressing his own text ("Philosophers' Hell: An Interview").

6   Jacques Derrida, *Of Grammatology,* trans. G. Spivak (Baltimore: Johns Hopkins University Press, 1976), 158.

7   See the remarks on this problem in Part 2, "Deconstruction at Auschwitz."

8   Philippe Lacoue-Labarthe, *Heidegger, Art, and Politics,* trans. C. Turner (Oxford: Blackwell, 1989), 74.

9   For an important study in the genealogy of European fascist ideology, see Isaiah Berlin, *The Crooked Timber of Humanity* (New York: Knopf, 1991).

10 See Derrida, *Limited Inc.* (Evanston: Northwestern University Press, 1988), 111ff. See also the articles on deconstruction mentioned in note 5.

11 See Derrida, "Biodegradables: Seven Diary Fragments," in *Critical Inquiry* 15 (Summer 1989): 812–73. On this point, see Reed Way Dasenbrock, "Taking It Personally: Reading Derrida's Responses," 261–79.

12 See Richard Bernstein's employment of this term in *The New Constellation: The Ethical-Political Horizons of Modernity / Postmodernity* (Cambridge: MIT Press, 1991).

13 See the anthology edited by H. Aram Veeser, *The New Historicism* (New York: Routledge, 1989).

14 Heidegger, "Overcoming Metaphysics," in *The Heidegger Controversy: A Critical Reader,* 68.

15 Pierre Bourdieu, *Heidegger's Political Ontology* (Stanford: Stanford University Press, 1990).

16 For the crucial texts, see Maurice Blanchot, *The Unavowable Community,* trans. Pierre Joris (Albany: Station Hill, 1988); Jean-Luc Nancy, *The Inoperative Community* (Minneapolis: University of Minnesota Press, 1991). Georges Bataille's *The Accursed Share,* trans. Robert Hurley (New York: Zone Books, 1988) is the urtext in this lineage. I develop the substance of these criticisms in Chapter 10.

17 See Derrida, "The Politics of Friendship," *Journal of Philosophy* (1988): 632–44. I cite from the much longer manuscript version of this essay, 48.

18 Fredric Jameson, *Postmodernism, or The Cultural Logic of Late Capitalism* (Durham: Duke University Press, 1991), 257. To be sure, as the title of his book implies, Jameson has shown himself to be quite critical of postmodernism, whose cultural manifestations he interprets in a reductive-Althusserian vein. It is his political affinities with postmodern approaches that I highlight here.

19 For a preliminary discussion of this concept, see Ernst Nolte, *Marxism, Fascism, Cold War* (Atlantic Heights, N.J.: Humanities, 1982), 193ff. See also my essay, "Left Fascism: Georges Bataille and Legacies of French Illiberalism," forthcoming in *Constellations* 2, 2 (October 1995).

20 See Karl Popper, *The Logic of Scientific Discovery* (New York: Basic Books, 1959).

21 Joseph de Maistre, *Considérations on the French Revolution*, trans. R. Lebrun (Montreal: McGill-Queens University Press, 1974), 97.

22 These developments have been traced by H. Stuart Hughes in *Consciousness and Society: The Reorientation of European Social Thought, 1890–1930* (New York: Vintage, 1977).

23 Edmund Husserl, "Philosophy and the Crisis of European Humanity," in *The Crisis of the European Sciences and Transcendental Phenomenology*, trans. D. Carr (Evanston: Northwestern University Press, 1970), 269–300.

24 See my discussion of these claims in Chapter 8. See also my earlier study, *The Politics of Being: The Political Thought of Martin Heidegger* (New York: Columbia University Press, 1990).

25 Heidegger, "The Word of Nietzsche: 'God is Dead,'" in *The Question Concerning Technology and Other Essays*, ed. and trans. William Lovitt (New York: Harper, 1977), 112.

26 Zeev Sternhell, *The Birth of Fascist Ideology*, trans. D. Maisel (Princeton: Princeton University Press, 1992), 257.

27 One of the standard discussions of these trends may be found in Hughes, *Consciousness and Society.*

28 Sternhell, *The Birth of Fascist Ideology*, 252.

29 Cited in Wolin, ed., *The Heidegger Controversy: A Critical Reader*, 47. The remarks in question were made to German students in November 1933, on the eve of a plebiscite called by Hitler on Germany's withdrawal from the League of Nations.

30 Tom Rockmore, *On Heidegger's Nazism and Philosophy* (Berkeley and Los Angeles: University of California Press, 1992), 33.

31 Heidegger, *Logica: Lecciones de M. Heidegger* (Spanish / German bilingual edition), ed. V. Farias (Barcelona: Anthropos, 1991), 38, 40.

32 On this point, see Manfred Frank, *Der kommende Gott.*

33 See Chapters 2 and 5.

34 Hans-Georg Gadamer, *Heidegger's Ways*, trans. John Stanley (Albany: State University of New York Press, 1994), viii. Gadamer uses these terms to indicate the way that the work of the later Heidegger is sometimes thought of.

35 Max Horkheimer and Theodor Adorno, *Dialectic of Enlightenment*, trans. J. Cumming (New York: Herder and Herder, 1972), xiii.

36 Ibid., xvi (my emphasis).

37 Cited by Frank, "Two Centuries of Philosophical Critique of Reason," 69.

38 Immanuel Kant, *The Moral Law*, trans. H. J. Paton (London: Hutchinson, 1948), 91. For a discussion of a hypothetical "emancipatory social interest," see Jürgen Habermas, *Knowledge and Human Interests*, trans. J. Shapiro (Boston: Beacon, 1971), 313ff. For a more recent formulation of this motif, see Habermas, "The Tasks of a Critical Theory of Society," in *The Theory of Communicative Action*, trans. T. McCarthy (Boston: Beacon, 1986), 2:374–403. The idea of an emancipatory human interest is clearly a residue from an earlier period of critical theory, especially the thought of Herbert Marcuse.

Kulchur Wars

1   In English the "Author's Introduction" appears in *The Protestant Ethic and the Spirit of Capitalism*, trans. Talcott Parsons (New York: Scribners, 1958), 13–31.

2   Here, attention should be called to the important parenthetic qualification "as we like to think." This phrase reminds us that what strikes us as "universal" only takes on this character from within the perspective of our own received value-orientation, and hence cannot fully lay claim to a more transcendent value-universality. Ultimately Weber's own (scientific) standpoint is *ethically relativistic:* ultimate ends cannot be rationally adjudicated therefore even with regards to the West.

3   Jürgen Habermas, *Theorie des Kommunikativen Handelns* (Frankfurt am Main: Suhrkamp, 1981), 2 vols. See especially the Weber interpretation, 225–365.

4   One can see that the fundamental achievements of this era receive their philosophical authentication in the three Critiques of Kantian philosophy, to which the aforementioned value-spheres correspond.

5   Cf. Max Weber, *Economy and Society*, ed. Guenther Roth and Claus Wittich (Berkeley and Los Angeles: University of California Press, 1978), 1:3–62.

6   Habermas's own reconstruction of Weber's system revolves around the attempt to reestablish the independent validity of the two neglected value-spheres of morality and art, and in this way overcome Weber's self-professed ethical relativism.

7   For the best survey of their writings, see Frank E. Manuel, *The Prophets of Paris* (New York: Harper Row, 1962).

8   Prototypical in this respect is Gilles Deleuze, *Nietzsche and Philosophy* (New York: Columbia University Press, 1983).

9   For a representative illustration of this perspective, see Jean-François Lyotard, *The Postmodern Condition* (Minneapolis: University of Minnesota Press, 1984).

10   See Walter Benjamin, "The Work of Art in the Age of Mechanical Reproduction," in *Illuminations* (New York: Schocken, 1969), 217–52.

11   Cf. Habermas, *Structural Transformation of the Public Sphere* (Cambridge: MIT Press, 1989), 60–69. See also *Habermas and the Public Sphere*, ed. C. Calhoun (Cambridge: MIT Press, 1992).

12   Although at this early point (1962) Habermas seemed in accord with Horkheimer and Adorno's view of the culture industry, in his most recent work he definitely is not. In *Theorie des Kommunakativen Handelns* he is of the opinion that rather than being a "one-way street," the mass media are at least as dependent on the way in which their communications are received by the community of recipients.

13   These are of course the chief lines of controversy in the Adorno–Benjamin dispute of the 1930s. For more on this debate, see Richard Wolin, *Walter Benjamin: An Aesthetic of Redemption* (Berkeley and Los Angeles: University of California Press, 1994), 163–212. For more on the dichotomy between "high" and "low" art, see C. Bürger, P. Bürger, J. Schulte-Sasse, eds., *Zur Dichotomiserung von hoher und niederer Literatur* (Frankfurt: Suhrkamp, 1982). See also Sandor Radnoti, "Mass Culture," *Telos* 48 (Summer 1981): 27–47. And for a classical discussion of these themes, see Leo Lowenthal, *Literature, Popular Culture, and Society* (Palo Alto, Calif.: Pacific Books, 1961).

14   Peter Bürger, *Theory of the Avant-Garde* (Minneapolis: University of Minnesota Press, 1984).

15 For more on this point, cf. Herbert Marcuse's essay "The Affirmative Character of Culture," *Negations* (Boston: Beacon, 1968), 88–133, in which he too argues for the overcoming of art in the domain of life-praxis.

16 Bürger, *Theory of the Avant-Garde,* 68ff.

17 See the volume edited by Wilhelm M. Lüdke, *"Theorie der Avantgarde": Antworten auf Peter Bürgers Bestimmung von Kunst und bürgerlicher Gesellschaft* (Frankfurt am Main: Suhrkamp, 1976).

18 Cf. F. Marinetti, *Selected Writings,* ed. R. W. Flint (London: Secker and Warburg, 1971).

19 Theodor Adorno, "Commitment," in *The Essential Frankfurt School Reader,* ed. A. Arato and E. Gebhardt (New York: Urizen, 1978), 301.

20 For a superb discussion of this episode in the history of the movement, see Maurice Nadeau, *The History of Surrealism* (New York: 1973), 169–88. Bürger might also take note of the title of the chapter of Nadeau's survey, which covers the years 1930–39: "The Period of *Autonomy*" (my emphasis), 191–229.

21 Benjamin, "Surrealism," in *Reflections* (New York: Harcourt Brace, 1978), 189.

22 Robert Hughes, *The Shock of the New* (New York: Knopf, 1981).

23 Lionel Trilling, "On the Modern Element in Modern Literature," in *Literary Modernism,* ed. Irving Howe (New York: Fawcett, 1967), 59–82.

24 For more on the technique of montage, which is of course originally derived from film, and which may be defined in terms of the anti-organicist ideal of the independence of the parts vis-à-vis the whole, see Bürger, *Theory of the Avant-Garde,* 98–111.

25 For one of the earliest proclamations of the crisis of the avant-garde, see H. M. Enzensberger, "The Aporias of the Avant-Garde," in *The Consciousness Industry* (New York: Seabury, 1974).

26 Cf. Hegel's *Aesthetics,* trans. T. M. Knox (London: Oxford University Press, 1975), 11: "In all these respects art, considered in its highest vocation, remains for us a thing of the past. Therefore it has lost for us genuine truth and life, and has rather been transferred into our *ideal* instead of maintaining its earlier necessity in reality and occupying its higher place. . . . The *philosophy* of art is therefore a greater need in our day than it was in days when art by itself as art yielded full satisfaction. Art invites us to the intellectual consideration, and that not for the purpose of creating art again, but for knowing philosophically what art is."

27 For a recent examination of the relationship between the European avant-garde and the New York School, see Serge Guilbaut, *How New York Stole the Idea of Modern Art* (Chicago: University of Chicago Press, 1983).

28 Though in retrospect the *nouveau roman* of Robbe-Grillet and Sarraute seemed to be legitimate harbingers of postmodern literature.

29 Arnold Hauser, *The Sociology of Art* (Chicago: University of Chicago Press, 1982), 651–53.

30 Irving Howe, "The New York Intellectuals," cited in Matei Calinescu, *Faces of Modernity* (Bloomington: Indiana University Press, 1977), 137–38. Calinescu's book contains many useful observations on the modernism/postmodernism dichotomy; see especially 120–44. For an incisive introduction to the thematic of postmodernism, see Fredric Jameson, "Postmodernism and Consumer Security," in *Anti-Aesthetic,* ed. Hal Foster (Port Townsend, Wash.: Bay Press, 1983), 111–26. The literature on the postmodernist controversy has become quite voluminous in recent years. For a useful introduction, see

the special issue of *New German Critique* 22 (Winter 1981), especially the contributions by Habermas, "Modernity and Postmodernity," 3–14; and Andreas Huyssen, "The Search for Tradition: Avant-Garde and Postmodernism in the 1970s," 23–40. For a critique of postmodernism from a more traditional perspective, see Gerald Graff, "The Myth of the Postmodernist Breakthrough," *Triquarterly* 26 (Winter 1973): 383–417, where Graff concludes: "A radical movement in art and culture forfeits its radicalism and impoverishes itself to the degree that it turns its back on what is valid and potentially living in the critical and moral traditions of humanism. In a society increasingly irrational and barbaric, to regard the attack on reason and objectivity as the basis of our radicalism is to perpetuate the nightmare we want to escape."

31 See Stuart Hall, "Cultural Studies and the Centre: Some Problematics and Problems," in *Culture, Media, Language*, ed. Stuart Hall et al. (London: Hutchinson, 1980), 15–47.

32 Andrew Ross, *No Respect* (New York: Routledge, 1989), 10. See also the work on "subcultures" by Dick Hebdige, *Subculture: The Meaning of Style* (London: Methuen, 1979).

33 Jim Collins, *Uncommon Cultures: Popular Culture and Post-Modernism* (New York: Routledge, 1989), 16–21.

34 For a perceptive account of the generational shift in critical theory (i.e., from the first generation to Habermas), see Agnes Heller, "The Positivist Dispute as a Turning Point in German Post-War Theory," *New German Critique* 15 (Fall 1978): 49–56.

35 See the essay by David Buxton, "Rock Music, the Star System and the Rise of Consumerism," *Telos* 57 (Fall 1983): 93–102. See also the response by David Scudder, "Structuralist Logic and the Conspiracy of Latent Functions," in *Telos* 59 (Spring 1984): 167–71.

36 See Alvin Gouldner, *The Coming Crisis of Western Sociology* (New York: Basic, 1970), vii.

37 Walter Benjamin, *Das Passagen-Werk* (Frankfurt: Suhrkamp, 1982).

38 See Adorno, "The Culture Industry Reconsidered," in *The Culture Industry: Selected Essays on Mass Culture*, ed. J. M. Bernstein (London: Routledge, 1991), 85–92.

39 For a classic statement of this theme, see Daniel Bell, *The Cultural Contradictions of Capitalism* (New York: Harper, 1977).

40 Leslie Fiedler, *The Collected Essays of Leslie Fiedler Reader* (New York: Stein and Day, 1971).

41 Fredric Jameson, "Reification and Utopia in Mass Culture," *Social Text* (Winter 1979), 141.

42 Ibid., 144.

43 John Fiske, *Understanding Popular Culture* (Boston: Unwin Hyman, 1989), 84–98.

44 See Linda Hutcheon, *The Politics of Postmodernism* (New York: Routledge, 1989).

45 Hal Foster, "(Post)modern Polemics," in *Recodings: Art, Spectacle, and Cultural Politics* (Seattle: Bay Press, 1985), 123.

46 For a number of analogous objections to postmodernism, see Terry Eagleton, "Capitalism, Structuralism, and Poststructuralism," in *Against the Grain* (London: Verso, 1986), 131–48.

47 Jameson, *Postmodernism or the Cultural Logic of Late Capitalism* (Durham: Duke University Press, 1991), 8–9.

48 Guy Debord, *Société du Spectacle* (Paris: Champs libres, 1971), 9. A new English translation of Debord's work has just been published by MIT Press. It is clear that Bau-

drillard's discussion of the "simulacrum" is in large measure derived from the analyses of Debord. See Baudrillard, "Simulacra and Simulations," in *Selected Writings*, ed. Mark Poster (Stanford: Stanford University Press, 1988), 166–84.

49   Jameson, *Postmodernism*, 9.

The Cultural Politics of Neoconservatism

1   Kramer has unabashedly titled a collection of essays on the art scene *Revenge of the Philistines* (New York: Free Press, 1985).

2   Hilton Kramer, "A Note on *The New Criterion*," *New Criterion* (September 1982): 1. Kramer's journal is funded by the Foundation for Cultural Review, an organization whose name is suspiciously absent from the leading foundation indexes. The title, of course, represents an unsubtle variation of T. S. Eliot's journal *The Criterion*.

3   For the definitive unmasking of this category, see Theodor Adorno, "Cultural Criticism and Society," *Prisms* (London: Neville Spearman, 1967), 17–34.

4   Walter Benjamin, "Edmund Fuchs: Collector and Historian," in *The Essential Frankfurt School Reader*, ed. A. Arato and E. Gebhardt (New York: Urizen, 1978), 233. In the same essay, Benjamin couples this claim with the oft-cited statement: "The products of art and science owe their existence not merely to the effort of the great geniuses that created them, but also to the unnamed drudgery of their contemporaries. There is no document of culture which is not at the same time a document of barbarism."

5   Kramer, "T. J. Clark and the Marxist Critique of Modern Painting," *New Criterion* (March 1985): 1–2.

6   Kramer, "A Note on *The New Criterion*," 2.

7   Peter Steinfels, *The Neoconservatives* (New York: Simon and Schuster, 1979), 55.

8   Kramer, "Professor Howe's Prescriptions," *New Criterion* (April 1984): 4.

9   Norman Cantor, "The Real Crisis in the Humanities Today," *New Criterion* (June 1985): 30.

10   Ferreting out left-wing influence in the academy is also one of Kramer's favorite pastimes. Art historian T. J. Clark and *Dissent* editor Irving Howe are two of his favorite targets. For a defense of Howe in the face of Kramer's jaundiced attacks, see Robert Boyers, "The Neoconservatives and Culture," *Salmagundi* 66 (Winter–Spring 1985): 192–204.

11   Cantor, "The Real Crisis in the Humanities Today," passim.

12   See, for example, Alvin Gouldner, *The Future of the Intellectuals and the Rise of the New Class* (New York: Continuum, 1979); Daniel Bell, "The New Class: A Muddled Concept," in *The Winding Passage* (New York: Harper Row, 1979); and with reference to Eastern European societies, Georg Konrad and Ivan Szeleny, *The Intellectuals on the Road to Class Power* (New York: Seabury, 1979). For Steinfels's discussion of the role played by the new class thesis in neoconservative ideology, see *The Neoconservatives*, 56–58, 285–90.

13   See Ronald Inglehart, *The Silent Revolution* (Princeton: Princeton University Press, 1977).

14   See Marshall Berman's book of this title (New York: Basic, 1982).

15   For the economic background to this argument, see Giacomo Marramao, "Theory of the Crisis and the Problem of Constitution," *Telos* 26 (Winter 1975–76): 143–64. In all

fairness to Bell, it should be acknowledged that in a more recent essay, he seems to have slightly altered his position on the relation between culture and the economic sphere. In "The New Class: A Muddled Concept," he remarks: "the machine of modern capitalism assimilated and commercialized these (countercultural) lifestyles. Without this hedonism created by mass consumption, the consumer goods industry would collapse. The cultural contradiction of capitalism ultimately amounts to the following: once capitalism lost its original legitimations, it adopted the legitimations of a formerly anti-bourgeois culture in order to maintain the stability of its own economic institutions"; see Bell, *The Winding Passage*, 163ff. For a classical treatment of the historical transition from a society of production to a society of consumption viewed through the prism of changing images of success in popular biographies, see Leo Lowenthal, "The Triumph of Mass Idols," in *Literature, Popular Culture and Society* (Palo Alto, Calif.: Pacific Books, 1961), 109–40.

16　For more on the failings of modernism, see Russell Berman, "Modern Art and De-sublimation," *Telos* 62 (Winter 1984–85): 31–57.

17　Kramer, "Postmodernism: Art and Culture in the 1980s," *New Criterion* (September 1983): 43.

18　See Suzy Gablik, *Has Modernism Failed?* (New York: Thames and Hudson, 1984); and Rosalind Krauss, *The Originality of the Avant-Garde and Other Modernist Myths* (Cambridge: MIT Press, 1986).

19　Cf. Kramer, "T. J. Clark and the Marxist Critique of Modern Painting," 1–2.

20　Adorno, "Cultural Criticism and Society," 20, 22.

21　Ibid., 19.

22　Ibid., 34: "Cultural criticism finds itself faced with the final stage of the dialectic of culture and barbarism. To write poetry after Auschwitz is barbaric. And this corrodes even the knowledge of why it has become impossible to write poetry today. Absolute reification, which presupposed intellectual progress as one of its elements, is now preparing to absorb the mind entirely. Critical intelligence cannot be equal to this challenge as long as it confines itself to self-satisfied contemplation." For some later reflections on this theme, see Adorno, *Negative Dialectics* (New York: Seabury, 1973), 362.

Reflections on Jewish Secular Messianism

1　Isaac Deutscher, *The Non-Jewish Jew and Other Essays* (New York: Hill and Wang, 1968), 26.

2　Ibid., 27.

3　Gershom Scholem, "Reflections on Jewish Theology," in *On Jews and Judaism in Crisis* (New York: Schocken, 1976), 284.

4　For example, in his excellent work, *Rédemption et Utopie: Le Judaïsme libertaire en Europe Centrale* (Paris: P.U.F., 1988), Michael Löwy identifies the French thinker Bernard Lazare as "l'exception qui confirme la regle," 224ff.

5　Anson Rabinbach, "Between Enlightenment and Apocalypse: Benjamin, Bloch and Modern German Jewish Messianism," *New German Critique* 34 (1985): 78.

6　Löwy, *Rédemption et Utopie*, 40.

7　Fritz Ringer, *The Decline of the German Mandarins* (Cambridge: Harvard University Press, 1969), 3.

8 See Ferdinand Tönnies, *Gemeinschaft and Gesellschaft* [1887] (New York: Harper Row, 1963); see also Harry Lieberzohn, *Fate and Utopia in German Sociology* (Cambridge: MIT Press, 1988).

9 Georg Lukács, *The Theory of the Novel* (Cambridge: MIT Press, 1971).

10 See Helmuth Plessner, *Der verspätete Nation* (Frankfurt am Main: Suhrkamp, 1959).

11 Rabinbach, "Between Enlightenment and Apocalypse," 82–83.

12 See, for example, my own study, *Walter Benjamin: An Aesthetic of Redemption* (Berkeley and Los Angeles: University of California Press, 1994), 246.

13 For Baader's influence on Bloch, see Arno Münster, *Utopie, Messianismus und Apokalypse im frühwerk Ernst Blochs* (Frankfurt am Main: Suhrkamp, 1982), 137.

14 Scholem, *The Messianic Idea in Judaism* (New York: Schocken, 1971), 3–4.

15 Ernst Bloch, *Geist der Utopie* (Frankfurt am Main: Suhrkamp, 1964), 347.

16 Scholem, *The Messianic Idea in Judaism*, 10–11 (my emphasis).

17 Ibid., 11.

18 Walter Benjamin, *Illuminations*, ed. Hannah Arendt, trans. H. Zohn (New York: Schocken, 1968), 264.

19 Scholem, *The Messianic Idea in Judaism*, 7.

20 See Ernst Cassirer, *The Myth of the State* (New Haven: Yale University Press, 1946).

21 Bloch, *Geist der Utopie*, 305, 346.

22 Benjamin, *Illuminations*, 253.

23 Benjamin, *Reflections* (New York: Harcourt Brace Jovanovich, 1978), 312.

24 Ibid., 313.

25 See the essay, "Critique of Violence," in *Reflections*, 277ff.

26 Bloch, *Geist der Utopie*, 344.

27 Theodor Adorno, *Minima Moralia* (London: New Left Books, 1974), 247.

28 Scholem, *On Jews and Judaism in Crisis*, 26.

29 On this theme, see the recent work by Ferenc Fehér, *The Frozen Revolution: An Essay on Jacobinism* (Cambridge: Cambridge University Press, 1988).

30 Benjamin, *Reflections*, 312.

Walter Benjamin Today

1 *Zur Aktualität Walter Benjamins*, ed. S. Unseld (Frankfurt am Main: Suhrkamp, 1972).

2 On the theme of redemptive political paradigms, see Ferenc Fehér, "Redemptive and Democratic Paradigms in Radical Politics," *Telos* 63 (Spring 1985): 147–56; Joel Whitebook, "The Politics of Redemption," *Telos* 63 (Spring 1985): 156–68; Paul Breines, "Redeeming Redemption," *Telos* 65 (Fall 1985): 152–58; Richard Wolin, "Against Adjustment," *Telos* 65 (Fall 1985): 158–63; and Moishe Gonzales, "Theoretical Amnesia," *Telos* 65 (Fall 1985): 163–70.

3 For two recent articulations of this position (which may be traced to John Locke's *Letter Concerning Toleration*), see John Rawls, "Justice as Fairness: Political not Metaphysical," *Philosophy and Public Affairs* 14 (Summer 1985): 223–51 and Richard Rorty, *Contingency, Irony, and Solidarity* (Cambridge: Cambridge University Press, 1990).

4 Irving Wohlfarth, "Re-fusing Theology: Some First Responses to Walter Benjamin's Arcades Project," *New German Critique* 39 (Fall 1986): 17.

5 Benjamin, *Gesammelte Schriften*, ed. Rolf Tiedemann and Hermann Schweppenhäuser,

with Theodor W. Adorno and Gershom Scholem (Frankfurt am Main: Suhrkamp, 1972–89), 5:592. All subsequent references to this edition will be cited as *GS*, followed by volume and page number.

6   Benjamin, "One-Way Street," in *Illuminations*, ed. Hannah Arendt, trans. H. Zohn (New York: Schocken, 1969), 84.

7   Benjamin, *GS*, 5:168.

8   Benjamin, "Theses on the Philosophy of History," in *Illuminations*, 258.

9   One of the best examples of this phenomenon is provided by postmodernist director Wim Wenders's 1988 film *Wings of Desire* (*Himmel über Berlin*), which is loosely based on Benjamin's "Theses on the Philosophy of History." The angel of Wenders's film descends to survey contemporary Berlin and its luckless inhabitants. It is a desolate and hopeless cityscape: literally a hell on earth, intended as an allegory for the ruins of modernity. Unlike Benjamin's essay, however, in Wenders's film, there is no allusion to that "strait gate through which the Messiah might enter." As a result, the film remains a testament to decline purely and simply. It is in no way an allegory of redemption, as is the case with Benjamin's "angel of history."

10 Benjamin, "Theses on the Philosophy of History," 263.

11 Susan Buck-Morss has commented on the relationship between Benjamin and postmodernism in *The Dialectics of Seeing* (Cambridge: MIT Press, 1989). According to Buck-Morss, the attempt to view him as "the precursor of such recent, postsubjective currents of thought as deconstruction and postmodernism" must fail, insofar as these schools are "characterized not infrequently by an anthropological nihilism which [Benjamin] criticized vehemently" (222). Toward the end of her impressive study, she makes the following (somewhat risky) claim: "Whereas modernism in philosophical terms is wedded to the Enlightenment dream of a substantively rational society, postmodernism takes its philosophical lead from Nietzsche, Baudelaire, and Blanqui. If the terms are defined this way, Benjamin must be counted as a modernist" (447 n. 35).

For an early debate on Benjamin's relation to deconstruction, see Irving Wohlfarth's response to Carol Jacobs, *The Dissimulating Harmony* (Baltimore: Johns Hopkins University Press, 1978), "Walter Benjamin's 'Image of Interpretation,'" *New German Critique* 17 (Spring 1979): 70–98.

12 Benjamin, "Theses on the Philosophy of History," 257.

13 For example, see Michael Taussig's attempt to generalize Benjamin's conception of the "state of emergency" (*Ausnahmezustand;* in truth, "state of exception") in *The Nervous System* (New York: Routledge, 1992); especially chap. 2, "Terror as Usual: Walter Benjamin's Theory of History as State of Siege"). Taussig speaks of "the violence in our own immediate life-worlds, in our universities, workplaces, streets, shopping malls, and even families, where, like business, it's terror as usual"; of "the irregular rhythm of numbing and shock that constitutes the apparent normality of the abnormal created by the state of emergency" (12–13).

14 For an account of the origins of the term *posthistoire*, see Lutz Niethammer, *Posthistoire: Ist die Geschichte zu Ende?* (Reinbeck bei Hamburg: Rowohlt, 1989). English translation: *Posthistoire: Has History Come to an End?* trans. P. Camiller (London: Verso, 1992).

15 Benjamin, *GS*, 5:570–71.

16 Friedrich Nietzsche, *The Will to Power*, trans. W. Kaufmann and R. J. Hollingdale (New York: Vintage, 1967), 9.

17 On this theme, see the important study by Stephen Aschheim, *The Nietzsche Reception in Germany, 1890–1990* (Berkeley and Los Angeles: University of California Press, 1992).

18 Scholem, *On Jews and Judaism in Crisis* (New York: Schocken, 1976), 194–95.

19 See, for example, Benjamin's letter of July 7, 1935, where he speaks of the Arcades Project as "destined to become the pendant to my study of the seventeenth century which appeared in Germany under the title *Origin of German Tragic Drama*" (*GS*, 5:1124).

20 For Nietzsche's distinction between active and passive nihilism, see *The Will to Power*, 17.

21 Benjamin, "Surrealism: The Last Snapshot of the European Intelligentsia," in *Reflections* (New York: Harcourt Brace Jovanovich, 1978), 187. Or, as he expresses his thought elsewhere: "the traditional image of humanity—ceremonious, noble, decked out with all the sacrificial offerings of the past" ("Erfahrung und Armut," *GS*, 2:216).

22 Benjamin, "Surrealism," 181–82; (my emphasis).

23 Benjamin, "The Destructive Character," in *Reflections*, 301.

24 Benjamin, "Karl Kraus," in *Reflections*, 272.

25 Benjamin, *Briefe*, ed. T. W. Adorno and G. Scholem (Frankfurt: Suhrkamp, 1966), 425.

26 On this theme, see Karl-Heinz Bohrer, *Ästhetik des Schreckens* (Munich: Hanser, 1978), where the works of Benjamin and Jünger are compared extensively. Of course, Benjamin recognized this problem in his critique of Jünger (*GS*, 3:240). See also the concluding sentences of his "Work of Art" essay, in *Illuminations*, p. 242, where Benjamin warns that in its glorification of war, fascism celebrates "destruction as an aesthetic pleasure of the first order."

   For a good discussion of the dangers of Benjamin's nihilist outlook, see John McCole, *Walter Benjamin and the Antinomies of Tradition* (Ithaca: Cornell University Press, 1993), 165ff. McCole correctly identifies a "liquidationist" component as prominent in all phases of Benjamin's thought. It can be traced as early as his involvement with the Youth Movement in the years 1910–1919, where his nihilistic attitudes toward the present age are prominent. But they are also evident in his later work: for example, his endorsement of the "decline of the aura" in the "Work of Art" essay; a thesis that relates destructively rather than conservatively to the dissolution of traditional culture and its semantic potentials.

27 On this question, see Fritz K. Ringer, *The Decline of the German Mandarins: The German Academic Community, 1890–1933* (Cambridge: Harvard University Press, 1969); and Fritz Stern, *The Failure of Illiberalism: Essays on the Political Culture of Modern Germany* (New York: Knopf, 1972).

28 The term *more real humanism* appears in his essay on Karl Kraus; see *Reflections*, 272. For the characterization of Klee's *Angelus Novus*, see 273.

29 Benjamin, "Surrealism," 192, 190 (second emphasis mine). For one of the most successful explorations of Benjamin's understanding of what surrealism might contribute to the Marxist tradition, see Margaret Cohen, *Profane Illumination: Walter Benjamin and the Paris of Surrealist Revolution* (Berkeley and Los Angeles: University of California Press, 1993). See also Josef Fürnkas, *Surrealismus als Erkenntnis* (Stuttgart: Metzler, 1988). Fürnkas's work is more specifically concerned with an analysis of Benjamin's short prose works.

Adorno was highly critical of Benjamin's employment of anthropological materialism. He saw this concept as essentially undialectical. Because of its surrealist-inspired
infatuation with the idea of "bodily collective exaltation," he viewed it as an expression
of immediacy in the Hegelian sense; even worse, it expressed an inclination toward
fetishizing the reified immediacy of given social relations. On this point, see Adorno's
letter to Benjamin of September 6, 1936 (Benjamin, *GS*, 7:864), where he accuses the
latter of flirting with "an undialectical ontologization of the body." In this sense,
Adorno's critique of anthropological materialism was very much akin to his critique of
surrealism in the 1950s. See Adorno, "Looking Back on Surrealism," in *Notes to Literature*, trans. S. W. Nicholsen (New York: Columbia University Press, 1991), 86–90.

30   Scholem, "Walter Benjamin," *Neue Rundschau* 76, no. 1 (1965): 19; reprinted in *On Jews
and Judaism in Crisis*, 195.

31   Habermas, "Consciousness-Raising or Rescuing Critique," in *On Walter Benjamin:
Critical Essays and Recollections*, ed. Gary Smith (Cambridge: MIT Press, 1988), 113,
124.

32   See Georg Stauth and Bryan S. Turner, "Ludwig Klages and the Origins of Critical
Theory," *Theory, Culture and Society* 9 (1992): 45–63. The authors claim that "the
Frankfurt School was closer to the tradition of Nietzsche and *Lebensphilosophie* in their
cultural critique than to Marxism" (45). This claim is certainly worth exploring. Yet the
authors fail to address the question of how, if substantiated, it would affect the contemporary relevance of critical theory. Moreover, in dealing with the Frankfurt School as a
whole, they fail to take into account the fact that a similar claim could in no way be made
for the critical theory of the 1930s, whose production revolved around the concept of
"interdisciplinary materialism." See also the predominantly biographical account in
Werner Fuld, "Walter Benjamins Beziehung zu Ludwig Klages," *Akzente* 28 (1981):
274–87.

33   Also see Axel Honneth's exploration of this problem in " 'L'Esprit et son object':
Parentés anthropologiques entre la 'Dialectique de la Raison' et la critique de la civilisa-
tion dans la philosophie de la vie," in *Weimar ou l'explosion de la modernité* (Paris:
Editions Anthropos, 1984), 97–111. Honneth argues that "in light of the contemporary
critique of reason it seems that *Dialectic of Enlightenment* is anchored more than one
would have thought in the tradition of a critique of civilization inspired by philosophy of
life." I agree with Honneth's characterization.

34   Richard Wolin, "The Frankfurt School: From Interdisciplinary Materialism to Philosophy of History," in *The Terms of Cultural Criticism: The Frankfurt School, Existentialism,
Poststructuralism* (New York: Columbia University Press, 1992).

35   Benjamin's letter to Schmitt may be found in *GS*, 1:part 3, 887. Some have pointed out
that the allusion to the *Ausnahmezustand* (the "state of exception") in the "Theses"
derives from Schmitt. But, given the precarious nature of European politics in 1940, it
would seem that the concept had an immediate historical point of reference.

36   The 1922 letter was reprinted in *TEXT + KRITIK* 31 and 32 (1971): 24. See Benjamin's positive evaluation of Klages's 1922 text in *GS*, 3:44.

37   Benjamin, "Johann Jakob Bachofen," in *GS*, 2:229–31. The Bachofen essay was unpublished during Benjamin's lifetime and written in French (at the behest of the
Nouvelle Revue Française, which eventually rejected it).

38   Benjamin, letter to Adorno, January 7, 1935, *Briefe*, 638ff.

39 Adorno, letter to Benjamin, December 12, 1934, cited in *GS*, 2:966.

40 See especially *Negative Dialectics*, trans. E. B. Ashton (New York: Seabury, 1973), 162–64. As Rolf Wiggershaus has remarked: "A major confrontation with Klages and his theory of the image appeared as an urgent task for both [Benjamin] and Adorno in the 1930s in order to clarify their own standpoint and the theory of dialectical images." Wiggershaus, *Die Frankfurter Schule: Geschichte, Theoretische Entwicklung, Politische Bedeutung* (Munich: Hanser, 1986). English translation: *The Frankfurt School: Its History, Theories, and Political Significance*, trans. Michael Robertson (Cambridge: MIT Press, 1994).

41 Reported by Wiggershaus, *Die Frankfurter Schule*, 224.

42 Klages, "Vom Traumbewusstein," in *Sämtliche Werke* (Bonn: Bouvier, 1974), 3:162.

43 Honneth, "Erschließung der Vergangenheit," *Internationale Zeitschrift für Philosophie* I (1993), 1–26. Honneth's analysis contains an interesting account of Jünger's diary, *Das Abenteuerliche Herz* (1929), as it relates to Benjaminian themes. See the reference to Bohrer in note 26.

44 See Bruce Detwiler, *Nietzsche's Aristocratic Radicalism* (Chicago: University of Chicago Press, 1990).

45 Jünger, *Das Abenteuerliche Herz* in *Sämtliche Werke* (Stuttgart: Klett-Cotta, 1978–83), 9:259.

46 Benjamin, *GS* 3:238–50.

47 Benjamin, *Illuminations*, 156–57, 202.

48 *Briefe*, 409.

49 Ibid., 515. For a brief discussion of Klages's relation to fascism (although he never joined the movement per se, many of his theories were taken up by Nazi ideologues such as Alfred Rosenberg), see Stauth and Turner, "Ludwig Klages and the Origins of Critical Theory," 57–59.

50 Benjamin, *GS*, 5:1161. See also the exchanges between Adorno and Benjamin on this subject, ibid., 5:1160–61. Since the publication of volume 5, new correspondence between Adorno and Horkheimer concerning Benjamin's relation to Jung and Klages has come to light; see 7:866–68.

51 For a discussion of the relationship between *Lebensphilosophie* and fascist ideology, see Herbert Marcuse, "The Struggle Against Liberalism in the Totalitarian Conception of the State," in *Negations* (Boston: Beacon, 1968), 3–42, and Lukács, *The Destruction of Reason* (London: Merlin, 1980).

52 Adorno, letter to Benjamin of August 2, 1935, in Ernst Bloch, *Aesthetics and Politics*, translation ed. Ronald Taylor (London: NLB, 1977), 113. See the discussion of the Adorno–Benjamin debate, 173–83.

53 For a good discussion of Benjamin's relation to Kommerell, see John McCole, *Walter Benjamin and the Antinomies of Tradition* (Ithaca: Cornell University Press, 1993), 176–78.

54 See the following remarks from the Arcades Project, *GS*, 5:493–94. Benjamin begins with a reference to "the forms of appearance of the dream-collective of the nineteenth century" and continues: "The 'critique' of the nineteenth century must begin here. Not as a critique of its mechanism and machinism, but instead of its narcotic historicism, of its mania for masks [*Maskensucht*], in which nevertheless is hidden a signal of true historical existence which the surrealists were the first to perceive. The project that

follows consists of an attempt to decipher that signal. And the revolutionary, materialist basis of surrealism is a sufficient guarantee that the economic basis of the nineteenth century has reached its highest expression in the signal of true historical existence—which is what concerns us here."

55 Kurt Sontheimer, *Antidemokratisches Denken in der Weimarer Republik* (Munich: Nymphenburger, 1962), 51.

56 The title of a book written by the national revolutionary thinker Hans Freyer in 1931.

57 Habermas, "Consciousness-Raising or Rescuing Critique," 113.

58 *GS*, 5:591–92.

59 See Michel Espagne and Michael Werner, "Les Manuscrits parisiens de Walter Benjamin et le Passagen-Werk," in *Walter Benjamin et Paris*, ed. H. Wismann (Paris: Cerf, 1986), 849–82, and Espagne and Werner, "Vom Passagen-Projekt zum 'Baudelaire': Neue Handschriften zum Spätwerk Walter Benjamins," *Deutsche Vierteljahrsschrift für Literaturwissenschaft und Geistesgeschichte* 68, no. 4 (December 1984): 593–657. In the latter work, the authors appear to modify some of the more far-reaching conclusions reached in "Les Manuscrits parisiens."

60 Benjamin, *Nachträge*, in *GS*, 7:870–72. See also Buck-Morss, *The Dialectics of Seeing*, 206–8.

61 Espagne and Werner, "Les manuscrits parisiens," 852.

62 Buck-Morss, *The Dialectics of Seeing*, 208: "Given that the planned Baudelaire book was first conceived as a chapter of the larger work, would it not be reasonable to assume that all of the 'chapters,' so condensed and abbreviated in both exposé descriptions, would ultimately have been extended to the point where each could, and indeed should, stand on its own? . . . The possibility that, in order to give himself space to develop the historical significance of what was now over a decade of research, Benjamin would have dissolved the 'Passages' into a series of works, all of which were within the same theoretical armature, does not indicate a 'failed' *Passagen-Werk*, but, on the contrary, one that had succeeded only too well" (the allusion to "a 'failed' *Passagen-Werk*" is directed critically to the Espagne-Werner interpretation).

63 Benjamin, *GS*, 5:1054.

64 *GS*, 5:574. See also 5:575 [N 2,6]: "A central problem of historical materialism that finally must be considered: whether the Marxist understanding of history must be unconditionally purchased at the expense of its [history's] visuality [*Anschaulichkeit*]? Or: how would it be possible to link heightened visuality with the carrying out of the Marxist method? *The first step of this way will be to incorporate the principle of montage in history.* Thus, to erect the largest constructions from the smallest, most sharply and keenly tailored elements [*Bausteine*]. Thereby, to discover the crystal of the total event in the analysis of small individual moments."

65 Tiedemann expresses doubts about Adorno's thesis in his introduction to the *Passagenwerk*, in *GS*, 5:13. Benjamin's description of the Baudelaire study as a "miniature model" of the Arcades Project may be found in *GS*, 5:1164.

66 Adorno, letter to Scholem of May 9, 1949, in *GS*, 5:1072–73.

67 Benjamin, letter to Gretel Karplus (Adorno) of August 16, 1935, in *GS*, 5:1139.

68 *GS*, 5:595.

69 *GS*, 5:583, 580.

70 *GS*, 5:495–96.

71   *GS*, 5:46–47.

72   From a philological standpoint, moreover, it is worth pointing out that there is considerable overlap between the notes to the "Theses" and those to section N of the Arcades
Project on the theory of knowledge and the theory of progress.

73   *GS*, 5:588.

74   *GS*, 5:595, 600.

75   Benjamin, *Illuminations*, 254.

76   Ibid., 260.

77   Ibid., 264.

78   *GS*, 5:573.

79   Bernd Witte, "Paris-Berlin-Paris: Personal, Literary, and Social Experience in Walter
Benjamin's Late Works," *New German Critique* 39 (Fall 1986): 57.

80   *GS*, 5:589.

81   *GS*, 5:1255. They go on to add that "the modifications vis-à-vis the older text [i.e., the
1935 version] are especially instructive concerning the development of Benjamin's theoretical views over the course of the four years that spanned the composition of the two
Exposés."

82   *GS*, 5:169. A slightly different account of the same reflections may be found in Benjamin, *Briefe*, 741–42. A number of these reflections found their way into the second
draft of the Arcades Exposé, in *GS*, 5:75.

83   *GS*, 5:76.

84   *GS*, 5:61. For an interesting discussion of Blanqui's importance for Benjamin, see
Miguel Abensour, "Walter Benjamin entre mélancholie et révolution," in *Walter Benjamin et Paris*, 219–49.

85   Ibid., 228.

86   Scholem, *On Jews and Judaism in Crisis*, 26.

Working through the Past

1   For confirmation of these trends, see Ingo Müller, *Hitler's Justice* (Cambridge: Harvard
University Press, 1991).

2   Gabriel Almond and Sydney Verba, *The Civic Culture: Political Attitudes and Democracy
in Five Nations* (Princeton: Princeton University Press, 1963). For example, consider
the following remarks, where the authors attempt to account for the lack of affective
commitment on the part of educated Germans to the FRG: "The German educated
middle classes were deeply compromised by National Socialism and in many cases
penalized (if only briefly) during the early phases of the Occupation. Their withholding
of feeling toward the German nation and toward the political process may be an expression of anxiety about being involved once again in a risky business. Perhaps both factors
are present: a sense of discomfort over the disorderliness and lack of dignity of democratic politics, and anxiety about any kind of political involvement, based on the Nazi
trauma" (153). It should be noted that in a later edition of the same book (1979),
German attitudes toward democracy rank on a par with those of other Western democracies.

3   "Was bedeutet: Aufarbeitung der Vergangenheit"; reprinted in *Gesammelte Schriften*
(Frankfurt am Main: Suhrkamp, 1977): 555–72. An English translation of the essay

("What Does Coming to Terms with the Past Mean?") has appeared in *Bitburg in Moral and Political Perspective*, ed. G. Hartman (Indianapolis: Indiana University Press, 1986), 114–29. Many of Adorno's observations are based on an empirical study of German attitudes toward the Hitler years that was undertaken by the Institute for Social Research in the early 1950s, entitled *Gruppenexperiment: Ein Studienbericht*, ed. F. Pollock (Frankfurt am Main: Suhrkamp, 1955). Adorno's own lengthy "qualitative analysis" of the study's findings has been republished as "Schuld und Abwehr," in *Gesammelte Schriften* 9:part 2, 121–324.

4   Alexander and Margarete Mitscherlich, *The Inability to Mourn*, trans. B. Placzek (New York: Grove, 1975), xxv. Another chief symptom of the German failure to work through its past according to the Mitscherlichs is a more general "impoverishment of object relations, i.e., of those processes of communication that involve feeling and thought" (8).

5   At the same time, as Saul Friedlander has pointed out, this generation, by attempting to extend their fascism-analysis to the contemporary West German political scene, ended up by overgeneralizing the concept and thus robbing it of much of its real meaning. Cf. Friedlander, "Some German Struggles with Memory," in *Bitburg in Moral and Political Perspective*, ed. G. Hartman, 29.

6   The standard account of those aspects of traditional German social structure that facilitated the mentality of popular obedience and passivity during the period of Nazi rule is Ralf Dahrendorf's *Society and Democracy in Germany* (Garden City, N.Y.: Doubleday, 1979). See also Hans-Ulrich Wehler, *The German Empire, 1871–1918*, trans. Kim Traynor (Leamington Spa, Warwickshire, U.K., and Dover, N.H.: Berg, 1985).

7   Mitscherlich and Mitscherlich, *The Inability to Mourn*, 12.

8   Or, as Holocaust historian Raul Hilberg has expressed this thought: "The bureaucrats who were involved in the extermination process were not, as far as their moral constitution is concerned, different from the rest of the population. The German wrongdoer was not a special kind of German; what we know about his mind-set pertains to Germany as a whole and not to him alone." A. Söllner, "Interview with Raul Hilberg," *Merkur* 413 (July 1988): 54.

9   It would of course be unfair to argue that no attempts have been made to deal honestly with the German past. Chancellor Willy Brandt's moving gesture of contrition before the Auschwitz memorial in Warsaw in 1972 will forever remain a memorable and courageous act on the road to reconciliation with the victims of Nazism.

  Ironically, the one event that seems to have triggered the greatest amount of national soul-searching was the showing of the U.S. television miniseries *Holocaust* in West Germany in 1979. However, serious doubts have been raised over the extent to which a four-part Hollywood-style dramatization can in and of itself serve as the vehicle of historical expiation that had been sought in vain for the previous thirty years. Cf. Siegfried Zielinski, "History as Entertainment and Provocation," *New German Critique* 19 (Winter 1980): 81–96. This entire issue is devoted to various appraisals of the West German reception of *Holocaust*.

10   Adorno, "What Does Coming to Terms with the Past Mean?" 117.

11   See the account in Richard Evans's superb book, *In Hitler's Shadow: West German Historians and the Attempt to Escape from the Nazi Past* (New York: Pantheon, 1989), 19.

12   According to official reports, when Bitburg had originally been selected as the site for President Reagan's visit in the winter of 1985, a snow-cover prevented German officials

from noticing the SS graves. Though most of the Bitburg debate has focused on the presence of the SS graves, Raul Hilberg has correctly pointed out that the German Wehrmacht or regular army was itself hardly an innocent bystander to the politics of genocide. Instead, they often provided logistical support to SS troops charged with exterminating the Jews. Its ranking officers (e.g., Field Marshall Keitel and General Jodl) were hanged as war criminals after the war. In truth, the German army was an integral part of Hitler's Reich and its crimes. See Hilberg, "Bitburg as a Symbol," in *Bitburg in Moral and Political Perspective,* ed. G. Hartman, 21–22.

13   See the remarks by Arthur Schlesinger Jr. on Reagan's performance at Bitburg: "Mr. Reagan in fact is the only American president who was of military age during the Second World War and saw no service overseas. He fought the war on the film lots of Hollywood, slept in his own bed every night and apparently got many of his ideas of what happened from subsequent study of the *Reader's Digest.*" "The Rush to Reconcile," *Wall Street Journal,* May 9, 1985.

14   For a good discussion of these events, see Charles Maier, *The Unmasterable Past: History, Holocaust, and German National Identity* (Cambridge: Harvard University Press, 1988); especially chap. 5, "A Usable Past? Museums, Memory, and Identity."

15   For a representative sample of views, see Charles Maier, "Immoral Equivalence," *New Republic* (December 1, 1986), 36–39. Saul Friedlander, *Reflections of Nazism: An Essay on Kitsch and Death* (New York: Harper Row, 1984); and Anson Rabinbach, "German Historians Debate the Nazi Past," *Dissent* (Spring 1988): 192–200.

16   Stürmer, *Dissonanzen des Fortschritts* (Munich: Piper, 1986), 12.

17   Stürmer, "Geschichte in geschichtslosem Land," *Frankfurter Allgemeine Zeitung,* April 25, 1986. Reprinted as "History in a Land without History," in *Forever in the Shadow of Hitler?* trans J. Knowlton and T. Cates (Atlantic Highlands, N.J.: Humanities Press, 1993), 16–18. This volume contains all the essential contributions to the Historians' Dispute.

18   Hillgruber, *Zweierlei Untergang: Die Zerschlagung des Deutschen Reiches und das Ende des europäischen Judentums* (Berlin: Siedler, 1986).

19   Habermas, *The New Conservatism: Cultural Criticism and The Historians' Debate,* ed. and trans. Shierry Weber Nicholsen (Cambridge: MIT Press, 1989), 212ff.

20   Cf. Raul Hilberg, "Bitburg as a Symbol," 22–23. See also the important study of Omer Bartov, *Hitler's Army* (Oxford: Oxford University Press, 1991), which, by showing the Wehrmacht's level of ideological commitment to the regime, explodes the long-standing myth that the German army was a predominantly professional, hence non-Nazified, fighting unit.

21   Peukert, "Die Genesis der 'Endlosung' aus dem Geiste der Wissenschaft," in *Zerstörung des moralischen Selbstbewußtseins: Chance oder Gefährdung* (Frankfurt am Main: Suhrkamp, 1988), 24–48.

22   Walter Benjamin criticized German historicism for its de facto writing of history from the standpoint of the "victors" rather than that of the downtrodden. See his "Theses on the Philosophy of History," *Illuminations,* trans. H. Zohn (New York: Schocken, 1969), 251ff. For a good account of the nationalistic convictions of German social scientists and historians during the Wilhelmine period, see Fritz Ringer, *The Decline of the German Mandarins* (Cambridge: Harvard University Press, 1969), 113–27. See also Georg Iggers, *The German Conception of History* (Middletown: Wesleyan University Press, 1983).

23 Nolte, "Between Myth and Revisionism? The Third Reich in the Perspective of the
    1980s," in *Aspects of the Third Reich*, ed. H. W. Koch (London: Macmillan, 1985), 17–
    38. Nolte uses the Weizmann declaration to justify his contention that "it can hardly be
    denied that Hitler had good reasons to be convinced of his enemies' determination to
    annihilate him"; a fact that in turn "might justify the thesis that Hitler was allowed to
    treat the German Jews as prisoners of war and by this means to intern them" (27–28).
       It is far from irrelevant to note in this context that the "Weizmann-declaration"
    argument has recently been resurrected by the French revisionist historian Robert
    Faurisson, who espouses the thesis that the Holocaust is a Jewish fabrication. Nor did
    the gas chambers ever exist, according to Faurisson. The crematoriums, moreover,
    served the "legitimate hygienic function" of protecting SS guards against the threat of
    infection and disease.

24 Nolte, "Between Myth and Revisionism?" 36. There are some eerie correspondences
    between Nolte's description of Nazi ideology as primarily anti-Bolshevik and Arno
    Mayer's discussion of the centrality of anti-Communism (rather than anti-Semitism) for
    Nazism in *Why Did the Heavens Not Darken?* (New York: Pantheon, 1988).

25 Nolte, "Between Myth and Revisionism?" 36.

26 Habermas, *The New Conservatism*, 236, 233.

27 Habermas develops this concept in the context of a reading of the developmental
    psychology of Piaget and Kohlberg. See his essay "Historical Materialism and the
    Development of Normative Structures," in *Communication and the Evolution of Society*,
    trans. T. McCarthy (Boston: Beacon, 1979), 95–129.

28 Within the context of this essay, it is difficult to give an adequate account of the signifi-
    cance that "geopolitical thinking"—the idea of Germany as a "nation in the middle"—
    has had in Germany's historical and political self-understanding over the course of the
    last two centuries. The explicit revival of the idea of Germany's "Mittellage," or being
    situated in the middle, as a prominent feature of the revisionist position, has been
    critically addressed by Hans-Ulrich Wehler, in *Entsorgung der deutschen Vergangenheit?
    Ein polemischer Essay zum "Historikersstreit"* (Munich: Beck, 1988); see especially 174–
    88. The Historians' Debate has spawned a mass of commentaries in the course of the last
    two years; Wehler's book is unquestionably one of the more reliable and intelligent
    works to have appeared on the subject thus far.

29 In his introduction to *Reworking the Past: Hitler, the Holocaust and the Historians' Debate*
    (Boston: Beacon, 1990), Peter Baldwin offers the following definition of the German
    Sonderweg thesis: "The *Sonderweg* approach maintains that it was the peculiar traditions
    inherited from the Wilhelmine Empire which left Weimar Germany unable to cope with
    the interwar crises. The continuing power of the aristocratic classes meant that the
    Junkers were among the main actors behind the downfall of the republic and Hitler's
    appointment to the chancellorship. The tradition of authoritarian and supposedly un-
    political government made the German middle classes willing to accept extraparliamen-
    tary solutions during the turbulence of the early 1930s" (12). In general, Baldwin's
    volume is an excellent sourcebook concerning the historical stakes of the Historians'
    Debate.

30 Nolte, *Der europäische Bürgerkrieg, 1917–1945: Nationalsozialismus und Boschewismus*
    (Munich: Propylaen, 1987).

31 Habermas, *The New Conservatism*, 227.

32 For a more detailed account of Habermas's distinction between "conventional" and "postconventional" identities with reference to the issues at stake in the Historians' Dispute, see "Historical Consciousness and Post-traditional Identity: Orientation Towards the West in West Germany," in *The New Conservatism*, 249–68.

See also the following pertinent remarks by sociologist M. R. Lepsius: "And essential change in the political culture of the Federal Republic lies precisely in the acceptance of a political order which defines and legitimates itself through individual participation in constitutionally certified political forms. Conversely, the traditional idea that a political order should be tied to the collective identity of a nation as a 'community of fate' [*Schicksalgemeinschaft*] . . . has faded. The growth of a 'constitutional patriotism,' the approval of a political order based on the right of self-determination, and the refusal of an idea of order based on an ethnic, cultural, collective 'community of fate,' are the central results of the delegitimation of German nationalism"; in Lepsius, "Der europäische Nationalstaat," in *Interessen, Ideen und Institutionen* (Stuttgart, 1990), 256.

33 Habermas, "Neoconservative Cultural Criticism," in *The New Conservatism*, 22–47.

34 "Life Forms, Morality, and the Task of the Philosopher," in *Habermas: Autonomy and Solidarity*, ed. P. Dews (London: Verso, 1986), 196. "There was no break in terms of persons or courses," observes Habermas; a remark that applied to two of his philosophy teachers, Oskar Becker and Ernst Rothacker.

35 For a classical statement of this perspective, see Arnold Gehlen, *Man and the Age of Technology* (New York: Columbia University Press, 1980).

36 For the historical and political background of the "Berufsverbot," see the special issue of *New German Critique* 8 (Spring 1976), 21–53.

37 Habermas, "Neoconservative Cultural Criticism," in *The New Conservatism*, 22–47.

38 "The German autumn" refers to the whirlwind of terrorist-related events that rocked the Federal Republic in the fall of 1977: the kidnapping of Hans-Martin Schleyer, head of the German employers' association, by the Red Army Faction; the hijacking by RAF terrorists of a Lufthansa jet to Mogadishu, Somalia; the rescue of the plane by West German commandoes, at which point Schleyer was executed by his captors; and the mysterious suicides in Stahlheim prison of the RAF leaders Ulrike Meinhof and Andreas Baader.

One of the most sinister aspects of these events was a renewed accusation by leading figures on the German right that critical intellectuals undermined the value-system of the Federal Republic and thus fostered attitudes conducive to terrorism. And thus in the fall of 1977, the CDU's Alfred Dregger, appearing on national television, accused the Frankfurt School of direct responsibility for the recent wave of German terrorism. For Habermas's response to these accusations, see "A Test for Popular Justice: The Accusations Against the Intellectuals," *New German Critique* 12 (Fall 1977): 11–13. The same issue of *New German Critique* also contains observations by Herbert Marcuse and Rudi Dutschke on the German autumn.

Schmitt's remarks were made during a Social Democratic Party congress in Hamburg. He went to observe, "Trivialization [of terrorism] would be dangerous, but it would be just as dangerous to let panic, exaggeration, and hysteria get the upper hand. What we need is a restful, considered decisiveness." Cited in W. Röhrich, *Die Demokratie der Westdeutschen* (Munich: Beck, 1988), 134–35.

39 Cf., for example, the collection, *Complexio Oppositorium: Über Carl Schmitt*, ed.

H. Quaritsch (Berlin: Duncker und Humblot, 1988); and G. Maschke, *Der Tod Carl Schmitts* (Vienna: Karolinger, 1987). For Habermas's critique of Schmitt, see the essay, "The Horrors of Autonomy: Carl Schmitt in English," in *The New Conservatism*, 128–39. For an explanation of the continuities between Schmitt's authoritarian political philosophy of the 1920s and his partisanship for National Socialism in the 1930s, see my essay "Carl Schmitt, Political Existentialism, and the Total State," in *The Terms of Cultural Criticism: The Frankfurt School, Existentialism, and Poststructuralism* (New York: Columbia University Press, 1992), 83–104.

40   See for example Ulrich Oevermann, "Zwei Staaten oder Einheit?" *Merkur* 44 (February 1990): 91–106, and Karl Heinz Bohrer, "Und die Erinnerung der beiden Halbnationen?" *Merkur* 44 (March 1990): 183–88. See also the dossier on German reunification in *New German Critique* 52 (Winter 1991): 31–108.

41   See the controversial essay by Botho Strauss in the February 1993 of *Der Spiegel*, where these positions are adumbrated.

42   "Modernity versus Postmodernism" first appeared in *New German Critique* 22 (Winter 1981): 3–14. The German original was entitled "Die Moderne: Ein unvollendetes Projekt" and appeared in *Kleine Politische Schriften*, 1–4 (Frankfurt am Main: Suhrkamp, 1981), 444–64. It was delivered by Habermas on the occasion of his receiving the Adorno Prize, awarded by the city of Frankfurt on September 11, 1980.

43   Habermas, "Modernity versus Postmodernity," 11.

44   Weber's clearest articulation of this perspective—implicit in all his work—may be found in "Religious Rejections of the World and Their Directions," in *From Max Weber*, ed. H. Gerth and C. W. Mills (New York, 1946), 323–59.

45   For Habermas's treatment of the problem of the modern need for self-legitimation (*Selbstvergewisserung*), see *The Philosophical Discourse of Modernity: Twelve Lectures*, trans. Frederick G. Lawrence (Cambridge: MIT Press, 1987), 1–22 ("Modernity's Consciousness of Time and its Need for Self-Reassurance").

46   Habermas analyzes the Nietzschean origins of postmodernism in *The Philosophical Discourse of Modernity*, chap. 4, "The Entry into Postmodernism: Nietzsche as a Turning Point," 83–195.

47   Cf. *Theory of Communicative Action*, 2:311–96, passim.

48   Habermas, "Neoconservative Cultural Criticism," 45.

49   Habermas, "The New Obscurity: The Crisis of the Welfare State and the Exhaustion of Utopian Energies," in *The New Conservatism*, 66–67.

Carl Schmitt

1   Carl Schmitt, *Staat, Bewegung, Volk* (Hamburg: Hanseatischer Verlaganstalt, 1933), 32.

2   Max Weber, *Economy and Society* (Berkeley and Los Angeles: University of California Press, 1968), 127ff.

3   One of the first to comment on Schmitt's remarks on the relationship between Hegel and Hitler was the philosopher Herbert Marcuse, who refers to the "profound comprehension" of Schmitt's judgment, but then immediately points out the retrograde implications from the standpoint of prospects for German freedom. For Marcuse, the "death of Hegel" signifies not only the demise of a specific philosophical system, but *the death of German idealism tout court;* more specifically, it presages the obsolescence of the strong

concept of reason (*Vernunft*) that was the cornerstone of this magisterial philosophical enterprise begun by Kant. See Marcuse, "The Struggle Against Liberalism in the Totalitarian State," in *Negations: Essays in Critical Theory,* trans. Jeremy Shapiro (Boston: Beacon, 1968). Many of the implications of Marcuse analysis have been drawn out by Georg Lukács in *The Destruction of Reason* (New York and London: Humanities, 1980).

4   Hannah Arendt, *The Origins of Totalitarianism* (New York: Meridian, 1958), 339.

5   Kurt Sontheimer, "Anti-Democratic Thought in the Weimar Republic," in *The Road to Dictatorship,* trans. Lawrence Wilson (London: Oswald Wolff, 1964), 42–43. Sontheimer's essay represents a condensed version of his book-length study, *Anti-Demokratisches Denken in der Weimarer Republik* (Munich: Nymphenburger, 1962), a work that contains a number of valuable discussions of Schmitt's thought in relation to the conservative revolutionaries. For a discussion of the conservative revolutionary movement in English, see Jeffrey Herf, *Reactionary Modernism: Technology, Culture, and Politics in Weimar and the Third Reich* (New York: Cambridge, 1984); and Fritz Stern, *The Politics of Cultural Despair* (New York: Anchor, 1965). For an attempt to downplay Schmitt's affiliations with the conservative revolutionaries, see Joseph Bendersky, "Carl Schmitt and the Conservative Revolution," *Telos* 72 (1987): 27–42.

6   Hence, this is true of the works by Herf and Sontheimer cited in note 5. It is also true of a significant number of other works that treat the conservative revolution. Among them, one would have to include Christian von Krockow, *Die Entscheidung: Eine Untersuchung über Ernst Jünger, Carl Schmitt, Martin Heidegger* (Stuttgart: F. Enke, 1958); Armin Mohler, *Die konservative Revolution* (Stuttgart: F. Vorwerk, 1950); and George Mosse, *The Crisis of the German Ideology: The Intellectual Origins of the Third Reich* (New York: Grosset Dunlap, 1964).

7   One of the classical articulations of this perspective is a militaristic tract composed by Werner Sombart during World War I entitled *Händler und Helden* (*Merchants and Heroes*) (Munich, 1915). For a good discussion of the way this opposition permeated the mind-set of the German intellectual mandarinate in the early decades of the twentieth century, see Fritz Ringer, *The Decline of the German Mandarins: The German Academic Community, 1890–1933* (Cambridge: Harvard University Press, 1969), 183.

8   Herf, *Reactionary Modernism,* 1ff.

9   Schmitt, *Der Wert des Staates und die Bedeutung des Einzelnen* (Tübingen: J.C.B. Mohr, 1914), 101.

10   Ibid., 108.

11   Joseph Bendersky, *Carl Schmitt: Theorist for the Reich* (Princeton: Princeton University Press, 1983), 12ff.

12   Friedrich Nietzsche, *The Will to Power* (New York: Vintage, 1967), no. 254.

13   Nietzsche, *On the Genealogy of Morals,* trans. Walter Kaufmann (New York: Vintage, 1967), 79.

14   On Spengler, see Herf, *Reactionary Modernism,* 49ff. In all fairness, though, it seems that Herf's study exaggerates Spengler's sympathies for the forces of technocracy in modern society, especially in his late work, *Man and Technics.*

15   Schmitt, *Political Theology,* trans. George Schwab (Cambridge: MIT Press, 1985), 5.

16   Ibid.

17   Hans Saner, "Grenzsituation," in *Historisches Wörterbuch der Philosophie* (Basel: Schwabe, 1974), 3:877.

18   Schmitt, *The Crisis of Parliamentary Democracy,* trans. E. Kennedy (Cambridge: MIT Press, 1985), 71.

19   Schmitt, *Political Theology,* 12, 31 (my emphasis).

20   Franz Neumann, *Behemoth: The Structure and Practice of National Socialism, 1933–1944* (New York: Oxford University Press, 1967), 145–46.

21   Schmitt, *Political Theology,* 15.

22   Karl Heinz Bohrer, *Ästhetik des Schreckens* (Munich: Carl Hanser, 1978), 334ff.

23   Schmitt, *Political Theology,* 12 (my emphasis).

24   Ibid., 15. See also the commentary by Bohrer on the passage in question in *Äesthetik des Schreckens,* 342–43.

25   In this sense, Schmitt would find little to disagree with in the critique of modernity set forth by Weber in the concluding pages of *The Protestant Ethic and the Spirit of Capitalism:* "Specialists without spirit, sensualists without heart; this nullity imagines it has attained a level of civilization never before achieved." Cf. Weber, *The Protestant Ethic and the Spirit of Capitalism* (New York: Scribner, 1958), 182.

26   Schmitt, *The Crisis of Parliamentary Democracy,* 67.

27   Chapter 1 of *Political Theology* ends with an encomium to an unnamed "Protestant theologian [Kierkegaard] who demonstrated the vital intensity possible in theological reflection." Schmitt goes on to cite approvingly the following gloss on the relation of the "exception" to the "general" from *Repetition:* "The exception explains the general and itself. And if one wants to study the general correctly, one only needs to look around for a true exception. It reveals everything more clearly than does the general. Endless talk about the general becomes boring; there are exceptions. If they cannot be explained, then the general also cannot be explained. The difficulty is usually not noticed because the general is not thought about with passion but with a comfortable superficiality. The exception, on the other hand, thinks the general with intense passion."

28   Schmitt, *Political Theology,* 36. For a refutation of Schmitt's endorsement of the "secularization hypothesis," see Hans Blumenberg, *The Legitimacy of the Modern Age* (Cambridge: MIT Press, 1983).

29   Neumann, *Behemoth,* 47.

30   Schmitt, *The Crisis of Parliamentary Democracy,* 70.

31   Ibid.

32   Ibid., 71.

33   See the anthology edited by Ernst Jünger, *Kreig und Krieger* (Berlin: Junker Dunnhaupt, 1930), in which Jünger first published his influential essay on "total mobilization." Walter Benjamin wrote a highly critical review of the volume, which has been reprinted in his *Gesammelte Schriften,* (Frankfurt am Main: Suhrkamp, 1972), 3:238–50.

34   Schmitt, *The Crisis of Parliamentary Democracy,* 173.

35   Schmitt, *Political Theology,* 48.

36   Ibid., 65–66.

37   For more on Schmitt's philosophy of history, see "Das Zeitalter der Neutralisierungen und Entpolitisierungen," in *Der Begriff des Politischen* (Berlin: Duncker und Humblot, 1979), 96–115.

38   Schmitt, *Parliamentary Democracy,* 75 (my emphasis).

39   Ibid., 75–76.

40   Schmitt, *Der Begriff des Politischen* (Berlin: Duncker und Humblot, 1963), 71.

41 Ibid., 75.

42 Schmitt, "Weiterentwicklung des totalen Staats in Deutschland" (1933), in *Positionen und Begriffe* (Hamburg: Hanseatischer Verlaganstalt, 1940), 185.

43 Ibid., 186.

44 Ibid.

45 Schmitt, "Die Wendung zum totalen Staat," ibid., 152. It should be noted that the praise of Jünger as a "remarkable representative of the German *Frontsoldaten*" cited above has been omitted from the reprint of this essay in *Positionen und Begriffe*. See the original publication in *Europäische Revue* 7, no. 4 (April 1931): 243.

46 Ernst Jünger, "Die totale Mobilmachung," *Werke* (Stuttgart: Klett, n.d.), 5:130.

47 See Bendersky, *Carl Schmitt*, 199ff.

48 Schmitt, *Positionen und Begriffe*, 110 (my emphasis).

49 Schmitt, *Der Begriff des Politischen*, 67.

50 Strauss, "Comments on Carl Schmitt's *Der Begriff des Politischen*," in Schmitt, *The Concept of the Political*, trans. George Schwab (New Brunswick, N.J.: Rutgers University Press, 1976), 90.

51 Jünger, *Kampf als inneres Erlebnis* (Berlin: E. S. Mittler, 1922), 57.

52 Schmitt, *Der Begriff des Politischen*, 49.

53 Ibid., 33.

54 Ibid., 28, 33.

55 See Benjamin, *Gesammelte Schriften*, 3:240: "This new theory of war . . . is nothing other than a reckless transposition of the theses of *l'art pour l'art* to war."

56 Schmitt, "Reich, Staat, Bund," in *Positionen und Begriffe*, 198.

"Over the Line"

1 Sheehan, "Heidegger and the Nazis," *New York Review of Books*, June 16, 1988, 47. For Sheehan's earlier defense of Heidegger (in response to Stephen Eric Bronner's "Martin Heidegger: The Consequences of Political Mystification," *Salmagundi* 38–39 [Summer–Fall 1977]), see *Salmagundi* 13 (Winter 1979): 173–84.

2 See, for example, Hans-Georg Gadamer, "Back from Syracuse?" *Critical Inquiry* 15, no. 2 (1989): 427–30.

3 Pöggeler, "Den Führer führen? Heidegger und kein Ende," *Philosophische Rundschau* 32 (1985): 26–67.

4 The phrase Heidegger uses in *An Introduction to Metaphysics* (New Haven: Yale University Press, 1959), 199.

5 In his biography of Heidegger, *Martin Heidegger: Unterwegs zu seiner Biographie* (Frankfurt am Main: Campus, 1988), Hugo Ott has reproduced the report of the Freiburg University denazification commission on 305ff.

6 Cited in Ott, *Martin Heidegger*, 316–17.

7 See for example Jürgen Habermas's essay, "Work and Weltanschauung: The Heidegger Controversy from a German Perspective," in Habermas, *The New Conservatism: Cultural Criticism and the Historians' Debate*, ed. and trans. Shierry W. Nicholsen (Cambridge: MIT Press, 1989).

8 Löwith, "My Last Meeting with Heidegger in Rome, 1936," reprinted in *The Heidegger Controversy: A Critical Reader*, 140–43.

9   Pöggeler, *Martin Heidegger's Path of Thinking*, 272.

10 Heidegger, *An Introduction to Metaphysics*, 199 (translation slightly altered).

11 See Martin Heidegger, "Letter to the Rector of Freiburg University, 4 November 1945," reprinted in *The Heidegger Controversy: A Critical Reader*, part 1, "Political Texts, 1933–1944." The allusion to 30 June 1934 is of course a reference to the so-called night of the long knives: the Nazi purge of the Röhm faction (the SA) and the "socialist" wing of the National Socialist movement, centered around the brothers Gregor and Otto Strasser.

12 See Heidegger, *Das Rektorat, 1933–34: Tatsachen und Gedanken* (Frankfurt am Main: Klostermann, 1983), 23. And the Spiegel interview, "Only A God Can Save Us," reprinted in *The Heidegger Controversy: A Critical Reader*, 91–115.

13 See, for example, the contributions by Emmanuel Levinas and Maurice Blanchot in the dossier entitled, "Heidegger et la pensée Nazie," *Le Nouvel Observateur*, January 22–28, 1988, 41–49.

14 For a discussions of the conservative revolutionary world-view, see Jeffrey Herf, *Reactionary Modernism: Technology, Culture and Politics in Weimar Germany* (Cambridge: Cambridge University Press, 1984); and Jerry Z. Muller, *The Other God that Failed* (Princeton: Princeton University Press, 1987).

15 Nietzsche, *The Will To Power*, ed. Walter Kaufmann (New York: Vintage, 1967), no. 809.

16 See the excellent discussion of this theme in Michael Zimmerman, *Heidegger's Confrontation with Modernity* (Bloomington: Indiana University Press, 1990), 113: "Beginning in the mid-1930s . . . Heidegger concluded that the work of art could help to make possible the non-representational, non-calculative, meditative thinking which would usher in the post-metaphysical age."

17 Heidegger, *Hölderlins Hymnen "Germanien" und "Der Rhein."* Gesamtausgabe 39 (Frankfurt am Main: Klostermann, 1980).

18 Heidegger, *Existence and Being* (Chicago: Regnery, Gateway, 1949), 287.

19 See Heidegger, "Only a God Can Save Us," in *The Heidegger Controversy: A Critical Reader*, 106.

20 Heidegger, *Discourse on Thinking* (New York: Harper, 1966), 47.

21 Heidegger, *Nietzsche: the Will to Power as Art*, trans. D. F. Krell (New York: Harper Row, 1979), 85–86.

22 See H. W. Petzet, *Auf einen Stern zugehen: Begegnungen und Gespräche mit Martin Heidegger, 1929–1976* (Frankfurt am Main, Societät, 1983), 232; and Heidegger, *Was Heißt Denken?* (Tübingen: M. Niemeyer, 1954), 65.

23 Heidegger, *Beiträge zu Philosophie* (Frankfurt am Main: Klostermann, 1989), 38 (my emphasis). See the superb analysis of this text of the mid-1930s by Nicolas Tertulian, "The History of Being and Political Revolution: Reflections on a Posthumous Work of Heidegger," in *The Heidegger Case: On Philosophy and Politics*, ed. Tom Rockmore and Joseph Margolis (Philadelphia: Temple University Press, 1991), 208–27.

24 Heidegger, *Basic Writings* (New York: Harper and Row, 1977), 96 (translation altered).

25 "Arbeitsgemeinschaft Cassirer-Heidegger," in Guido Schneeberger, *Ergänzungen zu einer Heidegger Bibliographie* (Bern: Suhr, 1960), 20–21 (my emphasis). English translation in *The Existentialist Tradition: Selected Writings*, ed. N. Lagiulli (Garden City, N.Y.: Doubleday, 1971).

26 For the best discussion of this theme in Heidegger, see Winfried Franzen, "Die Suche

nach Härte und Schwere," in *Heidegger und die praktische Philosophie*, ed. A. Gethmann-Siefert and O. Pöggeler (Frankfurt am Main: Suhrkamp, 1988), 78–92.

27   Heidegger, "The Self-Affirmation of the German University," in *The Heidegger Controversy: A Critical Reader*, 30.

28   Heidegger, *An Introduction to Metaphysics* (New Haven: Yale University Press, 1959), 47.

29   Heidegger, "The Self-Affirmation of the German University," 33–34.

30   Heidegger, *Basic Writings*, 210.

31   Heidegger, "The Word of Nietzsche: 'God is Dead,' " in *The Question Concerning Technology and Other Essays*, ed. and trans. William Lovitt (New York: Harper, 1977), 112.

32   Karl Löwith, *Heidegger: Denker in dürftiger Zeit* (Stuttgart: Metzler, 1984), 173–74.

33   Heidegger, *Logica: Lecciones de M. Heidegger* (bilingual edition) (Barcelona: Anthropos, 1991).

34   Löwith, "My Last Meeting with Heidegger in Rome, 1936," in *The Heidegger Controversy: A Critical Reader*, 142.

35   Heidegger, *Being and Time* (New York: Harper and Row, 1962), 436.

36   Heidegger, *Gesamtausgabe* (Frankfurt am Main: Klostermann, 1986), 48:138.

37   Ibid., 205.

38   Heidegger, *Logica*, 40.

39   Heidegger, *An Introduction to Metaphysics*, 38–39.

40   Ibid., 42.

41   Heidegger, *Hölderlins Hymnen "Germanien" und "Der Rhein,"* 134.

42   Heidegger, *Hölderlins Hymne der "Ister,"* in *Gesamtausgabe* (Frankfurt am Main: Klostermann, 1984), 54:106.

43   Heidegger, *Das Rektorat, 1933–34*, 39.

44   Heidegger, *Heraklit*, in *Gesamtausgabe* 55 (Frankfurt am Main: Klostermann, 1979), 55:123.

45   Heidegger, "Overcoming Metaphysics," in *The End of Philosophy* (New York: Harper and Row, 1973), 86.

46   Heidegger's letter to Marcuse is reprinted in *The Heidegger Controversy: A Critical Reader*, 163.

47   Martin Heidegger, "Insight into That Which Is," cited in Wolfgang Schirmacher, *Technik und Gelassenheit* (Freiburg and Munich: Albers, 1983), 25.

48   Cf. Ernst Tugendhat, *Self-Consciousness and Self-Determination* (Cambridge: MIT Press, 1986), 187 (translation slightly altered). For more on this point, see his essay, "Heidegger's Idea of Truth," in *The Heidegger Controversy: A Critical Reader*, 245–63.

49   Adorno, *The Jargon of Authenticity* (New York: Seabury, 1973), 8.

50   Söllner, "Left Students of the Conservative Revolution," *Telos* 61 (1984): 59.

51   Heidegger, letter to Herbert Marcuse of January 20, 1948, in *The Heidegger Controversy: A Critical Reader*, 162.

52   Heidegger, *Das Rektorat, 1933–34*, 25.

53   An observation from Heidegger's 1936 Schelling lectures, cited by Pöggeler in "Den Führer führen," 56.

54   See Kurt Sontheimer, "Anti-Democratic Thought in the Weimar Republic," in *The Road to Dictatorship*, ed. Lawrence Wilson (London: Oswald Wolff, 1964), 42ff.: "It is hardly a matter of controversy today that certain ideological predispositions in German

thought generally, but particularly in the intellectual and political climate of the Wei-mar . . . prepared the intellectual soil for the growth of National Socialism." For more on the intellectual origins of Nazism, see Fritz Stern, *The Politics of Cultural Despair: A Study in the Rise of the Germanic Ideology* (New York: Knopf, 1972) and George Mosse, *The Crisis of the German Ideology: The Intellectual Origins of the Third Reich* (New York: Grosset and Dunlap, 1964). For a thorough account of Heidegger's intellectual indebt-edness to the paradigm of conservative revolutionary thought that attained prominence in Germany between the wars, see Pierre Bourdieu, *Heidegger's Political Ontology* (Stan-ford: Stanford University Press, 1990).

55   On this point see the two important books by Michael Löwy, *Georg Lukács: From Romanticism to Bolshevism* (London: New Left Books, 1978); and *Utopie et rédemption: Le Judaïsme libertaire en Europe centrale* (Paris: PUF, 1988).

56   Heidegger, *The End of Philosophy*, 85–86.

57   See his remarks to this effect in *Was heißt Denken* (Tübingen: M. Niemeyer, 1954), 65, and "Only a God Can Save Us," in *The Heidegger Controversy: A Critical Reader*, 104.

58   For the classical account, see Helmuth Plessner, *Die verspätete Nation* (Frankfurt am Main: Suhrkamp, 1974). See also Ralf Dahrendorf, *Society and Democracy in Germany* (New York: Norton, 1979).

59   Leo Strauss, "An Introduction to Heideggerian Existentialism," in *The Rebirth of Classi-cal Political Rationalism*, selected and intro. T. Pangle (Chicago: University of Chicago Press, 1989), 30.

French Heidegger Wars

1   The most important of these speeches have been included in *The Heidegger Controversy: A Critical Reader*, ed. Richard Wolin (Cambridge: MIT Press, 1993), part 1, "Political Texts, 1933–1934."

2   See the debate in the 1946–47 issues of *Les Temps Modernes* that was spurred by Karl Löwith's essay, "Les Implications politiques de philosophie de l'existence chez Heideg-ger" (November 1946), reprinted in *The Heidegger Controversy: A Critical Reader*, 167–85. See also the further discussions of this theme by Alphons de Waelhens and Eric Weil in the July 1947 issue of *Les Temps Modernes*. The second debate, which occurred in the Parisian journal *Critique*, was provoked by a review essay by François Fédier that at-tacked three books critical of Heidegger: Guido Schneeberger's *Nachlese zu Heidegger* (Bern: Suhr, 1962); Theodor Adorno's *Jargon der Eigentlichkeit* (Frankfurt am Main: Suhrkamp, 1964); Paul Hühnerfeld's *In Sachen Heidegger: Versuch über ein deutsches Genie* (Hamburg: Hoffmann und Campe, 1959). Fédier's essay, which appeared in the February 1967 number, was rebutted in articles by Robert Minder, Jean Pierre Faye, and Aimé Patri, all of which appeared in *Critique* in July of the same year. An overview of this debate can be found in Beda Allemann, "Martin Heidegger und die Politik," in *Martin Heidegger: Perspektiven zur Deutung seines Werk*, ed. Otto Pöggeler (Königstein: Athe-näuum, 1969), 246–60.

3   Among Ott's researches, the most important are as follows: "Martin Heidegger als Rektor der Universität Freiburg," *Zeitschrift für die Geschichte des Oberrheins* 132 (1984): 343–58; "Martin Heidegger als Rektor der Universität Freiburg i. Br.—die Zeit des Rektorats von M. Heidegger," *Zeitschrift des Breisgau-Geschichtsvereins* 103 (1984):107–

30; and "Martin Heidegger und die Universität Freiburg nach 1945," *Historisches Jahr-buch* 1–5 (1985): 95–128. Most of Ott's findings have been incorporated in his recent book, *Martin Heidegger: Unterwegs zu seiner Biographie* (Frankfurt: Campus, 1988).

4 Heidegger's own accounts of his rectorship can be found in the "The Rectorship, 1933–34: Facts and Thoughts," trans. Karsten Harries, *Review of Metaphysics* (1985): 481–502; his "Letter to the Rector of Freiburg University, 4 November 1945"; *Der Spiegel* interview of May 1976: "Only a God Save Us: the Spiegel Interview." The latter two documents have been reprinted in Richard Wolin, ed., *The Heidegger Controversy: A Critical Reader.*

5 It is of more than passing interest to note that Farias first tried repeatedly to publish his manuscript in Germany—the country that has been his home for a number of years now; he himself is a former Heidegger student and currently lives in Berlin where he teaches at the Free University—but met with rejection from all quarters. That the renewed debate over Heidegger's past has exploded in France had been no small source of embarrassment to German intellectuals, who are only now beginning to formulate their own interpretations concerning "Der Fall Heidegger."

6 See note 4.

7 As Ott explains, this telegram contributed significantly to a Freiburg University de-nazification committee ruling in 1946 that stripped him both of his right to teach and "emeritus" status, by virtue of which he would still have been allowed to participate in university activities.

8 The existing translation of the Rectoral Address (see note 4) is woefully anodyne. I have therefore retranslated all references from the recent German edition, *Die Selbstbehaup-tung der deutschen Universität* (Frankfurt am Main: Klostermann, 1984).

9 Cf. Heidegger, *An Introduction to Metaphysics* (New Haven: Yale University Press, 1959), 48, where Heidegger observes that "the state of science since the turn of the century . . . has remained unchanged despite a certain amount of *Sauberung*."

10 The usual English rendering of the Greek (in both the Grube and Shorey translations) is "everything great is at risk" or "is precarious." Heidegger therefore has willfully dis-torted the Greek *episphala*—in order to give it an ideological twist—by translating it as "Sturm," thereby rendering it compatible with the militaristic tone of the speech and the times.

11 On this point, see the analysis of Heidegger's speech, "Deutsche Männer und Frauen!", in Karl Löwith, "Les implications politiques."

12 These events are cited in Ott, "Martin Heidegger als Rektor der Universität Freiburg i. Br.," 117–18.

13 Ibid., 124–26.

14 Ott, "Martin Heidegger als Rektor der Universität Freiburg," 356.

15 The disagreements fall into the category of unpleasant harassment rather than anything more serious. Krieck—with whom Heidegger made common cause in the spring of 1933 in the interest of the *Gleichschaltung* of the Association of German University Rectors—published several public attacks on Heidegger's philosophy as being ultimately incom-patible with National Socialist doctrines. Rosenberg seems to have been interested in suppressing the publication of a 1942 Heidegger essay, "Plato's Doctrine of Truth." The essay was eventually published, very likely owing to the intervention of Benito Mus-solini [!], who was informed about the matter by the Italian philosopher Ernesto Grassi.

For more on the Heidegger–Mussolini connection, see *Heidegger et le Nazisme,* (Lagrasse: Verdier, 1987), 273–82 ("Heidegger et il Duce"). See also the extremely informative interview with Ernesto Grassi in *Liberation,* March 2, 1988, 40–41.

16 "Heidegger at Eighty," reprinted in *Heidegger and Modern Philosophy,* ed. Michael Murray (New Haven: Yale University Press, 1978), 292–303.

17 See note 4.

18 Heidegger, *An Introduction to Metaphysics,* 197.

19 See, for example, the epistolary responses to the original essay of October 14, 1987, in the October 30, 1987 issue of *Le Monde.*

20 For example, see the following remarks by Derrida: "As for the essentials of these 'facts,' I have found nothing in this inquiry that was not already known for quite some time by those who were seriously interested in Heidegger." The Derrida interview, which originally appeared in the November 6–12, 1987, issue of *Nouvel Observateur,* appeared in the first edition of *The Heidegger Controversy: A Critical Reader* (New York: Columbia University Press, 1991), 264–73. It was deleted from subsequent editions at Derrida's request.

21 For comments on the part of the most loyal Heidegger devotées, see the contributions by Pierre Aubenque, Henri Crétella, and François Fédier in the dossier published in *Le Débat* 48 (January–February 1988). For a countervailing perspective, see the observations by Stéphane Moses and Alain Renaut in the same dossier.

22 Cf. Fédier's contribution to the *Nouvel Observateur* dossier on "Heidegger et la pensée Nazie," January 22–28, 1988, 50. See also his diatribe against Farias, *Heidegger: L'Anatomie d'un scandale* (Paris: Laffont, 1988).

23 Cf. note 21.

24 Paul Celan, in his poem "Todtnauberg," tells the story of his pilgrimage to the philosopher's Schwarzwald mountain ski hut and of his disappointment over Heidegger's refusal to utter a single word upon being asked about the Holocaust. A similar tale has been recounted by the theologian Rudolph Bultmann, who upon suggesting after the war that Heidegger publicly recant his Nazi past, received only a cold, silent stare in return (cf. the article by Robert Maggiori in *Libération,* October 16, 1987).

25 *Nouvel Observateur,* January 22–28, 1988, 43–45. Blanchot's comments, "Thinking about the Apocalypse," have been translated in *Critical Inquiry* 15, no. 2 (1989): 475–80.

26 *Nouvel Observateur,* January 22–28, 1988, 49. An English translation of Levinas's article, "As If Consenting to Horror," may be found in the issue of *Critical Inquiry* 15, no. 2 (1989): 485–88.

27 *Nouvel Observateur,* January 22–28, 1988, 45. An English translation of Gadamer's article, "Back From Syracuse?" may be found in the issue of *Critical Inquiry* 15, no. 2 (1989): 427–30.

28 Faurisson's argument is largely based on the fact that he has personally never met a Jew who actually *saw* the gas chambers. That Jews who did see the inside of the chambers were asphyxiated within three to four minutes might go far toward explaining the peculiar lack of eyewitness accounts Faurisson has encountered.

29 Cf. the report by Robert Maggiori in *Libération,* January 7, 1988, 43.

30 See Michel Tibon-Cornillot, "Heidegger et le chainon manquant," *Libération,* February 17, 1988, 41–42, for a comprehensive treatment of the relations between Heidegger and Fischer. In a follow-up letter the next day, Fischer would write: "The faculty

defends [Heidegger] as a spiritual Führer and a thinker. . . . We really do not have many great philosophers, let alone National Socialist philosophers." The fact that the papers of both Heidegger and Fischer are closed to public viewing represents a significant obstacle to a more detailed investigation of their relations.

31 Farias, *Heidegger et le nazisme*, 79.

32 Both have recently been translated into English. Jacques Derrida, *Of Spirit: Heidegger and the Question* (Chicago: University of Chicago Press, 1989) and Philippe Lacoue-Labarthe, *Heidegger, Art and Politics* (Oxford: Blackwell, 1990).

33 Cf. Derrida's essay, "The Ends of Man," in *Margins of Philosophy* (Chicago: University of Chicago Press, 1982), 109–36.

34 This contention has been subjected to a thoroughgoing rebuttal by Luc Ferry and Alain Renaut in *Heidegger and Modernity* (Chicago: University of Chicago Press, 1990).

35 Cited in *Der Spiegel*, August 18, 1986, 167.

36 See the remarks by Jean-Michel Palmier cited in *Der Spiegel*, August 18, 1986.

37 Cf. "Heidegger, l'enfer des philosophes" (interview with Jacques Derrida), *Nouvel Observateur*, November 6–12, 1987, 171–72; see note 20.

38 The category of the "will to will" dominates Heidegger's critique of traditional metaphysics and its nihilistic implications in his *Nietzsche*, 2 vols. (Pfullingen: Neske, 1962). A four-volume English translation has recently appeared from Harper and Row (1989).

39 Cited in "Neue Forschungen und Urteile über Heidegger und Nationalsozialismus," *Der Spiegel*, August 18, 1986, 169.

Democracy and the Political
in the Thought of Hannah Arendt

1 See Arendt, *The Origins of Totalitarianism* (New York: Meridian, 1958), 437ff.

2 Margaret Canovan, *Hannah Arendt: A Reinterpretation of Her Political Thought*, (Cambridge: Cambridge University Press, 1992), 20. Of the innumerable works that have recently appeared on Arendt, this book is undoubtedly one of the most useful. The accusation Canovan makes contra Arendt would also hold for Horkheimer and Adorno's *Dialectic of Enlightenment* (New York: Continuum, 1972).

3 On the discontinuities within Italian fascism, see Roger Griffin, *The Nature of Fascism* (New York: Routledge, 1993), 67: "Its next incarnation [in 1925] as a constitutional party operating as an integral part of a coalition government . . . was a radical contradiction of its palingenetic myth, as the 'intransigents' of all denominations pointed out vociferously. It had now been metamorphosed, almost against its leader's own will or better judgment, into an authoritarian regime exercising power in the name of a populist revolution."

4 For a classic study of the relationship between Germany's belatedness as a nation and its subsequent turn toward fascism, see Hans-Ulrich Wehler, *The German Empire, 1871–1918* (Leamington Spa, Warwickshire, U.K., and Dover, N.H.: Berg, 1985).

5 Martin Jay, "The Political Existentialism of Hannah Arendt," *The Permanent Exiles: Essays on the Intellectual Migration from Germany to America* (New York: Columbia University Press, 1985), 240. Jay's essay represents a very important, if often neglected, discussion of these themes. For a critique of Jay's treatment of these themes, see Mauri-

zio Passerin d'Entrèves, *The Political Philosophy of Hannah Arendt* (New York: Routledge, 1994), 87ff. While certain of d'Entrèves's points are well taken, in the end, he does not accord the valid aspects of Jay's criticisms their full due.

6   Arendt, "What is Existenz Philosophy?" *Partisan Review* 13, no. 1 (Winter 1946): 34.

7   See L. and S. Hinchman, "Existentialism Politicized: Arendt's Debt to Jaspers," in *Hannah Arendt: Critical Essays*, ed. L. and S. Hinchman (Albany: State University of New York Press), 140–145: "In particular, Karl Jasper's notion of *Existenz* or authentic selfhood is crucial, for it inspired Arendt's distinctions between action versus behavior and the 'who' versus the 'what' of a person, as well as her concepts of meaning of mass society. . . . This link between *Existenz* and action points to a crucial congruence between Jasper's and Arendt's theories."

8   Nietzsche, *Beyond Good and Evil* (New York: Vintage, 1966), section 208. For an excellent account of Nietzsche's concept of "great politics," see Bruce Detwiler, *Nietzsche and the Politics of Aristocratic Radicalism* (Chicago: University of Chicago Press, 1990).

9   I have discussed the stages involved in Heidegger's commitment to National Socialism in *The Politics of Being: The Political Thought of Martin Heidegger* (New York: Columbia University Press, 1990); see especially 96ff. In this respect, moreover, Heidegger's postwar confession that he viewed contemporary politics largely through the prism of Ernst Jünger's influential 1932 work, *The Worker,* should be kept in mind.

10   Arendt, *The Human Condition* (Chicago: University of Chicago Press, 1958), 205.

11   Canovan, *Hannah Arendt,* 134.

12   Arendt, *The Human Condition,* 179.

13   Ibid., 188.

14   Arendt, *Between Past and Future* (New York: Penguin, 1968), 154.

15   Arendt, *The Human Condition,* 187. For more on this point, see Seyla Benhabib, "Models of Public Space: Hannah Arendt, the Liberal Tradition and Jürgen Habermas," *Situating the Self* (New York: Routledge, 1993): "The distinction between the 'social' and the 'political' makes no sense in the modern world, not because all politics has become administration and because the economy has become the quintessential 'public,' as Hannah Arendt thought, but primarily because the struggle to make something public is a struggle for justice."

16   Arendt begins these observations by citing Isak Dinesen: " 'Let physicians and confectioners and the servants of the great houses be judged by what they have done, and even by what they have meant to do; the great people themselves are judged by what they are.' " Arendt herself continues: "Only the vulgar will condescend to derive their pride from what they have done; they will, by this condescension, become the 'slaves and prisoners' of their own faculties and will find out, should anything more be left in them than sheer stupid vanity, that to be one's own slave and prisoner is no less bitter and perhaps even more shameful than to be the servant of somebody" (*The Human Condition,* 211).

17   See Heidegger, "The Essence of Truth," in *Existence and Being* (South Bend, Ind.: Gateway, 1949), 292–324; and "The Origin of the Work of Art," in *Poetry, Language, and Truth* (New York: Harper Row, 1971), 15–88.

18   Arendt, *The Human Condition,* 192.

19   See George Kateb, *Hannah Arendt: Politics, Conscience, Evil* (Totowa, N.J.: Rowman and Allanheld, 1983), 30–31: "insofar as Arendt confines her thought to the action of the

polis, she severs the whole point of political action—its revelatory existential achievement, its creation of human identity—from moral motivation or intention. . . . Arendt talks about particular acts in a way that seems to strengthen one's alarmed sense that her general theory of action can too easily accommodate great substantial evils, even the system of evil known as totalitarianism." I believe that Kateb, who embraces a frightened liberalism, takes this argument much too far.

20   Arendt, *The Human Condition,* 180.

21   Carl Schmitt, *Political Theology,* trans. George Schwab (Cambridge: MIT Press, 1985), 15.

22   Arendt, *On Revolution* (New York: Penguin, 1963), 262 and 264. For a discussion of this aspect or Arendt's thinking, see John F. Sitton, "Hannah Arendt's Argument for Council Democracy," in *Hannah Arendt: Critical Essays,* 307–34.

23   Arendt, *On Revolution,* 275.

24   Ibid., 277.

25   Ibid., 278.

26   Ibid., 279–80.

27   Canovan, *Hannah Arendt,* 135.

28   Arendt, *The Human Condition,* 199.

29   Cited in Canovan, *Hannah Arendt,* 136.

30   Arendt, *On Revolution,* 28.

31   Cited in Canovan, *Hannah Arendt,* 137.

32   Ibid., 142.

33   Sheldon Wolin, "Hannah Arendt: Democracy and the Political," in *Hannah Arendt: Critical Essays,* 289–306.

Antihumanism in the Discourse of French Postwar Theory

1   Tony Judt, *Past Imperfect: French Intellectuals, 1944–1956* (Berkeley and Los Angeles: University of California Press, 1993), 9.

2   Raymond Aron, *Elusive Revolution: The Anatomy of a Student Revolt* (New York: Praeger, 1969), 125.

3   For more on the relation between surrealism and the critique of the subject, see Jerrold Seigel, "La Mort du sujet: Origines d'un thème," *Le Débat* (February 1990): 160–69.

4   André Breton, *Manifestos of Surrealism* (Ann Arbor: University of Michigan Press, 1969), 26.

5   A good example thereof is the militant Sinophilia of the *Tel Quel* group (J. Kristeva, P. Sollers, M. Pleynet) in the late 1960s and early 1970s.

6   On the notion of the "intellectual field," see Pierre Bourdieu, "The Genesis of the Concepts of *Habitus* and of Field," *Sociocriticism* 2 (1985): 11–24; and "Intellectual Field and Creative Project," *Social Science Information* 8 (April 1969): 89–119.

7   September 1945 report of the Freiburg University denazification commission concerning Martin Heidegger; cited by Hugo Ott, *Martin Heidegger: Unterwegs zu seiner Biographie* (Frankfurt am Main: Campus, 1988), 305–6.

8   For the best discussion of the circumstances surrounding the French publication of Heidegger's "Letter," see Anson Rabinbach, "Heidegger's Letter on Humanism as Text and Event," *New German Critique* 62 (Spring–Summer 1994): 3–38.

9 Heidegger, "Letter on Humanism," in *Basic Writings* (New York: Harper Row, 1977), 232.

10 Reprinted in Sartre, *Essays in Existentialism* (Seacaucus, N.J.: Citadel, 1965), 31–62.

11 Heidegger, "Letter on Humanism," 214.

12 Ibid., 219, 220.

13 Ibid., 220.

14 The details of this episode are recounted by Ott in *Martin Heidegger*, 294ff.

15 Rabinbach, "Heidegger's Letter on Humanism"; Heidegger's sons eventually returned unharmed.

16 Heidegger, *Das Rektorat, 1933–34: Tatsachen und Gedanken* (Frankfurt am Main: Klostermann, 1983), 25.

17 Cited in Richard Wolin, *The Politics of Being: The Political Thought of Martin Heidegger* (New York: Columbia University Press, 1990), 148.

18 Heidegger, *Nietzsche* (New York: Harper Row, 1982), 4:221.

19 Ibid., 215.

20 Heidegger, "Overcoming Metaphysics," in *The End of Philosophy* (New York: Harper Row, 1973), 82.

21 Heidegger, "Letter on Humanism," 210.

22 See Heidegger, "Only a God Can Save Us: The *Spiegel* Interview," in *The Heidegger Controversy: A Critical Reader*, ed. Richard Wolin (Cambridge: MIT Press, 1993), 91–116.

23 For an informative, Bourdieu-inspired analysis of Sartre's role in the contemporary intellectual "field," see Anna Boschetti, *The Intellectual Enterprise: Sartre and Les Temps modernes* (Evanston: Northwestern University Press, 1988).

24 Rabinbach, "Heidegger 2."

25 See Heidegger's remarks to Herbert Marcuse in a letter of May 12, 1948, where the philosopher observes that he made common cause with Nazism insofar as he "expected from National Socialism a spiritual renewal of life in its entirety, a reconciliation of social antagonisms, and a deliverance of Western *Dasein* from the danger of communism." Heidegger's letter may be found in Wolin, *The Heidegger Controversy: A Critical Reader*, 162–63.

26 Vincent Descombes, *Modern French Philosophy* (Cambridge: Cambridge University Press, 1980), 31.

27 On the relationship between Freud and the surrealists, see Margaret Cohen, *Profane Illuminations: Walter Benjamin and the Paris of Surrealist Revolution* (Berkeley and Los Angeles: University of California, 1993), 57ff. As Freud expressed it in a 1932 letter to Breton: "Although I receive so many testimonies of the interest that you and your friends show for my research, I am not able to clarify for myself what surrealism is and what it wants." *Les vases communicants* (Paris: Gallimard, 1981), 176.

There was also a strongly nationalist or chauvinist reception of Freud's doctrines in the 1920s that, focusing on the theory of the unconscious, opposed itself to the ego-psychological reading of Freud by Heinz Hartmann and others. For a while Lacan was a protégé of the leading member of these right-wing Freudians, Edouard Pichon. See the account of their relation in Elisabeth Roudinesco, *La Bataille des cents ans*, vol. 1 (Paris: Ramsay, 1982). For more on the relation between Pichon and Bataille, see also Jeffrey Mehlman, translator's foreword to Roudinesco, *Jacques Lacan & Co.: A History of*

Psychoanalysis in France, 1925–1985 (Chicago: University of Chicago Press, 1990), xii–xv. See also Mehlman, "The Suture of an Allusion: Lacan with Léon Bloy," in *Legacies of Anti-Semitism in France* (Minneapolis: University of Minnesota, 1983), 23–33; and Mehlman, "The Paranoid Style in French Politics: Léon Bloy and Jacques Lacan," *Oxford Literary Review* (1990), 39–47.

28   For a critique of Lacan's reading of Freud, see Ferry and Renaut, *French Philosophy of the Sixties*, 185–207. See also Joel Whitebook, "Rethinking the Subject: Lacan and Adorno," unpublished manuscript.

29   Freud, *Outline of Psychoanalysis* (New York: Norton, 1969); *New Introductory Lectures on Psychoanalysis, Standard Edition of the Complete Works of Sigmund Freud* (London: Hogarth, 1953), 22:80.

30   The reception of Freud as a proponent of ego psychology in France had been led by Marie Bonaparte and Rudolph Loewenstein. For an account of their influence, see Roudinesco's *Jacques Lacan & Co.* In the United States this view of Freud was advanced by Heinz Hartmann and others. In his *New Introductory Lectures on Psychoanalysis* (New York: Norton, 1965), Freud would criticize Hartmann for repressing those aspects of the analytic approach that were of greatest interest.

31   Lacan, *Ecrits* (Paris: Seuil, 1966), 374.

32   Peter Dews, *Logics of Disintegration: Post-Structuralist Thought and the Claims of Critical Theory* (London: Verso, 1987), 70.

33   Lacan, *The Seminar of Jacques Lacan: Book II, The Ego in Freud's Theory and in the Technique of Psychoanalysis, 1954–1955*, trans. S. Tomaselli (New York: Norton, 1988), 7.

34   Ibid., 16.

35   Lacan, "The Mirror Stage as Formative of the I," in *Ecrits: A Selection* (New York: Norton, 1977), 1–7.

36   Lacan, *The Seminar of Jacques Lacan: Book II*, 8.

37   Lacan, *Séminaire* (Paris: Seuil, 1978), 2:286.

38   *Ibid.*, p. 92.

39   Whitebook, "Rethinking the Subject," 17.

40   Lacan, *Séminaire*, 2:11.

41   The motif linking violence and metaphysics comes through clearly in Levinas's main philosophical work, *Totality and Infinity*, trans. A. Lingis (Pittsburgh: Dusquesne University Press, 1969). For an especially clear statement of this theme, see "Ethics as First Philosophy," in *The Levinas Reader*, ed. S. Hand (Oxford: Blackwell, 1989), 75–88.

42   Whitebook, "Rethinking the Subject," 19.

43   For example, see the important discussion of "The Analytic of Finitude" and "Man and His Doubles" in Foucault's *The Order of Things* (London: Tavistock, 1970), 312ff.

44   See J. G. Merquior, *From Prague to Paris* (London: Verso, 1986), 11: "Nowadays [Saussure's *Course in General Linguistics*] is rightly deemed the theoretical fountainhead of modern structuralism."

45   Vincent Descombes, *Modern French Philosophy*, 100.

46   See Paul Ricoeur, "Symbole et temporalité," *Archivio di filosofia*, 1–2 (1963): 24.

47   Lévi-Strauss, *Anthropologie Structurale* (Paris: Plon, 1958), 71. The rendering of this passage in the English-language edition (see the note that follows) is fully inadequate.

48   Lévi-Strauss, *Structural Anthropology* (New York: Harper, 1963), 58–59.

49   Lévi-Strauss, "History and Dialectic," in *The Savage Mind* (Chicago: University of Chicago Press, 1966), 249.

50   Lévi-Strauss, *Tristes Tropiques*, trans. J. and D. Weightman (New York: Penguin, 1992), 52.

51   Ibid., 58.

52   Ibid., 3.

53   Lévi-Strauss, "History and Dialectic," 249.

54   Ibid., 253.

55   Hans-Georg Gadamer, *Truth and Method* (New York: Seabury, 1974).

56   Lévi-Strauss, "History and Dialectic," 252.

57   Adorno, "Letters to Walter Benjamin," in *Aesthetics and Politics* (London: New Left Books, 1977), 110–33.

58   Lévi-Strauss, "History and Dialectic," 255–56.

59   See my analysis of this problem in Heidegger in *The Politics of Being: The Political Thought of Martin Heidegger* (New York: Columbia University Press, 1990), 160ff.

60   Steven B. Smith, *Reading Althusser: An Essay on Structuralist Marxism* (Ithaca: Cornell University Press, 1984), 200.

61   Lévi-Strauss, *Tristes Tropiques*, 37–38.

62   Lévi-Strauss, "Race and History," in *Structural Anthropology*, trans. M. Layton (Chicago: University of Chicago Press, 1976), 2:323–62.

63   Todorov, "Lévi-Strauss entre universalisme et relativisme," *Le Débat* 42 (November–December 1986): 173–92. See also his important new book *On Human Diversity: Nationalism, Racism, and Exoticism in French Thought* (Cambridge: Harvard University Press, 1993).

64   Lévi-Strauss, *Tristes Tropiques*, 55.

65   See Derrida's important essay, "Violence and Metaphysics: An Essay on the Thought of Emmanuel Levinas," in *Writing and Difference*, trans. A. Bass (Chicago: University of Chicago Press, 1978), 79–154.

66   Derrida, "Structure, Sign and Play in the Discourse of the Human Sciences," in *Writing and Difference*, 279.

67   Manfred Frank, *What is Neostructuralism?* (Minneapolis: University of Minnesota Press, 1989), 59–60.

68   Derrida, "Structure, Sign and Play," 279.

69   See Ernst Bloch, *Natural Right and Human Dignity*, trans. D. Schmidt (Cambridge: MIT Press, 1986).

70   See Derrida, "Racism's Last Word," in *Critical Inquiry* 12, no. 1 (Autumn 1985): 290–99. See also his attempt to trace the roots of Heidegger's Nazism to a "voluntarist metaphysics" in "Philosophers' Hell," in *The Heidegger Controversy*, 164–73.

71   See his more recent comments on this problem in *The Other Heading: Reflections on Today's Europe* (Bloomington: Indiana University Press, 1992).

72   Hannah Arendt, *The Origins of Totalitarianism* (New York: Meridian, 1958), 170.

73   Ibid., 173.

74   Derrida, "Racism's Last Word," 298. See also his attempt to account for Heidegger's Nazism in terms of the philosopher's overzealous attachment to a metaphysics of subjectivity in *Of Spirit: Heidegger and the Question* (Chicago: University of Chicago Press, 1989), 39–40: According to Derrida, a concept of "subjectivity" "reigns over the major-

ity of discourses which, today and for a long time to come, state their opposition to racism, to totalitarianism, to nazism, to fascism, etc., and do this in the name of (the) spirit, in the name of an axiomatic—for example, that of democracy or human rights—which, directly or not, comes back to this metaphysics of *subjectivity*. All the pitfalls of the strategy of establishing demarcations belong to this program, whatever place one occupies in it. The only choice is the choice between the terrifying contaminations it assigns. Even if all forms of complicity are not equivalent, they are *irreducible*."

75 See Michael Walzer, "The New Tribalism," *Dissent*, 39, no. 2 (Spring 1992): 164–71.

76 For the best accounts of this movement, see Pierre-André Taguieff, *La Force du préjugé* (Paris: Editions la Découverte, 1988); Taguieff, "Le Néo-Racisme différentialiste," *Langage et société* 34 (December 1985), 69–98; Taguieff, "Cultural Racism in France," *Telos* 83 (Spring 1990): 109–23.

   For the German context and background, see John Ely, " 'Similar Enough to Mistake Them' ": 'Black' and 'Brown' Versions of National-Conservatism in Germany Today," unpublished manuscript. As Ely observes with reference to the national conservative journal *Junge Freiheit*, "the ties between poststructuralist thought (under the influence of Nietzsche and Heidegger) and Armin Mohler [Ernst Jünger's former secretary and editor of the new right journal *Criticon*] are important. We see a significant influence (if not merely claim) of poststructuralism on the new right thinking. . . . [T]he publisher Matthes & Seitz, is an apparently left publisher which publishes not only Baudrillard, Bataille and de Sade, but also Gerd Bergfleth and Günter Maschke" (20).

77 This is more or less the thesis of a number of influential books written in France over the previous six or seven years that have sought to redress the new politics of ethnicity that has been a direct result of the rejection of cosmopolitanism. See, for example, Alain Finkielkraut, *The Defeat of Thought* (New York: Columbia University Press, 1995); Julia Kristeva, *Nations without Nationalism* (New York: Columbia University Press, 1993) *Strangers to Ourselves* (New York: Columbia University Press, 1991). Finally, see the important book by Todorov cited in note 63.

78 Kristeva, *Nations without Nationalism*, 2, 16.

79 See note 1.

80 Thomas Pavel, *The Freud of Language: A History of Structuralist Thought* (New York: Blackwell, 1989), 148.

81 Luc Ferry and Alain Renaut, *French Philosophy of the Sixties* (Amherst: University of Massachusetts Press, 1990).

82 For the new philosophers, see André Glucksmann, *The Master Thinkers* (New York: Harper Row, 1978); and Bernard-Henry Lévy, *Barbarism with a Human Face* (New York: Harper Row, 1979).

83 See Tony Judt, *Marxism and the French Left* (Oxford: Oxford University Press, 1986), 186: "Until 1948, by reference and by metaphor, Communist discourse set the Party firmly in the Jacobin-nationalist tradition of revolutionary patriotism, adopting as its own the whole of the republican pantheon (with the addition of Stalin)."

84 François Furet, *Interpreting the French Revolution*, trans. E. Forster (Cambridge: Cambridge University Press, 1981), 1ff. It is a telling measure of the new intellectual politics that, ten years after the appearance of Furet's influential book, as it came time to celebrate the revolutionary bicentennial, the only bit of "revolutionary" heritage that the ruling Socialists had to fall back on was the eminently "liberal" "Declaration of the

Rights of Man and Citizen" of 1789. It is, then, terrifically ironic to see Furet and others (Jacques Julliard and Pierre Rosanvallon) protesting the emergence of *La République du centre* (Paris: Calmann-Lévy, 1988); that is, the creation of a political climate of timorous centrism that he very much helped foster.

For a recent attempt to situate the importance of Furet's work in terms of its relation to French neo-liberalism, see Sunil Khilnani, *Arguing Revolution: The Intellectual Left in Postwar France* (New Haven: Yale University Press, 1993).

85   Cited in Pavel, *The Feud of Language*, 149. For an elaboration of the idea of "French philosophy of the eighties," see Ferry and Renaut, *Heidegger and Modernity*, trans. F. Philip (Chicago: University of Chicago Press, 1990), 16ff.

86   Ferry and Renaut, *French Philosophy of the Sixties:* "What is happening to Heidegger today, happened to Marxism in the 1970s" (xv). In *The Feud of Language*, Thomas Pavel goes so far as to describe the Heidegger controversy as having brought about "*a new cultural equilibrium . . . in France*" (viii). I have discussed the intellectual stakes involved in this debate in Chapter 8.

87   An important way station in this process was the French publication in the early 1970s of Robert Paxton's book, *Vichy France: Old Guard and New Order, 1940–1944*, which, along with Marcel Ophul's film of two years prior, *The Sorrow and the Pity*, triggered a widespread debate and much national soul-searching. See the account in Henry Rousso, *The Vichy Syndrome* (Cambridge: Harvard University Press, 1991), 252ff.

88   On Barbie's trial, see Alain Finkielkraut, *Remembering in Vain* (New York: Columbia University Press, 1993). Finkielkraut shows effectively how the definition of "crimes against humanity" was watered down in the trial to include crimes against resistance leaders and other offenses.

89   In April 1993, Le Pen's party has recently been denied electoral representation in France's National Assembly. Nevertheless, the extent to which the National Front has forced the other major parties to address their concerns—above all, the question of immigration—has been chilling. In other words, the damage has been done and is still being done. Le Pen has succeeded at least in fundamental, regrettable respect: he has made attitudes of racism and xenophobia politically respectable.

90   Philippe Lacoue-Labarthe, *Heidegger, Art, and Politics*, trans. C. Turner (Oxford: Blackwell, 1990), 95.

91   See Heidegger's remarks to this effect from his 1935 lecture course, *An Introduction to Metaphysics* (New Haven: Yale University Press, 1959): "This Europe, in its ruinous blindness forever on the point of cutting its own throat, lies today in a great pincers, squeezed between Russia on one side and America on the other. From a metaphysical point of view, Russia and America are the same; the same dreary technological frenzy, the same unrestricted organization of the average man" (37).

92   Pavel, *The Feud of Language*, 147.

93   Bourdieu, "Back to History: An Interview," in Wolin, ed., *The Heidegger Controversy: A Critical Reader*, 266.

94   Robert Holub, "The Uncomfortable Heritage," in *Crossing Borders: Reception Theory, Poststructuralism, Deconstruction* (Madison: University of Wisconsin Press, 1992), 182.

95   Todorov, *On Human Diversity*, xi.

96   Sartre, *Critique de la raison dialectique* (Paris: Gallimard, 1960), 29.

97   See the famous argument to this effect in Carl Schmitt, *The Crisis of Parliamentary Democracy* (Cambridge: MIT Press, 1985).

98   For more on the concept of privatism, see Jürgen Habermas, *Legitimation Crisis*, trans. T. McCarthy (Boston: Beacon, 1975), 75ff. More generally, see A. Arato and J. Cohen, *Civil Society and Political Theory* (Cambridge: MIT Press, 1992), especially 568ff.

99   See Donald Kelley, *Renaissance Humanism* (Boston: Twayne, 1991), 49ff.

100 For the essential works of this movement, see, in addition to the works of Ferry and Renaut cited above, Ferry, *Political Philosophy I: Rights, The New Quarrel between the Ancients and the Moderns* (Chicago: University of Chicago, 1990); Alain Finkielkraut, *The Defeat of Thought;* Renaut, *L'Ere de l'individu: Contribution à l'histoire de la subjectivité* (Paris: Gallimard, 1989).

     See also the excellent anthology edited by Mark Lilla, *New French Thought: Political Philosophy* (Princeton: Princeton University Press, 1994), which, in addition to an important selection of primary texts, contains a useful introduction by Lilla situating French thought of the 1980s in relation to prior competing intellectual tendencies and trends.

101 Ferry and Renaut, *French Philosophy of the Sixties*, xvi.

102 This is especially true of the major neoliberal philosophical attempts to rethink the subject. In *L'Ere de l'individu*, Renaut's reconstruction of the epistemological origins of the modern individual has recourse to Leibniz (as well as Berkeley, Kant, and Nietzsche). He concludes that, in an era where the limits to subjective self-assertion are progressively eroded, the result is, ironically, a dissolution of subjectivity itself. It is Ferry, who in *Political Philosophy I*, has recourse to Fichte's philosophy of reflection for the purpose of reestablishing a viable notion of individual autonomy.

     For a sympathetic discussion of the work of the neoliberals, see Alexander Nehamas, "The Rescue of Humanism," *New Republic* 23, no. 2 (November 12, 1990): 27–34. See also the review of their work by Mark Lilla in the *Times Literary Supplement*, November 17–23, 1989, 1255–56.

103 Max Horkheimer and Theodor Adorno, *Dialectic of Enlightenment*, trans. J. Cumming, (New York: Continuum, 1972).

104 George Herbert Mead, *Mind, Self, and Society* (Chicago: University of Chicago Press, 1934), 174.

105 George Herbert Mead, "The Social Self," in *Selected Writings*, ed. A. Reck (Chicago: University of Chicago Press, 1964), 149.

Deconstruction at Auschwitz

1   For Blanchot's case, see Jeffrey Mehlman, *Legacies of Anti-Semitism in France* (Minneapolis: University of Minnesota, 1982), 6–22.

2   Jeffrey Mehlman, quoted in *Newsweek*, February 15, 1988.

3   According to Reed Way Dasenbrock in "Reading Demanians Reading de Man," *South Central Review* 11, no. 1 (Spring 1994), "What the de Man affair provides is the fullest display we are likely to have of how deconstructive critics actually read texts" (23).

4   Habermas, *Theory and Practice*, trans. J. Viertel (Boston: Beacon, 1973), 32.

5   Jacques Derrida, *Positions* (Chicago: University of Chicago Press, 1981), 93.

6   See Jeffrey T. Nealon, *Double Reading: Postmodernism After Deconstruction* (Ithaca: Cornell University Press, 1993), a work that attempts to explore the dilemmas involved in the institutionalization of deconstruction. See also David Kaufmann, "The Profession of Theory," *PMLA* 105, no. 3 (1992): 519–30.

7   Harold Fromm, *Academic Capitalism and Literary Value* (Athens: University of Georgia Press, 1991), 252. See also Russell Jacoby's important discussion of these themes in *Dogmatic Wisdom: How the Culture Wars Divert Education and Distract America* (New York: Doubleday, 1994). As Jacoby remarks, "In the 'culture wars' little is more striking than the ease with which the new professors defend professional reputations and language, sophisticated theories and distinguished friends, heaping contempt on journalists and critics as backward outsiders" (164).

8   Thus Duke English professor Frank Lentricchia: "The real problem of the de Manians is hero worship—the spectacle of grown men and women idolizing another person." In his view, de Man was the "godfather" of the Yale "mafia." Cited in D. Lehman, *Signs of the Times* (New York: Poseidon, 1991), 212.

9   J. Hillis Miller, "An Open Letter to Jon Wiener," in *Responses: On Paul de Man's Wartime Journalism*, ed. W. Hamacher, N. Hertz, and T. Keenan (Lincoln: University of Nebraska Press, 1989), 334–35.

10 See Dasenbrock, "Reading Demanians": "The failure of deconstructive critics to read de Man's wartime journalism deconstructively tells us a good deal, not just about deconstruction, but about the relation between literary theory and critical practice" (24).

11 *Times Literary Supplement*, no. 4446, June 17–23, 1988, 676.

12 Ibid.

13 De Man, *Wartime Journalism, 1939–1943*, ed. W. Hamacher, N. Hertz, and T. Keenan, (Lincoln: University of Nebraska Press, 1988), 66.

14 Ibid., 158.

15 Cited by Stanley Corngold, in *Responses*, 81.

16 De Man, *Wartime Journalism*, 194.

17 Ibid., 29.

18 Miller, *Times Literary Supplement*, no. 4446, June 17–23, 1988, 676.

19 Derrida, "Like the Sound of the Sea Deep Within a Shell: Paul de Man's War," *Critical Inquiry* 15, no. 4 (Summer 1989): 647.

20 Ibid.

21 Ibid., 607.

22 De Man, *Wartime Journalism*, 43.

23 Quoted by the *New York Times*, December 2, 1987, 1.

24 Cited by Lehman, *Signs of the Times*, 182.

25 De Man, *Wartime Journalism*, 45.

26 See Dasenbrock, "Reading Demanians," 37: "Derrida insists in 'Limited Inc' on the openness of contexts, the necessary provisionality of any one reading. But there is nothing provisional in the least about Derrida's reading [of de Man] here. We are told that if we judge de Man, we are more than judges, we are censors, we are book burners, we are reproducing the exterminating gesture of the Holocaust. . . . In claiming interpretive privilege for his recontextualization and in ruling certain competing recontextualizations out of court, in claiming that his interpretation is privileged because it conforms to de Man's intentions, Derrida is here playing exactly the role of the policeman he is ascribing to unnamed others. Derrida is finally able to produce a member of the interpretive police 'ready to intervene' in the case: his name is Jacques Derrida." See also Dasenbrock, "Taking It Personally: Reading Derrida's Responses," *College English*, 56, no. 3 (March 1994): 261–79.

27 Derrida, "Like the Sound of the Sea," 625.

28   There is a terrible irony involved in Derrida's reference to the young de Man's text as "nonconformist," one of which he is apparently unaware. Among the pro-fascist French intelligentsia of the 1930s, "nonconformist" was a type of code word indicating a hatred of democratic institutions and a belief in the need for a revolution from the right. On this figure of the French right in the 1930s, see Jean-Louis Loubet del Bayle, *Les Nonconformistes des années trentes* (Paris: Editions du Seuil, 1969).

29   Cited in Alice Y. Kaplan, "Paul de Man, *Le Soir,* and the Francophone Collaboration," in *Responses,* 274–75. According to Kaplan, if one tries to understand de Man's anti-Semitism within the spectrum of other "respectable" contemporary forms of anti-Semitism, one perceives "not so much the slight disjunctions between positions, as a number of approaches to the anti-Semitic genre—cultural, racial, historical—which in their very disagreements, give the appearance of respectable 'debate.' What is more, all of them draw in some way on a critique of an 'incorrect' form of racist thinking that is beneath their dignity, and which is exemplified . . . by the pamphlets of Céline. As it turns out, Céline is useful to make everyone else sound better. All the positions [published in *Le Soir* in conjunction with de Man's 'The Jews in Contemporary Literature'] converge because of the existence of something more vulgar: de Man's article participates in this convergence, and in the legitimation of anti-Semitism."

30   Cited by Stanley Corngold, "On Paul de Man's Collaborationist Writings," in *Responses,* 80.

31   De Man, *Wartime Journalism,* 138.

32   See the discussion of cultural collaboration in Lehman, *Signs of the Times,* 179.

33   Sternhell, "The Making of a Propagandist," *New Republic* 200 (March 6, 1989): 31.

34   Kaplan, "Paul de Man," 268.

35   Sternhell, "The Making of a Propagandist," 32.

36   Cited by Jeffrey Mehlman in *Legacies of Anti-Semitism in France,* (Minneapolis: University of Minnesota Press, 1982), 108.

37   Bataille, "The Psychological Structure of Fascism," in *Visions of Excess: Selected Writings, 1927–1939,* ed. Allan Stoekl (Minneapolis: University of Minnesota, 1985), 143.

38   Peter Dodge, *Beyond Marxism: The Faith and Works of Hendrik De Man* (The Hague: Martin Nijhoff, 1966), 197–98, 201.

39   Derrida, "Like the Sound of the Sea," 628.

40   Jameson, *Fables of Aggression: Wyndham Lewis, the Modernist as Fascist* (Berkeley and Los Angeles: University of California Press, 1979). See also John R. Harrison, *The Reactionaries: A Study of the Anti-Democratic Intelligentsia* (New York: Schocken, 1967).

41   In Lawrence's case, one should consult *Aaron's Rod.* See the important study by Michael North, *The Political Aesthetic of Yeats, Eliot, and Pound* (Cambridge: Cambridge University Press, 1991).

42   De Man, *Wartime Journalism,* 331. For a discussion of de Man's relation to Jünger, see Ortwin de Graef, *Serenity in Crisis: A Preface to Paul de Man, 1939–1960* (Lincoln: University of Nebraska Press, 1993), 25–27; and de Graef, "A Stereotype of Aesthetic ideology: Paul de Man, Ernst Jünger," *Colloquium Helveticum* 11–12 (1990): 39–70.

43   Reed Way Dasenbrock, "Paul de Man: the Modernist as Fascist," in *Fascism, Aesthetics, and Culture,* ed. Richard Golsan (Hanover: University Press of New England, 1992), 238. Many of the essays in this volume shed essential light on the underresearched historical nexus between fascism and modernism.

44   Russell Berman, "Modernism, Fascism, and the Institution of Literature," in *Modern-*

ism: Challenges and Perspectives, ed. M. Chefdor, R. Quinones, and A. Wachtel (Champaign: University of Illinois Press, 1986), 94–102.

45   Geoffrey Hartman, "Looking Back on Paul de Man," in *Reading de Man Reading* (Minneapolis: University of Minnesota Press, 1989), 3–24.

46   Miller, "An Open Letter," 337, 339.

47   See de Man's essay, "Aesthetic Formalization: Kleist's *Über das Marionettetheater*," in *The Rhetoric of Romanticism* (New York: Columbia University Press, 1984), 263–89.

48   Jonathan Culler, "Paul de Man's War and the Aesthetic Ideology," in *Responses*, 780, 783.

49   Shoshana Felman, "Paul de Man's Silence," *Critical Inquiry* 15 (Summer 1989): 721.

50   Thomas Pavel, *The Feud of Language* (Oxford: Blackwell, 1989), 147.

51   De Man, *Blindness and Insight* (Minneapolis: University of Minnesota Press, 1983), 165, 35, 232.

52   See above all his essay on "Literary History and Literary Modernity," ibid., 142–65.

53   J. Hillis Miller, *The Ethics of Reading* (New York: Columbia University Press, 1987), 58.

54   For an excellent analysis of the problem of aesthetic ideology in de Man, see Martin Jay, " 'The Aesthetic Ideology' as Ideology: Or What Does It Mean to Aestheticize Politics," in *Force Fields* (New York: Routledge, 1993), 71–83.

55   Terry Eagleton, *The Ideology of the Aesthetic* (Oxford: Blackwell, 1990), 387.

56   M. H. Abrams, "The Deconstructive Angel," *Critical Inquiry* 3 (1977): 435.

57   Paul Jay, "Bridging the Gap: The Position of Politics in Deconstruction," *Cultural Critique* 22 (Fall 1992): 49.

58   See Nealon, *Double Reading*, 22. See also the remarks by Robert Holub in *Crossing Borders: Reception Theory, Poststructuralism, Deconstruction* (Madison: University of Wisconsin Press, 1992): "The decline of deconstruction as a theoretical force in the United States has been evident since the mid-eighties. . . . On one level, deconstruction simply lost its novelty for native critics. The general feeling pervading the academy was that the 'deconstructive movement' had exhausted itself. The seminal works had appeared during the late sixties in France and had been made accessible to the American public about a decade later; new impulses from abroad and novel adaptations domestically were lacking. Derrida had been read with interest in the late seventies, but his influence peaked at some point in the early eighties, and his more recent texts seemed to contain nothing radically new. . . . Deconstructors themselves contributed to their own self-deconstruction in the late eighties by persisting with their cliquish ways. They became increasingly intolerant of criticism. Even well-meant and intelligent questioning became anathema, and often writers perceived to be 'opponents' were simply dismissed as theoretical dinosaurs, unintelligent trespassers on a sublime critical turf, or reactionaries bent on persecuting an oppressed minority" (148).

59   Hayden White, *The Content of the Form: Narrative Discourse and Historical Representation* (Baltimore: Johns Hopkins University Press, 1987), 58–82.

60   For a rather defensive illustration of this indebtedness vis-à-vis the New Historicism, see his "New Historicism: A Comment," in *The New Historicism*, ed. H. Veeser (New York: Routledge, 1989), 293–302.

61   White, *The Content of the Form*, 75.

62   Ibid., 80 (my emphasis).

63   Carlo Ginzburg, "Just One Witness," in *Probing the Limits of Representation*, ed. Saul

Friedlander (Cambridge: Harvard University Press, 1992), 93. See also White's contribution to this volume, "Historical Emplotment and the Problem of Truth," 37–53.

In pursuing this line of thinking, White approximates Ernst Nolte's tasteless thought-experiment in "Between Myth and Revisionism," *Aspects of the Third Reich,* ed. H. W. Koch (London: Macmillan, 1985): "We need only imagine, for example, what would happen if the Palestine Liberation Organisation, assisted by its allies, succeeded in annihilating the state of Israel. Then the historical accounts in the books, lecture halls and schoolrooms of Palestine would doubtless dwell only on the negative traits of Israel; the victory over the racist, oppressive, even Fascist Zionism would become a state-supporting myth" (21).

64 Saul Friedlander, introduction to *Probing the Limits of Representation,* 10.

65 White, *The Content of the Form,* 74–75.

Afterword

1 Jacques Derrida, *Of Grammatology,* trans. G. Spivak (Baltimore: Johns Hopkins University Press, 1976), 158.

2 Derrida, *Glas,* trans. J. Leavey (Lincoln: University of Nebraska Press, 1986); see also Richard Rorty's reflections on these questions in *Philosophical Papers: Essays on Heidegger and Others* (New York: Cambridge University Press, 1990), 2:85–129.

3 Foucault, "My Body, This Paper, This Fire," *Oxford Literary Review* 4 (1979): 27.

4 Edward Said, *The World, the Text, and the Critic* (Cambridge: Harvard University Press, 1983), 203, 204, 207.

5 See, for example, Russell Berman, "Troping To Pretoria: The Rise and Fall of Deconstruction," *Telos* 85 (1990): 4–16.

6 Cited in *Les Fins de l'homme: À partir du travail de Jacques Derrida* (Paris: Editions Galilée, 1981), 514.

7 Derrida, "The Force of Law: The 'Mystical Foundation of Authority,'" in *Deconstruction and the Possibility of Justice,* ed. D. Cornell et al. (New York: Routledge, 1992), 7. For some critical observations on the translation and dissemination of Derrida's work, see Reed Way Dasenbrock in "Reading Demanians Reading de Man," *South Central Review* 11, no. 1 (Spring 1994); Dasenbrock, "Taking It Personally: Reading Derrida's Responses," *College English* 56, no. 3 (March 1994): 261–79. See also the excellent discussion in Ingrid Harris, "*L'affaire derrida:* Business or Pleasure?" *Philosophy and Social Criticism* 19, no. 3–4 (1994): 216–42.

For a work that argues for the importance of deconstruction as an ethical theory, see Simon Critchley, *The Ethics of Deconstruction: Derrida and Levinas* (Oxford: Blackwell, 1992).

8 Richard Kearney, "Deconstruction and the Other," in his *Dialogues with Contemporary Continental Thinkers* (Manchester: Manchester University Press, 1984), 124, 125.

9 Derrida, "The Force of Law," 15, 21, 25.

10 Sigmund Freud, *Civilization and Its Discontents,* trans. J. Strachey (New York: Norton, 1962), 56–57.

11 For the best account of the conservative revolutionaries in English, see Jeffrey Herf, *Reactionary Modernism: Technology, Culture and Politics in Weimar and the Third Reich* (Cambridge: Cambridge University Press, 1984).

12   For a good discussion of their alliance, see Bernd Rüthers, *Carl Schmitt im Dritten Reich,* 2d ed. (Munich: Beck, 1990). See especially, "Die Koalition grosser Zeitgeister 1933: Martin Heidegger und Carl Schmitt," 21–42.

13   Cited in Richard Wolin, ed., *The Heidegger Controversy: A Critical Reader* (Cambridge: MIT Press, 1993), p. 47.

14   I have tried to chronicle these implications in my book *The Politics of Being: The Political Thought of Martin Heidegger* (New York: Columbia University Press, 1990). I discuss Heidegger's ties to Schmitt and Jünger in chapter 2, "*Being and Times* as Political Philosophy." See also Anson Rabinbach, "Heidegger's Letter on Humanism as Text and Event," *New German Critique* 62 (Spring-Summer 1994), 3–38.

15   For a review of these developments, see Luc Ferry and Alain Renaut, *French Philosophy of the Sixties: An Essay on Antihumanism,* trans. M. Cattani (Amherst: University of Massachusetts Press, 1990). Also worth mentioning in connection with doctrines of left Heideggerianism are the works of Kostas Axelos, who in books such as *Horizons du monde* (Paris: Minuit, 1971) was one of the first thinkers on the French Left to attempt to fuse the doctrines of Heidegger and Marx.

16   Sartre, *Search for a Method,* trans. Hazel Barnes (New York: Vintage, 1963), 30 (translation altered).

17   Derrida, *Spectres of Marx,* trans. P. Kamuf (New York: Routledge, 1994), 13. A shortened version of Derrida's text appeared in *New Left Review* 205 (May–June 1994): 31–58.

18   See for example, J. Cohen and A. Arato, *Civil Society and Democratic Theory* (Cambridge: MIT Press, 1992). The literature on this theme has of late become enormous. For a recent attempt at synthesis, see Ernest Gellner, *Conditions of Liberty: Civil Society and Its Rivals* (London: Hammish Hamilton, 1994).

19   Derrida, *Spectres of Marx,* 75.

20   Aijaz Ahmad, "Reconciling Derrida: 'Spectres of Marx' and Deconstructive Politics," *New Left Review* 208 (November–December 1994): 102.

21   Martin Heidegger, "Only a God Can Save Us," in Wolin, *The Heidegger Controversy,* 107.

22   Derrida, *Spectres of Marx,* 15.

23   Derrida, "The Principle of Reason," *Diacritics* 19 (1983): 8.

24   Justin Barton, "Phantom Saviours, Phantom States," *Radical Philosophy* 65 (Autumn 1993): 63.

25   Derrida, *Spectres of Marx,* 37, 51.

26   Ibid., 52–53.

27   Ibid., 54.

28   Ibid., 55.

INDEX